THE REAL LIFE
OF
MARY ANN EVANS

ALSO BY ROSEMARIE BODENHEIMER

The Politics of Story in Victorian Social Fiction

The
Real Life
of
Mary Ann Evans

George Eliot, Her
Letters and Fiction

Rosemarie Bodenheimer

CORNELL UNIVERSITY PRESS

ITHACA AND LONDON

First published 1994 by Cornell University Press.

Library of Congress Cataloging-in-Publication Data

Bodenheimer, Rosemarie, 1946–
    The real life of Mary Ann Evans : George Eliot, her letters and
fiction / Rosemarie Bodenheimer.
        p.   cm.
    Includes bibliographical references (p.   ) and index.
    ISBN 0-8014-2988-9 (alk. paper)
    1. Eliot, George, 1819–1880. 2. Women novelists, English—
Correspondence—History and criticism. 3. Autobiographical
fiction, English—History and criticism. 4. Women and literature—
England—History—19th century. 5. Women novelists, English—
19th century—Biography. 6. Letter writing,   English—
History. 7. Self in literature. I. Title.
PR4681.B57   1994
823'.8—dc20
[B]   94-10513

Printed in the United States of America

For Andy

Contents

Illustrations

Frequently Cited Works

John Walter Cross. *George Eliot's Life as Related in Her Letters and Journals*. 3 vols. New York: Harper and Brothers, 1885. Cited as "Cross."

Gordon Haight. *George Eliot: A Biography*. Oxford: Oxford University Press, 1968. Cited as "Haight."

Gordon S. Haight, ed. *The George Eliot Letters*. 9 vols. New Haven and London: Yale University Press, 1954–1974. Cited in the text by volume and page in parentheses; in the notes as "*GEL*."

Thomas Pinney, ed. *Essays of George Eliot*. London: Routledge and Kegan Paul, 1963. Cited as "Pinney, *Essays*."

Ruby V. Redinger. *George Eliot: The Emergent Self*. New York: Knopf, 1975. Cited as "Redinger."

Because there are so many editions of George Eliot's novels, I have simply designated quoted passages by chapter number in the text. The footnotes indicate particular editions of less widely published works: short stories, essays, and poems.

Preface

Remember that what you are told is really
threefold: shaped by the teller, reshaped by the
listener, concealed from both by the dead man of
the tale. . . . And where is the third party? Rotting
peacefully in the cemetery of St. Damier.
Laughingly alive in five volumes.

—Vladimir Nabokov,
The Real Life of Sebastian Knight

"The best history of a writer is contained in his writings—these
are his chief actions," George Eliot wrote to a friend in 1879. "But
Biographies generally are a disease of English literature" (7:230). Her
acerbity covered a complex set of feelings. George Henry Lewes, her
life's companion, had been dead for only a year, and her correspondent was inquiring whether there was to be a biography. Lewes's efforts had supported her own persistent resistance to requests for biographical information about herself; now, at the end of her own
career, she was alone and increasingly exposed to a marketplace in
which readers were, she thought, more interested in personal gossip
about a writer than in reading her books. In one of her more lighthearted moods, I like to imagine, George Eliot would have taken
pleasure in Nabokov's *The Real Life of Sebastian Knight*, a novel about a
biographer in quest of the elusive truth about his half-brother, the
writer Sebastian Knight. The narrator-biographer of this tale burns
intimate letters unread, fails to interview the closest witnesses of his
subject's life, and discovers in the shimmering velleities of Knight's
prose his most suggestive autobiographical glimpses. Echoing Na-

bokov's, my title plays with the dubious promises of the biographical situation: the yearning to know which sends readers and writers on biographical quests, and the impossibility of knowing anything that is not somebody's fiction of the self in the guise of a story about another.

My own quest for something about George Eliot began when I read the extraordinary letters of the young Mary Ann Evans and found myself compelled to go on reading, through all the volumes in Gordon Haight's edition of the George Eliot letters. From the beginning Mary Ann Evans was highly conscious of her letters as pieces of writing. Her real life, as she imagined it then, took place in the moments when she could get free of household duties to read, write, and "take a deep breath in my own element," as she put it in a letter to Maria Lewis on her twentieth birthday (1:33). Some months later she announced to Lewis that she had made time "to prepare such a representative of myself for tonight's post as my rather dissipated brain will allow" (1:54). Her playful, literary notion of the letter as a representative of the self, rather than an expression or a confession, perfectly characterizes her lifelong practice of letter writing. The care with which she constructed her self-representations has led many readers of the correspondence to reject it as disappointingly dull and inexpressive, compared with the inventive genius displayed in the novels. My project in this book is to undo this dichotomy, and to suggest that a "best history" of George Eliot may be told by reading her letters in conjunction with her novels, stories, and poems.

I have found that this history is most usefully organized not as a chronological narrative but in a series of connected yet discontinuous chapters. Each chapter focuses on one of the intractable issues in George Eliot's mental and moral life, and each moves in some way between readings of a certain group of letters and readings of related published works. I have not attempted to give a full or comprehensive account either of George Eliot's letters or of her fictions. Certain periods of her life, certain correspondences, certain novels hardly come into play at all. The topics that became full-blown chapters did so because particular clusters of letters were especially compelling to me and because they suggested a fruitful dialogue with imaginative fictions. In addition, the chapters all bear in some fashion on two related patterns of consciousness which consistently emerge from my reading of George Eliot's texts. The first is a moral and emotional pattern in which acts of assertion, satire, or rebellion are followed by remorse or retreat. The second is George Eliot's peculiarly intense consciousness of audience, which caught her between scorn and defiance of public opinion and a strong dependence on it. Coming to the chapters as a group, the reader will see how often their stories and arguments intertwine along these central axes.

Although the chapters do form a roughly chronological sequence, I have been particularly interested in isolating certain critical junctures and unresolved issues in George Eliot's experience. Some chapters treat a short, well-defined period of biographical time, while extending their attention to works written at later periods. Chapter 2, "Constructing the Reader," concentrates on the adolescent letters written during the Evans family's residence at Griff; Chapter 3, "Mary Ann Evans's Holy War," investigates the period during which Mary Ann Evans lived with her father at Foleshill, Coventry; and Chapter 5, "The Outing of George Eliot," is concerned with the first three years of George Eliot's life as a pseudonymous novelist. Other chapters juxtapose disparate periods of life with one another: Chapter 4, "The Labor of Choice," focuses on Marian Evans's decision to live with George Henry Lewes, and on the marriage to John Walter Cross which occurred twenty-five years later, whereas Chapter 6, "Ambition and Womanhood," spans the whole career from adolescent writing to *Daniel Deronda*. The last two chapters, "George Eliot's Stepsons" and "Old and Young," widen the focus in order to look more broadly at the relationships with younger people which became important in the last two decades of George Eliot's life. The introductory chapter, "On Reading Letters," offers a context for this work on George Eliot's correspondence by making some general reflections on the history and methodology of letter reading.

Considering the letters along with novels and stories, I wish to suggest some ways in which George Eliot's works may be read autobiographically, as meditations on and transformations of the most intimate paradoxes of her very paradoxical experience. Because her mind reorganized autobiographical material in conceptual ways, it is rarely appropriate to identify her family or acquaintance directly with characters in her fiction, nor is it in my view desirable to read biography out of fictional representation, as some seekers after the lost truths of Mary Ann Evans's early life have done. What she does not represent in writing is not part of my concern, so I do not discuss her mother, Christiana Evans, the relative positions of her father, Robert Evans, and brother, Isaac Evans, in her interior life, or the successful intimate relationship with George Henry Lewes. Nevertheless this work has clarified for me the intense autobiographical charge of George Eliot's fictions and her great and flexible capacity for self-understanding, for transforming painful preoccupations into distanced fictional structures.

During the course of our century, various psychoanalytic languages have been developed which might be used to name some of the internal struggles that I delineate in these pages. Readers who are familiar with one or more of those languages may be tempted to apply them, or to wish that I had. My reluctance to learn and employ such a frame is based on the feeling that a retrospective application of any powerful terminology has the effect of disempowering the language of our predecessors. My desire in this book has been to effect just the reverse, to highlight the power of writing through which Mary Ann Evans managed both to express and to contain her strenuous affective life. Taken together, my chapters should create a general impression that the novelist George Eliot elaborated in fictional form both the probing self-analyses and the transcending self-idealizations that she tended to repress, or compress, in her correspondence. Yet to dwell for a moment on a given set of sentences in a certain letter is often to be overwhelmed by the reservoir of problematical feeling conveyed in the very phrases that attempt to master and present it for the consumption of others.

To imagine writing as the counterforce in a psychic life poised near the border of melancholy or depression may help to shift our perspective on the gender dualisms that have figured prominently in both Victorian and contemporary accounts of George Eliot's career. It is often said that George Eliot found her authority by writing like, or as, a man. I would prefer to say simply that George Eliot was a woman who found her authority in writing. Mary Ann Evans, a learned schoolgirl who cherished little hope of growing up to become anyone at all, was at sixteen already writing the complex, "masterful" sentences that her life of difficult feeling, ravenous reading, and evangelical piety stimulated in her. For an image of the George Eliot narrator ascendant, repressing in magisterial syntax the threats of weakness, silliness, or subordination represented by womanhood, I would substitute the picture of a woman battling not womanhood itself but internal threats of collapse into despair and loss of meaning, a woman using all the resources of her (immense) intellectual and imaginative capacity to redeem her life by reworking its elements within an aesthetic and moral order.

Nevertheless, the play between "Mary Ann/Marian Evans/Lewes" and "George Eliot" must concern everyone who writes about this woman and artist of many names, not least when it comes to making decisions about what to call her. I use George Eliot when the working novelist is in question, and I follow the lead of her signatures in naming her for any given period of her personal life. Mary Ann Evans becomes Marian Evans after her move to London in 1851, then Marian Lewes. (At the last she signed herself Mary Ann Cross, a move I allow myself to avoid.) For the sake of ease in writing, I also designate her sometimes by first name; to use either of her last names alone confuses her with others. I must confess, however, that I cannot call George Henry Lewes "George"—he rarely appears by that name in Marian Evans Lewes's letters, nor does he sign himself with his given name—so that I occasionally reproduce a situation in which the woman is called by her first name, the man by his last. I trust that my readers will forgive this practice.

I am indebted to the late Gordon S. Haight, whose long dedication to the collection and editing of the George Eliot letters made this book possible. The nine gray-bound volumes of the correspondence have been my companions for several years, during which I have appreciated on many occasions the careful attention to detail that is demonstrated on every page. Professor Haight was also responsible for leaving us the George Eliot and George Henry Lewes collection of letters and manuscripts in the Beinecke Rare Book and Manuscript Library at Yale University. The Beinecke staff made the correspondence readily available and gave me permission to quote from unpublished letters of the Lewes family. Portions of Chapters 3, 5, and 6 were previously published as articles in *Nineteenth-Century Literature* (© 1989, by the Regents of the University of California), *Dickens Studies Annual* (AMS Press, 1991), and *Victorian Studies* (1990); permission to reprint is gratefully acknowledged.

At various stages of this work I received crucial encouragement from scholars who had worked in the rich labyrinth of George Eliot studies well before I entered it. Neil Hertz, U. C. Knoepflmacher, George Levine, and Michael Wolff cheered me on when my direction was not yet clear and supported pieces of the work as it developed. Boston College gave me a well-timed faculty fellowship which enabled me to complete the book. The enthusiasm and curiosity of many friends who read initial pieces and wanted to hear more about George

Eliot made the writing a real delight. I thank in particular Harriet Ritvo, who gave me astute editorial advice about every chapter, and Jonathan Strong, who offered the welcome perspective of a novelist.

Andrew Von Hendy has, as always, been the best friend of this project. In thanks for everything he has contributed to its making, I dedicate the book to him.

ROSEMARIE BODENHEIMER

Chestnut Hill, Massachusetts

THE REAL LIFE
OF
MARY ANN EVANS

ONE

On Reading Letters

It is better to live quietly on under some degree of
misrepresentation than to attempt to remove it by
the uncertain process of letter-writing.
> —Marian Evans to Clementia Taylor,
> June 8, 1856

"A certain grayness of tone, something measured and subdued, as
of a person talking without ever raising her voice." That was how
Henry James characterized George Eliot's letters, as he reviewed the
volumes in which they first appeared under the title *George Eliot's Life,
as related in her Letters and Journals,* "arranged and edited by her husband, J. W. Cross."[1] James's polite description did not prevent his
sister, Alice, from responding to Cross's volumes with an intensity that
was anything but polite. Alice James recorded her reactions in a diary
entry dated June 28, 1889, with a relish that defied any specter of
reticence:

> Read the third volume of George Eliot's Letters and Journals at last.
> I'm glad I made myself do so for there is a faint spark of life and an
> occasional, remotely humorous touch in the last half. But what a
> monument of ponderous dreariness is the book! What a lifeless,
> diseased, self-conscious being she must have been! Not one burst of
> joy, not one ray of humour, not one living breath in one of her
> letters or journals, the commonplace and platitude of these last,
> giving her impressions of the Continent, pictures and people, is
> simply incredible! Whether it is that her dank, moaning features
> haunt and pursue one thro' the book, or not, but she makes upon
> me the impression, morally and physically, of mildew, or some mor-

bid growth—a fungus of a pendulous shape, or as of something damp to the touch. I never had a stronger impression. Then to think of those books compact of wisdom, humour, and the richest humanity, and of her as the creator of the immortal *Maggie*, in short, what a horrible disillusion! . . . What an abject coward she seems to have been about physical pain, as if it weren't degrading eno[ugh] to have head-aches, without jotting them down in a row to stare at one for all time, thereby defeating the beneficent law which provides that physical pain is forgotten. If she related her diseases and her "depressions" and told for the good of others what armour she had forged against them, it would be conceivable, but they seem simply cherished as the vehicle for a moan. Where was the creature's vanity! And when you think of what she had in life to lift her out of futile whining![2]

What did Alice James want? It is not enough to offer her sentences as lively examples of the late nineteenth-century reaction against the high moral tone of George Eliot, or even as examples skewed by the peculiarities of James's positions: as a woman whose sole visible occupation was the endurance of illness, as a writing woman who had no novels, no George Henry Lewes to "lift her out of futile whining."[3] James's envy and fear take the form of a recorded triumph over George Eliot the letter writer, but her disappointment also signals a more general structure of expectation about what great writers' letters are good for. That expectation is simultaneously moral and aesthetic. Published letters should offer a model of character which could turn envy into admiration and emulation; at least they should present an attractive character, not one that will create repugnance by reminding the ailing and depressive reader too much of herself in her worst moments. They should be entertaining, uplifting for the reader, and expressive in the writer of spontaneous feeling. A marked difference between the performed personae of the novels and the writer of the letters gives rise to a terrible feeling of "disillusion," as though the discovery that a toad had created a beautiful object had raised questions about the authenticity of the object.

It is worth examining the assumptions that shape such reactions, because they bear directly on the questions of method I want to raise in this chapter. What do we look for in letters? What do we do with them? Alice James's diary entry offers one starting point for some notes toward a history and methodology of letter reading. Like hundreds of other nineteenth- and twentieth-century letter readers, she turns to the writer's letters exactly because they are not her books, in order to find out something else about her "as a person." Yet she is appalled by the distance between the two forms of writing. She makes the assumption that "character" is to be found in letters, that they offer an index to a living being. Her inability to imagine the audiences for whom individual letters were written is partially created by Cross's patchwork manufacture of a continuous narrative from carefully selected excerpts, but her sense that a private correspondence ought really to speak to a public audience betrays itself in her wish that George Eliot had written of her headaches in a more exemplary fashion. The peculiar self-fashioning and self-covering which is the special opportunity of letters written to particular absent others at particular moments in time eludes her even though she, like most of us, has had more writing experience in the epistolary form than in any other.

The published letter, whether fictional or real, carries with it the cachet of violated boundaries and revealed secrets simply by virtue of circulating in print what was once (or is alleged to have been) written for an audience of one. In his judicious and generous review of Cross's *Life*, Henry James attributes the widely felt disappointment in the biography to just such expectations of "revelations" raised by the form itself. He knows perfectly well that George Eliot's letters are not a true index of her mind:

> George Eliot's letters and journals are only a partial expression of her spirit, but they are evidently as full an expression as it was capable of giving itself when she was not wound up to the epic pitch. They do not explain her novels; they reflect in a singularly limited degree the process of growth of these great works; but it must be added that even a superficial acquaintance with the author was sufficient to assure one that her rich and complicated mind did not overflow in idle confidences.[4]

Henry James was admirably equipped to sympathize with the reticences of a "rich and complicated mind." Nonetheless, in the course of his review he makes several judgments about the letters and the life which are simply more eloquent versions of his sister's commentaries. He understands letter writing as an art—of wit, of spirit, of entertainment—in which George Eliot failed to excel: "George Eliot was not a great letter-writer, either in quantity or quality; she had neither the spirit, the leisure, nor the lightness of mind to conjure with the epistolary pen." He gestures toward the possibility that letters might "explain" or bring some essential truth to bear upon the writer's published work, even though George Eliot's do not. The "remarkable, extraordinary" thing turns out in the closing sentences of the essay to be the gap between George Eliot as a personality and the novels themselves, though Henry James expresses the gap not, like Alice, as a disillusion but rather as a mystery of creation: it is "that this quiet, anxious, sedentary, serious, invalidical English lady, without animal spirits, without adventures or sensations, should have made us believe that nothing in the world was alien to her; should have produced such rich, deep, masterly pictures of the multiform life of man."[5]

Here and elsewhere Henry James displays a tendency to read the content of the letters as a true expression of character—that is, to believe what George Eliot the letter writer says of herself. This tendency is especially marked in the single passage that attends directly to the letters themselves, one in which James talks about the early letters written "on the threshold of womanhood, which form a very full expression of her feelings at the time." The feelings themselves, he asserts, "are rather wanting in interest—one may almost say in amiability." And he goes on to quote several of the most rigidly evangelical pronouncements of Mary Ann Evans, as single sentences lifted out of their contexts, in order to demonstrate "the provincial strain" of her young mind.[6] So Henry James, who knows all about letters as "partial expressions," falls himself into the familiar habit of understanding their assertions as represented truths of character.

Nineteenth-century readers of the George Eliot letters were understandably hampered by the deletions and scramblings of John Cross. By cutting the most exemplary fragments from the letters and journals and lacing them together with occasional connective comments, Cross produced an "autobiography" that was clearly intended both to monumentalize the public figure that George Eliot had become in her last decade and to forestall any more personal or less respectfully motivated attempts at biography which might have followed her death.[7] Once Cross had "pruned" the letters "of everything that seemed to me irrelevant to my purpose—of everything that I thought my wife would have wished to be omitted," the documents that might have promised an intimate view of the author's hidden life unveiled only the official portrait of an idealized figure.[8] Yet little changed when Gordon Haight, after twenty years of collection, restoration, and annotation, began to publish the first volumes of the meticulously edited correspondence in 1954. In his review V. S. Pritchett went straight for the gap between novels and letters: "Great writers are not necessarily good letter writers; George Eliot is one of the dullest. . . . We have only to read her novels to see how misleading the letters of a writer may be."[9] The familiar disappointment, that the letters were neither entertaining reading nor keys to the fiction, was echoed in a variety of reviews, which leave the strong impression that the reviewers do not much like the character they discover, especially in the early evangelical letters.[10] Irving Howe and Geoffrey Tillotson were the exceptions; their reviews briefly point the way toward a practice of letter reading which does not rest on a search for an admirably witty epistolary show. Howe reads the letters as a moving drama of intellectual development which offers us "an unexcelled portrait of the intellectual life of a century ago, which in its tones and tensions, if not in the specific problems that agitated it, bears an astonishing resemblance to our own time." He is interested in the development of the young writer's style, claiming that after the evangelical phase, "the writing becomes firm and supple, excellent in a wholly unliterary way."[11] As he cites examples of particularly strong sentences, one begins to question the "unliterariness" of this excellence; the ghost of the gap between fiction and letters hovers still. Only in Tillotson's review does it become possible to get a momentary glimpse of a deep connection between novelist and letter writer. Of the much-reviled early correspondence he asserts, "Her mind—the mind we know so well from the novels and admire so much—is already stretching itself in happy exercise, and already dealing with characteristic materials."[12]

My project here is to elaborate those "characteristic materials" by working with the gap between George Eliot's letters and her novels, while redefining the nature of the gap itself. Letters cannot "explain" novels or give us access to the writer "behind" the fictional narrative, nor can excerpts from letters reliably provide "facts" about a situation or a sensibility on which to ground a literary argument. Letters and novels are both acts of self-representation in writing and, as such, may both be taken, to begin with, as fictions. They differ markedly in genre, purpose, formality, and above all, in their establishment of relations with their readers. Nevertheless, it is possible, while granting each genre its appropriate and separate space, to discover characteristic objects of attention and characteristic gestures of style. In George Eliot's case, letters written to particular correspondents over a long period of time can also draw us closer to understanding the fruitful difficulty with which she struggled throughout her life—the problem of audience itself. Henry James said of her sequestered life, "If her relations with the world had been easier, in a word, her books would have been less difficult."[13] I believe the relation between literary style and complex "relations with the world" can be traced in letters written well before the emergence of the novelist called George Eliot. Both the act and the idea of performance before an audience preoccupied Mary Ann Evans/George Eliot, whether she wrote for an audience of one or for the illusory "far-off, hazy, multitudinous assemblage" that she makes fun of in *Impressions of Theophrastus Such*.[14]

The activity of reading a group of originally singular, handwritten, and dispersed letters that have been made into a narrative by virtue of editing and publication requires some methodological attention. If we are to go beyond a search for clues to literary interpretation or a quest for character, what exactly are we looking for? What sort of status or definition do letters have as texts? Considering all the theory and criticism trained upon nonliterary texts in recent years, there has been remarkably little theorizing about the familiar letter, especially in English studies.[15] When we look about at the ordinary treatment of letters in the contemporary literary landscape, we find, first, a tremendous amount of work devoted to the production of beautifully edited complete correspondences of writers. How are these volumes used? What kinds of discourse do they generate? Biography, of course, and reviews in literary periodicals, which characteristically comment on the quality of the editing before (or after) they fall into the belles-lettres mode of commentary on correspondences as windows on historical moments and as opportunities for speculation about character and relationships. The growing number of books that print correspondences between two friends, lovers, artists, or intellectuals attests to the popular recognition of letter writing as dialogue created between two epistolary voices; it also suggests that the public appetite for light reading in letters creates a profitable audience for such productions.

Letters have of course been given a good deal of play in current works of scholarship and criticism devoted primarily to studies of a writer's fictional art; such work increasingly recognizes the independent textuality of the letters themselves. We "know," apparently, that letters are fictions of a sort, self-presentations addressed to a particular reader under very specific conditions of time and place and relationship. Nevertheless, I would say that the very act of collecting small snippets from letters and marshaling them within a literary or cultural argument creates a rhetorical situation in which the letter excerpt is specially privileged as a "truth" or "fact" somehow different in status from the language of the literary work in question. Stanley Fish implies that letters are accepted as "evidence" when he (ironically) imagines the course a scholar would take to produce a new "nonironic" Jane Austen for critical consumption: "It would begin with the uncovering of new evidence (a letter, a lost manuscript, a contemporary response) and proceed to the conclusion that Austen's intentions have been misconstrued by generations of literary critics."[16] The excitement generated by the discovery of a newly published letter or by a new connection between a particular letter and a particular poem is an excitement about new light or new truth.

Clearly there are ranges of things that can be proven from the evidence of letters; if this were not the case, biography writing would lose all its grounding in the truth of relationships and events. The use of quotations from letters to make points about the writer's beliefs, neuroses, or even writing styles remains a somewhat different matter. Excerpting is inevitable, and inevitably distorting; when one is writing a text of one's own, whole letters can only occasionally be incorporated. Nevertheless, a criticism that does not privilege the letter fragment can be imagined. It requires, first, that the letter or correspondence play the role of a primary text under discussion. And it requires a vigilance about contexts that is sometimes difficult to maintain in the heat of critical argument: such contexts as dates, correspondents, and the histories of relationships with them; conventional letter-writing practices of the period; and the letter's place in the series of letters written around its time.

The difficulty of theorizing letter writing and reading may arise from the fact that letters are embedded in so many different kinds of cultural codes. To go searching for discourse about letter writing in the library catalog is to begin several different journeys at once. Letters are forms of social conduct and material signs of a certain level of gentility. They are objects moved around by historically evolving postal systems and then moved around again from one reader, pile, box, or attic to another. They figure in discourse about friendship, gossip, conversation, confidence. Invented letters fashion the narratives of epistolary novels and many nonfictional tracts, essays, and conduct books. They are—especially in eighteenth-century England—a high literary form. They are a debated—and underdebated—genre, loosely attached to discussions of the autobiography and the diary. Because they are neither primarily public nor essentially private writing they defy all attempts to maintain the theoretical boundary implied by the distinction.

All this crosscutting is exactly what makes the letter so interesting to think about and so difficult to pin down. The notion that letters, whether historical or invented, might provide the form and content of a published narrative is in itself an indication of their cultural position on the boundary of public and private discourse. For the sake of gathering some of these disparate possibilities together in one place, I will briefly survey the main kinds of "letter books" which have presented the form in modern times and have created the ordinary terms in which we have learned to respond to the publication of other people's letters.

The most popular form of the letter book in seventeenth- and eighteenth-century England was the "letter-writer"—a manual that combined advice on letter form and language with an anthology of fictional letters intended to serve as models for a "complete" range of common epistolary situations.[17] Although there were sixteenth- and early seventeenth-century predecessors, the acknowledged "father" of the English form was Samuel Richardson, the anonymous author of a letter manual published in 1741 and brought to light under Richardson's name in 1928 as *Familiar Letters on Important Occasions*.[18] A typical title page of one of Richardson's anonymous offspring looks like this: "The Complete Letter-Writer, containing Familiar Letters on the most common occasions in Life; also a variety of Elegant Letters for the direction and embellishment of style on Business, Duty, Amusement, Love, Courtship, Marriage, Friendship, and other subjects."[19] Most of the letter-writers begin with a brief essay on orthography, grammar, correct forms of address, and directness of style; some are attentive to such matters as proper writing paper and sealing wax. Several make it clear that letters are portraits, or later photographs, of the writer and that they are therefore particular signs of character. The universal dictum, which pervades all levels of discourse about letter writing, is that letters should sound like conversation; that they are in fact simply substitutes for conversation with an absent person. Most of the model letters themselves sound like anything but conversation; both the nature of occasions calling for letters and the language in which they are to be negotiated are highly formalized. The English letter-writers do address the "familiar" world in the sense that they offer models of correspondence between family members (to and from a child first going away to school, to a young man who is sowing his wild oats, etc.) and between masters and servants (letters of hiring, firing, advice, or recommendation).[20] The content of such letters turns the letter-manual into a conduct book that works by example to instruct parents on the diction and tone of advice to their children or servants, children and servants on the epistolary formulas of deference and request, lovers on discreet rituals of courtship, and so forth.[21]

The manuals' ubiquitous identification of letter writing with conversation has stuck stubbornly even to the most modern discourse on letters. William J. Dawson, a letter enthusiast who produced a popular collection titled *The Great English Letter-Writers* (1908), explains the special public privacy of tone in the good letter by calling the letter writer "a conversationalist who does not mind being overheard."[22] Contemporary eighteenth-century scholars Howard Anderson and Irvin Ehrenpreis turn the tables on the ordinary use of this trope, pointing out that "the stress laid upon the link between familiar letters and conversation indicates as much about the artful nature of the latter as the spontanaeity of the former"—an artful turn that connects the two activities all the more deeply.[23] Bruce Redford, who has written a critical book on letters, announces that his subject is "the familiar letter as intimate conversation," his method, the analysis of the performative techniques through which a letter writer devises rhetorical substitutes for the physical encounter of actual conversation.[24]

The stress on ordinary ways of speaking in early letter manuals and epistolary fictions did contribute to a general shift toward a preference for plain prose style.[25] And the pervasive metaphor of letter writing as conversation does have something to say about the nonargumentative, associative form of the letter as contrasted to the essay, about the choices of diction and tone which a letter writer makes, about the implicit expectation of response and counterresponse, and about a situation in which discourse addressed to a known audience of one may or may not be "overheard" by others. Still, this identification of speech and writing deserves not only to be theoretically deconstructed but to be challenged in other fundamental ways.[26] A letter writer may be responding to a received letter, but she has no inter-

locutor to alter and determine the course she takes from one sentence
to the next. The state of solitary writing is essentially different from
the action of dialogue. The act of writing creates by its nature a
different kind of self-representation than a conversation. In short,
the letter writer is in control of her discourse and may if she wishes
make representations that might be belied by a face-to-face social
encounter. Depending on the writer and the situation, these representations may take the form of greater confession or greater reticence. The letter writer is also constrained by whatever cultural conventions of letter writing she happens to have internalized, which are
necessarily different from the conversational manners she has
adopted. All this, and more, is well-known in practice to all of us, and
most of us probably have an intuitive preference, in tricky situations,
for either the control of the letter or the improvisatory interchange of
conversation. When it comes to developing a practice of letter reading, then, the standard of judging letters as interesting conversation
leaves out the formal and rhetorical qualities peculiar to the genre.[27]

   A different kind of generic crossing between letter-writing manuals
and conduct books also has a prolific history. Advice about epistolary
form made its way from the letter-writers into countless general etiquette books for women, which perpetuated their assumptions
throughout the nineteenth century and beyond. In later handbooks a
specifically Victorian sensibility was sometimes expressed in the special, emotionally charged attention paid to the writing of letters of
condolence.[28] A more intimate exchange of genre and content appears in the high proportion of the earlier conduct books addressed
to women which were written in epistolary form. Why should conduct
books disguise themselves as familiar letters? The frequent appearance of the letter form in many kinds of later eighteenth-century
prose writing suggests that this fiction, with its intimation of personal
contact and the public revelation of private character, had more popular appeal than the formal essay. But there is another important
reason: the feminization of the letter as the sole mode of writing
appropriate to the domestic sphere and the growing proscription of
female publicity or publication.[29] As the introductions to such volumes suggest, the letter form was intended to inscribe the discourse
of female conduct firmly within a domestic or familial context.

   That the subsequent Letters were written by a tender father, in a
   declining state of health, for the instruction of his daughters, and

not intended for the Public, is a circumstance which will recommend them to every one who considers them in the light of admoni-
tion and advice. In such domestic intercourse, no sacrifices are
made to prejudices, to customs, to fashionable opinions. Paternal
love, paternal care, speak their genuine sentiments, undisguised
and unrestrained.

Thus John Gregory began *A Father's Legacy to His Daughters*, published
in 1774.[30] John Bennet followed suit in 1818, addressing his *Letters to
a Young Lady* to a woman whose mother had commended her to his
care.[31] Hester Chapone dedicated her letters of advice to Mrs. Mon-
tague, asserting her own location within the domestic sphere: "I believe you are persuaded that I never entertained a thought of appearing in public, when the desire of being useful to one dear child, in
whom I take the tenderest interest, induced me to write the following
letters."[32] Jane West used only half of the myth, acknowledging "that
these letters were *originally written* for the purpose of publication,
although they are addressed to a young lady, the daughter of the
dearest friend of the author's early life."[33] Such fictions carried on the
tradition established by the letter-writers, in which the familial giving
of advice was linked with the writing of letters. At the same time they
used the ambiguous form of the letter to deny the "publicity" of
publication, as though it were essential to avoid the appearance of a
kind of performance they would forbid their feminine readers.[34]

If the letter manuals spawned a variety of intersections between
letters and conduct, they also produced more literary hybrids. As
Robert Adams Day tells us, "No very clear line . . . was drawn between
collections of letters intended as instructive models and miscellanies
of letters designed for entertainment, and these last bridged the gap
between Emily Post and epistolary fiction."[35] Model letters addressed
imaginary, if supposedly typical, situations; their writers created rudi-
mentary plots by presenting the letters in pairs, one letter responding
to the situation imagined in the other. For Samuel Richardson it was
just a step from the creation of such fictional dialogues to the extended epistolary narrative of *Pamela*; for others the letter-writers
were an inviting opportunity for the play of satire.[36] For my purposes
here, the inherently ambiguous boundaries between letters and novels are interesting in two particular ways. Individual letters, by inventing voices and situations, may more or less overtly make themselves
into fictions; the possibility of experimenting with fictional forms of

self-representation is always there. And a series of letters—even a group of two—immediately creates the possibility of narrative. As readers of correspondences, we are constructors of narrative no less than when we read epistolary novels. The plot lines are more intermittent, but they are there, and the conditions making for prolific nineteenth-century letter writing—after the penny post, before the telephone—make it more likely that we will get many stages of each story. If reading a correspondence seems to convey such stories better than biography—and it often does—then we must lace our awareness of fictionality into our theory of reception.

The letter manuals, with their peculiar intersections of letter and conversation, conduct and fiction, were not the only popular form in which published letters were circulated. A second common mode of letter book is the collection of selected individual letters by well-known writers, apparently intended as light reading matter for popular audiences.[37] Such volumes, which appeal to the reader's desire for windows that open on the private lives of the famous, take their stand on the notion of letters as moral inspirations and aesthetic entertainments. Like other books of extracted "gems," they commodify and perhaps seek to replace the practice of keeping individual commonplace books, in which selected favorite passages from literature are copied. They are also indicators of the market for their higher-brow source material, the publications of individual correspondences that became increasingly popular during the eighteenth and nineteenth centuries.[38]

Many of the Victorian and post-Victorian collections suggest an idiosyncratic randomness of selection, underlined by the categories invented to give the books some illusion of order. E. V. Lucas's *Gentlest Art* (1907), which went through many editions and overflowed into a successor, *The Second Post*, moves from "Children and Grandfathers" and "The News Bearers" to "The Familiar Manner," "The Grand Style," and "With a Spice"—a category filled entirely by the words of that perennial favorite, Jane Carlyle. Lucas also provides each letter with a running title: "Marjorie Fleming Writes Her First Letter" or "The Dean Tells Stella All." Other editors rely on historical order, though they all tend to recirculate a favorite group of names. Editorial introductions may be minimal, though it is possible to see a shift in descriptions of what such collections are good for. One T. Chamberlain, who edited an 1843 collection, announces that his primary object is "to bring together a mass of sound Christian advice and opinion bearing upon the daily concerns of human life."[39] By the early twentieth century, letters had frankly become valuable as keys to personality. William J. Dawson, who prefaced his two-volume collection with extensive and informative essays on the history and aesthetics of letter writing, emerges as a cheerleader for the familiar letter as the most intimate recording of the self. His letter writer

> must possess daring and freedom, for the last place where caution and reticence are required is in the familiar epistle; he must be resolutely sincere, for the moment he begins to pose his magic wand is broken, and he becomes tedious and offensive; he must above all possess the intimate note, for without it he will produce an essay, but not a letter. Of all these qualities, perhaps the last is the rarest, for a good letter is really a page from the secret memoirs of a man. . . . For this is the first aim of a true letter, self-revelation.[40]

It would be difficult to find a more stirring expression of the modern myth of the letter or of the notion of good writing as an essentially spontaneous, romantic act.

For Dawson, the letter may liberate the audience-conscious writer into "a free revelation of personality" which is also "a corresponding release of literary power." Like other editors, he praises the true letter as a document written without consciousness of a larger public; the stifling awareness of being a public personage is, in his view, responsible for the dullness of George Eliot's correspondence and the stiffness of Matthew Arnold's.[41] He is, however, one of the few editors to include George Eliot in his miscellany at all. Whereas the emotionally direct letters of Charlotte Brontë virtually dominate the collection, George Eliot is represented by a single famous letter, the one written to Cara Bray in September 1855 to defend the morality of her relationship with George Henry Lewes. The modern ethics of this choice may be appreciated by comparison with that of Dawson's contemporary Ada Ingpen, who was virtually required by her focus on women writers to include George Eliot. Her single entry is an impersonal excerpt that describes Spanish scenery in a manner calculated to enrage Alice James.[42]

When letter collecting is powered by the desire to revel in personality, George Eliot's productions do not make the cut. Nor does she figure in my next category of letter discourse, books of essays based on the correspondences of a selected group of writers. Books such as

Lyn Irvine's *Ten Letter-Writers* (1932), Cecil Emden's *Poets in Their Letters* (1959), and Elizabeth Drew's *Literature of Gossip* (1964) are literary meditations aimed at both general and scholarly readers.[43] Generically related to the review essay, each piece of twenty to twenty-five pages weaves together a thematic, stylistic, part biographical, part judgmental essay from brief letter excerpts. Along with the scholarly works, such essays constitute the main body of writing which takes published correspondence as its text, and they perpetuate many of the guiding assumptions we have encountered so far. Letters are particularly valued because they are not written for publication; they are "regardless of fame and futurity."[44] They are intimate keys to character and to the capacity for loving friendship, to be considered apart from the literary works of their writers: "The conscious and unswerving intention of the artist, so individual and so rarely communicated or shared, differs in root and branch from the mood of the letter-writer."[45]

The introductions of Irvine and Drew are particularly interesting because of their desire to claim the familiar letter as a female art and to feminize the epistolary activity of men.[46] In the assumptions of these twentieth-century essayists the Victorian linkage of the letter with the smallness, spontaneity, human connectiveness, and particularity of the domestic realm coexists with the eighteenth-century idea of the letter as an art form in its own right. Marian Evans herself, writing in male guise an anonymous review essay on seventeenth- and eighteenth-century French women of letters, shows a similar tendency to value the nonpublic, "feminine" modes of writing and salon conversation: she praises women's letters, memoirs, and private romances, "which left the feminine character of their minds uncramped by timidity, and unstrained by mistaken effort."[47] Such gendering of letters celebrates the literary talent that has expressed itself in epistolary forms, but it might also give us pause: does it miniaturize the female sphere? praise the inconsequentiality of its resident art form? set letters in a border country of their own? The feminine gendering of letters at any given period of history deserves further scrutiny, to uncover the ideological work that it performs in its particular context.[48]

Until recently, scholarly work on the familiar letter avoided that particular crossing, but it has often been concerned with another: to what extent are letters in general or particular letters to be considered pieces of literature?[49] Arrayed against the popular celebration of the letter as spontaneous expression are the studies that demonstrate that the good letter is particularly artful, rhetorically inventive, or brilliantly calculated to imitate spontaneity; such evidences of conscious artfulness are then used to qualify letters as literature. It is not surprising, considering that this conception was formulated in the eighteenth century, that most studies of epistolary art take eighteenth-century materials as their subjects.[50] William Henry Irving asserts in his first sentence, "As a literary phenomenon, English letter writing begins in the early seventeenth and ends in the early nineteenth century."[51] The literariness of the letter is defined by its achievement of a balance between the writer and his sense of audience, between the formal and the personal. Irving imagines that the literary letter is defined by its consciousness of a larger audience than one; Anderson and Ehrenpreis praise the way the eighteenth-century letter maintains a gracious sense of the reader through its urbane discussion of things outside the writer's self.[52]

The focus on audience is an important contribution to the study of letters, but it has largely been confined to eighteenth-century studies. After Byron, says Irving, letters are not literature but "business or fun between two people."[53] Even the more contemporary Anderson and Ehrenpreis share this animus against nineteenth-century letters, finding some of the most admired, "in their excess of responsiveness, their almost frantic exuberance (suggesting a flight from nervous depression), to blot out the recipient of the letter, making him an absorptive pad for their intellectual perspirations; a fever of observation, reaction, and self-analysis in them seems to underlie even their best anecdotes."[54] The excesses of nineteenth-century letter writing are sometimes blamed on the institution of the universal penny post in 1840, as though it sanctioned by its democracy the undignified proliferation of uncensored egotism in the mails.[55]

The main question raised by such studies does not, however, concern their refusal of literary status to the letters of lesser centuries. What does it accomplish to define letters as literature in the first place? It may give license to publish, read, and write about them, but one is left with the problem of what to say. Once launched into their subjects, scholars of letters produce a variety of analyses that—not unlike the more popular versions—mix biography, rhetorical and stylistic analysis, or psychological study in relatively brief essays that attempt to give the flavor and high points of a correspondence; once again, letters are treated as a genre separate from the other produc-

tions of the writer's pen. Bruce Redford, the latest of the scholars in
this line, rejects those predecessors who "treat the letter as a docu-
mentary source, a lode of anecdote and observation, not as a verbal
construct."[56] His work on the performative creation of voice in letters
is nonetheless interested in defining the epistolary skills that make for
"mastery" in the form. Though his criteria are modern, including, for
example, "autonomy," or a re-creation and sublimation of "the time-
bound I,"[57] he is both defining an art form and watching it at work in
a series of short, paired portraits, which necessarily involve some fine
work with character, biography, and the function of letters in the
stressed economy of the individual soul. It has been difficult, it seems,
to avoid writing a book that does not depend on some form of special
pleading for one's noncanonical choice of genre; it is even more difficult to write about letters without discussing character, praising qualities associated with entertaining conversation, or showing how spontaneity is really art.

At present, the criticism of letters—of women's letters in
particular—has begun to profit both from the elision of difference
between literature and other forms of writing and from the study of
discourse as cultural construction. So far, much of the published work
on women's private letters occurs in short pieces that focus on certain
rhetorical tendencies in longer correspondences.[58] As for theory and
methodology, some scholars continue to pay lip service to the development of "literary" criteria; thus G. B. Tennyson, ending a review
article on the Carlyles, imagines that we will "soon turn attention to
just what kind of literary undertaking letters really are," as we have
begun to do with autobiography; or Patricia Spacks notes that "the
larger question of appropriate literary standards for published letters
of any period has not yet been confronted."[59] I am not at all sure that
these are the right developments to await. A more promising line of
argument about letters and literature historicizes the terms in which
literariness and value are defined, as Janet Altman does in her account of the changes in French letter books from the sixteenth to the
eighteenth century.[60] Beyond that, we need to know how to read the
letters we have; there has been plenty of talk about good and dull ones
already. The problem is not to assimilate letters to "literature," whatever that might mean, but to read them as representations of a different sort. It is time to start other hares than "character" and "art" in
our chase through volumes of other people's correspondence.

I turn, then, in an attempt to move toward a methodological position for this book, to recent meditations on letters and related genres which most resist the history of assumptions I have outlined so far. We begin with definitions—definitions that rescue the letter from its entanglement with conversation and place it securely in the realm of writing.[61] As a genre the letter is immediately recognizable by its physical signs: its date, salutation, closing, signature, perhaps an envelope with its addresses, stamps, postmark. The characteristics of its discourse tend recently to be discussed by way of comparison to the two related forms of "I" narrative, the autobiography and the diary. In all these forms the writer and the narrator are identified, yet share the necessary split between the writing "I" and the subject "I" which makes any such narrative a partial fiction of self-representation. The differences among the three forms are crucial, however. The autobiographical "I" looks back in retrospection to create a continuous narration; the diarist and letter writer write relatively noncontinuous fragments from a dated point of the present, with no knowledge of what is to happen next. Dating proclaims diaries and letters to be works composed at a particular moment of time—although they may not in every case have been—and make it possible to place the writing in relation to a historical day when certain kinds of knowledge beyond that of the self would have been possible or impossible. At this point, diary and letter diverge on the crucial matter of audience. The diary may well be read by others and may therefore be composed for an imaginary audience beyond the self; yet that audience is not inherent in the conventions of the genre. The letter, on the other hand, is overwhelmingly defined by the presence of a particular, usually named, directly addressed reader or narratee.

This direct address subtly alters the way many dimensions of the letter discourse may be read. A particular pair of correspondents may, for example, develop a special epistolary language that requires special acts of interpretation. More universally, letters are written with intentions or purposes bearing on their recipients and thus present a far wider range of poses or even misrepresentations than would normally be found in diary writing. The function of letters is to establish an exchange between people separated by distance (which may include a psychological distance between two people inhabiting the same house), so that the writing of a letter implies or demands the probability of a return, one which may or may not meet the expectations of the writer. And although the dating of letters links them, as we have seen, with diaries, the distance separating the time and place of writer and recipient gives the dating of letters a somewhat different significance; they may, for example, be determined by the writer's sense of those gaps in time and space between writing, reading, and replying. Finally, the letter-as-object, exchanged between friends, lovers, or other significant pairs, has a meaning different from that of other written objects, a meaning that Mireille Bossis calls "a *real weight* different from that of the words in any other kind of writing. . . . It is this *real weight* which leads love letters to be treated as sacred objects, even as fetishes." This quality of tangibility, Bossis suggests, is responsible for the keeping of correspondence which makes it possible for us to read the letters of the past.[62]

Letters also differ from diaries in the kind of narrative they finally produce. A diarist may read earlier entries as a preparation for writing, creating the possibility of a continuous or at least partially connected narrative. Even if she does not, the dating of a diary signifies a ritual order of continued attention to a particular project of writing, which may come to an intentional ending. The letter writer cannot look back to earlier texts, except in very unusual circumstances; a series of letters, especially if it is dispersed among several correspondents, is necessarily fragmentary, discontinous, and unfinished. Its dates work by juxtaposition as well as sequence; for the reader, the meaning of a letter's date may change depending on whether it is read as a single document or together with certain other parts of the correspondence. Of all the forms of writing, a "correspondence" most resists the conventions that define narrativity.

Nevertheless, we are compelled by its nature to read correspondence as narrative. The language of emplotment has become fashionable. Can we say that letters emplot themselves, or is plot solely an interpretive framework? Can letters be caught up in common cultural plots, as of courtship or marriage? Or as Charles Porter puts the "fundamental question" we bring to letters, "Just exactly *what is the 'plot'* of a writer's correspondence?"[63] Such questions bring to a head the difficulties and perhaps the treacheries that arise when a missive letter is transformed into a page of published correspondence and read by a public audience. What are the implications of this transformation, and how might we responsibly negotiate them?

As everyone recognizes, a letter published in a collected correspondence becomes a new kind of object. As readers, says Charles Porter, "we are in a sense breaking into a confidence, uncovering something private, seeing something we were probably never meant to see. We must recognize that our understanding of these letters is mediated by the ways in which they have come before our eyes."[64] The primary mediation is, of course, that of the editor who collects, orders, decides whether and how to footnote, and writes introductory or contextual material; a correspondence exists only by virtue of these activities. As English Showalter puts it, "A correspondence is thus a strange genre, in which one of the central prerogatives of the author, that of conceiving and implementing a coherent organization, is denied.[65]

As letter readers, then, we are always in double jeopardy: we are invaders of privacy and creators of plots where none were intended. Patricia Spacks has made the most extensive exploration of the first dilemma. In a chapter titled "Borderlands," Spacks carries on the tradition of allying letters with conversation by concentrating on the highly permeable border between letter reading and gossip. For her, "personal letters, published, function for the reader . . . as moral equivalents of gossip," and our reading "partakes of the gossip's delight in secret knowledge and of gossip's titillation." Since gossip is at least partly a humane and connective activity in Spacks's view, this is not necessarily a bad thing; nonetheless, reading historical letters must "objectify the thinking, feeling, composing subject" as we make our own narratives about her. It is only when she reaches the end of her chapter that Spacks fully acknowledges the difference between talk and letter writing, admitting that reading a writer's sentences tells us about sentences and modes of self-presentation in writing, not about the person. Nevertheless, she folds her new position neatly into the old: both gossip and letter reading are fueled by a quixotic desire to "know" other people.[66]

This is probably true, but atavistic desire may, in the study of letters, be transformed by the reader's consciousness of letters as writing, and writing in a particularly coded genre. A respect for the writerly fictionality of letters may be our surest way of avoiding or mitigating the errors of exploitation in which other people's letters are either used in the service of our own ideological arguments or believed in as keys to personality. Mireille Bossis has made a useful list of methodological cares to be taken in such a project. One must be scrupulous in reading a writer's sentences only in the context in which they occur: "What is said in a given context, at a certain time, does not have the same significance in a different context, at another time." One must take into account whether a letter is really "written" or whether it is merely a response to a letter received. Meaning in letters must be read as "the product of collaboration" between the correspondents. The fiction-making power released by the absence of the reader must be given its due. And the objectification of the letter writer which disturbs Spacks is transformed by Bossis into a potential strength of method: "By a sort of affective asceticism, we must avoid the pitfalls of identification (positive or negative) with the author, identification which might lead us indiscriminately to credit everything. We must accept that the writer will always be to a large degree opaque as an individual."[67]

These are sound guidelines, supplemented by the equally sound dictum that the letters of any writer should be read against the prevailing social codes of letter writing which she has both absorbed and marked in her own way. In George Eliot's case, for example, the frequent writing about illness which Alice James and other readers of the correspondence have noted with horror or astonishment does not indicate anything peculiar or especially noteworthy about her. In writing unceasingly of their own bad health and inquiring solicitously after the health of their correspondents, Marian and George Henry Lewes were participating in epistolary rites practiced by most members of their culture and especially noticeable in the letters of other Victorian intellectuals. The notation of illness may be considered a synecdoche for all the other matters of bodily and psychological life which Victorian letter writers did not mention and a gesture of intimacy or sympathy with their correspondents. For people especially conscious of letter writing as a system of credits and debts, as George Eliot was, the articulation of illness served as an explanation for delays in correspondence. In the absence of aspirin, antibiotics, and diagnostic machines, discourse about ill health may also have stood in for all that could not be adequately named or controlled, including the psychological stress generated by the anxious internalization of ideological debates or family troubles. Marian Evans Lewes was depressive, subject to bad headaches, colds, and dyspepsia, often ill while in London, and usually ill under, or after, psychological stress. She was also strong, an energetic and enthusiastic country walker, and capable of long periods of concentration and enjoyment. Most of these propensities were shared, and discussed, by many other people of her time. There is, as Bossis observes, "no longer any question here of seeking the personal myth but rather of seeking the societal one."[68]

Bossis's methodological observations are important to my project in another way as well: she is another critic who has placed the study of letters in a dialectical relation with a study of the work. Such a strategy can lead us away from the quest for "character" or "art" and into a different territory. Bossis calls this an attempt "to locate the personal myths of writers or artists"; I would identify it as a phenomenological study of the narrative gestures that most deeply characterize the productions of a writer. But as Bossis points out, the game is not to identify letters and novels: "There is no direct correlation between them, but the confrontation of two separate registers—which must above all be kept separate—lets one develop a dialectic between public and private, a dialectic rich with insights, through the very divergence it reveals."[69] Her distinction between public and private is somewhat misleading, since letters may express particularly public and fictions particularly private versions of a contested site in the writer's consciousness; for George Eliot especially, the public-private distinction was itself the most volatile of those sites. But the point about divergence is important for exactly that reason. In moving between those "two separate registers," how does a writer transform personal into fictional conflict? To what extent are the limits of fictional imagination determined by what we can learn of her relations with the social and moral codes that shape her letters? To what extent does the fictional imagination break through those codes? What, above all, are the recurring activities of form or style, the patterns of response and assertion, which might establish for us the verbal structures with which the writer negotiated between public and private worlds?

To avoid the crudest impositions of "plot," such work might best be done in small pieces, each one confined to a defined part of the correspondence and to a particular aspect of the many-sided creature that goes under the name of "self." The chapters that follow are such pieces. Each begins its inquiry with a set of letters, either a cluster written during a short period or a linked group written over longer periods of time; each moves in some way between readings of letters and fictions. The sense of coherence lies not in a continuous story but in the accumulation of instances that suggest George Eliot's difficult negotiations among her imperative to express, her deeply internalized codes of social behavior, and her well-sharpened sense of audience.

The strenuousness of those negotiations, rather than a lack of talent for letter writing, accounts for the stretches of "grayness" in the George Eliot letters. On several occasions, Marian Evans Lewes had reason to develop her sense that letters are always in danger of becoming vehicles for misinterpretation once they reach the hands of their readers. That particular sense of audience is also dramatized at moments in her fictional narratives when characters send and read letters. In Jane Austen's novels, interpolated letters provide occasions for taking accurate readings of the letter writer's character: when Elizabeth Bennet reads Mr. Collins's letter she receives full and fair information, as do Emma and Mr. Knightley when they judge Frank Churchill's long letter of self-explanation. Charlotte Brontë, less devoted to the conduct-book morality of letters as emblems of character, makes them, in *Villette*, into fetish objects. We do not know what her characters' letters actually say; they are physical presences that function as lover substitutes for Lucy Snowe. In contrast to both of her predecessors, George Eliot focuses on the difference between the way a letter is written and the way it is read. Arthur Donnithorne's letter to Hetty Sorrel is written into the text of *Adam Bede* so that we may judge it, but the drama of the scene lies in the way Hetty reads a very different letter from the one we do. The letters that initiate the courtship of Dorothea Brooke and Edward Casaubon in *Middlemarch* are similarly misread according to the internal lights of their recipients. George Eliot, always aware that the writer has no control over the mental world into which her letter enters, shaped her styles of address with that truth in mind.

Each of her correspondents is an audience, and her epistolary performances—whether dull or amusing—cannot fail to tell us something about her many ways of directing and constructing her readership. Her modes of responsiveness were often elaborately polite, occasionally weary; especially after she began writing novels, letter writing was not a favored activity or essential to her need for utterance. Much of her letter style is more attentive to conventional social practices governing letter writing than that of other Victorian letter writers— including George Henry Lewes, whose letters are more voiced, more interested in the communication of personality, and less concerned to control his reader's range of response. That point will be apparent throughout this book, but I pay special attention to it in the next chapter, which brings the codes of letter writing formulated in early nineteenth-century conduct books to bear upon the adolescent letters of Mary Ann Evans and Charlotte Brontë. It is in such a context that the peculiarities of George Eliot's relations with her reading audiences begin to emerge in high relief.

TWO

Constructing the Reader

In gloomy weather I shall fancy you with your feet
on your fender, your double eye-glass over your
nose, looking at me with friendly scrutiny as I tell
you of my little affairs, or recall the impressions of
my day's thought and reading.

—George Eliot, "Letters from
a Town Mouse to a Country Mouse"

On October 20, 1854, the recently married Charlotte Brontë
Nicholls wrote a newsy note to her school friend Ellen Nussey, with
whom she had corresponded faithfully for twenty-three years. Her
final paragaraph begins:

> Arthur has just been glancing over this note. He thinks I have writ-
> ten too freely about Amelia, &c. Men don't seem to understand
> making letters a vehicle of communication, they always seem to
> think us incautious. I'm sure I don't think I have said anything rash;
> however you must BURN it when read. Arthur says such letters as
> mine never ought to be kept, they are dangerous as lucifer matches,
> so be sure to follow a recommendation he has just given, 'fire them'
> or 'there will be no more,' such is his resolve. I can't help laughing,
> this seems to me so funny.[1]

The Reverend Arthur Nicholls did not think the matter funny, however, nor would he leave it alone. A few days later Charlotte relayed
his ultimatum: either Ellen must pledge in writing to burn the letters,
or he "will read every line I write and elect himself censor of our
correspondence. He says women are most rash in letter-writing, they

think only of the trustworthiness of their immediate friend, and do not look to contingencies; a letter may fall into any hand" (4:157).

Ellen complied in a spirit of satire that maintained the fellowship of women against husbandly interference, directing her one-sentence note "To the Revd. The Magister" : "As you seem to hold in great horror the *ardentia verba* of feminine epistles, I pledge myself to the destruction of Charlotte's epistles, henceforth, if you pledge yourself to *no* authorship in the matter communicated" (4:157).[2] Charlotte responded with a tactful meditation on Arthur's motives, explaining that he mistrusted "the chances of war, the accidental passing of letters into hands and under eyes for which they were never written." Such fears—"a man's mode of viewing correspondence"—explain to her why men's letters are "proverbially uninteresting and uncommunicative. . . . As to my own notes, I never thought of attaching importance to them or considering their fate, till Arthur seemed to reflect on both so seriously" (4:158).

Five months later Charlotte Brontë was dead, and the fate of her letters had become a pressing question for her survivors, who were determined to control the posthumous public image of the controversial novelist. But Arthur Nicholls's earlier desire to censor his wife's "rash" letters seems to have had less to do with his consciousness of her as a public figure than with his absorption of more general cultural fears about the dangers attendant upon women's letter writing. Nicholls may have been protecting himself from becoming too vivid a character in his wife's letters; he had already had ample experience as the subject of her satire when he appeared as the curate Macarthy in *Shirley*. The terms in which his strictures were reiterated, however, echo notions that were repeatedly expressed in early nineteenth-century conduct books for women. Such advice manuals celebrate letter writing as a specifically feminine art and duty that cements the bonds of female friendship before marriage and those of family affection thereafter. At the same time they display intense fears that women's letters may violate the boundaries of domestic privacy and female modesty by making indiscreet revelations or by indulging in egotistical displays of stylistic prowess.

"This epistolary period of life" was Hannah More's wry phrase for the years of a young woman's life with which conduct books were especially concerned: the period between the end of formal schooling and settlement in marriage (or singleness), when female friendships, particularly those begun at school, might be deepened and extended through letter writing and mutual visiting.[3] Written for the most part by clergymen or pious middle-class women, conduct books were especially aimed at preparing young women for the highly moralized domestic role that developed with the expansion and prosperity of the middle class. Both Mary Ann Evans and Charlotte Brontë, whose young lives were shaped by clergymen and schoolteachers, would have read some of these books or have been taught their precepts during their attendance at boarding schools. Brontë attended the Misses Wooler's Roe Head school near Dewsbury, where the headmistress based her regime on Hester Chapone's *Letters on the Improvement of the Mind*;[4] Mary Ann Evans attended a series of three boarding schools, beginning at the age of five and continuing until she was sixteen.[5]

For the evangelical Hannah More, young ladies' letter writing was fraught with dangers inherent in the weaknesses of the female mind when unprepared by rigorous training in "scrupulous exactness" of expression:

> The habit of exaggerating trifles, together with the grand female failing of excessive mutual flattery, and elaborate general professions of fondness and attachment, is inconceivably cherished by the voluminous private correspondence in which some girls are indulged. A facility of style, and an easy turn of expression, are acquisitions said to be derived from an early interchange of sentiments by letter-writing; but these would be dearly purchased by the sacrifice of that truth, sobriety, and correctness of language, and that ingenuous simplicity of character and manners so lovely in female youth.[6]

More's stern distrust of female correspondence as a trivial waste of young ladies' time and their parents' money, and as an opportunity to develop style at the expense of moral rectitude, underlies many other representations of letter writing, even those that place it in a somewhat better light. Thomas Gisborne warned against the lures of "studied phrases" in women's writing: "Frequently, too, the desire of shining intermingles itself, and involves them in additional temptations. They are ambitious to be distinguished for writing, as the phrase is, *good* letters." According to Gisborne, vanity may be fed by letter writing until it invades other aspects of conduct as well, though a "lady" may write a good letter if it contains "the natural effusions of the heart, expressed in unaffected language. Tinsel and glitter, and laboured phrases, dismiss the friend and introduce the authoress."[7] Gisborne's strictures present the kinds of circularity and contradiction that appear in discussions of female modesty in general: "ladies" are supposed to be "natural" letter writers—indeed, letter writing was understood to be a special female domain—yet they are subject to elaborate anxious attempts to make their writing conform to a conventional art of "naturalness."[8] Gisborne's fear that writing may in itself issue a dangerous invitation to performative egotism is one that Mary Ann Evans, along with many other talented letter writers before her, internalized well.[9]

When they speak of letter writing, nineteenth-century conduct manuals often connect it with the cultivation of friendship; Sarah Stickney Ellis's pages on correspondence occur, for example, in a chapter called "Friendship and Flirtation."[10] Even when letter writing is not specifically discussed, the praise of trust and openness in female friendship is always checked by warnings against indiscretion. John Gregory, whose unexamined contradictions follow one another with appealing candor on the pages of *A Father's Legacy to His Daughters*, moves without blinking an eye from an array of arguments for reserve to "After all, I wish you to have great ease and openness in your conversation."[11] Hester Chapone too wants young ladies to value candor but fears what they may say to one another: "This confidence of friendship is indeed one of its sweetest pleasures and greatest advantages. . . . But we must not wholly abandon prudence in any sort of connexion, since, when every guard is laid aside, our unbounded openness may injure others as well as ourselves."[12] Sections on letter writing almost invariably warn their readers not to write anything they would not want others to see. Eliza Ware Farrar, after such a ritual warning, gives directions about the care of letters received: they are to be filed and then boxed with instructions to return them to the writer in case of death, or young girls should make pacts with their correspondents to burn each other's letters after they have been kept for a year.[13] An equally practical American imitation of the genre, "by a lady of Massachusetts," includes the cautionary tale of one "Celia," who wrote so unguardedly to a school friend that her suitor, who arranged to intercept her letters, discovered her frivolous, indecorous mind, humiliated her by circulating her letters among his friends, and then abandoned her to a miserable life as an old maid.[14] (His right to engage in these activities goes unchallenged by the account.)

Such fantasies of exposure received serious and extended consideration in a pamphlet called *Letter Writing,* produced by the evangelical tract writer and novelist Charlotte Elizabeth Tonna in 1843.[15] The narrative is written as an imaginary dialogue between a Mrs. Williams and her brother, who has heard his sister's reputation compromised after a letter of hers expressing religious doubt and self-accusation was read aloud to the receiver's circle of acquaintances. The first lesson is clear: it is not safe to write confessional letters at all. But Tonna goes on to develop her case against social indiscretion into a full-scale onslaught on the dangers of egotism inherent in the act of letter writing, with an intensity of evangelical cross-examination that matches—and throws light upon—the rigors of Mary Ann Evans's early letters. Mrs. Williams is accused of insincerity and vanity: her expression of doubt and self-accusation is exposed as an opportunity to display her literary style and create sympathy and admiration for herself in her reader. Writing itself, even diary writing, is presented as potential apostasy; the moment one is careful of one's style, egotism has unseated faith. But if thinking about style is wicked, it is even worse to abuse the gift of writing: "Every sheet of paper that we fill with idle words and superficial ideas, and mere commonplace remark, stands on record against us as a fearful abuse of one of God's most precious gifts."[16] The proper and reverent exercise of God's gift is clearly a difficult enterprise, demanding that one eschew bad writing while paying no attention to the practice of original expression which might make it good.

Tonna recommends that the excesses of private female correspondence be checked, for letter writing, like dancing, is so often unprofitable, time wasting, and vain; ladies are better occupied in caring for the poor.[17] Yet she knows that letter writing is essential to the discharge of some cherished duties, and she notes them in markedly sentimental language: letters must be sent "to soothe the sorrows of separation and to cherish the affection and sympathy of friends" or "to the absent member of a loving home circle."[18] Apparently remorseful after her vigorous critique, she then appends to the American edition of her pamphlet a long quotation from Sarah Stickney Ellis which offers more practical and educational solutions to the threat of vanity and triviality in young women's letter writing.

Ellis is equally ready to complain about the silly uses to which letters are put, but she is devoted to the notion that letter writing might be used as a kind of correspondence course that would prevent the minds of young girls from falling into disrepair after they have left

school. Without writing, "few persons, and especially women, think
definitely. The accustomed occupation of their minds is that of musing; and they are, consequently, seldom able to disentangle a single
clear idea from the current of vague thoughts which they suffer perpetually to flow."[19] Writing letters about serious matters provides
mental discipline, and Ellis recommends that young women "agree,
for their own improvement and that of their friends, to correspond
on some given subject." She is even ready to recommend topics: the
relation in the letter writer's own words of facts from reading, "peculiarities of plants and animals, different traits of character developed
by people of different countries and grades of society," and so forth.
In this way it will be possible "to displace from the page of female
correspondence, the trifling, the commonplace, or the more mischie-
vous gossip, which that page too generally unfolds."[20] The "daughters
of England" whom Ellis addressed were not to concern themselves
with anything in the way of higher education, but they could at least
help to prepare each other's minds for subsequent conversations with
their husbands.

The Reverend Arthur Nicholls was not, then, idiosyncratic either in
his distrust of his wife's correspondence or in his interference with it.
Charlotte Brontë's apparently genuine ability to forget that her private letters might reach other audiences speaks for the lack of self-
consciousness with which she conducted her emotional and epistolary
life with those she trusted; at the age of sixteen Mary Ann Evans had
already internalized the kind of self-censorship that seems to have
amused Brontë at thirty-eight. Yet the letters that both novelists wrote
in their late teens—between the ages of sixteen and twenty-one—are
deeply, if differently, affected by the instruction in letter writing each
would have received at boarding school and absorbed through her
reading. Born just three years apart, and at equally provincial distances from the center of English cultural life, Mary Ann Evans and
Charlotte Brontë understood themselves to be living double lives;
their imaginative and intellectual abilities acted in hiding while they
performed the strenuous domestic duties of young women in mother-
less households. Letter writing is a borderline activity: as writing addressed to one at a distance it might be a conduit for the hidden life;
as social behavior it must conform to the rules of epistolary discourse.
As they developed their first extended correspondences, each of the
young writers worked with and against such codes, and in the process
each invented characteristic ways of imagining and constructing her

audience which are predictive—if not formative—of her future narrative style. In Mary Ann Evans's case, the early evangelical letters display the particularly complex negotiations with internal and external audiences which are striking features of George Eliot's writing. Charlotte Brontë's adolescent letters provide a lively contrast, in which comparable experiences are very differently negotiated.

In addition to universal strictures on stylistic vanity, frivolity, gossip, and violations of privacy, young women beginning their "epistolary period of life" were likely to have been taught that neat and legible handwriting was a measure of social virtue.[21] Both Charlotte Brontë and Mary Ann Evans apologize regularly for bad handwriting in their early correspondence beyond the immediate family. The difference in the ways they do so makes an amusing initial prototype of the differences in their emotional apprehension of social rules. At sixteen, just beginning the correspondence with Ellen Nussey which was to last her lifetime, Charlotte Brontë makes her apologies in perfunctory orders she is confident her friend will accept: "Excuse all faults in this wretched scrawl," says a sentence in one postscript; in another, "Do not criticize the execrable penmanship visible in this letter" (1:104, 105). Two years later she is a bit more elegant and thoughtful—"If you can read this scrawl it will be to the credit of your patience"—or even more perfunctory: "Pray write soon; forgive mistakes, erasures, bad writing, etc" (1:122, 124). A year later, when her page has "got somehow disgracefully blotted," she begs Ellen "to excuse its slovenly appearance—please let no one else see it for the writing into the bargain is shameful" (1:129–30). Even the "shameful" does not carry much weight; Brontë trusts her friend to pay very little more than formal attention to the problem of legibility. Three years into the correspondence she may still apologize for what she says, but she stops worrying about handwriting altogether.

In the letters of Mary Ann Evans the question of handwriting betrays how much she thinks about how her letters will look in the eyes of her reader, and her embarrassment at this concern takes shape in elaborate sentences of excuse. In her first surviving letter, written at sixteen to her former teacher and evangelical mentor Maria Lewis while her mother was dying and her father stricken suddenly ill, news of the family trauma is painfully mixed with apologies for social incorrectness. The letter begins, all too characteristically, "I am grieved and ashamed that we should have appeared so unmindful of your kindly expressed desire to hear from us respecting our dear Mother's health"; already Mary Ann is making a distinction between feeling and appearing, but worrying about appearance nonetheless. A good part of her second paragraph is devoted to the appearance of the letter itself: "I need scarcely apologize for the disgraceful untidiness of my note, as you may well imagine that neither my hand nor my head is in a very favorable state for writing; but I must tell you that I am compelled to send you this paper that looks so poverty-stricken in consequence of Mr. Bucknill's [the doctor's] having drawn on my stock till it is quite exhausted" (1:3). The poignancy of this letter comes not only from the way her fear of social judgment competes with the family news of illness and anxiety but from the way the excuse itself turns into a metaphor for the weariness and depletion she feels. It is a fitting beginning for a career in which acute self-consciousness, combined with a need to justify herself to a possibly hostile or offended audience, is transformed into powerful writing.

At eighteen, Mary Ann's apologies for "untidiness" had not diminished; the repetition of the term suggests a more general criticism that she may have been familiar with since childhood.[22] In a letter of August 1838 she alludes to some unmentionable reason for "an extra portion of untidiness," produced by "a degree of perturbation that prevents my either thinking or writing as I should like," and she fears the trouble that her "almost undecipherable" letter will give to Maria Lewis (1:8). In fact, this letter is difficult to read not because of untidiness but because the writing is so densely packed on the page, with no margins and virtually no space between the lines. The handwriting, as throughout this early period, is large, with strong and craggy vertical strokes; the letters slant forward with a kind of impatience to go ahead. It is not an easily gendered handwriting, nor one that suggests ease in writing. (In the early anonymous correspondence with George Eliot's publisher, John Blackwood, handwriting gave him no clue about her gender. In fact, he told her that her handwriting had reminded him of that of a male acquaintance.)[23] The apologies for untidiness might stand in for her self-consciousness about a hand that is not pretty, rounded, elegant, or feminine, or for the willfulness and ambition that demands that so much matter be compacted within the bounds of a single folded sheet.

After this point, apologies for handwriting become less florid and are more often consigned to postscripts, usually written separately on one of the flaps folded over to make the envelope. But they do re-

Manuscript, letter of Mary Ann Evans to Maria Lewis, August 18, 1838. Beinecke Rare Book and Manuscript Library, Yale University.

main, often as comments on rereading the letter: "I am dismayed this morning to find many parts of my letter so illegible" (1:13); "I am fearful my hasty writing will be troublesome for you to read" (1:20); "In reading my letter I find difficulties in understanding my scribble that I fear are hopelessly insurmountable for another" (1:24); "Flaws of the least evil that disfigure my letter are those of ink, but they need a pardon" (1:31); "Hardened as I am by evil habits I positively cannot look at my letter now that candles are come in without shame. I will not tax you thus again" (1:33). In dramatizing her process of revision, she expresses her sense of the gap between her own immersion in writing and the deciphering demanded of other eyes. In marked contrast to Brontë's apologies, these assume that the reader, however familiar, remains at a difficult, ever-to-be-negotiated distance.

The different senses of audience which crop up in even so trivial a matter as ritual apologies might initially be explained by the household situations of the two young writers. However much her father may or may not have loved and supported her in childhood, Mary Ann Evans had never had a family member who understood or shared anything about her intellectual ambition or her emotional volatility. In her late teens her turbulent inner life was isolated in a working country household where, after her mother's death, she acted as housekeeper to her father and brother. Maria Lewis, her childhood teacher and mentor, had been her first important audience beyond the family; she had also inducted Mary Ann into strict evangelical piety and suppressed her Midlands dialect. While Mary Ann's correspondence with Maria served as an intellectual and expressive lifeline that reached out of the family, it was necessarily confined by a continuing deference to Lewis and by the discourse of evangelical piety within which Mary Ann had to contrive to speak her mind. It was a given of Mary Ann Evans's existence that she would not be understood without a complex mediation of her feelings in languages that others might be expected to read or hear.

Charlotte Brontë had had since early childhood the intimate audience and collaboration of her brother Branwell, with whom she created an intensely romantic and gothic imaginary world that she was hard put to let go of even in her early twenties.[24] Her secret life was shared not only with her brother but with the second pair of Brontë imaginists, Emily and Anne; from its beginnings her writing assumed the readership of a sympathetic and equally emotional audience, one to whom she could speak directly and abruptly. When she began her correspondence with Ellen Nussey, she did so in the most conventional way, as a school friend who kept her wilder inner life safely out of sight; it seemed that she was to be the single Brontë sibling who knew that she must practice the arts of communication and negotiation with the more ordinary world. As the correspondence with Ellen developed, however, Charlotte began to incorporate her auditor more intensely in her own epistolary outpourings, anticipating the creation of roles for her reader which she was to make in her fiction.

Charlotte's first letters to Ellen Nussey might have been conduct-book models of an "improving" correspondence.[25] She adopted the role of the wiser friend, filling her pages mainly with responses to Ellen's news, giving moral perspective on Ellen's descriptions of other people, recommending a course of literary reading, reminding her that they had agreed to write once a month, and attempting to initiate a correspondence in French which will, she tells Ellen, "contribute greatly to your improvement" (1:108). She responds to Ellen's request for her opinion "respecting the amusement of dancing," about which Ellen seems to have been harboring Calvinist fears, arguing solemnly that "for the exercise and amusement of an hour among young people" dancing may be "perfectly innocent" (1:123). After a visit between them, she speaks approvingly of Ellen's new interest in politics and indulges in some political "rodomontade" in the Brontë fashion (1:126).

These letters are almost entirely responsive, telling almost nothing of Charlotte herself and often mentioning the lack of news Haworth has to offer; only at moments are glimpses of the writer unleashed. When Ellen reacts to her reading of Scott's *Kenilworth*, Charlotte cannot restrain her literary expertise:

> I was exceedingly amused at the characteristic and naive manner in which you expressed your detestation of Varney's character, so much so, indeed, that I could not forbear laughing aloud when I perused that part of your letter; he is certainly the personification of consummate villainy, and in the delineation of his dark and profoundly artful mind, Scott exhibits a wonderful knowledge of human nature, as well as surprising skill in embodying his perceptions so as to enable others to become participators in that knowledge.
> (1:109)

It does not sound as though she thinks her friends's participation in the dark and artful knowledge is terribly profound, despite Scott's best efforts. Rather, Ellen plays the role of the admirably sane and religious other, as in one of Charlotte's rare descriptions of her relation with herself: "As I read it [your last letter] I could not help wishing, that my own feelings more nearly resembled yours: but unhappily all the good thoughts that enter *my* mind evaporate almost before I have had time to ascertain their existence, every right resolution which I form is so transient, so fragile, and so easily broken that I sometimes fear I shall never be what I ought" (1:110).

Much of the personal feeling in these earliest letters concerns Charlotte's surprise at Ellen's continuing friendship, on which she comments in rather conduct-book-like rhetoric. A few months after leaving the Roe Head school, where they had met, Charlotte writes, a bit monitorially, "I think, dearest Ellen, our friendship is destined to form an exception to the general rule regarding school friendships. At least I know that absence has not in the least abated the sisterly affection which I feel toward you" (1:105). About sixteen months later, again bemoaning her lack of news, she tells Ellen,

> My motives for maintaining our practical correspondence are in the first place to get intelligence from you, and in the second that we may remind each other of our separate existences; without some such medium of reciprocal converse; according to the nature of things *you*, who are surrounded by society and friends, would soon forget that such an insignificant being as myself, ever lived, I however in the solitude of our little hill village, think of my only *unrelated* friend, my dear ci-devant school companion daily, nay almost hourly. Now Ellen don't you think I have very cleverly contrived to make a letter out of nothing? (1:118)

Despite the lighthearted dismissal with which the passage is insulated, Charlotte's tendency to cast Ellen as the one who might be lured away by "society" returns four months later (June 19, 1834) when she welcomes Ellen back from a visit to London. This letter takes the form of a moral essay addressed to her friend, in which she congratulates her for having escaped the corrupting influence of the great city: "You are withdrawing from the world (as it is called) and bringing with you . . . a heart as unsophisticated, as natural, as true, as that you carried there. . . . Few girls would have done as you have done—

would have beheld the glare and glitter and dazzling display of London, with dispositions so unchanged, hearts so uncontaminated." If the rhetoric of the letter can be believed, Ellen's continuing affection has convinced Charlotte, who describes herself as "slow, *very* slow to believe the protestations of another," that she is a *"true* friend" (1:120). It is difficult, in any case, to disentangle the language of the letter from any actual confession of new trust that Charlotte may be making; up to this point she has continued to negotiate the relationship with Ellen through the convention of those model friendships recommended for young ladies of their age.

The correspondence took a dramatic turn when Charlotte was twenty, separated from her family audience, and in emotional crisis. In July 1835 the Brontë siblings were, as Charlotte woefully put it, "about to divide, break up, separate" (1:129); she returned to Roe Head as a teacher, where she suffered badly from the restrictions of freedom imposed by the discipline of the boarding school. By 1836 she was in the throes of a long and serious depression, which expressed itself in letters to Ellen as religious breast-beating and self-accusation. Ellen's role as the sane religious counterpart to her friend's wayward imagination was intensified to the point that she became incorporated as a major character in Charlotte's inward drama, and the conventional endearments that ornamented the earlier letters turned into passionate declarations:

> My darling if I were like you I should have my face Zionward though prejudice and error might occasionally fling a mist over the glorious vision before me for with all your single-hearted sincerity you have your faults, but I am *not like you.* . . . If you knew my thoughts; the dreams that absorb me; and the fiery imagination that at times eats me up and makes me feel Society as it is, wretchedly insipid, you would pity and I dare say despise me. (1:139)

> I am at this moment trembling all over with excitement after reading your note; it is what I never received before—it is the unrestrained pouring out of a warm, gentle, generous heart; it contains sentiments unrestrained by human motives, prompted by the pure God himself; it expresses a noble sympathy which I *do* not, *cannot* deserve. (1:139–40)

> What am I compared to you? I feel my own utter worthlessness when I make the comparison. I am a very coarse, commonplace wretch, Ellen. I have some qualities that make me very miserable,

some feelings that you can have no participation in, that few, very few people in the world can at all understand. I don't pride myself on these peculiarities, I strive to conceal and suppress them as much as I can, but they burst out sometimes, and then those who see the explosion despise me, and I hate myself for days afterwards. We are going to have prayers, so I can write no more of this trash, yet it is too true. (1:141)

Though it is not Ellen who has become "unrestrained" in these letters, Charlotte's need to address Ellen as a loverlike but entirely pure figure increases with the intensity of her confession:

In writing at this moment I feel an irksome disgust at the idea of using a single phrase that sounds like religious cant—I abhor myself—I despise myself—if the Doctrine of Calvin be true I am already an outcast—you cannot imagine how hard rebellious and intractable all my feelings are—When I begin to study on the subject I grow almost blasphemous, atheistical in my sentiments, don't desert me—don't be horrified at me, you know what I am—I wish I could see you, my darling, I have lavished the warmest affections of a very hot, tenacious heart upon you—if you grow cold—it's over— (1:143)

As though Ellen could be the religiously stable wife, the "comforter," who would save her from this agony, Charlotte fantasizes that they might live together "without being dependent on any third person for happiness" (1:147, 146). These astonishingly direct letters reveal the sexual turmoil that underlies the struggle with religious doubt; Ellen becomes a refuge and confessor figure not because Charlotte is in love with her but because she represents the negation of both the sexual charge and the corresponding despair that Charlotte could wish to erase in herself. At the same time she stands in, at her epistolary distance, for the lover whom Charlotte needs and wants, and the relationship with her takes the pattern of distance punctured by passionate confession which will later shape the romances of Charlotte's fiction. "Why are we to be divided?" Charlotte asks her rhetorically some months later. "Surely, Ellen, it must be because we are in danger of loving each other too well—of losing sight of the *Creator* in idolatry of the *creature*" (1:153). Jane Eyre will say the same of herself and Rochester on a later page of Brontë's.

The fictional re-creation of Ellen during that period of lonely pain may also be seen in retrospect as a precursor of Brontë's narrative relations with her reading audiences. The correspondence begins with Brontë in hiding, speaking in a reasonable, tutorial, social voice; it explodes in an episode of eloquent, sometimes gothic confessional language that trusts its audience to hear even as it seems to invite our disapproval. If Ellen Nussey could receive those letters without recoiling from the heat of that tenacious heart, she could be trusted. When Brontë invented the narrator Lucy Snowe it was precisely this about herself as a creator and tester of audiences that she reproduced as a fully developed fiction of narration.

Ellen Nussey passed the test, and soon after the crisis of 1836 the correspondence reached a new condition of normalcy in which Charlotte is neither the wise mentor nor the tortured supplicant. Her writing becomes supple, varied, and conversational; she addresses Ellen directly, as she might one of her siblings, in affection or rebuke; she feels free to jump from thought to thought or tone to tone as her mind moves. Charlotte Brontë had achieved what she understood—and practiced throughout her life—as a natural condition: to write to a friend as directly as she felt. That was a condition which Mary Ann Evans could almost never assume.

After the death of her mother in 1836 and the marriage of her elder sister in 1837, Mary Ann Evans kept house at Griff for her father, Robert Evans, and her brother, Isaac Evans, until March 1841, when, at twenty-one, she moved with her father to Foleshill, Coventry. The letters we have from the Griff period are written to three correspondents: Maria Lewis, Mary Ann's aunt and uncle Elizabeth and Samuel Evans (both lay Methodist preachers), and Martha Jackson, a school friend from Mary Ann's years at the Miss Franklins' school in Coventry (1832–1835).[26] The letters to the aunt and uncle are carefully religious in tone and content; family news and moral meditation are largely couched in language that imitates the pietistic discourse of the Methodist branch of Evanses. Those to Maria and Martha are regulated by two intertwined conventions: the evangelical and the educationally improving. The culturally "given" features of these early letters are, then, references of daily struggles to biblical texts, exhortations to faith, introspective self-cross-examinations about the temptations of ambition, reports on books and recommendations for reading (including a long set-piece essay on the dangers of novel reading), and the special discourse of female friendship. Mary Ann is scrupulous in her censorship of gossip and her respect for the privacy of the family; she almost never writes directly of her father or brother even during the prolonged and difficult negotiations among them that preceded the move to Foleshill, reserving what few complaints she allows herself for the household tasks that occupy much of her time. Given all these rhetorical and ideological constraints, she contrives within their terms an extraordinary representation of a passionate intellect at work.

These letters are dense with self-scrutiny and embarrassed by their own demands for attention. In the writer's most self-denying moments they berate the exhibitionism of performance in performative metaphorical prose; in other moments pietistic language appears to assuage the guilt of her interest in her own strong moods and conflicts of feeling. They are manifestly adolescent; at the same time they are visibly the stuff of which George Eliot novels were to be made. It is not altogether surprising that the chorus of reviewers who responded to them in the 1950s either dismissed them or felt moved to raise them, as Irving Howe did, to a George Eliot–like ideal: "I cannot recall having read any letters or diaries in which the idea of intellectual devotion is realized with such a blend of common humanity and selfless austerity."[27]

Much of the abundant intellectual and satirical energy at Mary Ann Evans's disposal is channeled into the making of metaphor. Through troping, she expands the trivial and fuses her emotional turbulence with intellectual and political life, as though she were, like her heroine Dorothea Brooke, determined to construct a life in which "everyday-things with us would mean the greatest things" (*Middlemarch*, chap. 3). Sometimes her metaphors express sheer play, the pleasure of writing, as in this reference to her kitchen duties: "I am about to commence the making of mince pies, with all the interesting sensations characterizing young enterprise or effort. Would that I could shield the medley of my feelings under so even and uniform a covering as that of the said pies! Had I not better assemble my friends at some Runnymede, that they may give me a Parva Charta ensuring to me the privilege of being silly or sillissima whenever I please?" (1:77). Characteristically, each of the three sentences is a critique of the one before, anticipating her reader's potentially judgmental response and transforming it into an artful acknowledgment hidden within the next metaphorical play. This motion of narrative, in which each sentence rereads and responds to the unstated implications of the one before, is to my mind a most striking (and lifelong) aspect of George Eliot's style. It creates both the dense and muscular demand of her prose, and its peculiar self-enclosure, which makes of the reader not so much a direct addressee as a reminder of other perspectives that the writer is compelled to incorporate, defuse, and transform.

Writing extended metaphor was also a way of relieving the pressure of rebellious feeling or frustration by comparing that feeling to immense universal processes. This example, one of Mary Ann's elaborated complaints about her domestic life, creates a geological image of just such internal pressure:

> I have lately led so unsettled a life and have been so desultory in my employments, that my mind, never of the most highly organized genus, is more than usually chaotic, or rather it is like a stratum of conglomerated fragments that shews here a jaw and rib of some ponderous quadruped, there a delicate alto-relievo of some fern-like plant, tiny shells, and mysterious nondescripts, encrusted and united with some unvaried and uninteresting but useful stone. My mind presents just such an assemblage of disjointed specimens of history, ancient and modern, scraps of poetry picked up from Shakespeare, Cowper, Wordsworth, and Milton, newspaper topics, morsels of Addison and Bacon, Latin verbs, geometry entomology and chemistry, reviews and metaphysics, all arrested and petrified and smothered by the fast thickening every day accession of actual events, relative anxieties, and household cares and vexations. (1:29)

It is remarkable how often such apparent self-criticism or discouragement becomes turned through exuberant writing into a vehicle for self-creation. The passage is an attempt to do what it complains of being unable to do: it fuses those fragments of reading and knowledge through an act of linguistic metamorphosis. The image of the mind as a geological field (containing a concealed threat to any religious definition of the self) seems to define the "petrified and smothered" being of the writer as a potential arena of transformative intellectual energy. The self evoked here is not, as in Brontë's letters, a romantic oppositional core but a field of mental activity; it is defined and brought into being by the act of describing itself as something else.

By incorporating her wide world of reading into the economy of the self, Mary Ann Evans overcomes her fear of intellectual insignificance: "Have you not alternating seasons of mental stagnation and activity? Just such as the political economists say there must be in a nation's pecuniary condition—all one's precious specie, time, going out to procure a stock of commodities while one's own manufactures are too paltry to be worth vending" (1:45–46). Such metaphors provide a partially concealed expression of the immensity of her own ambition, disguised as complaints about the burdens of home duties. So too does this far-from-abject apology to Maria Lewis play in George Eliot–like shifts and reversals with the importance of her own writing:

> You will think me interminably loquacious, and still worse you will be ready to compare my scribbled sheet to the walls of an Egyptian tomb for mystery, and determine not to imitate certain wise antiquaries or antiquarian wiseacres who "waste their precious years, how soon to fail?" in deciphering information which has only the lichen and moss of age to make it more valuable than the facts graphically conveyed by an upholsterer's pattern book. (1:64)

The sentence is in itself a little "pattern book" for certain idiosyncratic aspects of George Eliot's mature style. Starting with a defensive assumption about what her reader is thinking about her writing, she proceeds to turn the situation into a dizzying challenge to the reader's power of syntax, from which she emerges triumphant in her ironic historical equation of ancient hieroglyphics with the mundanity of contemporary fabric patterns. There is little for the reader to do but smile and applaud so highly condensed a display. And that is exactly, again, my point. The moment of apparent apology is the opportunity for the moment of self-enclosed, self-delighting narrative power.[28]

No one was more aware of the conflation of writing and egotism than Mary Ann Evans herself.[29] These early letters are full of apologies for egotism, for talking too much of herself, for "the frequent use of the personal pronoun" (1:23). Her difficulty with the beginnings of letters, especially in the earlier phases of her correspondences, suggests a related reluctance to impose her writing on her audiences, for fear that they will reject her epistolary overtures. She is very conscious of the debt incurred in sending or receiving a letter; in one opening of a letter to Martha Jackson this concern is transmuted into the metaphor of coinage:

> I am inclined to calculate the weight of feeling inversely to that of expression, and lest you should have adopted the same mathemat-

ics, I will secure myself against the suspicion of indifference to you by not once telling you that I was glad to see your delegate this morning, and by liquidating my debt to you "incontinent," as Knox would say, prove that I am desirous to have further traffic with you. It is true that all my cash is just now copper, and the payment is likely to prove both to you and me a heavy one; but if I waited till I could send you gold, you might confidently book mine as a bad debt. (1:35)

This is an especially tricky way of receiving and replying to a letter, but earlier examples attest to a long line of embarrassed and thus highly performative apologies: "I have in vain waited for an opportunity of reminding you of myself in a more modest way than that I am adopting . . ." (1:4); "My night thoughts are generally even more misty than my day thoughts; I would not therefore have inflicted them on you without good reason, especially as my letter-writing is, like my chess-playing, unpremeditated and quite at random . . ." (1:5); "Vain as I am I did not imagine that I had such a claim on your remembrance as to entitle me to an earlier proof of it than the welcome one I received yesterday . . ." (1:10). Martha Jackson seems to have elicited particularly elaborate rhetorical gestures in which the conventions of epistolary gratitude are both mocked and satisfied:

I pursue the same plan with my letter as I used when a little child with my pudding, that of dispatching the part for which I had the least relish first, and therefore I will dispose of such dry crust-like subjects as my reasons for not responding sooner to your welcome and undeservedly kind proof of your remembrance of me, and of my inability now to do so in a way that would satisfy my gratitude, as speedily as possible, that we may discuss without interruption the little sweetmeat my ill-furnished storeroom may afford. (1:8)

By May 1840 Mary Ann had become impatient of such games and began a letter to Maria: "If you are in health it is well. I am also well. I am so tired of *artful* simplicity, in modern vogue, that I have a mind to return to the antique fashion of simple formality" (1:50). Yet even this was a highly artful way of getting over the difficulty of beginning, though many beginnings had come and gone by this time. Although she finally worked her way out of such mannered openings, it would seem that Mary Ann's audiences were not easily taken for granted, that they had to be re-created, renegotiated, with each address in writing. Her need to foreground the conventions of gratitude and reciprocity suggests an uneasy sense of exchange with others which is channeled into elaborate constructions that express both the embarrassment and the opportunity of self-assertion.

The exclusion of her audience from a position of simple reciprocity is especially apparent when Mary Ann Evans is in pain or conflict herself. Like Charlotte Brontë, she had at the age of twenty a crisis in which family tension, religious rebellion, and sexual despair were mixed up together; the immediate cause was probably the prolonged family negotiation about who was to live where after Isaac Evans announced his engagement to marry. Mary Ann's tendency was to distance such conflicts in generalized religious meditation rather than to incorporate her friend into her emotional dramas. On October 30, 1839, announcing to Maria Lewis some unexplained "clouds and meteors that have appeared above my little horizon," she goes on to explain that "my troubles referred to have been of a very grovelling nature, but for that very reason they constitute the discipline most suitable for me." Thus begins a meditation on how our special trials are chosen by God as the best ones to teach us submission, couched in the pious general "we" so deep a part of George Eliot's repertoire. After two sentences of that, the "I" again demands its due: "If I were truly spiritually minded I should rather delight in an occasion of proving to myself the genuineness of my religious experience and of exercising a cheerful submission to the will of my Saviour, instead of acting as a bullock unaccustomed to the yoke, murmuring at the slightest opposition to my taste, the slightest mortification of my fleshly mind." This first appearance of the yoke image so familiar in George Eliot's work occurs as part of the ego's play of imagination and its subtle satire: "proving to myself the genuineness" of religious experience is hardly the same as feeling it. The next sentence, turning to the language of Saint Paul and then again to the "we," attempts to smother the "I" in the yoke of religious discourse, but the paragraph ends with a sigh of failure—"my mind a stranger to that continuous enjoyment of that peace that no man can take from its possessors" (1:31−32). All this is self-description located at a great remove from suffering; yet it makes in the alternations of pronouns and languages a syntactical representation of internal strife.

In October 1840, when she appears to have been most distressed, the letters verge on despair. Expressing her fear of perpetual loveless-

ness in a letter to Martha Jackson, Mary Ann casts it as a voice coming
to her from outside: "Every day's experience seems to deepen the
voice of foreboding that has long been telling me, 'The bliss of recip-
rocated affection is not allotted to you under any form. Your heart
must be widowed in this manner from the world, or you will never
seek a better portion; a consciousness of possessing the fervent love of
a human being would soon become your heaven, therefore it would
be your curse'" (1:70). Like Charlotte Brontë she casts her twenty-
year-old sexual frustration in terms of religious struggle, invoking the
same rejection of human idolatry in the name of faith. But the very
Brontëan voice that speaks here is at two removes from its audience
and set carefully apart from the writing self as well. For more direct
expressions of emotional chaos, Mary Ann Evans allowed her rage
and disgust to seep out around the edges of intellectual play, as in this
almost unreadable sentence:

> Carlyle says that to the artisans of Glasgow the world is not one of
> blue skies and a green carpet, but a world of copperas-fumes, low
> cellars, hard wages, 'striking,' and gin; and if the recollection of this
> picture did not remind me that gratitude should be my reservoir of
> feeling, that into which all that comes from above or around should
> be received as a source of fertilization for my soul, I should give a
> lachrymose parody of the said description and tell you all seriously
> what I now tell you playfully that mine is too often a world such as
> Wilkie can so well paint, a *walled-in* world, furnished with all the
> details which he remembers so accurately, and the least interesting
> part thereof is often what I suppose must be designated the intel-
> ligent; but I deny that it has even a comparative claim to the appella-
> tion for give me a three-legged stool and it will call up associations
> moral, poetical, mathematical if I do but ask it, while some human
> beings have the odious power of contaminating the very images that
> are enshrined as our soul's arcana, their baleful touch has the same
> effect as would a uniformity in the rays of light—it turns all objects
> to pale lead colour. (1:71)

The sentence is a virtual map of guilty rage, moving from the cen-
sored but still expressed desire to identify with the suffering of
working-class Glasgow, to disgust at the failure of "intelligence"
around her, to a direct attack on someone, perhaps Isaac, who has the
power to quench the lights of her inner world—all mediated through
the interruptive reminder that she should be grateful, the conditional

tense, the pretense of play, the use of comparison and fragments of other people's art. As the letter goes on it veers from Wordsworth to Shakespeare to Byron to George Sand in an effort to find a consolation, but none is forthcoming; instead, Mary Ann, seeking a moral generalization, produces one of brutal despair: "We should aim to be like plants in the chamber of sickness, dispensing purifying air even in a region that turns all pale its verdure and cramps its instinctive propensity to expand. Society is a wide nursery of plants where the hundred decompose to nourish the future ten, after giving collateral benefits to their contemporaries destined for a fairer garden" (1:71–72). If the form of these sentences calls for self-sacrifice, their images cry out for nourishment and room to expand. The charge of such writing comes at least as fully from its staging of the conflict between rage and conscience as it does from any directness of feeling. It is not a struggle into which any other human being is invited to enter; we watch as the writer herself watches, catches, and attempts to squelch her own insuppressible power.

For the modern reader of Mary Ann Evans's correspondence with Maria Lewis, the heavy, pious prose that guaranteed the contract of their epistolary relationship goes on nearly past the point of endurance. As Mary Ann privately began the process that was to lead to her rejection of organized religious belief, the letters to Maria seem more ritualistically religious; the juices of the writer's mind have begun to flow in other, still secret channels. At the same time Mary Ann plays with her two schooltime correspondents a new letter game initiated by Martha Jackson, who had come across *The Language of Flowers*, a dictionary that linked plants with mental or moral qualities (1:xlix). Martha names Mary Ann "Clematis," for intellectual beauty; Martha becomes "Ivy" (constancy); and Maria "Veronica" (fidelity in friendship). The apparent intensification of both evangelical and "young ladies'" conventions of letter writing signals an internal withdrawal during which letter writing becomes an activity maintained at least as much by politeness as by need.

The controlled play with the figuration of the reader in the later writing of George Eliot is a far cry from the embarrassed elaboration in some of the early letters, but it is made from the same source. The easy term for that source is the characterological one: self-consciousness, or perhaps hyperconsciousness of audience. To describe a kind of writing and not a kind of person, we would have to say

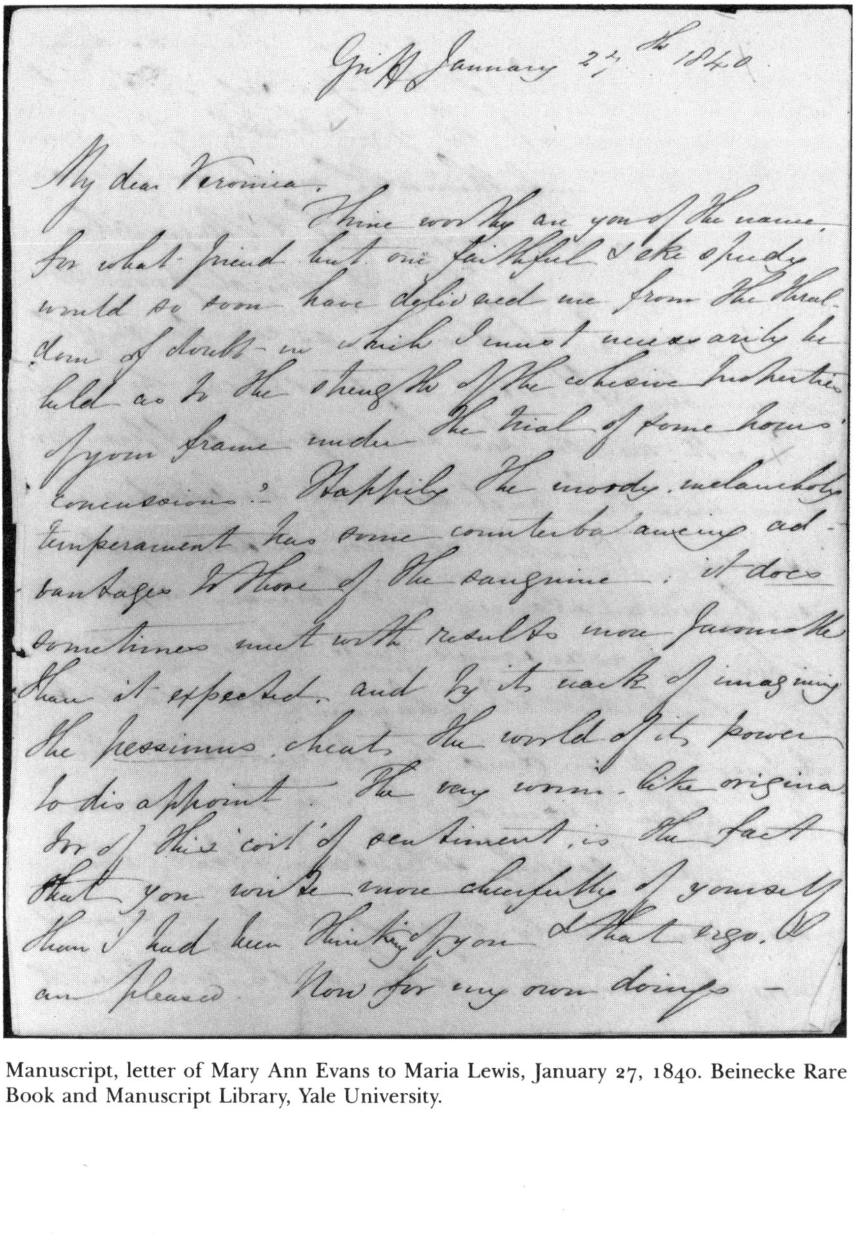
Griff January 27th 1840

My dear Veronica,

Thine worthy are you of the name, for what friend but one faithful & eke speedy would so soon have delivered me from the thraldom of doubt in which I must necessarily be held as to the strength of the cohesive tendencies of your frame under the trial of some hours' concussions? Happily the moody melancholy temperament has some counterbalancing advantages to those of the sanguine: it does sometimes meet with results more favorable than it expected, and by its mode of imagining the pessimus cheats the world of its power to disappoint. The very worm-like originator of this sort of sentiment, is the fact that you write more cheerfully of yourself than I had been thinking of you & that ergo I am pleased. Now for my own doings –

Manuscript, letter of Mary Ann Evans to Maria Lewis, January 27, 1840. Beinecke Rare Book and Manuscript Library, Yale University.

that this is prose generated from the act of rereading. If one sentence follows another, it is not always because the writer has her eye on an object; it may be that she is giving voice to what was silent, suppressed, or merely implied in the sentence before. The appeals to readers and the sudden shifts of perspective that are so central to the effect of George Eliot's prose originate in this always double activity, in which the writer both immerses herself in writing and assumes the position of a suddenly critical reading audience. If that is a defensive posture, it becomes in George Eliot's hands an immensely generative technique, for her mind is fertile in response to the imaginary opposition that she herself creates. As I want to show in a series of readings from her fictional work, the construction of the apparently oppositional reader comes into special play at moments when George Eliot feels moved to defend her artistic procedures. I begin with a brief fragment of writing in epistolary form, "Letters from a Town Mouse to a Country Mouse," in which the writer's relation to her reading audience is dramatized and fictionalized with particular emphasis.

"Letters from a Town Mouse to a Country Mouse" is a fragment written on two pages and two lines of large lined notebook paper. Gordon Haight includes it in his edition as a letter to Martha Jackson and says it was probably written in 1841 just before the move from Griff to Foleshill, but its features suggest a much later date, after the beginning of George Eliot's career. Haight bases his judgment on the appearance in the text of the name "Miss Jackson" and on the fact that the fragment beaks off with the announcement of a move (1:85–86; ms. Yale). There is, however, little evidence, either external or internal, that the piece is a letter to Martha. Its style, instantly recognizable as the earthy, sensory, nostalgic, yet satirical descriptive writing of George Eliot's early fiction, is entirely different from the usual bantering tones of Mary Ann Evans's letters to her school friend. The handwriting is noticeably different from the hand we see in George Eliot's letters until the late 1850s; during the first years of fiction writing her handwriting changed markedly, becoming smaller, more rounded, and more horizontally fluid. The hand in which the fragment is written is not visible in her letters until about 1858. Moreover, Mary Ann Evans did not write letters on large, lined, unfolded paper. The appearance of a Miss Jackson in the text suggests the rhetorical use of Martha's very common name in a passage about surroundings that enhance the appearance of human beings: "Who will pretend that a woman who is reached through a spacious entrance hall with

Letters from a Town Mouse to a Country Mouse.

Dearest Rusticus.

Your proposition that I should write my journal in the form of letters to you, smiles upon me invitingly. You say that scraps of thought & knowledge are hardly ever edifying to you except when they come to you associated with a personality, & that you shall get wiser on my scraps than by reading whole books of dead men who have neither face nor voice for you. That will stimulate me to write down the day's gatherings with more completeness than I have ever had resolution to do in the stiff sort of soliloquy that belongs to ordinary journal writing. In gloomy weather I shall fancy you with your feet on your fender, your double eye-glass over your nose, looking at me with friendly scrutiny as I tell you of my little affairs, or recall the impressions of my day's reading. In fair weather, I shall fancy that we are strolling together round your five acres, which you contrive to expand into a large farm by elaboration of thought & handiwork, throwing as much soul into your indignant spudding of a single thistle as any ordinary Ofellus would spend over a crop large enough to seed the worlds in the Milky Way. I, your companion, pause mechanically where you pause — look at a cow when you look at her — watch the flight of a straw which you toss aside with your leisurely speed, & all the while chatter egoistically about my own thoughts & doings, & complacently reflecting now & then, how very useful I am to you by keeping up your sympathy with a world where language is at a more sophisticated stage than Ba-a! Towzer's nose pushes itself against my fingers, & then my fingers wander about his rough coat as I write. I am in the country, without the trouble of packing up: I see the autumn berries, I snuff the peculiar pastiness of the autumn air between the hedge-rows in the green lane, & the new soil the plough is turning over in the next field; or I wrap my cloak round me & enjoy the December hoar frost that defines every lingering brown leaf on the

Manuscript, "Letters from a Town Mouse to a Country Mouse." Beinecke Rare Book and Manuscript Library, Yale University.

Indian matting can appear as utterly commonplace as Miss Jackson seen through the open parlour-door as you enter the passage?" The "Rusticus" to whom the imaginary letter is addressed is a small farmer, not apparently a female one. Rusticus is an auditor who represents the beloved country life that Marian Evans has left behind, and who marks a figure of difference from the language-obsessed, storytelling "I" of the piece. The "I" represents herself as a figure of "a little obloquy and a little celebrity," which may date the fragment at a point after the elopement with Lewes and the publication of *Adam Bede*. I conclude that the move referred to at the end of the piece may be the Leweses' move from Richmond to Holly Lodge, early in February 1859, after *Bede* had come out in three volumes but before the Liggins matter had begun to haunt George Eliot's "celebrity." In that case, the piece may be a preliminary and discarded sketch for what was to become the short first-person reminiscent opening chapter of *The Mill on the Floss*. The quality of the writing in portions of the sketch certainly resembles that curious chapter more than it does anything else in George Eliot's work.

When she toyed momentarily with the idea of Rusticus, George Eliot may have been experimenting with the possibility of writing an epistolary novel, a memoir in epistolary form, or simply a new kind of journal. The letter begins by imagining that Rusticus has proposed that the narrator write her journal in the form of letters to him, because "scraps of thought and knowledge are hardly ever edifying to you except when they come to you associated with a personality." The writer sees this as an invitation to write down her day's doings "with more completeness than I have ever had resolution to do in the stiff sort of soliloquy that belongs to ordinary journal writing." She imagines Rusticus as a friendly audience, "with your feet on your fender, your double eye-glass over your nose, looking at me with friendly scrutiny as I tell you of my little affairs." For this auditor, the writer will be a town mouse bringing culture to the country, "complacently reflecting now and then, how very useful I am to you by keeping up your sympathy with a world where language is at a more sophisticated stage than Ba-a!" But the first subject of her discourse is nostalgia, an evocation of the country in language. As in the opening of *The Mill on the Floss*, a physical sensation of the writing present is linked to the imaginative re-creation of the past. "Towzer's nose pushes itself against my fingers, and then my fingers wander about his rough coat as I write. I am in the country, without the trouble of packing up: I see the autumn berries, I snuff the peculiar freshness of the autumn air between the hedge rows in the green lane, and the new soil the plough is turning over in the next field . . ."; the list of sensory memories continues.

This writerly trance is suddenly broken by the recollection of a judging auditor who must be placated, advised, and amused. "You will almost accuse me of valuing you as I do some painter's figure—for the sake of the landscape in which you are placed," she observes, as though she were imagining how the characters in *Adam Bede* might complain to her if they could. "Well! I suppose we are all loved (or despised) a little for the sake of our circumstances as well as for our qualities." In full-blown George Eliot diction she illustrates: "The most heroic grocer would be under some disadvantage from the fact that you imagine him in company with pyramidal parcels of sugar, bladders of lard, and a general odour of tallow and the coating of cheese." This observation leads back to the "I," and the question of her attraction for the reading "you." As for her own "extrinsic charm," what does the writer have to make people care for her "a little more than my qualities might deserve"? Only, she concludes, that "little obloquy and a little celebrity"; and it is the obloquy to which she attributes "some of your interest in me."

The fragment breaks off at this interestingly autobiographical moment, as the writer promises her reader to explain, some day, how that obloquy has been useful to her in many other ways. The path through reminiscence has led to a potentially painful confrontation with the question of how those rural readers of *Adam Bede* and the even more intimately known readers of the projected new autobiographical novel might feel about her. The initial picture of the friendly rural auditor and the self-satirical writer has suddenly become fraught with the indirect admission that she hopes to be loved for "the circumstance" of her writing life, and her fear that "obloquy" still stands in her way. Turning corners of self-questioning at every paragraph, the fragment might stand as a condensed example of the internal dialogue of George Eliot as she veers between the work of imaginative re-creation and the specter of her attending audiences. Such alternations between the invocation of a sympathetic and an oppositional reader occur regularly in George Eliot's published fiction as well.

The first stories, *Scenes of Clerical Life*, are addressed to a "you" who is also called "reader," and even "dear reader." With this entity the narrator is on storytelling terms, indicated by such casual phrases as

"you see," "so that, you perceive," or "as you may imagine." Although
the narrator maintains a position of shared distance with the reader
as they jointly overlook the doings of the characters, he is also concerned to teach the reader how to read. Most simply, this strategy
takes shape in phrases that assume the reader has been drawing conclusions from the text and which attempt to direct those conclusions
properly: "You already suspect that the Vicar did not shine in the
more spiritual functions of his office" ("Gilfil," chap. 1), or "I dare say
the long residence of the Countess Czerlaski at Shepperton Vicarage
is very puzzling to you also, dear reader, . . . the more so, as I hope
you are not in the least inclined to put that very evil interpretation on
it which evidently found acceptance with the sallow and dyspeptic Mr
Duke" ("Amos Barton," chap. 7). The intimacy of tone thus established above and beyond the story is bought at the cost of condescen-
sion; this reader is addressed affectionately, but as a child. The tone is
interrupted, however, by a second construction, of the reader as a
lesser or narrower being who has entirely missed the point of the
narrator's immersion in the story. The appearance of this oppositional reader in the narrative seems essential to the project of defining
her art which George Eliot first performs in "Amos Barton" and
repeats in many novels thereafter. The alternation between images of
the audience as sympathetic and docile or distanced and critical will
also remain as a characteristic part of George Eliot's narrative procedure.[30]

The first of the imaginary misunderstanders is "a lady reader . . . Mrs Farthingale, for example," who declares Amos Barton "an
utterly uninteresting character!" George Eliot probably learned this
interruptive and confrontational technique from Thackeray, who also
used it to satirize readers of sentimental or sensational novels, but she
does not work it out in his way. Whereas Thackeray might go on to
confound the distinctions between life and art, George Eliot turns the
satire toward an articulated dogma of her realism, defined here as the
reader's moral discovery of "the poetry and the pathos, the tragedy
and the comedy, lying in the experience of a human soul that looks
out through dull grey eyes, and that speaks in a voice of quite ordinary tones" (chap. 5). My point here is not the nature of that definition or even its discomfiting position of double superiority to reader
and character but the means by which it is evoked. What we may call
the piety of George Eliot's realism is generated out of opposition to an
imaginary audience, the heightened rhetoric of persuasion made pos-

sible by the satirical anger first directed at Mrs. Farthingale, the reader of silly novels by lady novelists.

Adam Bede enunciates in its opening sentences a more defined relationship of narrator and reader which is carried through the novel with some consistency. "With a single drop of ink for a mirror, the Egyptian sorcerer undertakes to reveal to any chance comer far-reaching visions of the past. That is what I undertake to do for you, reader. With this drop of ink at the end of my pen, I will show you . . ." (chap. 1). The scenic mode of presentation which George Eliot develops here seems to situate narrator and reader on the outskirts of a setting that is drawn in pictorial detail by the narrator, then put into living motion by the dialogue of characters; it is a technique that calls attention to the novel as a fiction and yet manages to achieve a kind of intimate realism.³¹ The narrator plays the role of knowing guide: "Let me take you into that dining-room, and show you. . . . We will enter very softly, and stand still in the open doorway" (chap. 5). "Yes, the house must be inhabited, and we will see by whom; for imagination is a licensed trespasser: it has no fear of dogs, but may climb over walls and peep in at windows with impunity. Put your face to one of the glass panes in the right-hand window: what do you see?" (chap. 6). This construction of the reader offers more aesthetic respect than do the earliest fictions, but it, too, is ruptured by the famous excursus of chapter 17, "In Which the Story Pauses a Little." Although any responsive reader will have learned to like the clergyman Mr Irwine, the chapter opens with the narrator's fantasy of a lady's protest: "This Rector of Broxton is little better than a pagan!" and the great meditation on the moral value of artistic realism which follows is structured as an argument with a reader-antagonist who wants art to portray an ideal world of heros and villains and who is repulsed by the vulgarity of Dutch paintings. In response to this invented voice, the narrator is inspired to create an "I" who will drown the imaginary reader's qualms about easygoing clergymen in his own flood of eloquence. The flood is released, in dialogical fashion, by the direct confrontation with the narrow-minded upper-class taste that is staged in the text.

The invented oppositional reader is not intended to correspond with the actual reader; from the moment its voice is heard we are obliged by the narrative satire to resist it and to lend the weight of our resistance to the power of the narrative self-justification. As in some of the early letters, the reading audience is not so much addressed as called to witness a confrontation between the writer and an audience located in some fearful and scornful part of her consciousness. To be an actual reader, then, is to be audience to George Eliot's imaginary audiences; that is what her writing asks, and what it performs.

As she developed her narrative art, the direct addresses to the readerly "you" and the habit of scene setting begin to diminish. Vestiges remain in *The Mill on the Floss*, but for the most part the narrative tends to stay inside the story, and the critique of sentimental fiction is incorporated into the representations of characters' conflicts. Yet there are still junctures, explicit or implicit, when the overwhelming power of narrative persuasion depends on telling the imaginary reader that he is thinking something that an actual reader has most likely had little inclination to think. In *The Mill on the Floss* this dynamic becomes more interesting, because that something is directly linked to the narrator's own dark thoughts. As she opens book 4, "The Valley of Humiliation," the narrator confesses through the comparison of the Rhone and Rhine valleys her murderous fantasies about the "narrow, ugly, grovelling existence" that she has been exhorting her readers to love throughout her previous career. "I have a cruel conviction," she says, "that the lives these ruins are the traces of, were part of a gross sum of obscure vitality, that will be swept into the same oblivion with the generations of ants and beavers." And she goes on to imagine that her reader feels similarly oppressed by reading about the Dodsons and Tullivers: "You could not live among such people; you are stifled for want of an outlet towards something beautiful, great, or noble; you are irritated with these dull men and women, as a kind of population out of keeping with the earth on which they live." The "you" here is none other than the young Mary Ann Evans we have met in her letters, and the narrator's job is to stifle, in turn, this voice of rebellion.

She does so this time in a new way. Joining with the putative voice of the reader ("I share with you this sense of oppressive narrowness"), she creates a breathtaking series of widening intellectual perspectives that diminish and effectively silence the rebellious voice. First, feeling must be succeeded by a historical understanding of how this narrow life "has acted on young natures in many generations, that in the onward tendency of human things have risen above the mental level of the generation before them, to which they have been nevertheless tied by the strongest fibres of their hearts." Then this moving general description of her own conflict is further generalized and expanded to include "every town, and . . . hundreds of obscure hearths." Finally, historical understanding gives way to the further authority of science: if we think in this way, we are engaged in a scientific study that "shall bind the smallest things with the greatest" and "to which every single object suggests a vast sum of conditions." By the time she reaches the almost empty abstraction of the final sentences, the narrator has achieved an effective flight from the feared hatred she has projected upon her reader. Faced up close with the ordinary life that caused her so much pain, she virtually admits that she can endure it only as a distanced object of study. The action of intellectual energy triumphing over rage so intimately staged in the progression of these sentences is like a retrospective reenactment of the battles fought in the early letters.[32]

That narrative action is symptomatic of an unresolved relation to the past which is endemic to the telling of *The Mill on the Floss*. But the dialogical generation of high rhetoric from opposition may be observed in the prose of later novels as well. The most famous sentence in *Middlemarch* is doubtless this one: "If we had a keen vision and feeling of all ordinary human life, it would be like hearing the grass grow and the squirrel's heart beat, and we should die of that roar which lies on the other side of silence" (chap. 20). In the sequence of passages that demand the reader's sympathetic attention to the ordinary, this moment takes a new turn; instead of asking us to attend to the ordinary because it is our real life or our history, it suggests that the ordinary conceals the extraordinary and tragic intensity of hidden feeling. The shift in emphasis which has so often been studied in accounts of George Eliot's realism has taken place. But how does the narrator arrive at that astounding climactic sentence?

No explicit "you" has arrived on the scene to prompt it; yet the odd preceding shifts in narrative perspective and tone signal a familiar dynamic of readerly opposition. The drama begins with the description of Dorothea's response to the "weight of unintelligible Rome," in a paragraph that veers away from Dorothea, coming dangerously close to exposing the narrator's overwrought subjectivity. Roman art and architecture is said to impress Dorothea in terms that suggest a nightmare vision of her own condition in marriage to Casaubon: "All that was living and warm-blooded seemed sunk in the deep degeneracy of a superstition divorced from reverence"; the "eager Titanic life" is, like Dorothea, trapped and "gazing and struggling on walls and ceilings"; "all this vast wreck of ambitious ideals, sensuous and spiritual, mixed confusedly with the signs of breathing forgetfulness and degradation" figures the psychological confusion of her disillusion. The packing of a wide cultural life into metaphor for the psyche in turmoil is recognizable as a gesture developed from the earliest writerly impulses of Mary Ann Evans. But then the narrator, apparently describing Dorothea's postnarrative future, takes a turn into her own psyche, as she does several times in the novel when Dorothea suddenly becomes a site of meditation about the activity of memory. The forms that "took possession" of Dorothea's mind are said to prepare "strange associations which remained through her after-years . . . and in certain states of dull forlorness Dorothea all her life continued to see the vastness of St. Peter's, the huge bronze canopy, the excited intention in the attitudes and garments of the prophets and evangelists in the mosaics above, and the red drapery which was being hung for Christmas spreading itself everywhere like a disease of the retina." In its intellectual intention that last image is a brilliant imbrication of visual memory both with its original sensory experience and with the anguish of uncontrolled hallucination; it makes a sinister commentary on Wordsworth's "inward eye / Which is the bliss of solitude." In its affective quality, the image is frightening, suggestive of its speaker's intimacy with madness or hysteria. Having written it, George Eliot suddenly feels the power of other retinas focused disapprovingly on that display of morbidity. Her next sentence, dropping a thousand watts of intensity, begins the work of placating and then reconstructing those squeamish readers.[33]

"Not that this inward amazement of Dorothea's was anything very exceptional," she begins, belying the exceptional nature of the experience she has been describing; "many souls in their young nudity are tumbled out among incongruities and left to 'find their feet' among them." Her strategy of self-justification is to defuse her own heightened intensity by asserting in markedly colloquial language that Dorothea is just like every other newly married young woman. The next move is to rebuild the intensity in new terms: the reader who fails to regard Dorothea's situation as tragic because it is ordinary is wrong— ordinary inner experience is tragic—but this failure is understandable, for the intensity of ordinary hidden experience is unbearable: "We should die of that roar which lies on the other side of silence." The stages of this not entirely logical argument are puzzling if we take them seriously: first we are told that Dorothea's experience is common, as though to jolt us out of the strained emotionalism of the previous paragraph; then we are instructed that most people are not moved by what is not unusual, as though the problem had been that the Dorothea rhetoric was all too ordinary. The coldness of tone that accompanies these assumptions about the reader seems to imitate the coldness with which the narrator imagines our response to her evocation of psychic distress. It is just one indication of a contradiction between the defense of commonness and the defense of the specially gifted character which pervades and energizes the novel. Yet through these strange byways the passage arrives at a point where the reader is persuaded through the magnificent rhetoric of the closing lines to participate in and consent to the notion that inner life is as unbearably intense as the description in the previous paragraph has declared it to be. Having accomplished this overwhelming of an imaginary resistance, the narrator can assert a humorous fellowship with the limitations that protect everyone from knowing too much about other people's strong feelings: "As it is, the quickest of us walk about well wadded with stupidity."[34]

The existence of such proclamations depends—and here I return to my main theme—on the interpellation in the text of a resistance that must be overcome. It does not matter that the resisting reader so imagined is unlike most actual readers, though plenty of George Eliot's readers have recorded their annoyance at being addressed in the ways I have been describing here.[35] My point is rather that George Eliot was, and had always been, her own best resisting reader and that the creation of oppositional voices in the novels is a fictional development of a writing procedure she had practiced all her life. In the early letters, the existence of an actual correspondent often pales before the performative argumentative relations that her sentences set up with one another. In the novels, the reader who feels manipulated or excluded by the narrator's constructions of readers in the text is experiencing a related phenomenon. Those imagined readers are not really representations of ourselves; they are necessary embodiments of the many shadowy voices with whom George Eliot boxes in order to write.

This discussion will, I hope, complicate a common perception that the defensive postures and the self-justifying gestures of George Eliot's writing might be related to the beleaguered social position she assumed after her decision to live out of wedlock with George Henry Lewes. Henry James suggests something of this sort in his review of

Cross's *Life*. Considering the "sequestration" produced by her life with Lewes, James links the difficulty of her work with the "irregularity" of her life:

> Her deep, strenuous, much-considering mind . . . fed upon the idea of her irregularity with an intensity which doubtless only her magnificent intellectual activity and Lewes's brilliancy and ingenuity kept from being morbid. The fault of her work is the absence of spontanaeity, the excess of reflection; and by her action in 1854 . . . she committed herself to be nothing if not reflective, to cultivating a kind of compensatory earnestness. . . . If her relations with the world had been easier, in a word, her books would have been less difficult.[36]

Mary Ann Evans's "relations with the world"—that is, with all the other critical perspectives that might be brought to bear upon her at any given moment—had always been uneasy. The difficulty of a writing style that committed itself to negotiating with all those perspectives had been apparent since the first days she put pen to paper. "The idea of her irregularity" had been her constant companion since childhood. While it is possible that George Eliot's style might have developed more ease had her marriage to Lewes been a legal one, it is also likely that Marian Evans was empowered to make the decision to live with Lewes because she had already had strong experience in surviving the "irregularity" that resulted from her deep propensity toward "excess of reflection." As I have tried to suggest in this chapter, George Eliot's shadowy interlocutors were part of her mental equipment, and inseparable from the art of her writing.

THREE

Mary Ann Evans's Holy War

For my part, I wish to be among the ranks of that
glorious crusade that is seeking to set Truth's Holy
Sepulchre free from a usurped dominion. We shall
then see her resurrection!

—Mary Ann Evans to Elizabeth Pears,
January 28, 1842

On March 17, 1841, Robert Evans with his youngest daughter, Mary
Ann, moved to a house off the Foleshill Road just outside Coventry,
leaving his business and the family homestead at Griff in the hands of
his son, Isaac. During the four previous years, following the death of
her mother and the marriage of her elder sister Christiana—since the
age of seventeen—Mary Ann had been housekeeper to her father
and brother at Griff. The move to Foleshill was the result of an extended, wavering family negotiation about who was to live where, with
whom, and for whose sake, which had begun when Isaac announced
his engagement in May 1840.

Mary Ann's letters from May through October record the changes
of plan and the emotional turmoil they caused her. According to the
rule she scrupulously practiced in her correspondence she refrained
from complaining about any member of her family or even from
indicating the changing opinions and feelings of Robert or Isaac. Yet
the prolonged negotiation, in which she played the role of the
unmarried—possibly unmarriageable—daughter devoted to the best
interests of the father, was a painful confrontation with questions of
her own future and her own authority. On May 28 the matter first
surfaced in a letter to Maria Lewis, which reported on a subject that "I

forbear to put down on paper. . . . I will only hint that there seems a probability of my being an unoccupied damsel, of my being severed from all the ties that have hitherto given my existence the semblance of a usefulness beyond that of making up the requisite quantum of animal matter in the universe" (1:50). The defensive irony betrays her anger at the prospect of displacement, as well as her dependence on her family for an easily threatened social identity. In July she believes that she and her father will move to Coventry together; in September that she will be sent to live with her sister's family at Meriden. "Think you my elements are such as are likely to disturb the serenity of that atmosphere? or rather do you not think I shall be a stunted shrub?" she had queried when she first imagined the latter plan (1:51).

By October, however, it appeared that Robert and Mary Ann would stay at Griff and Isaac would move out: "My prospects have been long fluctuating so as to make it unsafe for me to mention them; *now* I believe I may say that I am not to be dislodged from my present pedestal or resign my sceptre. The secession has devolved on another and the *flutterer* is to leave the nest" (1:68). Self-mocking and triumphant, the political metaphors announce the reestablishment of stability: the fluctuating Isaac will go, father and daughter will stand together on firm ground. But Isaac's secession turned into a patriarchal succession in the end. Some weeks later news of the final reversal is accompanied by an acute sense of despair and disgust. Writing to enjoin Maria to visit her once more in the scenes she must soon leave, Mary Ann describes "a mindful of the accumulated scum of continued intercourse with the herd" and takes off into the brilliant, wild passage comparing her own sense of imprisonment and contamination by other human beings to Carlyle's description of working-class distress in "Chartism" (1:70–72). The tone is characteristically heard, labeled, and reproved—"it is time I check this Byronic invective"— but the despair continues to proliferate in images of society "in so chemically critical a state that a drop seems enough to change its whole form." The painful disruption of the home, refigured in political terms, erupts in images of turmoil and political revolution, and is finally quieted in a shift to the language of religious salvation. The easy slide from individual to social organism which occurs here was to recur with large consequences throughout Mary Ann Evans's thinking about her "Holy War."

The move away from Griff was shadowed by a sense of personal disruption and wrong. Although Mary Ann claimed in letters that her chief anxiety had been about her father's resistance to the change (1:83, 93), she continued to express her own sense of dispossession in her newly charged affection for the landscapes of Griff. She had retained her authority as her father's housekeeper and escaped the farmwife chores—managing the dairy, hiring and firing servants, organizing obligatory holiday feasts—that she had occasionally allowed herself to complain about in her letters to Maria. Yet Isaac had won a place that she had lost, and the family had fissured along its fault lines. The crisis *she* ignited, ten months after the move to Foleshill, was a four-month standoff with her father which she precipitated with her sudden announcement one Sunday morning that she would not accompany him to church as usual. It required no changes of place; yet it was read by her family in terms that extended and renewed the initial struggle. Then Mary Ann's story, one about an ideal quest for truth, came into conflict with the old stories of Robert and Isaac, about who was to live with whom, and why.

During the first eight months of the new life in Coventry, Mary Ann's correspondence with Maria Lewis proceeded apparently as before. In the "language of flowers" which she initiated with Maria on October 1, 1840, she was "Clematis," Maria "Veronica," and the religious tone of the correspondence seems if anything exaggerated during the year that followed. Yet there are subtle changes, which suggest at least in retrospect the newly venturesome thinking that Mary Ann was privately conducting in her new surroundings. Her diction, still heavily mannered at twenty-one, veers between pietistic sermonizing and Shakespearean banter, both styles revealing more interest in the production of powerful language than in their subject matters. Indications of her own concerns emerge indirectly, as commentaries on Maria's own unstable position; during this period Maria was looking for a new post as governess or teacher, and Mary Ann was trying to help her establish contacts. The threat to her own "pedestal" as vital caretaker to her father had made her sense of Maria's unemployment especially keen and underlined the strength of her own reluctance to operate in the public market as an independent figure. In July 1840 Mary Ann merges her own unsettled anxiety about Robert Evans's authority with Maria's troubles when she hopes that Maria "may have the assurance that 'your Father is at the helm'" (1:57). When in May 1841 Maria considers setting up a school for herself Mary Ann expresses her aversion to the plan, listing all the trials and headaches of that independent position. By August she seems to be attempting to

school herself in maintaining her intimacy with Maria, first suggesting that they should pray for each other daily "at Curfew time," then,
a few days later, confessing to an acute sense of isolation—"no one
with whom I can pour out my soul"—which is hastily retracted in the
next paragraph as she reminds herself of Maria's heavier trials
(1:101–103).

An unacknowledged shift in her religious orientation is especially
clear when she writes about potential religious barriers to Maria's
employment in dissenting families. In May, she describes with great
enthusiasm a freethinking dissenting family that may require a governess and opines, "Of course in Mr. W.'s family perfect freedom of
thought and action in religious matters would be understood as an
unquestioned right, but as education, to be such, implies aggression
on supposed error of every kind and incubation of truth it is probable
you would not choose to put yourself in a position apparently requiring the anomalous conditions of neutrality and command" (1:90–91).
It is all too clear that the writer's support lies with "perfect freedom of
thought and action" rather than with "aggression on supposed error,"
and Mary Ann's guilty sense that she has after all been making implications about her own education at Miss Lewis's hands expresses itself
at the end of her paragraph: "So much on this head which I fear I am
dilating unnecessarily." In October the subject comes up again, Mary
Ann requesting from Maria an indication of her willingness to take
employment with "*liberal spirited* nonconformity" (1:115), as though
she were indirectly testing the waters with regard to herself. By December 8 she had released herself from all tactful conformity to Maria's Evangelicalism, writing a diatribe against the divisiveness of reli
gious denominations—the "eternal dragons of Church and dissent"—
which, she imagines, would even if kept apart, "find abundant food
under the generic names Church and Dissent and these would begin
to bite and devour each other" (1:122).

By this time a vital new connection had made such dangerous satires possible. On November 2, Mary Ann paid her first visit to Charles
and Caroline (Cara) Bray at Rosehill, and her friendships with the
liberal ribbon manufacturer and his thoughtful Unitarian wife deepened immediately into something like family intimacy.[1] She had
found what she urgently required—people with whom she could
"pour our her soul" and thinkers who had preceded her on the journey of extrication from religious dogma. (Cara Bray had been con-

vinced by her brother Charles Christian Hennell's *Inquiry into the Origins of Christianity*, which concluded that the life of Christ was in no way miraculous and that Christianity was not a divine revelation but a natural religion. Charles Bray recorded in his autobiography that Mary Ann read this book before her intimacy with the Brays began).[2] The new family—soon expanded to include Cara's sister Sara Sophia Hennell—seems to have afforded an almost explosive release of feeling for Mary Ann Evans. In the summer of 1841 she had written a note of extravagant gratitude to an acquaintance of her sister's from whom she thought she had received "such exotic favors as those of purely affectionate attention" (1: 96); now her notes to Cara and Sara, immediately cured of their stilted syntax, were lavish with feeling and affectionate endearment. In Cara she had a new, concerned mother; in Sara, a new sister whose intellectual ambitions seemed at that time to match her own. The combination of freethinking and emotional receptivity which Mary Ann Evans found in the Brays was the necessary condition for the sudden eruption of her Holy War.[3] Within two months of acquaintance with their intense new friend, the Brays found themselves embroiled as nurturers and advisers in a bitter Evans family struggle.

On January 2, 1842, Robert Evans's journal records the fatal fact: "Went to Trinity Church in the forenoon. Miss Lewis went with me. Mary Ann did not go" (1:124). Why did Mary Ann choose to announce the change in her religious opinions in this fashion? The date suggests a New Year's resolution, a perhaps arbitrary or impulsive decision so to publicize the conviction that had been developing in the deep privacy of her mind for some time. Its abruptness—if we can assume that the refusal was her first outward sign—signals the depth of the gap between her inner life and her family life and the desperation or awkwardness in her attempt to negotiate it. The choice of a day when Maria Lewis was visiting presents other questions as well. Did she assume that Maria would act as a buffer, mitigating or explaining the shock to her father? Or that having a substitute companion at church would placate him? Or, conversely, did she count on her father's acceptance to buffer the blow to her friendship with Maria, which existed on the basis of shared religious commitments? Was she tacitly offering Maria a continuing intimacy with the family in place of their private religious dialogue? Whatever the case, her miscalculation is interesting; it represents the first time that the exigencies of her intellectual life were allowed to override the protective silences of family life or the veiled metaphorical excursions in intellectual rambunctiousness she had smuggled into her letters to Maria.

The impulsive refusal rested also on the assumption—at least the hope—that friendship and love are independent of opinion. On November 13 she had written a letter of veiled announcement to Maria, in which she mentions that her "whole soul has been engrossed in the most interesting of all enquiries" and proclaims that "my only desire is to know the truth, my only fear to cling to error." "Think," she implores, "is there any *conceivable* alteration in me that would prevent you coming at Christmas?" (1:120–21). The refusal to attend church may suggest a desire to test the two persons who had stuck with her the longest, who had shared with her the outer life of religious observance and the inner life of religious self-scrutiny. The structure of the test was equivalent to the structure of her own intellectual change: she had separated her reverential capacities and her sense of duty and adhesion from religious doctrine, and she was asking her father and friend to effect a similar separation in their relation to her. She could now risk such a test because there was, at last, an alternative conduit for her intellectual and affectional life in her new friendship with the Brays.

Robert Evans had no equipment that would allow him to understand his daughter's declaration in such terms. Mary Ann's heresy was a cause for social shame, a threat to his standing in the new community he thought he had entered for her sake. Considering all he had recently relinquished of his authority, the further provocation, defined in a realm beyond his frames of reference, may have been especially unacceptable. After two months of domestic coldness and a barrage of unsuccessful attempts at persuasion by family, clergymen, and friends, Robert reopened the housing battle that had so disturbed his daughter twenty months earlier: he made preliminary plans to move again. Both he and Isaac had already threatened Mary Ann with the argument that the Foleshill house had been taken entirely for her sake and that she had forfeited her right to the special expenditure by her antisocial behavior. For a short time Mary Ann planned to take lodgings in Leamington and support herself by teaching; Isaac, however, intervened with his father. As Caroline Bray recorded in a letter to one of her sisters, Isaac saw his sister's distinction between "setting herself up against the family" and "wishing for liberty to act according to her present convictions" (1:132); he persuaded Robert Evans to stay in Coventry and to allow Mary Ann to visit him at Griff for a time. After about five weeks at Griff, Mary Ann went home; in the interim father and daughter had reached an accommodation. Mary Ann acceded to her father's social demand that she attend church with him, and he silently conceded her right to think what she liked.

Isaac and his wife—perhaps because they had an interest in retaining the structure of households that had given them free rein at Griff—served during the crisis as translators, putting Mary Ann's positions into terms the father could (or would) understand. Yet Isaac was not above a further attempt to restart the family housing war when he found himself fearing the future burden of an eccentric unmarried sister. According to another secondhand report in a letter of Mrs. Bray's, Isaac returned to the charge in February 1843, when he tried to persuade his father to move to Meriden, where sister Chrissey lived with her family. Chrissey could, he reasoned, get Mary Ann away from the "radical" influence of the Brays, so that she would return to the church and find a suitable husband (1:156–57). Apparently Robert Evans was not to be moved; his standards of outward conformity—as well as his need for female tendance—had, perhaps, been adequately met.

Rendered in outline, the Holy War story raises some tantalizing questions for modern interpretation. What was the relation of the declaration of religious independence to the troubled negotiations about splitting the family? What was the family dynamic of decision? Was Mary Ann really innocent about, or blind to, her father's probable response to her unorthodoxy, or did she unconsciously will such a confrontation? Why did she not take the path of social as well as intellectual independence from relatives who refused to understand her? Was her eventual concession a humiliation or an achievement? And what, finally, did she learn from the Holy War?

Ruby Redinger gives the most extended analysis of the episode so far; she too sees it as a critical turning point, "both crucible and whetstone" for the genius of George Eliot.[4] Redinger understands the Holy War in the family context, as an unconscious act of aggression against Robert Evans: "Underlying her rebellion against her spiritual father lay the rebellion against her earthly father."[5] It was during the period of waiting for the Griff decision to be made, a time when Robert Evans's lack of authority in directing her destiny became manifest, that "she was fast preparing herself to reject another father,

God" (109). The "principled" decision not to attend church "provided her with what she was in need of without realizing it, a platform upon which to take her stand against her father" (118). And the family furor she created was a direct result of the father's and brother's sense of the "hostile aggressiveness of which she was unaware at the time" (119).

This account of unconscious rebellion forges a strong link between the family stress at Griff and its repetition in the Holy War. It was never, of course, Mary Ann Evans's way of interpreting herself, nor did she imagine herself in the early stages to be rejecting God. As her letters indicate, her rejection of Christian religious doctrine was undertaken in a militantly religious spirit, as a quest for truths worthy of God. The recollections of Mary Sibree, printed in Redinger's own pages, make that quite clear; in them we see a deeply moved Miss Evans exclaim that people of all faiths have "the strongest possible claim on God" (112). In a letter to her neighbor Elizabeth Pears, she writes on January 28, in the thick of the Holy War, "I fully participate in the belief that the only heaven here or hereafter is to be found in conformity with the will of the Supreme; a continual aiming at the attainment of that perfect ideal, the true Logos that dwells in the bosom of the One Father" (1:125–26). In the remarkable explanatory letter she wrote to her father, she lays out her position on the Bible: "I regard these writings as histories consisting of mingled truth and fiction, and while I admire and cherish much of what I believe to have been the moral teaching of Jesus himself, I consider the system of doctrines built upon the facts of his life and drawn as to its materials from Jewish notions to be most dishonourable to God and most pernicious in its influence on human and social happiness" (1:128). And she closes: "If ever I sought to obey the laws of my Creator and to follow duty wherever it may lead me I have that determination now" (1:130).

What God might be is, however, part of her question, and part of this story. The names she chooses—Creator, Supreme Being, even "the One Father"—signal an internal move from the evangelical to the romantic pole of her imagination. A tribute to Wordsworth written on her twentieth birthday (November 22, 1839) captures the polarity: writing to Maria, Mary Ann piously wishes "an indication of less satisfaction in terrene objects, a more frequent upturning of the soul's eye." But she cannot refrain from adding, "I never before met with so many of my own feelings expressed just as I could ⟨wish⟩ like them" (1:34). The crossed-out "wish" suggests an uncomfortable recognition that the two "wishes" do not exactly wish the same thing. By October 1, 1841, three months before her "heresy," she is writing in an unabashedly romantic vein, taking comfort for sadness not in pious meditation but in poetic fancy: "Is this not a true autumn day? Just the still melancholy that I love—that makes life and nature harmonize. The birds are all consulting about their migrations, the trees are putting on the hectic or the pallid hues of decay." The usual self-reflexive check is not long in appearing; she delivers Maria "by a good bye from more of this trash" and, in her next letter, apologizes for a misuse of the pen in writing those "silly nothings" (1:111–13). The person who wrote of her life in July 1840 as "this vestibule to life's theatre" (1:56) was in December 1841 exulting in a deity "who has originated and sustains our existence to be harmonizing notes in the great chorus of praise ever ascending from every part of the universe" (1:123). The romanticism of her new earth-loving credo takes Keatsian form in a later letter to Sara Hennell, who replaced Maria Lewis as her principal correspondent after the Holy War: "I think there can be few who more truly feel than I that this is a world of bliss and beauty, that is, that bliss and beauty are the end, the tendency of creation, that evil is the foil to the jewel, the intaglio without which there could be no cammeo, the shadows that are the only conditions of light in the picture" (1:146).

The welcome of release from perpetually checked romantic thoughts emerges strongly in the letters to the Reverend Francis Watts—one of the clergy unsuccessfully called in to bring Mary Ann back into the fold—which were written during and just after the Holy War. Tentatively trying out a new position, Mary Ann rejects the idea of God as "figure" and calls "prayer, beyond that involved in culture, . . . a vain offering." Having by now returned to her father, she has redefined prayer as a social practice; her idea of God is suspended. Overwhelmingly, her focus is not on the problem of Deity but on the release of romantic feeling and intellectual freedom. "I confess to you," she continues to Watts, "that I find it an inexpressible relief to be freed from the apprehension . . . that at each moment I tread on chords that will vibrate for weal or woe to all eternity. I could shed tears of joy to believe that in this lovely world I may lie on the grass and ruminate on possibilities without dreading lest my conclusions should be everlastingly fatal" (1:143–44). To confine such feelings—and their latent satire—to the category of rebellion against

God or father obscures the driving force of intellectual curiosity that
claimed its recognition in the Holy War.

In Redinger's development of the "lessons" of the Holy War, the
psychological reading gives way to a conclusion borrowed from
George Eliot's moral language. Redinger maintains that the standoff
with Robert Evans resulted in Mary Ann's confrontation with her own
aggressive egotism and a subsequent commitment to tolerance. In the
return to her father and to church, Mary Ann recognized that the
former action of her conscience was "no more than an outburst of the
very egoism she had sought for years to discipline" (123). The fear of
voluntarily leaving her father which Mary Ann expresses in her letter
to him is, Redinger suggests, the dawning recognition of her own
aggression and the realization that leaving would only be "a continua-
tion of that act"(123). The reward of that recognition, then, is the
reward of substituting self-control for rebellion: "At last she had
made the discovery which had eluded her for many years of anguish:
that the conscious suppression of self can lead to greater release from
the burden of self than the most drastic attempts to reduce the latter
by venting it outward" (125–26). At the same time, Redinger points to
a "new ego strength, a new sense of identity," discovered as Mary Ann
became "without arrogance, a law unto herself," a person who would
"never again submit to external pressure . . . as a reason for action"
(127).

Here we are reading the story of a George Eliot heroine at the
paradoxical turning point of maturity, when interior freedom becomes linked with apparent submission to others' minds. There is a
biographical truth in this story; yet this heroine is also stripped, as
George Eliot heroines are, of precisely the intellectual ferocity that
created and sustained the conflict of the Holy War. It is that drive, and
its implications for George Eliot's doctrines of sympathy and tolerance, that I wish to recover in turning to the Holy War letters.

Although it is probable that she discussed the growth of her religious skepticism with the Brays and with those who wished to dis-
suade her from it, neither Mary Ann Evans nor George Eliot ever told
that story in writing. We might suspect a strong resistance to telling
any version of it, from the complete silence in *Middlemarch* about what
happens to Dorothea's Evangelicalism after her engagement to Casaubon. Considering that the loss of faith story was a staple of Victorian literary production, this taciturnity is in itself interesting. It can
be explained, I think, by the way that the story turned so quickly into

another kind of narrative, one George Eliot was never to cease telling: the story of a "wide" idealistic mind coming into collision with the intractable prejudices around it and finding its heroism in bending to that narrowness in the name of common humanity. This story is implicit not only in George Eliot's theory of art ("If Art does not enlarge men's sympathies, it does nothing morally" [3:111]) but also in her theory of social change as a process that can occur only through the internal widening of each individual sensibility. The Holy War experience, then, became a story that commandingly patterned the thought of George Eliot. Yet it must be understood as a cover story, a shape of moral experience that has at its heart the necessity of erasing a model of change based on the concept of liberation and putting in its place another, in which the central revolution is a turning back.

The letters in which we can watch this transformation at work are powerful and few—seven, falling into three groups (and excluding the more doctrinal letters to the Reverend Mr. Watts which I have drawn on already). The first group, written before Robert Evans threatened to leave the house in Foleshill, are addressed to the Evans's neighbor Elizabeth Bray Pears (January 28, 1842), to Maria Lewis (February 18), and to Robert Evans himself (February 28). Of the second group of three, the first is written to Mrs. Caroline Bray from Foleshill (March 12); the second and third, to Mrs. Pears and Mrs. Bray, are dated from Griff during the period Mary Ann spent with Isaac and his wife (March 31 and April 20). The final letter, written eighteen months later, is addressed to Sara Hennell, by this time Mary Ann's main correspondent (October 9, 1843). In this letter the not-yet-twenty-four-year-old Mary Ann formulates sentences about the possibilities for spiritual and social change which are immediately recognizable as precursors of George Eliot's practice.

The first letters, of January and February 1842, are written in the full flush of liberated intellectual energy. The obsessive apologies of the earlier letters—for "untidy" or illegible handwriting, for "egotistical" attention to her own concerns, for the reiteration of "I"—are gone. The self-conscious literariness, the trying-on of styles, which marks her adolescent correspondence is abated. Gone, above all, is the fear of the recipient's judgment which renders the earlier letters exercises in balancing powerful needs for intellectual and emotional self-expression with equally strong needs to placate or imitate her correspondent's characteristic views and language. The Holy War letters are landmarks because Mary Ann Evans has allowed herself to forget her audience; or to put the same point a different way, the others have become audiences for newly unapologetic performances of herself.

The first letter to Elizabeth Pears (1:124–26) comes to a climax with Mary Ann's self-enlistment in the Holy War: "To *fear* the examination of any proposition appears to me an intellectual and moral palsy that will ever hinder the firm grasping of any substance whatever. For my part, I wish to be among the ranks of that glorious crusade that is seeking to set Truth's Holy Sepulchre free from a usurped dominion. We shall then see her resurrection!" It is her revolutionary clarion call. The religious metaphors in which she conducts the Holy War as a search for a God unobscured by human dogma should not blind us to the animus in her scorn for others' fears of thought and in the language of political liberation. In the full flush of her confidence she closes the letter, first with a smile at herself which is not a doubt or a retraction, then with a priestlike blessing: "I hardly know whether I am ranting after the fashion of one of the Primitive Methodist prophetesses, with a cart for her rostrum, I am writing so fast. Goodbye, and blessings on you, as they will infallibly be on the children of peace and virtue." For the moment she has discovered a place for herself in a female family tradition apart from her father's: though preaching rather different doctrines, she imaginatively allies herself with her aunt Elizabeth Evans, formerly a well-known Methodist preacher. From her new figural standing ground on the cart, in league with "infallibility," she takes the authority to bless her friend.

The rhetoric of the whole letter is imbued with a similar vision; Mary Ann has now aligned herself with a large abstract idea that will encompass her and give her a safe position from which she can look down on the fears and weaknesses of others. She "can rejoice in all the joys of humanity." Though she must "of course . . . desire the ultimate downfall of error," she believes that she need not proselytize but only show her love of truth in "a calm confidence" in its eventual attainment of "universal empire." Even the image that most betrays her fear of losing her family support is confident: thanking Pears for having entrusted her with the care of her two-year-old child, she comments, "I was beginning to get used to the conviction that, ivy-like as I am by nature, I must (as we see ivy do sometimes) shoot out into an isolated tree." If ivy has the vigorous capacity to "shoot out," there need be no excessive fear of losing the walls on which it normally climbs.

Three weeks later the audience-blind quality of her confidence takes on a painfully strained form in a letter to Maria Lewis (1:126–28). Here, refusing to acknowledge that Maria has any cause for doubting her, Mary Ann casts herself as a religious martyr to public opinion, attempting to elicit sympathy and admiration from the very person whose Evangelical mentorship she has so dramatically cast off. She speaks of bearing up bravely under "*cooled* glances" at home and attacks on her pride from an acquaintance, and she denies the pain of isolation: "The mind that feels its value will get large draughts from some source if denied it in the most commonly chosen way"—all the while pretending to assume that nothing has changed in her relations with Maria. Meanwhile, she is heedlessly trampling on Maria's carefully cultivated Evangelical garden by rejecting the concept of self-denial in favor of the intrinsic virtue in a "being of moral excellence" and redefining "ego"—for the first time—as a potentially glorious motive force. The wish to hold on to her friend's affection at the very moment when she is kicking it away could not be more apparent, to anyone but the writer of this document.

Yet the same attitudes—the pose of intellectual martyrdom to the social world, paired with the insistence that religious opinion be separated from love—are beautifully controlled in the extraordinary letter to Robert Evans dated ten days later. The decision to write a letter to the person with whom she shared a house indicates Mary Ann's will to break the silent impasse between them by raising Robert Evans out of the conventional social world and transforming him into the audience that her letter requires. As she puts it, the letter is an attempt to liberate "judgements" from the obstructions of feeling which make domestic conversation impossible. Needless to say, the letter is not unobstructed by feeling; instead, it deliberately challenges Robert Evans to respond to a different kind of feeling from the kinds he had been exhibiting.

Carefully composed and organized, the letter's three paragraphs move from a clear declaration of her new beliefs to a rejection of the family's reaction and finally to an emotional appeal for the father's love and loyalty. At each stage Mary Ann reiterates her refusal to bow to social or family pressure that she attend church, and separates her disregard for her "worldly interests" from the "very strong convictions" she is not prepared to sacrifice. She also—and this is the basis of her appeal—is intent to separate the love and duty between father and daughter from the "worldly" question of what Robert Evans might be expected to do for her. Two absolutes reign: her convictions

Manuscript, letter of Mary Ann Evans to Robert Evans, February 28, 1842. Beinecke Rare Book and Manuscript Library, Yale University.

and the moral relationship between parent and child. The social world in which those absolutes manifest themselves is scornfully excluded.

Thus she claims, "I could not without vile hypocrisy and a miserable truckling to the smile of the world for the sake of my supposed interests, profess to join in worship which I wholly disapprove. This and *this alone* I will not do even for your sake—anything else however painful I would cheerfully brave to give you a moment's joy." Her anger at the family interpretation of her position turns into a proud scorn for the family attitude to money: if both Isaac and Robert have insinuated that the expensive Foleshill house has "no other object than to give me a centre in society," if she has now placed "an insurmountable barrier to my prosperity in life," she is glad to know it, since she could not "remain as an incubus or an unjust absorber of your hardly earned gains which might be better applied among my Brothers and Sisters with their children." The hurt she feels at being considered a social problem on which family money is going to waste turns to devastating satire on the family's way of thinking.

When she comes to her final appeal, however, she writes the financial story another way. If Robert Evans wants to punish her "for the pain I have most unintentionally given you," she will "joyfully submit" to his giving the others money intended for her support. If she has offended against love, rather than against social aspiration, she is ready to take the blame. "I fear nothing but voluntarily leaving you," she says; and she offers to do anything her father wants—live at his cottage in Packington if it will comfort him, leave him if he desires it. She declares her love for her father and her resolution to follow duty "though every being on earth were to frown upon me." By all these rhetorical means, she insists that her need for a place in family life is as strong as her intellectual conviction, and separate from it. At the same time she attempts to make of Robert Evans a man who knows what he feels about his daughter apart from the social and religious rules of behavior in a small provincial city.

If this is rebellion against the father, it must be understood in a very specialized way, one that grants Mary Ann Evans's consistent wish to retain the structure of paternal authority as she wished to maintain the order of the original household. She is—at least rhetorically— ready to sacrifice her life to Robert Evans, as she is ready to martyr herself to the pursuit of God's truth. It is simply that she has claimed a flagrantly independent right to discover, define, and interpret the path to God's truth and a corresponding right to serve her father in her own way, on her own terms, and with the assurance that he is a figure of tolerant authority rather than a creature of social custom. But the Robert Evans she tried to create in her letter did not exist.

The father responded to the daughter's letter in the language of houses. Three days later he alerted the landlord of his Packington cottage that he intended to move into it. Nine days after that he informed his Coventry landlord of imminent departure and ordered his house agent to find a new tenant for Foleshill. Two weeks later, persuaded by Isaac, he temporized, telling the agent to stop advertising the Coventry house, as he was planning to stay for a year or so until the Packington cottage was renovated (1:129, 131, 132n.). The protracted ambivalence recalls the period of indecision at Griff, suggesting that Robert Evans's emotional turbulence about making social arrangements between aging parent and grown child had been reawakened.

The second group of letters, written in March and April, show Mary Ann Evans sorting out the gains and losses entailed by her initial high-minded position; in particular they replace the goal of maintaining visible intellectual integrity at any cost with that of maneuvering back into a domestic relationship with her father. The change, and the shift of tone that accompanies it, appear in a short note to Cara Bray, written when Mary Ann had decided to take rooms by herself in Leamington: "There is but *one* woe, that of leaving dear Father. All else, doleful lodgings, scanty meals, and *gazing-stockism* are quite indifferent to me" (1:131). Her principles are intact: domestic love is important; the opinion of the world is not. Her martyrlike stance is intact as well. But the terms are being wielded in a new arena, one in which intellectual principle and its ideal language no longer play a starring role.[6] And, beginning in this note, Robert Evans becomes a person it is necessary to "handle" according to his prejudices, moods, and idiosyncracies.

In the subsequent letters from Griff, the note of martyrdom disappears as well. Now adhesiveness is the dominant tone; domesticity and affection prevail. The term "Holy War" is coined, ironically set in a domestic context that makes it look quite silly: "Oh, if I could transport myself to your dining-room, where I guess you and Mr. Pears are sitting in anticipation of tea, carrying on no 'Holy War,' but at peace with the world and its opinions, or if ever you do battle in the happy ranks of the majority, I could kiss you into sublime liberality!" Mary

Ann begs for letters, visits; she makes play with Caroline Bray's new hairstyle; she even returns to her old habit of apology for the egotism of her topics. (1:133–34; 137–39). Her audience has once again become her lifeline, and she is anxious lest any emotional connection be broken. Separated from her father, awaiting his decision, martyrdom melts in confession: "On a retrospection of the past month I regret nothing so much as my own impetuosity of feeling and judging"; she fears she has irrevocably severed the primary connection with him.

Retuned to human frailty, she now follows the hope of discerning her father's wishes as one might follow the weather reports; yet she is also insistent that he be brought to recognize her right to a home and an integral place in the family. Her position might best be described as that of an obedient manager of her father's recalcitrant feelings; although she is "disposed to be lamb-like" in the matter of where they shall live, she is "warm and decided" about her feeling that she cannot remain at Isaac's, where she is merely an adjunct and where she has gone only "in compliance with my Father's wish" that she retire from a place where she had made a public spectacle of herself. She is not above devising all manner of strategies to bring the situation to conclusion. In the letter to Mrs. Pears she asks her neighbor to send her word of "how he seems disposed"; later she tells Mrs. Bray, "It is important, I know, for him as well as myself that I should return to him without delay, and unless I draw a circle around him and require an answer within it, he will go on hesitating and hoping for weeks and weeks." With the help of Isaac's wife, she has already brought her father most of the way around by arguing that "he could not place a more effective barrier to my 'conversion' than by making my apparent worldly interests dependent on it." In effect, Mary Ann was ready to dish up a vulgarized view of her own "prideful" psychology in order to make her father believe that his efforts to bully her into conversion by withholding her worldly security were precisely those which would prove most counterproductive.

Only a step or two separates this strategy from the decision to resume churchgoing. The war of the houses had clarified both the principle and the personal need that required Mary Ann to live with her father. She agreed to misrepresent herself in the eyes of the world in order to maintain both the household and the private integrity of her mind. Her scornful view of "worldly interests" and the opinions around her was acutely tested and survived in the altered form of a willingness to allow others to think what they might about her pride and her capitulation. This shift, the submission to worldly opinion from which she is internally independent, was at the center of Mary Ann Evans's experience in the Holy War.

Its importance can be gauged against the preoccupation with "good opinion" in her earlier letters. "Ambition, a desire insatiable for the esteem of my fellow-creatures" is "my besetting sin," writes the nineteen-year-old Mary Ann to her aunt Elizabeth Evans (1:19); in her earliest known composition, "Affectation and Conceit," the fourteen-year-old berates herself, in the guise of the world at large, for affectations designed to make others give adulation and praise.[7] Now, writing to Elizabeth Pears from Griff at twenty-two, she begins to understand that the Holy War has been a genuine testing ground for that "besetting sin." Her acquaintances are smiling upon her in spite of her heresy, she tells her friend. "All these things, however, are but the fringe and ribbons of happiness. They are *ad*herent, not *in*-herent, and without any affectation I feel myself to be acquiring what I must hold to be a precious possession, an independence of what is baptized by the world external good." The sentiment belongs to the future Marian Evans Lewes, who had prepared herself well in her youth for the endurance of an anomalous social position.

Yet the same experience that helped prepare the emotional possibility of a happy marriage outside the law created the intellectual necessity for the set of unresolvable tensions which we call George Eliot's social conservatism. These tensions are collected in the strange, abstract letter to Sara Hennell in which Mary Ann Evans recorded the moral and intellectual conclusions of her Holy War (October 9, 1843; 1:161–63). The letter is immediately striking for its initial sounding of the George Eliot doctrine of fellowship. Rejecting speculative truth as "but a shadow of individual minds," Mary Ann postulates "the *truth of feeling* as the only universal bond of union." And she asks "Are we to remain aloof from our fellow-creatures on occasions when we may fully sympathize with the feelings exercised, although our own have been melted into another mould? Ought we not on every opportunity to seek to have our feelings in harmony though not in union with those who are often richer in the fruits of faith though not in reasons, than ourselves?"[8] If, however, we read the familiar language of sympathy as it arises within the taut, impersonal thinking of the letter as a whole, the matter takes on its more problematic aspects.

There is, to begin with, the appearance of the George Eliot "we," which represses the positive "I" of the Holy Warrior in more ways than one. Mary Ann now presents her experience as one in a common category: "I am inclined to think that such a change of sentiment is likely to happen to most persons whose views on religious matters undergo a change early in life. The first impulse of a young and ingenuous mind is to withhold the slightest sanction from all that contains even a mixture of supposed error." (A difference of eighteen months separates this writer from the "young and ingenuous mind.") The tremendous self-distancing in this lofty perspective becomes truly baffling, however, in sentences that make it grammatically impossible to know whether Mary Ann is referring to her own experience or to that of the people around her. After "a year or two of reflection," the young person discovers that the exultation of liberation "from the wretched giant's bed of dogma on which [the soul] has been racked and stretched ever since it began to think" has turned to something else: "We find that the intellectual errors which we once fancied were a mere incrustation have grown into the living body and that we cannot in the majority of causes [*sic*], wrench them away without destroying vitality. We begin to find that with individuals, as with nations, the only safe revolution is one arising out of the wants which their *own progress* has generated. It is the quackery of infidelity to suppose that it has a nostrum for all mankind, and to say to all and singular, 'Swallow my opinions and you shall be whole.'"

Whose errors have grown into the living body? Presumably—in the actual experience—those of her family? Was her own revolution, arising most certainly from the wants which her own progress had generated, not a "safe" one according to this definition? Yet the letter suggests it was dangerous, dangerous at least to whoever was threatened by a destruction of vitality. And what is "the quackery of infidelity"? Is infidelity a new name for religious heresy or for the disloyalty to others inherent in talking of one's own new opinions? Moreover, why is she talking as if her error had been to proselytize, when the serious proselytizing was aimed by her family and friends at her? The diction represses these questions. Its grammar fuses the writer with a universal "we," while its images say that someone has threatened someone else's life, that someone has been disloyal to others. The Holy Warrior was bent on testing her father's fidelity and tolerance; now she implicitly shifts to herself the failure of his performance. She is guilty of her "own progress" the moment it has social ramifications in others' lives.

The subsequent paragraphs of the letter return to worry the question of responsibility in new ways. The second begins with the exhortations to harmony in feeling and slides, as if to explain the necessity for that harmony, into a parable abstracted from the Evans family experience:

> The results of non-conformity in a family are just an epitome of what happens on a larger scale in the world. An influential member chooses to omit an observance which in the minds of all the rest is associated with what is highest and most venerable. He cannot make his reasons intelligible, and so his conduct is regarded as a relaxation of the hold that moral ties had on him previously. The rest are infected with the disease they imagine in him; all the screws by which order was maintained are loosened, and in more than one case a person's happiness may be ruined by the confusion of ideas which took the form of principles.

In this sad tale Mary Ann takes the step of separating the liberated individual from the mass and then runs them syntactically together again in potential ruin. Who is responsible for this disastrous scenario? The individual for failing to make his reasons intelligible? The rest for infecting themselves with imaginary diseases? The individual for making himself an imaginary source of those imaginary diseases? Mary Ann's scorn for others' stupidity is closer to the surface here, yet it only makes the danger more acute. A singular revolution may generate collective anarchy, which may in turn render a safe revolution unsafe. Now the doctrine of sympathy, or tolerance, begins to appear in a new light. Although we cannot feel what others feel, we must sympathize ("have our feelings in harmony though not in union") lest we loose a torrent of irrational and destructive behavior. Sympathy in this guise is tolerance running in scorn and fear of its object.

In the final paragraph Mary Ann seems at least partially to recognize the bleakness of this vision and to make some efforts to retrieve it. How can change occur? she asks; "Are we to go on cherishing superstitions out of a fear that seems inconsistent with any faith in a Supreme Being?" Her replies may be taken as her cautious revision of the original mission of the Holy War: "I think the best and the only way of fulfilling our mission is to sow good seed in good i.e. prepared ground, and not to root up tares where we must inevitably gather all the wheat with them. We cannot fight and struggle enough for freedom of enquiry and we need not be idle in imparting all that is pure and lovely to children whose minds are unbespoken." But the replies

double back upon the question of change itself. Where is that prepared ground, and who has prepared it? Is there such a thing as an
isolated child with an unbespoken mind? The quest for a virgin territory in which to seed restates the social despair in a new way: only
when nothing is there already can change safely occur.

These organic metaphors for change mark the beginning of a long
and troubled George Eliot discourse, in which the life of plants figures the human potential for social evolution.[9] Here, as in a well-
known sentence from her essay "The Natural History of German
Life," the problem lies in the relationship between the need to protect
the roots of the past and the desire to sow the seeds of the future:
"The nature of European men has its roots intertwined with the past,
and can only be developed by allowing those roots to remain undis-
turbed while the process of development is going on, until that perfect ripeness of the seed which carries with it a life independent of the
root."[10] The young Mary Ann Evans could only imagine sowing in
newly prepared fields where the root is absent or invisible; the older
essayist understands the necessary connection between root and seed
but is still unable to close the gap, either syntactically or organically.
The seed has no verb; it is pure ideal potential. As soon as it falls into
the ground it will be implicated once again with all those roots.

Although the organic metaphor proved its usefulness as a guilt-free
model of social progress, it did not settle the concerns of the twenty-
three-year-old writer, who returned to the question of responsibility.
All her abstraction and syntactical conflation had failed to evade the
nagging question: "Who was at fault in the family struggle?" She finds
temporary closure in an appeal to the authority of Saint Paul, citing
his "reasoning about the conduct of the strong toward the weak in the
14 and 15 chapters of Romans." Paul answers her question thus: "We
then that are strong ought to bear the infirmities of the weak, and not
to please ourselves." He warns the strong in faith against weakening
their brothers by offending them on doctrinal points thay are not yet
ready to accept. The moral is clear: the nonconforming member of
the family is responsible for the moral disorientation of the others.
The strong must not only bear the infirmities of the weak but must
prevent the weak from falling into their own weaknesses. The application of Christian doctrine to an antidoctrinal movement of intellectual liberation is an ironically appropriate closure for a mission conceived throughout in the language of Christian martyrdom.

The appeal to Paul solidifies the movement of the whole letter; now

the independently running soul freed from the wretched giant's bed
of dogma has made a 180-degree revolution, taking on its own shoul-
ders the weight of all it yearned to leave behind. This revolution,
encompassing the shift from superior intellectual enlightenment to
superior strength and responsibility, becomes George Eliot's model
for change.

Although the Holy War had sensitized her to the sympathy and
sacrifice required for the maintenance of family relations, Mary Ann
Evans was more than eager to loose her mind and her latent revolutionary fervor on a sufficiently distant object. Less than five years
after the October 1843 letter to Sara, we find a small group of letters
to a young friend, John Sibree, Jr., written early in 1848 during the
period of release after the two-and-a-half-year work of translating
David Friedrich Strauss's *Das Leben Jesu* and before the onset of mortal
illness in Robert Evans turned his daughter into a nurse. The letters
to Sibree sparkle with the energy of intellectual freedom, intellectual
flirtation, and the self-projecting fantasy that the young man will be
able to live out what the young woman has had to compromise or
repress. Sibree merits a bluntness of expression that is otherwise virtually absent in the George Eliot correspondence; to him Mary Ann
can refer to Victoria as "our little humbug of a queen" (1:254), and
she can triumph over her own religious compromise when John's
religious doubts lead him away from the ministry: "It was impossible
to think of your career with hope while you tacitly subscribed to the
miserable etiquette (it deserves no better or more spiritual name) of
sectarianism" (1:261).

Wrapping her personal involvement in the protective mantle of
mentorship, she also rejoices in the 1848 Revolution in France: "I am
all the more delighted with your enthusiasm because I didn't expect
it. I feared that you lacked revolutionary ardour. But no—you are just
as sansculottish and rash as I would have you. You are not one of those
sages whose reason keeps so tight a rein on their emotions that they
are too constantly occupied in calculating consequences to rejoice in
any great manifestation of the forces that underlie our everyday existence" (1:253–54). The displaced fervor of the Holy Warrior finds its
special image in the possibility of a spiritually led revolution: she
would consent "to have a year clipt off my life for the sake of witness-
ing such a scene as that of the men of the barricade bowing to the
image of Christ 'who first taught fraternity to men.'" And the dutiful,

silenced daughter revels in the thought of freeing the world from the hegemony of father and son: "I have little patience with people who can find time to pity Louis Philippe and his moustachioed sons. Certainly our decayed monarchs should be pensioned off: we should have a hospital for them, or a sort of Zoological Garden, where these worn-out humbugs may be preserved."

Such explosions of repressed animus, distanced as they are, raise the danger signals. In the next paragraph the inevitable turn occurs, in a carefully drawn distinction between the socially educated "mind of the people" in France and the retrograde quality of the English, whose "selfish radicalism and unsatisfied, brute sensuality" would render a revolutionary movement "simply destructive." Revolution must be kept far from home and associated with an idealized view of mental development; nevertheless, the energy for it is still alive. Well recognizing that it is, Mary Ann closes the letter with cautious words that recall her anxious absorption of conduct-book warnings. She asks John Sibree to burn her letters when he has read them so "there would be no risk of a critical third pair of eyes getting a sight of them." That the caution coexists with a strong need for such "clandestine" exchange she reveals by projecting her own case upon his: "But I will be as careful for you as if I were ultra-cautious on my own behalf, so I say again utter, utter, utter, and it will be a deed of mercy twice blest, for I shall be a safety-valve for your communicativeness and prevent it from splitting honest peoples' brains who don't understand you and moreoever it will be fraught with ghostly comfort to me." The ghostly comfort of providing a safety valve for a surrogate male life of the mind is not much comfort at all. Perhaps there is more in the opportunity for her own blunt utterance and in the reassuring evidence that the Holy War between expressive intellectual exploration and the social yoke of sympathy, if never to be won, was never to be lost.

The last of the Sibree letters was truncated by a new crisis and a new phase of that alternating current. April 1848 marked the beginning of the last year of Robert Evans's life. During that year all Mary Ann's activities were halted by his severe illness and increased dependency; she became a full-time nurse. Her need to act out the full meaning of her Holy War in self-sacrificial responsibility for her father is indicated by the intensity of her immersion in this task and by the severe repression of her own intellectual and emotional life. The spiritual self-discipline of the Evangelical years was renewed and refurbished in Mary Ann's struggle against the threats to her own mental and physical health which she invited by taking the full burden of nursing upon herself.[11] Because she achieved her own spiritual goals during that year—that is, because she knew she had given everything to Robert Evans by the time of his death and had been rewarded with a few belated indications of his gratitude—she learned to regard herself as a person whose passion was to be spent only in the fullness of devotion to a single other human being.

Years before this final test, Mary Ann expressed her full participation in the Victorian worship of woman's special mission in the sickroom. When Sara Hennell was nursing a tubercular family member in January 1843, Mary Ann wrote to her, "I think it almost enviable as far as one's self is concerned not of course when the sufferer is remembered, to have the care of a sickroom, with its twilight and tiptoe stillness and helpful activity. I have always had a peculiarly peaceful feeling in such a scene" (1:156). She was attracted to a duty so necessary as to quiet inner conflict and offering such clear authority to the nurse. When her father became severely ill in April 1848, however, her feelings were anything but peaceful. The alarm "has been a greater trial to me than I have ever had to see him suffering for so many weeks together," she wrote to her stepsister Fanny Houghton (1:258).

When Robert Evans became well enough to travel to St. Leonard's on the coast, his daughter's concern turned to serious depression as she recognized the implications of his debility. "He makes not the slightest attempt to amuse himself, so that I scarcely feel easy in following my own bent even for an hour," she reported to the Brays (1:263). Attempting to conquer her depression by taking charge of it in writing, she described to them a state of mind in terms that were later to figure in the scene of Dorothea's disillusioned return to Lowick Manor after her marriage to Casaubon: "Alas for the fate of poor mortals which condemns them to wake up some fine morning and find all the poetry in which their world was bathed only the evening before utterly gone—the hard angular world of chairs and tables and looking-glasses staring at them in all its naked prose. It is so in all the stages of life—the poetry of girlhood goes—the poetry of love and marriage—the poetry of maternity—and at last the very poetry of duty forsakes us for a season and we see ourselves and all about us as nothing more than miserable agglomerations of atoms" (1:264). For six years she had fulfilled "the poetry of duty" to her father; now it looked as though it might swallow up her life entirely. For Charles Bray she borrowed tropes from Scott, whose novels she read endlessly to her father: "The enthusiasm without which one cannot even pour out breakfast well (at least *I* cannot) has forsaken me. . . . But for the present my address is Grief Castle, on the river of Gloom, in the valley of Dolour" (1:265). Her smothered rage turned to cynical social meditation in a letter to Sara Hennell: "You will wonder what has wrought me up into this fury—it is the loathsome fawning, the transparent hypocrisy, the systematic giving as little as possible for as much as possible that one meets with here at every turn. I feel that society is training men and women for hell" (1:267). Three days later she professed to be feeling a bit better, but her own situation covertly fueled a critique of *Jane Eyre*: "All self-sacrifice is good—but one would like it to be in a somewhat nobler cause than that of a diabolical law which chains a man soul and body to a putrefying carcase" (1:268).

Near the end of that depressed June, however, she announced to Sara a "metamorphosis," for which the "sickly feelings" had been merely a preparation. "I am entering on a new period of my life which makes me look back on the past as something incredibly poor and contemptible. I am enjoying repose strength and ardour in a greater degree than I have ever known and yet I never felt my own insignificance and imperfection so completely. My heart bleeds for dear Father's pains, but it is blessed to be at hand to give the soothing word and act needed" (1:269–70). With the help of Thomas à Kempis, she had invented a revised form of her former Evangelical ardor, the more effective because of her greater maturity and the more urgent demand of her situation.[12] Although her letters during the extended period of her father's acute illness send out dire bulletins from the front—"I am suffering perhaps as acutely as ever I did in my life" (1:274) or "I am living unspeakable moments and can write no more" (1:282)—they give primarily the impression of someone so immersed in her task, so physically and psychologically exhausted by it, that she can do little more than write notes about her father's condition to family members or surface occasionally to produce a few rushed paragraphs of literary and spiritual meditation that was otherwise confined to inner monologue.

It is in the light of this second phase of religious self-discipline that we must read the words Mary Ann Evans wrote as she saw her father approach the day of his death. "Strange to say I feel that these will ever be the happiest days of life to me. The one deep strong love I have ever known has now its highest exercise and fullest reward—the worship of sorrow is *the* worship for humans," she wrote to Charles Bray sometime in May (1:283–84). Her satisfaction arises from her knowledge that she has met her own highest standards for love, as she sees her long ordeal coming to its close. The other side of the same coin emerged in a letter to the Brays written after the last sleepless night she would spend at her father's side. "What shall I be without my Father? It will seem as if a part of my moral nature were gone. I had a horrid vision of myself last night becoming earthly sensual and devilish for want of that purifying restraining influence" (1:284). That "purifying restraining influence" had never been Robert Evans himself; it was the activity of her own remorseful conscience. Because she had once been made to suffer for the liberating announcement of independence from her father's social and religious rigidities, her anticipation of liberation from his care took an inverted form, as a nightmare fear of the desires and pleasures she had pent up so deliberately during the year of nursing. The desire for the indulgence of intellectual freedom and romantic inclination which had burst forth in the first stage of the Holy War had threatened her with homelessness. With her father's death she was facing the same threat—and the same opportunity. But in that semidelirious moment of exhaustion it looked like a threat only to her own ability to maintain the carefully cultivated discipline that had produced the moral self-satisfaction of the previous months.[13] She had finished the Holy War with a complete demonstration of her ability to endure the boredom and the tediousness of loving service to another suffering and imperfect being. She had borne the infirmities of the weak and maintained her mental strength. Her reparation was complete—her future a mystery.

As that future developed, the 1843 letter to Sara Hennell proved to be only the first intimation of a discourse that would continue throughout Mary Ann Evans's life as George Eliot. The tremendous fertility of its stated ideas and buried feelings was something she had sensed as she brought the letter to a close: "But I have not said half what I meant to say. There are so many aspects in which the subject might be presented that it is useless to attempt to exhaust it. I fear I have written very unintelligibly, for it is rather late and I am so cold that my thoughts are almost frozen" (1:163). She was right: this first pronouncement of the official creed in the official voice contains in frozen, abstract nuggets some of the central tensions that animate George Eliot's novels.

Once released into dramatic fictional motion, these tensions were repeatedly to be enacted in the central narrative gesture of turning back. Memory itself, so frequently invoked or described as a moral activity in its own right, is an actor in this drama. In the careers of George Eliot's good characters, liberation, followed by flight, is succeeded by the critical turn. The moment when Romola in flight from Tito's betrayal is quite literally turned around in the road by Savonarola is a dramatic physical rendition of the central gesture, as is Maggie's return to St. Ogg's after her flight with Stephen.[14] Dorothea's mental flights into anger or scorn at Casaubon and Ladislaw are internally turned around into re-visions that bring the rejected figures back into sympathetic focus. The vision that takes Felix Holt off the blindly followed hereditary course also turns him homeward to take charge of his mother. For such characters the meaning of tolerance is also defined in the Holy War pattern: the "widening of sympathy" central to George Eliot's philosophy of art is not a conversion of the narrow-minded but a transformation that occurs in the consciousness of those who are already free of what she would call hereditary prejudice; it involves the absorption of a shocked recognition of the intractibility of others, who are then to be re-seen, perhaps succored, in their narrowness.[15]

The action of moral revolution is not confined to characters' stories; it is the controlling force in the rhythm of George Eliot's narratives. Again and again the stories satirize provincial "opinion," offering up ironically detailed exposures of its absurdity, its blind self-righteousness, its complacent prejudices, and its capacity for harm— only to take a remorseful turn back, to dissolve the satire in demands for sympathy or sentiment which neither address nor deny the implacable power of those public voices. The first story of all, "The Sad Fortunes of the Reverend Amos Barton," erases all its critique of gossip, judgment, and opinion in a sentimental death. The Dodsons, so thoroughly satirized in *The Mill on the Floss*, are allowed to redeem themselves in a few incidents at novel's end.[16] In *Middlemarch* the movement is more subtle, but it is there: if we allow ourselves to despise "Middlemarch opinion," we are aligned with Lydgate's blindness to the facts controlling his life; if we allow ourselves to despise Casaubon, the narrative insists on its remorseful turn to look again.

If every mental step forward requires a moral turn back, the question of social evolution becomes a vexed one. George Eliot has a genius for gradualism when she is talking about deteriorations—of a marriage, a moral relationship with the self, a person's standing in the community. How things might improve is a more difficult matter for one so conscious of the power of roots and the environments of seeds. The "inward revolution" of even so optimistically conceived a character as Esther Lyon is grounded in a backward look at the affections of the past and the sacrifice of a narcissistic idea of the future. More often, positive changes are created by instant narrative interventions, deaths that open a prisonlike existence to a glimpse of something better. Gradual enlightenment may be postulated in the George Eliot world, but it is not very often put into action. A life may be saved from moral wreckage; a person may be revered in memory. The medium remains resistant.

Thus the stories remain perpetually haunted and energized by the unlaid ghosts of the Holy War. "Safe revolution" occurs in the privacy of the individual mind; moral learning is communicated to others only at specially charged moments through acts of confession that effect some human relief without being fully understood. As in the opening chapters of *Impressions of Theophrastus Such,* the action of "Looking Inward" is followed as though necessarily by that of "Looking Backward." The necessity that drives those George Eliot "revolutions," the vision that accentuates not the initial moment of change but the turning around to see it again, was inscribed by 1843 in the letters of Mary Ann Evans. When she became a writer, her messages to the world found their irresistible truth less in the liberation of free enquiry than in a perpetual repetition of the bold setting forth and the chastened return which marked the trajectory of her Holy War.

FOUR

The Labor of Choice

I have counted the cost of the step that I have taken
and am prepared to bear, without irritation or
bitterness, renunciation by all my friends.

—Marian Evans to John Chapman,
October 15, 1854

Eleven days before she died, George Eliot wrote the last significant letter of her life to Elma Stuart, one of several younger women who made up the coterie of followers attending the famous novelist's later years. Whereas the other letters of December 1880 give dutiful attention to the social responsibilities of letter writing, this one is notable for its extended outburst in defense of a Mrs. Menzies, a close friend of Stuart's who had unexpectedly announced her conversion to Catholicism. Remonstrating with Stuart about her reaction to the unwelcome news, George Eliot wrote:

> I for my part would not venture to thrust my mind on hers as a sort of omniscient dictatress, when in fact I am very ignorant of the inward springs which determine her action. That she has not spoken to you of her intention until now is no proof that it has not been long ripening, and in fact I see in her letter the expression of a long-felt dissatisfaction and yearning—a thirst which has found the longed-for water. To insist on ideas or external reasons in opposition to such deeply-felt inclinations is no more effective than the swallowing of a paper prescription. (December 11, 1880; 7:346)

Amid illness and anxiety, George Eliot's writing energies were aroused by a situation that had been central to both her life and her art. On at least three crucial occasions—the Holy War, her elopement with George Henry Lewes, and her marriage with John Cross—her own prolonged secret or intimate debate had been followed by a sudden public action for which most of her friends, as well as a larger audience of onlookers, were unprepared. The dangers inherent in this pattern of action had shown up clearly enough in the Holy War episode; yet George Eliot was compelled to repeat the pattern each time she made an important and controversial choice. It was, she might have said, "the story of her life"; it was also the story that she told and retold in one fictional variation after another, of how a character's intense inner debate results in a choice or action imagined in terms that are incomprehensible to its audiences.

Marian Evans's choice of George Henry Lewes has always been retrospectively read as the act that made her fiction writing possible. Earlier accounts emphasize Lewes's role as mentor, muse, mother, protector, and literary agent; more recent ones concentrate on Marian Evans's liberating choice of an "outlaw" sexual situation. Nina Auerbach, who gives the most dramatic of such readings, suggests that George Eliot released her artistic capacity by tapping into the demonic power of fallenness itself: "The role of fallen woman was so pivotal in Eliot's life, functioned so powerfully as the crucible in which unpromising beginnings were forged into unprecented triumphs, that it is tempting to read her life as a mythic work of Victorian fiction."[1] While both kinds of explanation address certain truths about her situation, it seems to me that Marian Evans's creativity was released by her resistance to any conventional or unconventional myth of fallennness; she felt she was not a fallen woman, and she knew that her culture defined her as one. What she gained from her choice of Lewes was a story that had to be told, an obsession as powerful as Dickens's compulsion to tell stories about innocent children who are tainted or distorted by a guilty adult world. Through characters from Amos Barton to Gwendolen Harleth, she would tell it, dramatizing in innumerable variations the gap between her characters' private choices and the fatal or comic misreadings of their communities. Though an element of self-justification helped to fuel this inventive fire—the art making up for the life, so to speak—she had created a plot that was interesting and compelling enough to sustain her private expenditures of intellectual and imaginative energy over the twenty years of her life as a novelist.

This chapter concentrates on the ways that George Eliot constructed choice, in the letters that cluster around her liaisons with Lewes and later with Cross and in the fiction, particularly *The Mill on the Floss,* which most fully devotes itself to the problematics of choice. Although George Eliot's heroines often end up on a more obviously sacrificial side of their choices than Marian Evans did, I believe that George Eliot's representation of choice is about the essence of her experience, about how it was internally structured and how it was externally read and misread by others. Although we will never have access to the private determinants of choice in George Eliot's mind, we know how she chose to present important decisions to others, in diplomatic letters and exploratory fictions; and as Phyllis Rose has observed, "the formulas with which we choose to present our actions are by no means a negligible part of them."[2] In the configurations that emerge from these texts, George Eliot's insistence on the inviolability of the "inward springs which determine action" is mixed with her knowledge that others experienced her choices as personal betrayals and with her growing awareness that important choices would inevitably breed misinterpretation and misrepresentation.[3] That pattern of experience, played out as we have seen in the Holy War, was to be recapitulated on a larger scale and with a new set of actors in the months that followed July 20, 1854, when Marian Evans and George Henry Lewes departed for the Continent to travel, write, and research Lewes's biography of Goethe.[4]

When John Cross came, in his *Life* of George Eliot, to "the most important event in George Eliot's life—her union with Mr. George Henry Lewes," he meticulously followed the protocol established by Lewes and Marian Evans during their eight-month stay in Germany. He represents the event by quoting from a single letter written to Cara Bray fourteen months after the "elopement," by reprinting pages of the travel journal in which Marian Evans recorded her memories of Weimar and Berlin, and by writing a brief note deflecting the question of moral judgment with an appeal to results: such a judgment can best be made, he asserts, "by consideration of the whole tenor of the life which follows, in the development of which Mr. Lewes's true character, as well as George Eliot's, will unfold itself."[5] Marian Evans's letters from Germany covered the bare fact of her union with the legally married Lewes by appealing to results, in writing that attests to the richness of a new life of travel and intercourse with eminent persons of culture and talent.

Her first letters home were written to John Chapman and Charles

Bray, the two men in whom she had confided her relation with Lewes, and on whom she depended as mediators of her professional and financial affairs, which included the receipt of her half-yearly income from Isaac Evans. (Chapman's address was to serve as a forwarding station for letters from her family for the next three years.)[6] She also wrote to her friend Bessie Rayner Parkes, who initiated the correspondence against the will of her parents and was one of the first to visit the Leweses when they returned to England.[7] These early letters are exuberant, confident, and focused on the pleasures of travel and meetings with interesting people. They could easily be characterized as the letters of a traveling companion who had been cheered up by a badly needed vacation, and they seem intended to be read in that way. The "I" predominates over the "we"; Lewes's name is not mentioned. "I have had a month of exquisite enjoyment, and seem to have begun life afresh. I am really strong and well and have recovered the power of learning in spite of age and grey hairs," she wrote to Bray on August 16 (2:170–71). The last phrase was repeated a month later in a letter to Bessie Parkes in which Marian Evans describes her happy year, "full of the seeds of future activity, in spite of age and grey hairs" (2:174). Her emphasis on intellectual renewal at the advanced age of thirty-four suggests that she wished to see her life as exempted by "grey hairs" from the possibility of sexual fallenness; the model that lurks behind her story is the life of Margaret Fuller, which Marian had commented on in an 1852 letter: "I am thankful, as if for myself, that it was sweet at last" (2:15). By far the most personal revelation in this early group of letters to England was written to Chapman at the end of August: "I am happier every day and find my domesticity more and more delightful and beneficial to me. Affection, respect, and intellectual sympathy deepen, and for the first time in my life I can say to the moments 'Verweilen sie, sie sind so schön'" (2:173).[8]

The "seeds of future activity" which attended this rebirth included a new interest in writing about the lives of European women, as if Marian Evans now desired to redefine "woman" in more generous terms than Victorian England allowed. Her essay "Woman in France: Madame de Sablé" was written during this period and published by Chapman in the October *Westminster Review*;[9] in January she proposed another on the history of German women, but Chapman did not respond (2:190). In a burst of frolicsome parody she began her first letter to Chapman, "It is the immemorial fashion of lady letter-writers to be glad and sorry in the same sentence, and after all, this feminine style is the truest representation of life" (8:115). Her new life with Lewes allowed her to play, and play with, the feminine part; her entrancement with Franz Liszt, whom they met and befriended, was deepened by the German acceptance of his liaison with the married Princess von Sayn-Wittgenstein, whose physical unattractiveness was detailed with fascinated amazement in Marian Evans's journal (2:169).

If the early letters from the German adventure strike the largely impersonal note the eloping pair desired to maintain, they also established a careful ambiguity about what the journey was all about, probably to prepare for the possibility that one of them might return alone, as though he had served as a convenient traveling escort, and she as a helpful companion for an ailing writer on a research trip.[10] This was the line taken by Charles Bray, who found himself engaged in defending Miss Evans from the suspicions of George Combe, the Edinburgh phrenologist and *Westminster Review* supporter who had worked closely with her in her role as Chapman's assistant editor. The Combe-Bray correspondence forms a little subplot that helps to specify the aspects of the scandal that began to develop at home—not, however, until two months of companionship had allowed the travelers' "affection, respect, and intellectual sympathy" to deepen into further commitment.

The published part of the Combe-Bray dialogue begins touchingly, with a letter from Caroline Bray to Mrs. Combe, who had written to inquire about a disaster rumored to have befallen Miss Evans. Cara Bray's response makes it quite clear that she believed her husband's representation of the journey as a reviving vacation for which Lewes had provided escort: "You are aware doubtless that she travelled to Weimar under Mr. Lewis's escort, who had been suffering from congestion of brain and required change. . . . I feel quite sure we should have heard if any mishap had befallen her" (September 23, 1854; 8:119). It seems likely that Charles Bray had agreed with Marian to describe the journey in this way or that he designed the explanation in order to cover for her in what he perceived as a mistake that was sure to end in failure as well as scandal.[11] In any case, he held to this version for as long as he could, while Combe sent him increasingly interrogatory letters. On October 8 Bray described the journey as an exchange of favors: Lewes was ill and needed a companion; he had "offered to introduce her to friends of his in Germany and leave her there for 12 months, which is what she wished." He had, he added, not previously seen anything in the plan to disapprove. On October

18 he responded to a tone of accusation in Combe's letters by defending his wife and Sara Hennell: "Miss E's going had not their sanction, because they knew nothing at all about it" (8:122–23, 126). This line sheds some light on Marian's failure to confide in the two female friends who had for so long maintained a familial and caretaking relationship with their unhappy and sometimes difficult protégée: Cara in particular would disapprove and feel implicated in the sexual harm to Marian were she to be told.

In the late October days that followed, Charles Bray did his best to stave off George Combe's almost fanatical interest in Marian Evans's fall. Twice he retailed parts of Marian's letters to Combe, excising clauses that named the fact that she was living with Lewes (8:127, 128); then he found himself appealing to her devotion as a daughter and her general moral nature in a way that implicitly conceded Combe's suspicions: "As a daughter she was the most devoted I ever knew, and she is just as likely to devote herself to some *one* other, in preference to all the world, and without reference either to the regularity or legality of the connection" (8:128). Such arguments were meant to persuade Combe to "let the matter drop," but they succeeded only in fanning the flames. On November 15 Combe finally found out what he wanted to know from Robert Chambers, one of the two friends to whom Lewes himself had written, and his response bordered on hysteria: "We are deeply mortified and distressed; and I should like to know whether there is insanity in Miss Evans's family; for her conduct, with *her* brain, seems to me like ⟨insanity⟩ morbid mental aberration" (8:129). Combe's sense of betrayal had in part to do with his phrenological pride in "knowing" Marian Evans well, but it concealed a variety of other agendas. He had lost faith in Chapman's work on the *Westminster* and wished to dissociate himself from it or hire a new editor; he was horrified that he had allowed Marian into intimacy with the women in his family circle; and he affected to fear that she had "inflicted a great injury on the cause of religious freedom" (8:129).[12] Bray continued to soothe him, attempting to turn his ire into creativity. "I quite agree with you in every word," he wrote after receiving Combe's frantic letter, but he goes on to remind Combe of the distinction between conventional law and "a natural law" that would presumably admit the Lewes case. "We want a good book or article on the subject of marriage and divorce. Could you not write one for the Westminster? *it would do great good just now*" (8:130–31). His efforts to rope Combe back into the liberal fold of the *West-*

minster are amusing, but they do suggest that reputations other than Marian Evans's personal one had been threatened by her liaison with Lewes.

Bray's attempt to elevate the terms in which the liaison might be considered built directly on a postscript Combe had added to his November 15 letter: "I think that Mr. Lewes was perfectly justified in leaving his own wife, but not in making Miss Evans his mistress" (8:130). This distinction staked out a position in the debate of gossip and rumor which flourished on the question of whether the man or the woman was most at fault in the Evans-Lewes matter. Was Lewes a feckless seducer, likely to leave Marian in the lurch? Or was Marian Evans responsible for breaking up the Lewes marriage? Had the Leweses been formally separated before the journey, or was a separation being negotiated from the Continent? Had Lewes "run away" from his wife and children? Had Marian Evans written an offensive message to Harriet Martineau before her departure? This last irrelevant and unfounded rumor, apparently circulated by Martineau, was the only one that could be *simply* denied. For the rest, the two companions responded to news of the gossip and appeals from Chapman and Bray for advice on how to answer it by following some simple principles. He would defend her; she would defend him; about their own relationship they would remain silent. Thus Lewes, having received a friendly response from Thomas Carlyle to a letter explaining his separation from Agnes Lewes, wrote again to vindicate Marian from the charge that she had caused the breakup, and to deny the existence of the Martineau letter. "Thus far I give you a solemn denial of the scandal. Where gossip affects a point of honour or principle I feel bound to meet it with denial; on all private matters my only answer is *silence*" (October 19, 1854; 2:177). In the letters Marian wrote, however, some of these principles proved less simple to negotiate than she might have desired.

The letters she wrote to John Chapman on October 15 (8:123–25) and to Charles Bray on October 23 (2: 178–79) were designed to provide them with facts that would allow them to correct the rumor that Lewes had "run away" from his wife and children. That part was easy to write; it had already been true for some years that, as she wrote to Bray, Lewes's "conduct as a husband has been not only irreproachable, but generous and self-sacrificing to a degree far beyond any standard fixed by the world." Part of the immediate generosity lay in Lewes's unwillingness to justify himself by naming his family situa-

tion with any specificity, for fear of bringing further scandal to bear
on Agnes Lewes, his own three sons, or the several children Agnes
had borne his old friend and colleague Thornton Hunt. Marian
Evans took the occasion of these letters to align herself with Lewes's
determination to continue supporting his wife and all the children—a
responsibility that would prove to outlive Lewes himself.

The difficult part of the letters was writing about herself. She was
caught between declaring that she was personally indifferent to gossip
because the matter was no one's business but her own and the knowledge that she had threatened the friendships of others who genuinely
cared for her. She began her letter to Chapman with a fine display of
the first stance, assuming the role of one who has inadvertently created a minor trouble for her correspondent: "I am sorry that you are
annoyed with questions about me. Do whatever seems likely to free
you from such importunities. About my own justification I am entirely indifferent." After the paragraphs defending Lewes and denying
that she had written to Harriet Martineau, however, she felt compelled to begin again from the beginning: "You ask me to tell you
what reply you shall give to inquiries. I have nothing to deny or to
conceal. I have done nothing with which any person has a right to
interfere. I have surely full liberty to travel in Germany, and to travel
with Mr. Lewes. No one here seems to find it at all scandalous that we
should be together." These sentences are experimental stance-takers;
they teeter back and forth between maintaining the fiction of
"traveling"—a form of denial—and the proud but entirely vague "I
have nothing to deny or to conceal," a line considerably more disturbed and defensive than Lewes's "on all private matters my only
answer is *silence*." They fail to answer Chapman's practical question
because they are addressed to an internally imagined audience that is
being treated with defiance.

Characteristically, Marian hears her own tone and develops her
answer: "But I do not wish to take the ground of ignoring what is
unconventional in my position. I have counted the cost of the step
that I have taken and am prepared to bear, without irritation or
bitterness, renunciation by all my friends. I am not mistaken in the
person to whom I have attached myself. He is worthy of the sacrifice I
have incurred, and my only anxiety is that he should be rightly
judged." This remarkable shift of ground is not really addressed to
Chapman either, except insofar as it returns him finally to the charge
of vindicating Lewes. Instead it leaps to a position that grants her

audience everything they may see in her—the outcast, the fallen woman—and recasts herself as the heroic chooser. She has "sacrificed" her other relationships for a higher calling—surely a womanly thing to do? And she has chosen, not fallen, for she has "counted the costs," assessed the consequences, prepared herself to bear them, and made her move. The heroic chooser is, moreover, better than her friends because she will not judge them for judging her. These elements—the construction of choice as sacrifice rather than selfishness, the emphasis on the consideration of consequences, and the moral superiority of the chooser to her audiences—are central to George Eliot's imagination of choice. What makes her representations truly interesting, however, is her further knowledge of how these positions fail. That knowledge entered the case when Marian Evans applied her heroic stance to her actual friendships with Cara Bray and Sara Hennell.[13]

In the letter to Chapman, Marian had implicitly acknowledged that the fiction of "fellow travellers" could no longer be sustained. When she wrote a parallel letter to Charles Bray a week later, she was faced with a somewhat different problem. Charles passed her letters on to Cara and Sara; she did not know if they had yet realized the nature of her choice, or how they would react when they did. After she had finished her defense of Lewes's reputation, her dilemma produced some quite astounding sentences: "Of course many silly myths are already afloat about me, in addition to the truth, which of itself would be thought matter for scandal. I am quite unconcerned about them except as they may cause pain to my real friends. If you hear of anything that I have said, done, or written in relation to Mr. Lewes beyond the simple fact that I am attached to him and that I am living with him, do me the justice to believe that it is false." The introduction of that "simple fact" in a subordinate clause is a stroke both rhetorically masterful and personally self-defeating. It is not just the fact but the treatment of the fact that would be shocking to old friends; it is shocking enough to come upon it as a twentieth-century reader. By subordinating her life decision to the problem of false gossip, Marian was in a sense being true to the principles she and Lewes had worked out: their own relationship was not be discussed. But, as she knew perfectly well when she wrote that sentence, she was in fact finessing the far more complex situation she had created when she deliberately misled her friends and covered her tracks with secrecy. It was the secrecy, rather than "the simple fact," which counted as betrayal—even though, as I have suggested, the secrecy was probably designed to insulate her friends from her unconventional conduct.

The end of the letter returns to deal with the consequences she had
announced with abstract grandeur in her letter to Chapman. "I am
ignorant how far Cara and Sara may be acquainted with the state of
things, and how they may feel towards me. I am quite prepared to
accept the consequences of a step which I have deliberately taken and
to accept them without irritation or bitterness. The most painful consequence will, I know, be the loss of friends. If I do not write, therefore, understand that it is because I desire not to obtrude myself."
From her point of view, this formulation was a generous way to release Cara and Sara from association with a social outcast. From
theirs, it was a further betrayal of the intimacy and confidentiality that
Marian Evans had at least rhetorically sustained in her many letters to
them during the years of her sojourn in literary London—letters that
often and affectionately returned to a distinction between real
friends, who understood one's renegade nature, and the conventionally judging world.[14]

Sara Hennell responded immediately to the implicit invitation to
renew the friendship under its new conditions, but not without registering a strong protest against Marian Evans's apparent willingness to
abandon her past connections without a qualm. By October 31, Marian was already composing her response to Sara's accusations (2:181–
82). She professes herself shocked by the reading given to her self-
sacrificial stance: "I am so deeply conscious of having had neither the
feeling nor the want of feeling which you impute to me that I am quite
unable to read into my words, quoted by you, the sense which you put
upon them." As it would not require a great effort of imagination to
read those words as Sara had, her utterly nonapologetic response
must be taken as a careful effort to retain her relation with the Bray
circle, while placing the friendship at a certain distance. Her way of
doing so was to go on the attack: "When you say that I do not care
about Cara's or your opinion and friendship it seems much the same
to me as if you said that I didn't care to eat when I was hungry or to
drink when I was thirsty. One of two things: either I am a creature
without affection, on whom the memories of years have no hold, or,
you, Cara and Mr. Bray are the most cherished friends I have in the
world. It is simply self-contradictory to say that a person can be indifferent about her dearest friends; yet this is what you substantially say

when you accuse me of 'boasting with what serenity I can give you up,' of 'speaking proudly,' etc." This is angry rather than explanatory logic, and evasive logic at that; clearly Marian Evans did not like having her moral pieties punctured by Sara's accurate descriptions of their overtones, nor could she broach the accusation that she could forget her past. It was as if Sara had moved herself and Cara into the position formerly occupied by Robert and Isaac Evans, except that Marian felt enough power in her relation to a slightly-less-than-equal woman friend to express her anger directly. Her fence mending later in the letter moves significantly to an emphasis on the Bray circle as the familial repository of her past: "Cara, you and my own sister are the three women who are tied to my heart by a cord which can never be broken and which really *pulls* me continually. My love for you rests on a past which no future can reverse."

The metaphor of tied affection was to figure in *The Mill on the Floss* as a highly ambiguous image of confinement and connection. But that kind of fence mending with Sara was not a new activity; it would seem that Sara was apt to express her (accurate) feeling that Marian Evans was ambivalent about her. Two and a half years earlier Marian had written a similar letter reassuring Sara of her devotion; it too defines Sara and Cara in familial terms and avers, "It is certain that I can never have any friend—not even a husband—who would supply the loss of those associations with the past which belong to you" (2:19). The end of the 1854 letter, however, makes sure that "those associations with the past" are placed in proper relation to the present connection with Lewes: "While I retain your friendship I retain the best that life has given me next to that which is the deepest and gravest joy in all human experience." She did not hesitate to make it clear that she had traveled into realms that must remain in mystery for the unmarried Sara Hennell.

Marian was equally unwilling to concede that her secrecy might have been experienced as a betrayal of the friendship, and she answers Sara's charge that she wishes to be in communication only with Charles in a way that vaguely suggests she had been protecting Lewes's interests during the early months of their German sojourn: "The reason why I wrote to Mr. Bray and not to you and Cara is simply this. Before I left England, I communicated, by Mr. Lewes's desire, certain facts in strict confidence to Mr. Bray and Mr. Chapman and I did so for special reasons which would not apply to any female friend. . . . There is now no longer any secrecy to be preserved about

Mr. Lewes's affairs or mine, and whatever I have written to Mr. Bray, I have written to you." She denies that she is "standing on stilts of any kind" and maintains the principle of silence about her relationship with Lewes: "I wish to speak simply and to act simply but I think it can hardly be unintelligible to you that I shrink from writing elaborately about private feelings and circumstances." If the friendship is to continue, it must do so in letters about "things not personal, in which I know you would feel a common interest."

Sara accepted the terms of this letter and returned to an affectionate correspondence about literary matters. "But," she noted on November 15, "I have a strange sort of feeling that I am writing to some one in a book, and not to the Marian that we have known and loved so many years. Do not mistake me, I mean nothing unkind" (2:186). Sara may have been following up on a reference to Charlotte Brontë's *Villette* which had appeared in a mysterious and abrupt sentence inserted in a letter written just a few days before Marian departed for the Continent with Lewes: "I shall soon send you a good-bye, for I am preparing to go to 'Labassecour'" (2:165). Marian had read the novel immediately after its publication in February 1853 and had recommended it to the Bray group with an oddly uncritical fervor. "There is something almost preternatural in its power," she wrote in mid-February; and a month later she sounded an impatient call: "Villette—Villette—have you read it?" (2:87, 92). It is easy to see how Brontë's story of Lucy Snowe and the forbidden soul mate Paul Emanuel might have seemed a "preternatural" figure for her relationship with Lewes at just that period. When Sara followed up on the comparison, however, she sounded a warning note about a situation that Brontë herself had been unable to imagine as a sustainable life. Her sense that she was writing to a different Marian puts succinctly the actual break in continuity that her friend's rhetoric was at pains to deny, along with a tinge of suggestion that this new Marian was attempting to live a fantasy. Thus she nudged her friend, however gently, to see that her high-minded positions were being read with critical eyes.

If Sara complicated the position of heroic choice by rehumanizing it, Cara Bray took a path that might have recalled Robert Evans's response to the Holy War: she maintained a cold resistance to Marian's conduct by sending a letter of remonstrance and then remaining silent for a year.[15] By September 4, 1855, Marian Evans was able to write a controlled defense of her choice, taking the opportunity of response to a brief note of Cara's inquiring about bedding she had left at Rosehill (2:213–15). By this time she was in an internally strong position: Lewes had not, after all, abandoned her, and they had successfully weathered several months of living openly in London.[16] She was therefore able to retake the theoretical ground and to address Cara's concerns about the principles of her conduct; the letter suggests that Cara had accused her of succumbing to levity and pride in her stubborn attachment to a relationship that could not have any enduring status outside the laws of marriage.

What is striking about this letter—the one that both Cross and Haight quote at length as a representation of her moral position—is how little of its significant length is devoted to an actual vindication of that position.[17] Two brief groups of sentences perform that function. The first is frequently quoted: "Light and easily broken ties are what I neither desire theoretically nor could live for practically. Women who are satisfied with such ties do *not* act as I have done—they obtain what they desire and are still invited to dinner." These trenchant statements represent her public choice of Lewes in a way that distinguishes her from women who would not even consider the possibility of sacrificing social approval for a personal commitment. The telling uses of the word "desire" define Marian's as a principled position to which she has adhered in practice, while other women's desires for more casual love affairs are defined as selfish greed: they "are satisfied"; they "obtain what they desire" along with their dinners. It is such hypocritically respectable women, she manages to imply, who are fallen, while her own ability to tie herself to Lewes and take the consequences returns her to the position of heroic chooser. The obvious virtue of their position is emphasized in the next paragraph by her definition of their relationship as one of family support: "We are leading no life of self-indulgence, except indeed, that being happy in each other, we find everything easy. We are working hard to provide for others better than we provide for ourselves, and to fulfil every responsibility that lies upon us. Levity and pride would not be a sufficient basis for that." In their own way, she rightly suggests, they are going far beyond the conventional ethics of marriage laws in their mutual support of Agnes and her children; once again work, unselfishness, and reponsibility are called on to erase the possibility that *their* liaison might be interpreted in sexual terms.

These powerful nuggets lie at the center of a letter that is otherwise preoccupied with the problem of writing and misinterpretation. Although the letter was written as an effort to clarify misinterpreted words previously sent between the two women, its import is that Marian Evans has recognized the true cost of her choice: it is not that she will not be invited to dinner but that she can never again expect other people to interpret or represent her correctly. As she had written to Bessie Parkes the previous March, "Believe no one's representations about me, for there is not a *single person* who is in a position to make a true representation" (2:196). (Her italics would seem to include herself and Lewes, who had refrained from explaining themselves by retailing the story of Agnes Lewes and Thornton Hunt). Writing to Cara, she returns constantly to the lack of information which skews all interpretations of others. The letter opens on that note: "No one has better reason than myself to know how difficult it is to produce a true impression by letters, and how likely they are to be misinterpreted even where years of friendship might seem to furnish a sufficient key." Signs go awry in the reader's hand; Marian's attack on George Combe's petty fears for his own reputation in an earlier note to the Brays had, she fears, been read as her serious opinions on the marriage laws. As she goes on it becomes clear that her aim is not to explain but simply to list the gaps of information that make misinterpretation necessary. Cara does not know Lewes; she does not know what has transpired in Marian's intellectual and moral life; nor does Marian know Cara's views: "*How far* we differ I think neither of us know," she declares, but that is not matter for discovery in letters; she can only write "in few words" those powerful sentences of self-justification. Despite her declared distrust of letters, as Alexander Welsh aptly notes, she has taken good advantage of the distance writing allows: "Her feelings have been armored in the kind of argument one can only construct in writing, and the defense of her actions is predicated on distance and the withholding of personal confrontation."[18]

Once having allowed herself the sarcasm about women who obtain what they desire without sacrificing dinner invitations, Marian is roused to a stronger formulation of her dilemma: "That any unworldy, unsuperstitious person who is sufficiently acquainted with the realities of life can pronounce my relation to Mr. Lewes immoral I can only understand by remembering how subtle and complex are the influences that mould opinion. But I *do* remember this, and I indulge in no arrogant or uncharitable thoughts about those who condemn us, even though we might have expected a somewhat different verdict. From the majority of persons, of course, we never looked for anything but condemnation." Reestablishing a position of moral superiority to her audiences, she claims that the judged will not judge her misinformed jurors, all the while leveling a covert attack on Cara Bray for her presence among "the majority." Along with the representation of choice as sacrifice made in full awareness of its consequences, these sentences define her relation to close observers and a more general audience constrained by thoughtless morality, completing the cluster of attitudes I have linked with the idea of choice. They might also stand as an agenda for the novels of George Eliot, which were to track the "subtle and complex influences that mould opinion" with the precision of objective scrutiny and the overtone of distant superiority.

Having stated these positions for Cara, however, Marian Evans recognizes and attempts to repair the further gaps they may have created by covering the problem of misinterpretation with the language of love and memory. "Whatever I may have misinterpreted before, I do not misinterpret your letter this morning, but read in it nothing else than love and kindness towards me to which my heart fully answers yes." And she devotes a paragraph to her keen memory of Cara's past generosity, her recognition of her own past faults, and her determination to make the present better than than her past. It is not a present that fully includes Cara, however; the paragraph's close has the sound of an epitaph for a friendship: "But if we should never be very near each other again, dear Cara, do bear this faith in your mind, that I was not insensible or ungrateful to all your goodness, and that I am one amongst the many for whom you have not lived in vain." Although the many kinds of powerful appeal in the letter did serve to reopen the correspondence between Marian Evans and Cara Bray, its actual invocation of the power of memory serves, as in the letter to Sara Hennell, to emphasize an internal break with an outgrown past. Under the pressures placed on Marian Evans's loyalty to the Bray circle, the romance of memory emerged as an antidote or counterforce to what the narrator of *The Mill on the Floss* was to call "the labour of choice."

Piety about the past became a persistent theme in Marian's letters to Cara Bray, as though the reiteration of the language of memory itself had become a substitute for the actual relation. Thus, in March 1858 Marian wrote, "The feeling that you and Sara have been and always will be the women I have loved best in the world—the women I have had most reason to love and admire—strengthens instead of fading with time and absence. It is impossible ever to revive the past, and if we could recover the friend from whom we have parted we should perhaps find that we could not recover precisely the old relation. But that doesn't hinder the past from being sacred and belonging to our religion" (8:199–200). The past had become a religion because it was an occasion for the production of sacramental language to fill an interpretive and experiential gap.

Moving as they do between representations of sacrificial choice, public misunderstanding, and the pietistic language of memory, these letters of self-explanation stake out a familiar terrain for the reader of George Eliot's novels. It was not comfortable territory for Marian Evans, who was capable of scathing formulas about public opinion exactly because she was incapable of remaining unscathed herself. Ultimately she, like most of her interpreters, relied on the consequences of her choice in order to justify it to herself. It was not until the first two stories in *Scenes of Clerical Life* had appeared in *Blackwood's* that she could bring herself to inform her brother Isaac Evans, her sister Chrissey Clarke, and her stepsister Fanny Houghton of her marriage with Lewes. On May 26, 1857, she wrote the letters that were to result in Isaac's severance of communication with her (2:331–33, 346). Several days later Sara Hennell received a letter that articulated a new economics of choice. Marian informed Sara that she had told her family, and that she had "learned to see how much of the pain I have felt concerning my own family is really love of approbation in disguise." Her next sentence reveals that her writing—which was at this time yet another secret from Sara and the Brays—plays a crucial role as a compensation for that lost approbation. "If I live five years longer, the positive result of my existence on the side of truth and goodness will outweigh the small negative good that would have consisted in my not doing anything to shock others, and I can conceive no consequences that will make me repent the past. Do not misunderstand me and suppose that I think myself heroic or great in any way. Far enough from that! Faulty, miserably faulty I am—but least of all faulty when others most blame" (2:342). She could hardly have put herself in a more complex position. The renewed pressure built up by her decision to inform Isaac has led her to a new moral mathematics in which writing will put her "on the side of truth and goodness" and outweigh the effect of her scandalous behavior; all the while she is concealing from Sara that truth which she desires so much so tell.[19]

Having made a grand and mysterious assertion about her importance to the world, she is hard put to follow it with disclaimers that will put Sara off the scent again. She appeals, finally, to the topos of misinterpretation: "least of all faulty when others most blame." Her new mode of self-justification has landed her in the old fix; she writes herself into the role of a specially moral being who cannot represent herself against others' misrepresentations.

George Eliot's narrators are Marian Evans's answer to a life about which "there is not a *single person* who is in a position to make a true representation." They provide, within the controlled representations of fiction, the human, yet larger-than-human perspective that can give voice to a multiplicity of interpretations within a single discourse. I have written in Chapter 2 about the habit of critical self-reading which shapes George Eliot's style and necessitates her disruptive addresses to her reader. In relation to her characters, however, George Eliot's narrative strategies were determined by the desire to achieve an interpretive justice and flexibility that she knew to be unavailable in life. It is a kind of justice in which verdicts are endlessly deferred, their outlines blurred and complicated by further twists of perspective, further bits of evidence, further explanations. Although the interpretations of morally flawed characters or of ignorantly gossiping communities are ironically rendered so as to make the reader superior to them, the narration itself does not reside in a fixed position of judgment or approval even in relation to the admirable characters, whose choices are also subject to questioning and whose idealism is rendered in ambiguous narrative tones that mark it as a form of heroic rhetoric. This refusal of singleness, which makes almost every critical interpretation a story of lesser complexity than the one George Eliot tells, is her primary mode of depicting a world of observers and observed in which "true representation" is impossible.

The particularly intense narrative attention given to moments of choice details the many conflicting formulations of claims, valid or questionable, through which individual characters must pass before the decisive moment of action, and then shows how the meaning of that choice may be altered in that moment when it is performed before an audience. The reader, meanwhile, is drawn to judgment of a character less on the grounds of the choice itself than through the narrator's description of how the process of choice is internally experienced. Thus, we have a very different sense of the meaning of

Lydgate's vote for Tyke than do the hospital board members before whom it is, nightmarishly, staged; we also know that an important moral difference between Dorothea and Lydgate is exemplified in her willingness to see that she is confronted with choices that she must make within intensely discomfiting constraints.[20] But if George Eliot's primary morality lies in her sense that characters must embrace choices in the face of relentlessly determining histories and circumstances, she is equally interested in the invisibility of such moralities to the naked eye.

For Maggie Tulliver, George Eliot's most overtly autobiographical heroine, true representation is impossible. Maggie is systematically misinterpreted by others, and haplessly colludes in the system of misrepresentation by forming secret relationships that make her actions increasingly open to hostile interpretations once they are discovered. *The Mill on the Floss* has an especially intense relation to Marian Evans's life because it compacts so much material, making a continuous line of the actual discontinuity between her provincial family experience and her later choice of Lewes. Maggie's decision to return to St. Ogg's after her escape with Stephen Guest has, for example, frequently been read as some sort of commentary on Marian Evans's elopement with George Henry Lewes. But what sort? Barbara Hardy imagines it as a self-justifying apologia that reads: "Had human ties been involved, I would not even have broken the faintest commitment; since there were none, I was prepared to break social laws and commandments."[21] Janice Carlisle, on the other hand, reads the novel as a self-condemnation: "By allowing Maggie to refuse to sacrifice her ties with the past and her family despite the strength of her desires, George Eliot created what she could not be, a noble, self-sacrificing character." In her reading, the novel "holds up the glass of public opinion and assents to its verdict against her own unconventional choices."[22] Alexander Welsh reads the peculiar complexity of Maggie's situation on the river with Stephen as necessitated by George Eliot's determination to create "the same balance of undeserved shame and moral achievement that she hinted to her friends when she secretly designed to become a novelist";[23] one could bring that same formula to bear on her original secret, the illegal marriage with Lewes. The novel allows for such variant readings, as it allows us to feel that Maggie's final choice is simultaneously an act of moral heroism and one of masochistic self-destruction. It is really this bafflement of interpretation which most interests me about *The Mill on the Floss*, its replication of structures of misunderstanding rather than its rendering of particular autobiographical stories.[24] If we look at the way the novel constructs moments of choice without attempting to derive interpretations that tell us a certain story, we see George Eliot immersed in dramatizing the hopelessly tangled stresses of competing claims which constitute acts of choice.

In the broadest sense, choices are structured as conflicts between loyalty and old commitments and acceptance of new ones, or—roughly—between self-limitation and self-expansion. As in Marian Evans's life, new ties become old ones in subsequent stages of choice. In the first stage the conflict between service to the father and Mary Ann Evans's intellectually expansive relationship with the Bray circle is represented by the conflict between the Tulliver family code (with the brother acting in the role of police enforcer) and Maggie's culturally expansive but asexual relationship with Philip Wakem. In the second stage Marian Evans's "betrayal" of Cara Bray and Sara Hennell in her secret relationship with Lewes and her redefinition of them as a past made sacred by memory are transformed into Maggie's mental redefinition of Philip as the "sacred place" with "its roots deep down in her childhood" where her conscience must reside as she encounters the sexuality, mobility and largeness of life offered by Stephen Guest (bk. 6, chap. 7). The second-stage offenses are forgiven by the immediate victims (the Bray circle; Philip and Lucy), but their intensity derives from the original structure of conflict: the figure of Philip in Maggie's dream turns into the figure of Tom; behind the tension with the Brays lay, in George Eliot's retrospective imagination, Isaac Evans's absolute severance of ties with his sister after she finally announced to him her union with Lewes.

The difficulty of the narrative lies in the fact that it is still caught up in the struggle it is attempting to depict. Throughout the novel the valorizing of memory and continuity takes place against the repeated demonstration that the choice of the "familiar" is equivalent to the choice of death.[25] This is not true for Maggie alone; Mr. Tulliver's decision to stay on at the mill and submit himself to work for Wakem is most strongly influenced, the narrator explains, by "the love of the old premises where he had run about when he was a boy. . . . he felt the strain of this clinging affection for the old home as part of his life, part of himself. He couldn't bear to think of himself living on any other spot than this" (bk. 3, chap. 9). Apart from the interesting ambivalence in the phrase "strain of this clinging affection," the narrator desires her readers to feel and sympathize with this pull; yet the self-suppression necessitated by the decision leads directly to Mr. Tulliver's violent outbreak against Wakem and his subsequent death. It is as if the Marian Evans Lewes of 1859 was intent on filling up the rifts in her life with a persuasive defense of her power to adhere in memory, while demonstrating that an actual choice based on loyalty to the past would have killed her.[26] The strained perspective into which this position leads her can be represented by the passage in which she sounds the thematic term, "the labour of choice," and contrasts it to the Edenic condition of unity with an original place.

The passage appears at the end of the long chapter titled "Tom's First Half" (bk. 2, chap. 1), a chapter that might otherwise serve to qualify George Eliot as a modern feminist. It includes the passages about Tom's structural feminization under the unfamiliar rules of schooling and the several episodes in which Maggie's imaginative reading and reasoning collide with cultural definitions of women's minds as "quick and shallow."[27] Whereas many of the novel's chapters end in ways that mark the tensions explored in the previous pages, this one retreats from its especially pungent social critiques, returning to Tom the chapter that Maggie had co-opted and recording Tom's intense yearning for home. The passage soon modulates into a general meditation:

> There is no sense of ease like the ease we felt in those scenes where we were born, where objects became dear to us before we had known the labour of choice, and where the outer world seemed only an extension of our own personality: we accepted and loved it as we accepted our own sense of existence and our own limbs. Very commonplace, even ugly, that furniture of our early home might look if it were put up to auction; an improved taste in upholstery scorns it; and is not the striving after something better and better in our surroundings, the grand characteristic that distinguishes man from the brute—or, to satisfy a scrupulous accuracy of definition, that distinguishes the British man from the foreign brute? But heaven knows where that striving might lead us, if our affections had not a trick of twining round those old inferior things—if the loves and sanctities of our life had no deep immovable roots in memory.

The Edenic condition described here is one in which one can love without choosing; to be ejected from it is to be condemned to "the labour of choice." The absence of choice is also described as an idyllic continuity of self and audience, whereas the action of choice would open a gap between "personality" and "the outer world." As so often in these pseudo-Wordsworthian passages, George Eliot shifts from the love of persons to the love of objects or places to release her rhetoric of memory,[28] but as the passage moves along its nostalgia for childhood furniture unfolds some other tonalities. "Striving after something better" is cast in a satirical role, invoking the decision to educate Tom, the Dodson family obsession with household goods, and thoughtless nationalistic prejudices. We are enjoined to prefer the inferior, entwined with affection; in a later sentence the narrator satirizes "those severely regulated minds who are free from the weakness of any attachment that does not rest on a demonstrable superiority of qualities." All this preparation can support the narrator's treatment of Tom's education, making the argument that such strivings could be dangerous—heaven knows where they might lead—if a person like Tom were not affectionally linked to others by memories of home. Read as a commentary on Maggie's frustrated strivings, or on the narrator's position, the passage has more troubling implications because it offers no field of action for "the labour of choice" apart from a satirized, futile, and diffusely dangerous aspiration. "There is no better reason," the narrator concludes, "for preferring this elderberry bush than that it stirs an early memory—that it is no novelty in my life . . . but the long companion of my existence, that wove itself into my joys when joys were vivid." To announce such a preference blurs the narrator's actual separation from the world she depicts and attempts to erase the traces of distanced social satire which have just been inscribed on the page.[29]

   The drama of Maggie's choices sets out a similarly claustrophobic arena, in which Maggie takes on the hard labor of choice without developing the psychic or social means to break her original ties. In a simple overview, we could say that Maggie gets trapped in a relatively clear pattern of desire: she gives up, then she takes, then she is punished for taking. Following scenes that foreground choice, from the division of the jam puff to the choice of Philip to the escapade with Stephen, we could readily argue that by the end of the novel Maggie is imposing on herself the punishment that has formerly been carried out by Tom. In the actual reading, however, the scenes construct choice as a battle between the power of Maggie's internal decision-making process and those who seek to deny her that power.[30]

The childhood scene in which Tom allots the unequal halves of a coveted jam puff pits Maggie's version of choice against Tom's. It is quite clear how Maggie has chosen: she wants the smaller piece, so as to please Tom, and she says so both before and after Tom gives her the larger. Had Tom simply held out the two pieces, Maggie would have taken her choice and the matter been amicably settled. But Tom cannot allow Maggie the power of choice or the consciousness that she has taken the more generous path along with the smaller piece. His version of choice is blind chance: Maggie must close her eyes and pick a hand, so that the responsibility of choosing resides only in Tom's own choice "to be fair." Yet after Maggie "wins" according to Tom's lottery, she is condemned as "a greedy" because she fails to share the larger bit with him; that is, she is treated as if Tom had chosen to sacrifice the larger piece and deserved recompense. When she momentarily forgets Tom in the dreamy bliss of jam eating, she is instantly vulnerable to his punishment. The scene establishes a structure in which Maggie is compelled to sacrifice the terms in which she would choose; then a pleasurable act that follows from her submission to another's needs is interpreted as her choice of greed, selfishness, and forgetfulness. The plot of *The Mill on the Floss* is a machine that replicates this structure in increasingly complicated ways.

In its specific characterization of Tom Tulliver as a brother unable to allow his sister to exercise choice and prone to generate irrational double binds, George Eliot formulated in fiction what she forbade herself otherwise to put into writing about her brother Isaac. A single letter briefly violates that contract with herself; it suggests a remarkably similar situation. The letter was written to the Bray-Hennell group on December 31, 1852, after Marian Evans had returned to London from a visit to her sister Chrissey Clarke following the sudden death of her husband, Edward. "I had agreed with Chrissey that, all things considered, it was wiser for me to return to town," she writes. "Isaac, however, was very indignant to find that I had arranged to leave without consulting him, and thereupon flew into a violent passion with me, winding up by saying that he desired I would never 'apply to him for anything whatever'—which, seeing that I have never done so, was almost as superfluous as if I had said that I would never receive a kindness from him." The rather vicious twist at the end of the sentence gets its due repentance in the next: "But he is better than he shewed himself to me and I have no doubt that he will be kind to Chrissey, though not in a very large way" (2:75). This tiny glimpse into the history of the relationship between brother and sister is enough to suggest what painfully twisted strands of feeling compelled George Eliot to create the nostalgically compensatory story of a sister who cannot let go of her attachment to her brother.[31]

In her text Tom Tulliver remains consistent in his advocacy of blind justice and in his inability to countenance any choices that Maggie might make without his permission. When Tom discovers the clandestine meetings between Maggie and Philip Wakem, he produces an alternative that makes a mockery of choice:

> "Now, then, Maggie, there are but two courses for you to take; either you vow solemnly to me, with your hand on my father's Bible, that you will never have another meeting or speak another word in private with Philip Wakem, or you refuse, and I tell my father everything; and this month, when by my exertions he might be made happy once more, you will cause him the blow of knowing that you are a disobedient, deceitful daughter, who throws away her own respectability with the son of a man that has helped to ruin her father. Choose!" (bk. 5, chap. 5).

Tom's idea of choice is blackmail, and his use of it restores Maggie to his control. Compared with the elaborate moral debates through which Maggie has succumbed to the meetings with Philip, it is a parody of choosing. Maggie manages to get more room by promising only that she will not see Philip without Tom's permission, a revision that complies with Tom's primary need to be in charge. By the end of the scene, however, this central episode in the brother-sister conflict has set off George Eliot's feeling about Isaac Evans's response to her marriage with Lewes, and she finishes the chapter by staging a debate that rings of her recent experience. Maggie is roused to eloquence in an attack on Tom's moral narrowness and his failure to see who she is: "You have no pity: you have no sense of your own imperfection and your own sins. . . . You have not even a vision of feelings by the side of which your shining virtues are a mere darkness!" Tom answers only in the language of conduct: if your conduct was right, why have you kept it secret? How can good feeling end in conduct that is disobedient and deceitful? (bk. 5, chap. 5). The debate ends in a deadlock—its only answer lying in the writing of a narrative that goes to great lengths to render "conduct" as the product of intensely specific moral and emotional histories.

The internal and external debates that constitute the greater parts
of Maggie's narrative relations with both Philip and Stephen pull in
many directions at once. They dramatize all the factors activated by
Marian Evans's choice of Lewes: the opportunities and dangers of
secrecy, the conflict between new life and the betrayal of old connections, the definition of choice as sacrifice, the imagination of consequences, the debate over whether women have choices at all, and the
subsequent public hysteria about "conduct." These scenes are so constructed that the reader is prevented from resting on one or another
side of a question, while they retain the essential structure established
in the jam puff scene: Maggie's choices are co-opted by others, but her
actions are read as those of a greedy—in adult terms, a sexually
reprobate—woman.

Both Philip and Stephen pressure Maggie to abandon deliberately
made choices to renounce their company. Maggie decides not to see
Philip because their meeting violates the Tulliver family code and
would require secrecy and concealment; she understands the painful
consequences of discovery. Philip shakes her resolve by adducing other, equally plausible consequences: "Seeking safety in negations" will
result in a violent reaction to self-repression, and "every rational satisfaction of your nature that you deny now, will assault you like a savage
appetite." Maggie is derailed enough by that vision to assent silently to
Philip's sophistry: "If I meet you by chance, there is no concealment in
that?" (bk. 5, chap. 3). The narrator is quick to moralize on this lapse
from the responsibility of choice, calling it "the defeat we love better
than victory," but it is Philip's rationalization and motive on which she
focuses the reader's judgment and sympathy. Maggie herself has
struggled with the two voices that contend in her and made her
choice; she is given a full awareness of Philip's strategy: "She felt there
was some truth in what Philip said, and yet there was a deeper consciousness that, for any immediate application it had to her conduct, it
was no better than falsity" (bk. 5, chap. 3). Although both Maggie and
Philip clothe their own desires in terms of providing help for the
other, it is Maggie who has a fuller consciousness that there is a serious choice to be made, or betrayed.

Stephen Guest is represented as someone who fails to grasp the
nature of choice as George Eliot imagines it. He is introduced in an
ironic narrative passage that foregrounds his self-satisfaction in
"choosing" Lucy Deane as his future wife. "Perhaps he approved his
own choice of her chiefly because she did not strike him as a remark-

able rarity," the narrator comments wryly. For Stephen, inclination and choice mean the same thing. "He meant to choose Lucy: she was a little darling, and exactly the sort of woman he had always most admired" (bk. 6, chap. 1). Maggie throws him into moral confusion because "he would never have chosen her himself" (bk. 6, chap. 6); unschooled by internal conflict, his only recourse is to impose his demand on Maggie against her every act of resistance and persuasion, until he allows their boat to drift too far down the river and earns Maggie's reproach: "You have wanted to deprive me of my choice" (bk. 6, chap. 13). Like Tom and Philip, he will not credit the terms of her decisions. Thus Maggie is perpetually in the position of making choices she does not act upon, acting upon choices framed by others' needs, and being judged as the agent of her actions. This is not simply a pattern in which Maggie's noble choices are undermined by her own desire but one in which George Eliot demonstrates how human decisions are necessarily shaped and defined by collisions between the internal needs of more than one person.

Meanwhile the reader is drawn into the moral dilemmas posed by the choices themselves. What, for example, is the status of secrecy in the novel? We are drawn simultaneously to a disapproval of the principle and to an endorsement of its possibilities: it is difficult to disapprove of Maggie's wish to protect her family from knowledge of her meetings with Philip when they are her only source of mental life and growth. When Maggie tells Lucy that she would choose Philip as a husband in order to conceal her feeling for Lucy's fiancé, we are torn between judgments about her sincere duplicitousness; she hopes to protect more than to deceive. And what of Maggie's inclination to validate her choices as sacrifices? It is often difficult to know whether the narrative endorses her sacrificial thoughts on behalf of others or whether they are presented as Maggie's way of describing to herself what she most wants or needs to do. Nor does the capacity to consider consequences determine the morality of a choice. How does one weigh Maggie's knowledge that secrecy may harm her family and herself against Philip's argument that Maggie's self-suppression will have explosive future implications? Or Maggie's claim that she cannot live with her conscience if she betrays Lucy and Philip against Stephen's argument that they cannot sincerely love their intended spouses after the explosion of their feeling for each other? Playing the game of consequences is clearly a move in a deeper struggle of motives and character; the future of a choice remains an unknown quantity, and we are left to judge the quality of the arguments largely on the grounds of the extent to which they are immediately self-serving or more widely considered.

Maggie's impassioned arguments about why she must leave Stephen and return to St. Ogg's come, in the end, not to a definitive clarity about the rights and wrongs of the case but to an action that recalls her power of choice to herself and to the advocacy of the past she has learned to espouse. She has, she argues, "never deliberately consented" to the creation of sorrow in other minds. "It has never been my will to marry you." What she finally declares, regardless of consequences, is her right to a woman's power of choice. And she is immediately punished for it; Stephen exclaims, "What a miserable thing a woman's love is to a man's. I could commit crimes for you—and you can balance and choose in that way" (6:14). To retain the right of choice, to wear it in the face of her society, is to be misread in several ways at once; Maggie is accused both of rational coldheartedness and unwomanly sexual license.

The Mill on the Floss requires its readers to accept and admire Maggie's choice if they are to be true to "the inward springs that determine her action." It also, however, presents us with conflicting messages about how to assess those particular inward springs. Reverence for memory is a touchstone of the narrative; there is a strong moral pull in Maggie's words to Stephen, "The real tie lies in the feelings and expectations we have raised in other minds" (bk. 6, chap. 12). The narrative makes it equally clear that Maggie is rooted to the spot in St. Ogg's because she cannot let go of her repetitive need to be judged and then forgiven. The narrator who opened the novel with a prose poem celebrating the re-creative power of memory closes it with an assertion of pastoral reunion which belies and forgets the actual stress of conflict rendered in the narrative of childhood. Memory itself has become suspect in the writing of this work.[32] But there is a moment that more accurately records George Eliot's relation to her past. At the end of *The Mill on the Floss* the narrator displaces herself into the significantly *written* voice of Philip Wakem in his letter of forgiveness to Maggie. "Perhaps I feel about you as the artist does about the scene over which his soul has brooded with love," Philip writes, identifying himself directly with the distanced perspective of the narrative voice. He has mysteriously disappeared from sight in St. Ogg's, for it is only in the act of writing that he can repair the damage in his relation with Maggie and rise to that ultimate George Eliot rhetoric of sympathy which marks his moral evolution: "The new life I have found in caring for your joy and sorrow more than for what is directly my own, has transformed the spirit of rebellious murmuring into that willing endurance which is the birth of strong sympathy" (bk. 7, chap. 3). Such idealistic rhetoric is made possible by an ambiguous physical relation to Maggie: "I shall not go away. The place where you are is the one where my mind must live, wherever I might travel." Philip, the "revisiting spirit" of the conclusion, is not rooted to any spot.

So might Marian Evans, in letters and fictions, repair her past connections from the enabling distance of her mental, moral, and physical travels. She had chosen to surprise the feelings and expectations she had raised in other minds; she had persuaded herself that she could stand to be judged and largely unforgiven. We may read the novel as an autobiographical account of her young and guilt-ridden struggle between loyalty and self-development, of all that kept her rooted to the spot in Warwickshire until her father's death. We may read it as a full rendering of the nostalgic desire for forgiveness, an apology for a felt betrayal of her past, even a wish to be released from the labor of a choice that altered the tone of every day of her life as Marian Evans Lewes. And we may read it as her declaration of a woman's life as a rich and strenuous process of choice, invisible to a world in which she is defined by requirements about conduct. All these readings would be true.

The end of George Eliot's life bears an uncanny resemblance to the fantasies that conclude *The Mill on the Floss*. She married John Cross—an unexpected decision that raised yet another episode of surprise and scandal. She was married in a church, surrounded by the several new sisters and brothers she had acquired. She erased all the names that had signified her self-making and signed herself with the names her father and husband gave her: Mary Ann Cross. She had a reconciliation with Isaac Evans. And she died. It is impossible to know whether she understood the inward spring of these actions as a fundamental need to go home again at the last. The letters that announce and interpret her marriage to Cross do, however, indicate how deeply the tensions generated by her choice of Lewes twenty-five years earlier still pressed on her consciousness.

George Eliot's marriage to John Walter Cross was decided and carried out in a way that repeated the scenario of her union with George Henry Lewes. The young banker had become a close friend of the

Eliot-Lewes household during the years that preceded Lewes's death on November 30, 1878. George Eliot, who had affectionately familial if not mildly flirtatious feelings for him, called him "Nephew." Along with her other friends and worshipers, Cross was excluded from her presence during her first intense months of mourning and saw her for the first time at the end of February 1879 (7:107). On April 22, faced with several financial decisions, George Eliot wrote an urgent note of summons: "I am in dreadful need of your counsel." "From this time forward," Cross wrote, "I saw George Eliot constantly. My mother had died in the beginning of the previous December, a week after Mr. Lewes, and, as my life had been very much bound up with hers, I was trying to find some fresh interest in taking up a new pursuit."[33] The new pursuit, in which George Eliot insisted on joining him, was reading Dante. By January 1880 Cross could record, "She was in the habit of going with me very frequently to the National Gallery, and to other exhibitions of pictures, to the British Museum sculptures, and to South Kensington. This constant association engrossed me completely, and was a new interest to her. A bond of mutual dependence had been formed between us."[34] As with Lewes, a consolatory friendship had deepened into intimacy. And as with Lewes, it was represented as if it were an ordinary companionship or escort, while its intimate fluctuations were concealed from others.[35] John Cross was not mentioned in George Eliot's letters to her other friends.

On April 9, 1880, George Eliot's journal notes, "My marriage decided" (7:259). During the following month no one was told of the decision except the Cross family and Lewes's eldest son, Charles (who learned of it a week before the wedding), although several friends were mysteriously informed in late April or early May that George Eliot was "going abroad for a little while" (7:265, 9:305). The wedding took place on May 6, after which the pair departed immediately for the Continent. On May 5, George Eliot wrote letters to several friends—including Cara Bray—in order to inform them of the marriage before they read about it in the newspapers. Charles Lewes was designated to break the news to several others. Once it had spread, gossip exhumed the scandal of the Lewes elopement. As Edith Simcox recorded in her journal on June 30, "The things that are said of her hurt me. They go back to the old story. I cannot believe that she built her happiness upon a separation, that but for her need not have come" (9:313). She was referring to the old debate about whether Marian Evans had broken up the Lewes marriage.

For George Eliot herself, the "old story" had recurred too, but it was defined differently. It had to do with finding herself once again in a position that pitted a new connection against adherence to memory, one that would be read, regardless of her actual feeling, as a betrayal of her now-revered attachment to Lewes. Once again a choice of hers had set her in a relation to public opinion which she found impossible to negotiate through means other than secrecy, action, and flight, even though she was fully convinced that her friends would experience her concealment as betrayal. Edith Simcox, whose love for George Eliot has provided us with the most detailed account of those days, wrote up a conversation with Cross's sisters about Cross's spectacular illness during the honeymoon. Cross, they told her, had been worn out; he "had to continue all his business to the last because she would not let anyone be told and he shrank from the responsibility, if her friends were likely to take it as she thought they would, of coming between her and them" (July 12, 1880; 9:314). It is difficult to know whether it is Simcox's intensity or George Eliot's that most pervades this passage, but it does suggest that George Eliot had experienced the repetition of her earlier choice as traumatic and had accordingly been compelled to repeat her style of managing it as well. Delegating Charles Lewes to mend her fences seems a particularly questionable demand to have placed on his filial devotion and loyalty; it reveals a ferocious need to assert a continuity with Lewes, as well as a truly fearful avoidance of her friends' responses. Charles Lewes provided the further clue that George Eliot worried about her choice of Cross in terms of its effect on her audiences; he told Anne Thackeray Ritchie that George Eliot had "confided in [her physician] Paget who approved and told her that it wouldn't make any difference in her influence" (7:284). Yet no one should have known better than George Eliot that one might spend twenty years teaching one's readers to sympathize with the peculiar dynamics of human choice, only to be misunderstood again.

In fact, the Cross marriage is still perfectly misunderstandable because it had no history that would allow us to interpret a choice according to its consequences. George Eliot died eight months after her marriage, before the couple had had a chance to establish any regular life together. Because the precise timing of a person's death can be psychosomatically suggestive, it is tempting to imagine that she had learned in those months that her emotional solitude was unbroken and that she had finished the work of her life. The letters written in her last months suggest a retreat into affectionate familial politeness, laced with many expressions of gratitude; an occasional glimpse of strain can be sensed in moments like this one in a letter to Elma Stuart: "My soul is often too full of past and present together and seems hardly strong enough for the double weight, but no woman could be helped more than I am" (7:323). Because we have no further record, twentieth-century readers of the life remain in positions like those of George Eliot's contemporaries when it comes to imagining motives for her choice of a man twenty years her junior whose strongest previous tie had been with his mother. Gordon Haight deals with this question by repeating Charles Bray's now-infamous line, "She was not fitted to stand alone," and by adducing George Eliot's "essential conservatism" as the basis of her inducement to marry conventionally; he also points significantly to Cross's virtues as "those her father would have admired."[36] Phyllis Rose emphasizes the sexual and emotional appeal of a handsome and devoted young man who could be loved in a different way from Lewes, and the pleasurable guilt of another socially dubious attachment.[37] Ruby Redinger creates a George Eliot who "was afraid of losing her power to love" and was trying to evade the lesbian advances of Edith Simcox.[38]

Reading the letters of the period between Lewes's death and the Cross marriage draws me toward another kind of speculation, however. George Eliot experienced during those months the legal peculiarities of her position as the nonwidow of George Henry Lewes, as well as the kind of work that must be done after the death of a person of letters. All her considerable financial assets were in Lewes's name; amid the complex procedures of transferring her own property to herself she signed a "Deed of declaration adopting the surname of Lewes in addition to the name of Evans." Two months after Lewes's death, therefore, "Mary Ann Evans, Spinster," legally changed her name to "Mary Ann Evans Lewes."[39] (Mary Ann, it would appear, had always been retained as her Christian name for legal purposes.)

The new Miss Evans Lewes had, she felt, not only to complete Lewes's unfinished *Problems of Life and Mind* and to establish a scholarship in his name but to sustain the financial arrangements with Agnes Lewes, decide how to deal with the poor and importunate widow and children of Lewes's youngest son, Bertie, and take over the endless minutiae of two authorial careers, which Lewes had managed during his life. During the larger part of 1879 she was ill with the renal disease that was soon to kill her; Cross had attended her. Charles

Lewes was the only competent adult in her life who was legally related to George Henry Lewes, and much of the burden of his father's affairs fell on him. She would have realized with great clarity that in her own case there was not even a Charles Lewes; there was no adult conversant with her complex affairs with whom she had a legal relationship. Marrying John Cross, who already managed her investments and venerated her work as well as her privacy, was the most practical step she could have taken. It is quite possible that Charles Lewes appreciated that point as well as anyone could.

It was, however, not a point that could be expressed, at least not directly. In the group of explanatory letters that George Eliot wrote to her friends about her marriage, she recurred to a series of formulas, each of which suggested that she had abrogated the power and pride of choice. For if her last decision was in many ways a repetition of her earlier one, it also marked a significant change in her self-representation.

A few days after the decision was made, George Eliot wrote two notes to John's sister, Eleanor Cross, an unmarried woman in her early thirties. They express doubt and fear, as well as a kind of yearning to be taken again into the bosom of a family. "You can hardly think how sweet the name Sister is to me, that I have not been called by for so many, many years," she begins. "Without your tenderness I do not believe it would have been possible for me to accept this wonderful renewal of my life." These notions, that she is the passive recipient of the Cross family generosity and that she has been given a last-minute chance at life when her own direction was deathward, were to pervade her correspondence. As she put it in the second note to Eleanor, "The inward struggle, the doubt, the final word—all has been a trial, and I have often wished that my life had ended a year ago. But now what remains of it must have a new consecration in gratitude for the miracle of his love." The extreme difficulty of making that "miracle" a practical reality pains her, however. "Yet I quail a little in facing what has to be gone through—the hurting of many whom I care for," she wrote; and "I am still agitated—terrified, perhaps because I am not well" (7:259–60). The idea that she would once again be accused of betrayal was very much on her mind. It may have been intensified by her knowledge that her own feeling for Cross was very different in kind from the feeling she had heroically defended twenty-five years earlier.

In the letters of announcement written on May 5 and others written in response to congratulations after her marriage, George Eliot did not of course allow herself such extreme expressions of doubt, but she continued to develop the formulas she had begun in the notes to Eleanor Cross. It was, she managed to imply, John Cross's heroic and sacrificial choice rather than her own, a choice that developed in a continuous line from his friendship with Lewes. "He has been a devoted friend for years, much loved and trusted by Mr. Lewes, and now that I am alone, he sees his only longed-for happiness in dedicating his life to me," she wrote to Georgiana Burne-Jones (7:269). The phrase "much loved and trusted by Mr. Lewes" was repeated in several other letters, as if to underline the fact that she was violating no long-standing trusts. A month after the marriage she praised Cross more directly to Barbara Bodichon, who had produced a characteristically generous response to the news even though the May 5 letter intended for her had never arrived, having been mistakenly locked in George Eliot's drawer. Wishing that Barbara could know Cross's delicacy and generosity firsthand, George Eliot added, "But you will have inferred something of this from his desire to dedicate his life to the remaining fragment of mine" (7:290). To Isaac Evans, who had broken the long silence between them with a stiff little note of congratulation, she was pointedly explicit about the matter of Cross's choice: "His affection has made him choose this lot of caring for me rather than any other of the various lots open to him" (7:287). Such formulations make it quite clear that she was announcing her resignation from the position of "strong-minded woman."

She also tried to lessen her own agency by casting the story as a kind of miraculous romance tale, in which the heroine, rescued from death and restored to life at the last minute, is still too dazed to know quite what has happened to her. "A great momentous change is taking place in my life—a sort of miracle in which I could never have believed, and under which I still sit amazed," she wrote to Georgiana Burne-Jones (7:269); to Maria Congreve, "The whole history is something like a miracle-legend" (7:296). Everything had moved so quickly, she implied, that she was prevented from writing until "the eleventh hour" (7:267 and 269). Such romantic language was designed to placate the female friends who were most likely to feel both offended by her secrecy and shocked at her marriage, but a more straightforward version of the story went also to Barbara Bodichon: "All this [including the Cross family welcome] is wonderful blessing falling to me beyond my share after I had thought that my life was ended and that, so to speak, my coffin was ready for me in the next room. Deep down below there is a hidden river of sadness but this must always be with those who have lived long—and I am able to enjoy my newly-reopened life. I shall be a better, more loving creature than I could have been in solitude" (7:291). She might almost have said "my newly reopened coffin"; to Barbara she allows herself the faintest of suggestions that it might have been easier to lie in that coffin and suffer her sadness without the restorative kiss of a young prince. In the last sentence of the last letter she wrote to Cara Bray, on November 28, 1880, that mixture of notes may be heard again: "If it is any good for me that my life has been prolonged till now, I believe it is owing to this miraculous affection which has chosen to watch over me" (7:341).

The argument that the marriage will make her better and less selfish, that "the springs of affection are reopened in me" (7:259), was also repeated several times in the letter group.[40] Her alliance with Lewes had been described as an action that filled her with happy energy and made her fertile with ideas. This latter choice was, on the other hand, to redeem her for human community. In her mourning she had become a sort of Silas Marner, and now, miraculously, an Eppie had walked into her life, inducing her to reforge her ties with ordinary people and behaviors. For the sake of the friends who had come to know and revere her as George Eliot, she produced a George Eliot fable.

The letters about her union with Lewes cast her proudly as the heroic chooser; the later group represent her as a person who has done something apart from her own will, something she is doubtful and perhaps even slightly ashamed of, for the sake of another's active need.[41] But how can we account for the passivity in this stance? Why was it necessary to cast herself as a Maggie Tulliver who could not help it, one whose "rescue" had come, not in the form of a flood but as a romantic tale of eleventh-hour revival? Perhaps it was because she understood her marriage as unraveling all her life's labor of choice, as an act that symbolically restored the Edenic situation of immersion within an accepted and acceptable family code. She had made a contract with her audiences and admirers to be George Eliot, great writer and infamous woman, and now she had broken that promise to the expectations she had raised in others' minds. She had given up her special status and the names that marked it in order to end her life within the pale of her father's world. If she embraced the legality, respectability, and practicality of that world with some relief, it could not have been unmixed with the discomfort of being seen in an action that could be read as a pathos-ridden fantasy of return.

The night George Eliot died, John Cross's first instinct was to write to Isaac Evans, whom he had never met. "I feel you should be written to first of all," he said. "The Brother 'who leaned soft cheeks together' with her in the old old days" (9:322). It was as if he had read to perfection his function in George Eliot's life. He was to be the loving retrospect, the action of repair, the conduit to her origins. He was to be the editor who excised the sharp separateness of her letters, and strung them together in a continuous narrative.

FIVE

The Outing of George Eliot

Yet to hide a passion totally (or even to hide, more
simply, its excess) is inconceivable: not because the
human subject is too weak, but because passion is in
essence made to be seen: the hiding must be seen: *I
want you to know that I am hiding something from you,*
that is the active paradox I must resolve: *at one and
the same time* it must be known and not known: I
want you to know that I don't want to show my
feelings: that is the message I address to the other.
Larvatus prodeo: I advance pointing to my mask: I
set a mask upon my passion, but with a discreet
(and wily) finger I designate this mask.

—Roland Barthes, *A Lover's Discourse*

Throughout her life Marian Evans wrote elaborate notes of remorseful apology to people with whom she had allowed herself to
speak harshly or critically of others. A remarkable sample of this
genre, sent by the twenty-nine-year-old Mary Ann to her stepsister,
Fanny Houghton, illustrates the nature of her struggle against the
satirical bent of her intellect. "I am in that mood which, in another
age of the world, would have led me to put on sackcloth and pour
ashes on my head, when I call to mind the sins of my tongue—my
animadversions on the faults of others, as if I thought myself to be
something when I am nothing." Written during the last months of
Robert Evans's life, when Mary Ann was attempting to subdue herself
to her nursing tasks, the sentences attest to the moral disciplines she
was imposing on herself: "Though my 'evil speaking' issues from the
intellectual point of view rather than the moral,—though there may

be gall in the thought while there is honey in the feeling, yet the evil speaking is wrong. We may satirize character and qualities in the abstract without injury to our moral nature, but persons hardly ever" (1: 276). "Evil speaking"—that puritanical phrase for gossip or uncharitable words about absent others—was always to remain an active term in her vocabulary. "I shrink, perhaps superstitiously, from any written or spoken word which is as strong as my inward criticism," she confided to John Blackwood in February 1859, while conceding the justice of a critique of Carlyle running in the current *Blackwood's Magazine* (3:23). From an author whose first novel had been published three weeks earlier, these words might suggest how closely her ban on evil speaking was connected to a fear of exposure to others' judgments of herself.

It is not difficult to see what fiction writing offered to a mind whose keenest instincts were so often to be suppressed or transformed into more acceptable utterances. In stories both "the gall in the thought" and "the honey in the feeling" could be dramatized in a way that preserved the reputation of the writer's "moral nature." George Eliot's first story, "The Sad Fortunes of the Reverend Amos Barton," which satirizes its eponymous hero and then replaces the satire with pity, enacts just such a victory over the power of evil speaking. At the same time, writing the story allowed George Eliot to re-create in masked form her own position as the subject of gossip, while inventing a narrative voice that has the power to unmask and triumph over gossip with pathos and exhortations to sympathy. The untalented curate Amos Barton struggles haplessly to create an audience in his congregation, becoming instead the victim of gossip. His creator, appearing in the guise of a male narrator, offers himself to his new audience as Barton's antithesis: a speaker who can imagine his audience, adapt his language to its needs, and bring it to see the injustices perpetrated by community talk. "Amos Barton" makes George Eliot's first "realist" claims for sympathetic attention to the ordinary and the mediocre and dramatizes them by insisting on the difference between the ordinary sad story of the Bartons and the melodramatic gossip about them. The privileged reading audience understands that Barton's story—much like the Leweses' in 1856—is about poverty, whereas the gossiping characters turn it into one about sexual scandal, only to be disabused by the sad death of Amos's angelic and long-suffering wife, Milly Barton. When Milly's death occurs, the lips of gossip are shut up in pity and remorse.

In this first act of fiction making, George Eliot activated both her internal struggle against evil speaking and her protest against the misrepresentations she had incurred by choosing to live with George Henry Lewes. The story contains the implicit hope, or wish, that literary eloquence might have the power to overcome social stigma and the gossip that elaborates on it.

Quite a different sequence was, however, to attend the story's fate in the world. "Amos Barton" and its successor stories in *Scenes of Clerical Life*, first published anonymously in *Blackwood's Magazine*, generated a new storm of literary gossip and misrepresentation which came to a head after the publication of *Adam Bede* in 1859. Through a kind of fateful irony, the mysterious "George Eliot," who burst so spectacularly upon the reading public with *Adam Bede*, was tracked to her lair by people who read her stories as retailed gossip about the Warwickshire models on whom Amos Barton and some of her other characters were based. George Eliot, who began her fiction-writing career with a kind of exuberant pleasure in hiding, was thus bombarded within the first three years of that career with gossip and rumor to which she responded far more vehemently than she had to the earlier talk about her social status; the events of 1859 were permanently to determine her relation with the literary marketplace. The story of those three years, and the fictional transformations they produced, is the subject of this chapter.[1]

On November 6, 1856, George Henry Lewes submitted "The Sad Fortunes of the Reverend Amos Barton" to John Blackwood, the publisher with whom he most frequently worked.[2] "Meanwhile I trouble you with a m.s. of 'Sketches of Clerical Life' which was submitted to me by a friend who desired my good offices with you," he told Blackwood and reported "what I am commissioned to say to you about the proposed series," which included Lewes's high praise as well as "his"— the writer's—plans for future sketches in the series (2:269–70). Blackwood quickly wrote to report that "your friend's reminiscences of Clerical Life will do"; although he had several reservations about the story, he welcomed the new writer, begging "to congratulate him on being worthy of the honours of print and pay" (2:272). Lewes went immediately to the defense, reporting that his "clerical friend," though a bit discouraged by Blackwood's letter, would submit the second story when it was ready. He went on to explain why he rated "the story much higher than you appear to do" and then covered the tracks of his special pleading by introducing another friend—a named one—who wished to publish a scientific paper in Maga (2:273–74). "I am glad to hear that your friend is as I supposed a Clergyman," Blackwood replied, and produced the higher praise Lewes had elicited (2:275–76).

Thus began, by proxy, the honeymoon period of Marian Evans's relationship with John Blackwood, who was—except in the case of *Romola*—to remain her publisher to the end. After being corrected in his assumption that the "clerical friend" was a clergyman, Blackwood made some other attempts at guessing "his" identity and reported the speculations of other readers of "his" work, but his London correspondents were adamant on the subject of anonymity. "I am not at liberty to remove the veil of anonymity—even as regards social position. Be pleased therefore to keep the whole secret—and not even mention *my* negotiation or in any way lead guessers," Lewes insisted (2:277). When the first part of "Amos Barton" appeared, however, Blackwood directed the issue of Maga "To the Author of Amos Barton," and Marian replied to the firm, signing herself in the same way. Blackwood's next letter, accompanying the second part and reporting on mixed opinions of the story, saluted her as "My dear Amos" (2:290). On February 4, 1857, Marian responded to Blackwood's unstated problem. "Whatever may be the success of my stories, I shall be resolute in preserving my incognito, having observed that a *nom de plume* secures all the advantages without the disagreeables of reputation. Perhaps, therefore, it will be well to give you my prospective name, as a tub to throw to the whale in case of curious inquiries, and accordingly I subscribe myself, best and most sympathizing of editors, Yours very truly, George Eliot" (2:292). Her handwriting, Blackwood mused, reminded him of a friend's—a Captain George Warburton's, though he doubted that "a good artillery man" could have written "Amos Barton" (2:294).

Blackwood agreed to tell inquirers that "the Scenes are by one George Eliot of whom I know nothing" (2:308) and received a confirmation from the mysterious writer: "For several reasons I am very anxious to retain my incognito for some time to come, and to an author not already famous, anonymity is the highest *prestige* . Besides, if George Eliot turn out to be a dull dog and an ineffective writer—a mere flash in the pan—I, for one, am determined to cut him on the first intimation of that disagreeable fact" (2:309–10). The first fruit of the collaborative invention of "George Eliot" was the three-way correspondence that ensued among Blackwood, Lewes, and the new author. Well before the name "George Eliot" was printed on any title page—which did not occur until January 1858, when Blackwood published *Scenes of Clerical Life* in book form—all the participants took pleasure in playing on the boundaries of the fiction. For a while, Marian enjoyed the "prestige" of anonymity and the secret thrill of hearing both Blackwood and Lewes repeat others' opinions and gossip about the stories and their unknown writer. The play between "I" and "George Eliot" was not repeated in later letters to Blackwood, but his status on the boundary between knowing and not knowing made for the possibility of teases. Lewes, announcing his departure for a zoologizing journey, told Blackwood in February 1857 that he had "great hopes of having the company of Eliot" during the latter part of his trip (2:295), and Marian, having been with him the whole time, continued the fiction in May by promising to send proof "from Jersey, where on a strict promise that I am not to be dissected, I shall shortly join our friend Lewes" (2:324). Blackwood was asked to make out his payment checks to Lewes, who was to endorse them and hand them over to George Eliot; in June, Marian asked him simply to pay her money into Lewes's account (2:336). Furthermore, Lewes wrote in August, "G.E. begs me to ask you not to draw a checque again for George Eliot, as it will be revealing to his banker who George E. really is" (2:378). The fiction allowed Blackwood to surmise "who George E. really is" without having to face the implications of that particular "disagreeable fact."

The pleasure of anonymity was doubled by the play on gender boundaries. Marian's sense of literary fun had always been released by imaginary cross-dressing situations: the woman who was considered to harbor a man's mind and display a man's strong facial features liked to resist Victorian gender stereotyping in verbal play. She and Sara Hennell had written to one another during some of the Coventry years as "husband and wife," which generated a good deal of what Marian liked to call her "silliness"; and she had once written the Brays a fictional account of her engagement as simultaneous wife and translator to a Professor Bücherwurm, who "prefers as a female garb a man's coat, thrown over what are justly called the *petti*coats, so that the dress of a woman of genius may present the same sort of symbolical compromise between the masculine and feminine attire of which we have an example in the breastplate and petticoat of the immortal Joan" (8:15). This moment reads as a playfully proleptic description of George Eliot's early narrators, who announce themselves in male

Portrait of George Eliot in 1864, etched by Paul Rajon after a drawing by Frederic Burton

coats while displaying an intimate knowledge of domestic and emotional detail which bespeaks the petticoat.[3]

Marian Evans's early letters to John Blackwood are energized by a similar freedom to play between genders authorized by the signature of "George Eliot"; they move readily between a very easily assumed authority of authorship and an appealing charm that bound him into her service. "If I don't write better and better, the fault will certainly not lie in my editor, who seems to have been created in pre-established harmony with the organization of a susceptible contributor," she wrote as she sent him the first section of "Janet's Repentance" (2:335). But when Blackwood criticized the harshness of the picture painted by that story, he encountered the polite wrath of an unbending writer: "As an artist I should be utterly powerless if I departed from my own conceptions of life and character. There is nothing to be done with the story, but either to let Dempster and Janet and the rest of them be as I *see* them, or to renounce it as too painful. I am keenly alive, at once to the scruples and alarms an editor may feel, and to my own utter inability to write under any cramping influence, and on this double ground I should like you to consider whether it will not be better to close the series for the Magazine *now* " (2:348). Blackwood was horrified—"I do not fall in with George Eliots every day"—and retracted his objections (2:352). George Eliot's charm returned: "Thanks for your kind letter. It shows that you have understood me, and will give me confidence for the future" (2:353).

By the time Blackwood finally met Marian Evans face to face, on February 28, 1858, he had been well trained by both members of the household. From "Eliot" he had learned that all but his most trivial objections would be sternly resisted in the name of artistic integrity. From Lewes, in confidential letters, he had learned of "Eliot's" extreme diffidence, his liability to get discouraged and stop writing if Blackwood persisted in making any but the most serious objections (2:363, 372). Assailed on one side by the manly defiance of George Eliot and on the other by the hidden specter of Marian Evans's sensitivity, Blackwood complied: he learned to write paragraphs of praise in response to every new piece of manuscript. Even after he met Marian Evans, however, the George Eliot fiction was sustained in their letters. Lewes continued to refer to "E." as "he"; Blackwood continued to address himself to George Eliot, and Marian to sign herself with that name. The pleasure they felt in their fiction was lined with an unstated anxiety: they all wanted to keep "George Eliot" publicly

separate from the woman who lived with Lewes. While the pseudonym held, the honeymoon with Blackwood could be extended.

On December 6, 1857, awaiting the publication of *Scenes* in volumes, Marian wrote in her journal an extended account of what she
could not reveal to any of her friends, titling it "How I Came to Write
Fiction" (2:406–10). The narrative is as interesting for what it does
not include as for what it does: it recounts in detail Lewes's doubts and
his encouragement when he discovers that she does after all have
"dramatic power" as well as the power of description, and then it
moves to a summary of the negotiations with Blackwood, with a full
recording of the specific praises and speculations which the anonymous author had stimulated. There is no discussion of the pseudonym, or of the sources of the stories, which are described simply as
"drawn from my own observation of the Clergy." The story of how a
long-cherished dream is finally realized depends, in this account, on
the validating responses of her audiences; it is told in a tone of quietly
modulated triumph. Her new secret wanted only to be told; in the
mood of 1857 it seemed to carry with it the promise of pleasure and
praise.

In her letters to friends she kept the secret, while pointing to her
mask. Sara Hennell, a primary correspondent during this period, was
herself becoming an author of books on religious topics in which she
imagined Marian still to be interested. In her patient editorial handling, Marian wrote with a double mind, withholding her own authorial concerns by displacing them in responses to Sara's or by emphasizing Lewes's newly successful writing career. The question of authorial
signatures was in the air: she reported to Sara that George Combe,
that inveterate Lewes-hater, had written to praise an article signed
only with the initials G.H.L.: "We should all of us pass very different
judgments now and then, if the thing to be judged were anonymous"
(2:264). After Sara won a prize for her essay "Christianity and Infidelity" she was advised of Lewes's opinion: "He says, by no means put
Sara, but S. S. Hennell. He thinks that Sara would do harm" (2:282).
Meanwhile, she reported herself to be very much occupied, though
she would not say how. In January 1857 she offered to review Sara's
book as an exception, adding the surprising fact that Lewes "forbids
me to do any reviewing now" (2:289); she had recently written to
Charles Bray, "You needn't observe any secrecy about *articles* of mine.
It is an advantage (pecuniarily) to me that I should be known as the
writer of the articles in the Westminster" (2:287). Once again she

leaned on Bray to disseminate a current policy about secrets, leaving him to speculate about its meaning. Cara, too, was told in June about how hard Marian and Lewes were working for *"present* money" (2:339), and Bessie Parkes heard in January 1858 that Marian could not write for her new feminist journal, "from the complete occupation of my time and faculties in a peremptory manner elsewhere." A few days later she explained the refusal: "I have given up writing 'articles,' having discovered that my vocation lies in other paths. In fact *entre nous,* I expect to be writing *books* for some time to come"(2:428, 431). John Chapman, who had come to depend on her as a reviewer for the *Westminster,* was told on January 12, 1858, that she was giving up a review of Newman she had promised "and that I have no ground for my negations but inability"; this mysterious refusal had also to be explained in a later letter as "simply an inability to do two things at once, for you do not suppose I am turning fine lady and doing nothing" (2:420, 427).

What was she doing then? The mystery was only emphasized by moments when Marian could not refrain from suggesting that she had reached a point in her life when her sad past was to be redeemed. On her thirty-seventh birthday (November 22, 1856), she admitted to Sara that she had forgotten their double birthdays,[4] but "life seems worth twice as much to me now as it was even last November" (2:276). To her former Coventry pupil Mary Sibree Cash, she wrote on June 6, 1857, "I feel, too, that all the terrible pain I have gone through in past years partly from the defects of my own nature, partly from outward things, has probably been a preparation for some special work that I may do before I die" (2:343). The day before she had formulated for Sara her new sense of balance: "If I live five years longer, the positive result of my existence on the side of truth and goodness will outweigh the small negative good that would have consisted in my not doing anything to shock others" (2:342). Full of a sense that her new secret was wholly positive, awaiting only further confirmations of her success, Marian practically dared her friends to understand what it was.

The possession of a new secret power may be indirectly connected with Marian's decision to end the silence that had kept her marriage hidden from her family. On May 26, 1857, she wrote to Isaac Evans: "You will be surprized, I dare say, but I hope not sorry, to learn that I have changed my name, and have someone to take care of me in the world. The event is not at all a sudden one, though it may appear sudden in its announcement to you" (2:331). A month earlier Isaac had received a note signed "Marian Evans," asking anxiously for news of sister Chrissey's illness and requesting Isaac to deflect part of Marian's half-yearly income to her "to spend in taking a change of air" (2:317). An immediate impetus for the decision to break the news was concern for Chrissey's health; Marian feared that further lies and floating rumors about her marital state would interfere with her ability to help her sister. So she intimated when she informed Sara Hennell about the step: "I feel satisfied to have done this, for they are now acquainted with what is *essential* in my position, and if any utterly false report reaches them in the first instance, their minds will be prepared not to accept it without reserve. I do not think Chrissey will give up correspondence with me in any case, and that is the point I most care about, as I shall still be able to help her as far as my means will allow" (2:342).

This rather naive effort at rumor control, three years after her liaison with Lewes began, was probably allied with other motives. Marian wanted to clear up her financial affairs by having Isaac—like Blackwood—pay her income into Lewes's account; to that end, she had to announce a change of name. She also wanted, now that she would stop writing for him, to free herself from the entanglement of using John Chapman as a forwarding address; she relieved Chapman of that duty the next day, informing him that she was now Mrs. Lewes to her relatives.[5] Her correspondence with her family was conducted from the cottage in the Jersey fishing village where she and Lewes spent the summer, and she offered them no London address, intimating that she and Lewes had no fixed residence. This evasiveness, along with the sudden announcement of a change of name and an assurance to Isaac that "we are both workers, and shall have enough for our wants" (2:332), suggests that she was primarily interested in announcing a further stage of independence from her brother, so long as it could be done without endangering her access to Chrissey. The new probability that she would continue to make money as a novelist underwrote that assurance.

Marian could not have been entirely surprised, then, when her letter was answered by Isaac's lawyer Vincent Holbeche, who was one of the joint trustees of her inheritance. Isaac was "so much hurt" at her failure to communicate her "intentions and prospects" that he could not write "in a Brotherly Spirit"; in his name Holbeche requested details of the marriage and facts about Lewes (2:346). These facts (excepting an address other than that of Lewes's bank) were easier to write to Holbeche, and Marian did so on June 13, 1857, explaining the reason for the nonlegal marriage. "My brother has judged wisely in begging you to communicate with me," she wrote. "If his feelings towards me are unfriendly, there is no necessity for his paining himself by any direct intercourse with me; indeed, if he had written to me in a tone which I could not recognize (since I am not conscious of having done him any injury) I must myself have employed a third person as a correspondent" (2:349). There is at least as much relief as hurt in this haughty dismissal of a direct correspondence. But it failed to achieve another objective: sister Chrissey and stepsister Fanny Houghton (who had received an announcement of the marriage enclosed with Isaac's) were also enjoined to cut off communication. "So now there is nothing to be concealed from any one, and the greatest service my friends can do is to tell the truth in contradiction to false rumors," Marian summarized for Sara (2:364). She meant that Sara, presumably in the dark about Marian's other secret, did not have to keep further silence about the liaison with Lewes. The double motive for this sentence from Marian's point of view does, however, suggest the close connection of the two secrets in her own consciousness.

The family excommunication determined a shift of signature from Marian Evans to Marian Lewes—a change that followed close upon the adoption of the pseudonym George Eliot.[6] Until 1857 "Mrs. Lewes" was used primarily for the sake of landladies; Marian signed her personal letters "Marian," "Marian E.," or "Marian Evans." After announcing to Isaac that she had changed her name, however, she began to use "Marian Lewes" or "Marian E. Lewes" and insisted to Bessie Parkes that she "please not call me *Miss Evans* again" in an introduction (2:384). The signature gradually evolved to "M. E. Lewes," or sometimes "M.E.L." But the connection between the fictional married name and the pseudonym is a tantalizing one. If she could be George Eliot, why not Marian Lewes? On the other hand, if George Eliot were to be unmasked, it was better that the morally dubious woman sheltered by the pseudonym be Marian Lewes than Marian Evans. Marian Evans was also the name known in Warwickshire, which had begun to recognize itself in the new stories by George Eliot; it was preferable to maintain some distance from that, as well as from the family name. All these issues were waiting in the wings in 1857, and the drama that was to bring them fully onstage was initiated by the rumor of yet another name: the name of Liggins.

Liggins entered Marian's consciousness through an appropriate provincial channel: a letter from Fanny Houghton, written to acknowledge the change-of-name announcement before Isaac cut off correspondence between them. Apparently struck by the familiarity of the figures and stories in "Clerical Sketches," Fanny reported Warwickshire gossip that a Mr. Liggins had written them. "You are wrong about Mr. Liggins, or rather your informants are wrong," Marian returned, acknowledging that she too had "recognized some figures and traditions connected with our old neighbourhood. But Blackwood informs Mr. Lewes that the author is a Mr. Eliot, a clergyman, I presume. *Au reste*, he may be a relation of Mr. Liggins's or some other 'Mr.' who knows Coton stories" (2:337). She and Lewes had probably amused themselves in concocting this reply; since the name of George Eliot had not yet been attached to the *Scenes*, there was little cause for anything but a mild correction and some ingenuous play on the gender of the "unknown" author. The implicit agreement that the writer was likely to be a clergyman and closely connected with the neighborhood was innocent sport enough. But had she known what "Liggins" had in store for her, Marian might not have engaged even in this playful fanning of gossip's flames.

As George Eliot settled into the writing of *Adam Bede* during 1858, other consequences of the happy incognito began to make themselves felt. Suddenly the friends whom she had tantalized with her reticences threatened to become perpetrators of rumors she tried haplessly to control. The Bray circle received her first warnings. "Apropos, when do you bring out your new poem?" Marian teased Bray on March 29. "I don't see why I shouldn't suppose you are writing a poem, as well as you suppose that I am writing a novel. . . . Seriously, I wish you would not set false rumours, or any other rumours afloat about me. They are injurious" (2:442–43). True rumors, she implied, would be equally damaging. On October 6 Sara too had to be chastised: "Do not guess at authorship—it is a bad speculation. I have *not written a word* in the Westminster" (2:486).

The real threat, however, came from John Chapman, a central channel of London literary gossip and a person with plenty of cause for speculation. Herbert Spencer, who was in on the secret, told the Leweses on November 5 that Chapman had asked him directly if Marian had written *Scenes of Clerical Life*. "I wrote at once to the latter to check further gossip on the subject," Marian wrote in her journal (2:494n). Her stern note to Chapman is a perfect example of the futility of that mission; it exudes the kind of anger and vulnerability that could only have confirmed Chapman's sense of power in his supposition. "A little reflection in my behalf would have suggested to you that were any such rumours true, my own abstinence from any communication concerning my own writing, except to my most intimate friends, was evidence that I regarded secrecy on such subjects as a matter of importance. Instead of exercising this friendly consideration, you carelessly, certainly, for no one's pleasure or interest, and to my serious injury, contribute to the circulation of idle rumours and gossip, entirely unwarranted by any evidence" (2:494).

Chapman had been a trustee of the Leweses' first secret. This time he had been excluded and had lost one of his best writers; yet his own friendship and loyalty were being both appealed to and questioned in censorious tones. It was not likely to work, and it did not. On February 12, 1859, some days after the publication of *Adam Bede*, Lewes took up the pen against Chapman's further speculations: "Not to notice your transparent allusion in your last, would be improperly to admit its truth. . . . your continuing to impute those works to Mrs. Lewes may be *meant* as a compliment, but it *is* an offence against delicacy and friendship. As you seem so very slow in appreciating her feelings on this point, she authorizes me to state, as distinctly as language can do, that she is not the author of 'Adam Bede'" (3:13). He could hardly have invented a more effective admission of her authorship. The effort to control rumors that were in fact true, by responding to them in high-minded tones, was to be a consistent choice of the Leweses in the months that followed; it most frequently acted as a stimulant for the gossip they were trying to suppress.

By late November 1858 so many rumors had reached them from both Warwickshire and London that immediate publication of *Adam Bede* seemed urgent if it was to benefit by the "mystery" of its authorship. Blackwood, who was especially afraid of a direct link between George Eliot and Marian Lewes, hoped that the pseudonym would hold at least through the publication of the book to follow *Bede* (3:73); the pressure of the "bad" secret on the "good" secret began to cloud the initial joy of anonymity. Yet the attachment of "George Eliot" to someone other than Marian Lewes—to Liggins, or Liggers as he was sometimes miscalled—pointed up the paradoxes of pseudonymity with a fiendish twist. In the first place, Marian fiercely cherished the praise she got for her writing. When Dickens wrote in high praise of *Scenes of Clerical Life,* including his confident assumption that the writer was a woman, Marian relayed her message through Blackwood: "There can hardly be any climax of approbation for me after this, and I am so deeply moved by the finely-felt and finely expressed sympathy of the letter, that the iron mask of my incognito seems quite painful in forbidding me to tell Dickens how thoroughly his generous impulse has been appreciated" (2:424). Other significant letters of praise, from Jane Carlyle and James Anthony Froude, also put pressure on her anonymity (2:425–26, 481–82). Her own hunger for approbation, clarified as it had never been before, caused Marian to see very precisely the nature of her dilemma. She wrote to Blackwood in November 1857, "Unhappily, I am as impressionable as I am obstinate, and as much in need of sympathy from my readers as I am incapable of bending myself to their tastes" (2:400); and again in the following January, on the eve of *Bede*'s publication, "I perceive that I have not the characteristics of the 'popular author,' and yet I am much in need of the warmly expressed sympathy which only popularity can win" (3:6). Yet with a slight shift in perspective, the "iron mask" that prevented George Eliot from responding to Dickens's "sympathy" became an "iron chest" which protected her identity from the mills of gossip and rumor. Wishing *Adam Bede* "to be judged quite apart from its authorship," Marian wrote to Blackwood of her decision—based on Walter Scott's—that direct questions about her authorship be met with absolute denials: "One ought to say 'No' to an impertinent querist as one would decline to open one's iron chest to a burglar" (2:505). Her metaphor was prophetic: by the end of 1859 she was to feel personally violated by the world *Adam Bede* had taken by storm.

The rumor that Liggins was the author of *Scenes of Clerical Life* was not simply an ironic reminder of her desire to be acknowledged; the matter carried with it a troubling question about George Eliot's use of her Warwickshire sources. As early as February 1857 Blackwood's London agent Joseph Munt Langford heard that "Amos Barton" was "the actual life of a clergyman named Gwythir" (2:298). Blackwood kept this piece of gossip to himself, but in August he forwarded to George Eliot a letter from the Reverend W. P. Jones, who insisted that Mr. Tryan in "Janet's Repentance" was a portrait of his deceased brother and was "utterly at a loss to conceive who could have written the statements or revived what should have been buried in oblivion" (2:374–75). George Eliot replied that Tryan was not a portrait and that Jones, "misled by some similarity in outward circumstances, is blind to the discrepancies which must exist where no portrait was intended." But the question—a mere rehearsal for what was to come—upset her. "I should consider it a fault which would cause me lasting regret, if I had used reality in any other than the legitimate way common to all artists who draw their materials from their observation and experience. It would be a melancholy result of my fictions if I gave *just* cause of annoyance to any good and sensible person," she argued, implying that Jones was not such a person and that his annoyance was unjust (2:375). The accusation that she had "revived what should have been buried in oblivion" was a direct threat to the practice of realism she had announced in "Amos Barton." It suggested that fiction based on the observation of ordinary folk from a particular past was a violation of personal privacy—was, in fact, the kind of practice she herself was fiercely resisting in her battle to retain the pseudonym. It also gave check to the exuberant sense that her writing was a redemption of her painful past: the past, it seemed, could talk back to her, and chastise her use of it.

The Liggins rumor flourished on the assumption that no one except a long-standing local resident could possibly have known the personal facts from which the stories in *Scenes* and *Adam Bede* had been made. In May 1858 Blackwood heard the Warwickshire gossip when he met Charles Newdegate—Warwickshire member of Parliament and nephew to Robert Evans's former employer at Arbury Hall—at the Derby. Newdegate claimed to know the originals for every character in the *Scenes* and said he "knew the author, a Mr. Liggers" (2:457). George Eliot responded with her usual point that readers who find "certain points of coincidence" leap mistakenly to identify a portrait. "That is amusing enough to the author, who knows from what widely sundered portions of experience—from what combination of subtle shadowy suggestions with certain actual objects and events, his story has been formed" (2:459). Off in Munich, where the Leweses were spending the summer, the problem seemed more remote, and Lewes could see Liggins as a useful decoy: "It is well that Liggers, or any one else, should be the supposed author; because the more confidently such reports are spread, the more difficult will be the detection of the real culprit" (2:461). But when *Adam Bede* was finished, George Eliot was very conscious of the "portrait" problem. On November 30 she wrote in her journal a "History of 'Adam Bede,'" companion piece to "How I Came to Write Fiction." This time the first half of the narrative concentrated on the story's sources, in her aunt's and her father's early lives, "but Adam is not my father any more than Dinah is my aunt. Indeed, there is not a single *portrait* in 'Adam Bede'; only the suggestions of experience wrought up into new combinations" (2:503). As she wrote these defensive lines, she was planning a new novel based on her own immediate family experience. Would it, too, be read as an unwarranted violation of personal privacy?

"The Lifted Veil" came into being at just this juncture. Its title suggests a direct connection with the breaking of the pseudonym, and by the time it was finished in April 1859, George Eliot was in the thick of the battle against the Liggins imposture. But the story itself was begun before February, and its existence was announced to Blackwood in a letter of March 31, as a "slight story of an outré kind" that could be ready in a few days (3:41). Its emotional context, as well as its plot, is more directly familial: Marian was apparently feeling the guilty stress of permanent estrangement from her family in conjunction with her plan to write so intimately about them. This state of mind was painfully exacerbated by the death of Chrissey Clarke. On February 24 Marian received a letter from her sister, who was dying and "regretting that she ever ceased to write to me. It has ploughed up my heart" (3:23). Chrissey died on March 15, without seeing her sister again. Marian, who took what people said about her most deeply to heart when she denied it most strongly, created the strange narrator of "The Lifted Veil" as a melancholy image of the way she thought herself to appear in Warwickshire eyes: as a satirical violator of other people's secret lives.

"The Lifted Veil" might usefully be considered a sort of dumping ground for feelings about the Evans family's mutual rejections, which had to be exorcised before *The Mill on the Floss* could be written. Latimer, the story's first-person narrator, gives voice in the most direct way to self-pity and bitterness over his family's rejection of his poetic and hypersensitive nature. At the same time he represents himself as a kind of dangerous incubus whose alienated and preternaturally keen vision preys on the moral privacy of everyone close to him. Through techniques of gothic fiction borrowed in particular from Mary Shelley,[7] George Eliot exaggerates her own bitter satirical insight as a special visionary and auditory power that comes unbidden into Latimer's life, but the story suggests quite powerfully that the excoriating insight on Latimer's part both causes and results from the dismissive withholding of love by others. Latimer's single memory of happiness in early childhood links his own temporary blindness with his mother's physical tenderness.

Latimer expresses not so much George Eliot's guilt at authorship as her guilt about what she saw, and how she saw, during the long period of her life when her vision, like Latimer's, was unconnected with any creative activity.[8] Latimer sees "the souls of those who were in a close relation to me . . . as if thrust asunder by a microscopic vision, that showed all the intermediate frivolities, all the suppressed egoism, all the struggling chaos of puerilities, meanness, vague capricious memories, and indolent make-shift thoughts, from which human words and deeds emerge like leaflets covering a fermenting heap."[9] His disgust at human nature is briefly lifted only when sympathy for his father's grief and his father's dying lifts him to a higher moral plane. Despite his Prague vision of a world deadened by the stony gaze of father-statues, his brief sympathetic identification with the father is identified as his only escape from his own morbidity. Mary Ann Evans's nursing of her father had been retained in her imagination as an episode of self-exemption from the circular traps of her family life; yet the story demonstrates only the repetition and intensification of Latimer's dilemma in his complex relationship with Bertha.[10]

This relationship lays itself open to intricate theorizing about projections of gender. It was typical of George Eliot to reverse the genders when she took on the darkest and most alienated parts of herself; she was to do so again when she invented Silas Marner and Edward Casaubon. Latimer, who is "held to have a sort of half-womanish, half-ghostly beauty" (20), is an obverse image of the gender-blurred George Eliot and a figure of the woman writer who suffered behind the mask of the male pseudonym. Bertha takes her place in a sequence of beautiful and unreadable female characters—Hetty, Rosamond, Gwendolen—whose beauty acts as a mask or veil, giving no reliable "sign" of their inward self-absorption. Such characters might be read—as Mary Jacobus suggests—as indicators of George Eliot's complicity with male visions of the dangerous or castrating female.[11] But in the context of a biographical reading like this one, it makes sense to assign gender crossings equally to the figures of Bertha and Latimer. Fascinating because unreadable, Bertha becomes Latimer's beloved oppressor, even though "she was the very opposite . . . of the ideal woman"; the terms in which the dependency is described could easily suggest a version of Mary Ann Evans's sibling relationship with

Isaac: "But there is no tyranny more complete than that which a self-centred negative nature exercises over a morbidly sensitive nature perpetually craving sympathy and support" (22). Bertha is implicated with the brother figure whom Latimer hates and envies: Latimer loves her because he hates his brother, to whom she is engaged, and his desire is created by the primary rivalry with the brother. He describes his intoxication with her as "poison" but is unable, despite his vision of future anguish, to prevent himself from guiltily marrying her after his brother's "accidental" death. So long as Latimer cannot see into Bertha's soul, he remains addicted to the poison of psychological subjection to her.

Latimer finally sees into Bertha's soul just after his father's death—that is, at the moment when he is no longer entangled in family duty and sympathy. The first thing he sees is a vision of how she sees him: "I know how I looked at that moment, for I saw myself in Bertha's thought as she lifted her cutting grey eyes, and looked at me: a miserable ghost-seer, surrounded by phantoms in the noon-day, trembling under a breeze when the leaves were still, without appetite for the common objects of human desire, but pining after the moonbeams" (48). This vision of himself as he appears to her eye is a turning point for both characters: Latimer is freed from his subjection to her, while she comes to hate him for his intrusive assessment of her. Now Bertha (Latimer sees) "meditated continually how the incubus could be shaken off her life—how she could be freed from this hateful bond to a being whom she at once despised as an imbecile, and dreaded as an inquisitor" (51). All the elaborated psycho-gothic generality comes, in the end, to a more intense version of Latimer's relationship with his original family: he hates her because of the way she sees him, and yet, he is precisely the hateful inquisitorial being she sees. The final twist of the tale, in which Bertha's maid comes back to life and accuses her of a plan to poison Latimer with the maid's connivance, is a gothic externalization of Latimer's own situation. He is telling his accusatory tale at an equivalent moment—between the knowledge of his death and its arrival—and he too has nothing to say except that he has been complicit with Bertha in an act of moral self-poisoning. The circularity of the story admits no satisfactory exit from the depressive condition of feeding on the self-mirroring vision of other people's rejections.

While George Eliot was writing "The Lifted Veil" and mourning her sister, the news of her immense popular success began to come in.

A second edition of *Adam Bede* was called for by mid-March, just six weeks after initial publication, and the sales figures soared from that point. It was a propitious time for a powerful new voice. Dickens, ascendant for some twenty years, was nearing the end of his career. Thackeray's star was fading with the publication of *The Virginians*. The Brontës were dead, and Elizabeth Gaskell was current as Charlotte Brontë's controversial biographer. *Adam Bede*'s combination of detailed pastoral portraiture and sexual melodrama was, after all, a bid for the popularity that George Eliot both wanted and scorned. But for her it was a complicated success. "The effect upon G.E. has been almost sad, instead of joyful—but the sadness lies near joy—and you will understand the effect on such a nature," Lewes wrote to Blackwood (3:36). The news could not be shared with anyone except Lewes and Blackwood; moreover, it was shadowed by family sadness and by the knowledge that pressure on the pseudonym could only increase in the coming months. "I am like a deaf person, to whom someone has just shouted that the company round him have been paying him compliments for the last half hour," Marian explained to Blackwood (3:34). Her "deafness" suggests that she had a more-than-usually loud chorus of internal voices to attend to.

By mid-April the Liggins imposture had come into prominence; it was to play itself out in the next two months. The truth about why this impoverished, ne'er-do-well Nuneaton clergyman was credited with the authorship of George Eliot's fiction is unknown to this day, but it seems likely that Liggins himself was not the originator of the myth. In a letter forwarded to George Eliot by Charles Bray in July, Charles Holt Bracebridge, one of Liggins's most tenacious (and unreliable) supporters, claimed that Liggins "has never asserted or denied that he was the author. He has *let people suppose so*" (3:110n). Rumors that Liggins had shown a manuscript of *Scenes of Clerical Life* to his supporters were never substantiated. Haight implies that the party responsible for promoting the rumor was the gullible James Quirk, curate of Attleborough, whom he calls "the real 'inventor' of Liggins"; Redinger suggests that Liggins may have been bribed by persons— perhaps London journalists, enemies of Lewes's from his *Leader* days—who wanted to smoke George Eliot out of hiding.[12] The several attacks on George Eliot's anonymity in the London press give her supposition some credibility, though the Leweses' public responses to Liggins did in themselves invite the kind of journalistic backbiting they received. Whatever the truth may have been, the Liggins affair could hardly have been better designed to crack open the issues covered over by pseudonymity.

Liggins remained a farcical matter for the Leweses so long as his claim reached them in random rumor. Sara Hennell, who had written Marian an account of Liggins—including the story that he had freely donated the manuscript of *Adam Bede* to Blackwood's and received no profit from it—was treated to Marian's evasive implication that Lewes had read and admired *Bede*, but she had not yet, "so *I* must refresh my soul with it now" (3:46). But on April 13 a notice appeared in the *Times*—which had run an enthusiastic review of the novel the day before—announcing that Joseph Liggins of Nuneaton was the author of *Scenes of Clerical Life* and *Adam Bede* (3:48). (The signatory, one Henry Smith Anders, later apologized via Blackwood, alleging that the publication had been "unintentional" [3:66]). Lewes, the veteran journalist, felt it was time to go into action. Two days later a letter under the signature "George Eliot" appeared in the *Times*, denying Anders's claim and adding a gratuitously provocative challenge: "Allow me to ask whether the act of publishing a book deprives a man of all claim to the courtesies usual among gentlemen? If not, the attempt to pry into what is obviously meant to be withheld—my name—and to publish the rumours which such prying may give rise to, seems to me quite indefensible, still more to state those rumours as ascertained truths" (3:50). Although Blackwood laughed over this letter and thought it would stop "all the better class papers" from publishing further rumors (3:51), Lewes brought on a diatribe in the *Leader*, describing "such concealments as a species of literary fraud. . . . Let him tell the truth as to his name, and shame Mr. Anders" (3:62n).

When Marian heard the rumor that a subscription had been established to raise money for the indigent Liggins, her own ire was roused. Blackwood refused her request that he should write another rebuttal to the *Times*, saying it would look like puffery for the novel and probably meaning that he was content to let any imposture flourish so long as the secret could be kept. But he and his newly famous writer were beginning to diverge on this point. "While I would willingly, if it were possible—which it clearly is not—retain my incognito as long as I live, I can suffer no one to bear my arms on his shield," she wrote Blackwood on April 29 (3:60). Her own "shield"—no longer only a mask or an iron chest—had taken on the charge of a warrior proud in battle. It was the first indication of her desire to come out of hiding. By June 5, on the impetus of yet more published Liggins matter, Blackwood did publish a joint rebuttal with George Eliot, indicating that if Liggins were receiving charitable donations he was doing so under false pretences. George Eliot's letter suggested that if Liggins's supporters could "induce Mr. Liggins to write one chapter of a story, that chapter may possibly do what my denial has failed to do" (3:75).

The only tangible effect achieved by these letters was to stimulate "Amos Barton" to rise up out of obscurity. On June 13 the Reverend John Gwyther of Yorkshire declared himself to Blackwood, in order to suggest yet another candidate for the author of what he frankly described as "an episode in my own life." He admitted that he had been hurt by reading his own story two years earlier in *Blackwood's Magazine*, but "time passed away, and my pained feelings at the making public my private history abated." He now asked that his "kind remembrances" be conveyed to the man he thought had written the story, former Nuneaton curate W. H. King, "although I thought it unkind and taking a great liberty with a living Character" (3:83–84). Through this ingenuous letter, George Eliot was confronted with the necessity of responding to a person who claimed that her fictional attack on gossip and rumor had in fact been unwarranted gossip about his own life.

Her reply was constructed in two elaborate sentences which would have been difficult for the awkwardly literate Gwyther to follow; they display an evident embarrassment at her own attempt to deny him the validity of his hurt feelings. She informs Gwyther that she is not Mr. King but "a much younger person," who wrote "under the impression that the clergyman whose long past trial suggested the groundwork of the story was no longer living," and goes on to declare that, because of the writer's imperfect knowledge of the episode, "any one who discerned the core of truth must also recognize the large amount of arbitrary, imaginative addition." Her conclusion mixes remorse with her own growing annoyance at the pressure the Liggins affair was putting on her own private existence: "But for any annoyance, even though it may have been brief and not well-founded, which the appearance of the story may have caused Mr. Gwyther, the writer is sincerely sorry" (3:85–86). It is unlikely that Gwyther derived any comfort from this note; certainly George Eliot did not. Gwyther had forced her to confront the fact that she had, indeed, been writing "portraits."

This was not the kind of recognition with which she wanted to celebrate the success of her new art. In fact there was only one person who had seen through the pseudonym in the way that Marian had most wished when she played cat and mouse with her personal friends. That person was Barbara Bodichon, who on April 26 exploded in a moving letter from Algiers: "My darling Marian! Forgive me for being so very affectionate but I am so intensely delighted at your success. . . . I can't tell you how I triumphed in the triumph you have made. It is so great a one." As Barbara went on it became clear that she had not even read *Adam Bede*, only seen excerpts in reviews, but one of them "instantly made me internally exclaim that is written by Marian Evans, there is her great big head and heart and her wise wide views." And she listed the special sources of her pleasure: "1st. That a woman should write a wise and *humorous* book which should take a place by Thackeray. 2nd. That YOU *that you* whom they spit at should do it! I am so enchanted so glad with the good and bad of me! both glad—angel and devil both triumph!" (3:56). With these words Barbara Bodichon—feminist and painter, herself an illegitimate child—became a heroine of the drama: she saw exactly what Marian would have wanted her friends to see, and she expressed the feelings Marian could not herself openly express.

In her warmly grateful response to this letter, Marian called Barbara "the first friend who has given any symptom of knowing me—the first heart that has recognized me in a book which has come from my heart of hearts." She also expressed surprise that none of her Coventry friends had done so, speculating that the Liggins rumor had put them off the track (3:63–64). Her desire to be "seen" is evident; she reminds Barbara of the importance of the incognito but imagines that it will only last "a few months longer." (Blackwood, on the other hand, was writing, "KEEP YOUR SECRET" [3:68]). By mid-May Marian's sense of alienation from the Coventry trio expressed itself in a veiled wish for the kind of recognition Barbara had given her: "You live—all of you—and 'make no sign,' which is far more inexcusable than dying with the same omission. Why do you all collapse into utter silence?" (3:68). A month later, just after she had had to respond to Gwyther's painful "recognition," she was ready to include them in her secret and invited them to London for that purpose. The meeting, which took place on June 20, was fraught with discomfort and required several follow-up letters of apology and explanation. "This experience has enlightened me a good deal as to the ignorance in which we all live of each other," Marian wrote in her journal (3:90n); their surprise had clearly taken her aback. Bray, placed once again in the position of deputy gossip controller for Warwickshire, was issued instructions about what to say, and Sara Hennell, who had come hoping that the focus of attention would be on her own writing, had to be placated. By this time the pressure of rumor and gossip from every direction had grown so acute that Marian's sensitivity to all talk about absent others had risen to a fever pitch. In one of her characteristic letters of remorse, she apologized to the Brays even for "having listened with apparent acquiescence to statements about poor Agnes [Lewes] which a little quiet reflection has convinced me are mingled with falsehood—I fear of a base sort." She wrote, she said, "to satisfy myself by protesting against a momentary acceptance of gratuitous evil speaking either by myself or others" (3:91).

Matters were reaching a crisis from every direction. The Leweses were angry at Chapman and Spencer, who were suspected of stirring up London gossip and imagined as serious betrayers of friendship. The news from Warwickshire on June 26 ran that "Miss Evans" had replaced Liggins as the subject of George Eliot gossip. At the same time letters about Liggins announced that he was showing manuscripts in his own hand of George Eliot's works, and the Leweses, against Blackwood's wish, sent another, more fiery letter to the *Times*, accusing Liggins of being an impostor and a swindler and daring him to deny it (3:92–93). J. T. Delane, the *Times* editor, did not publish the letter before consulting Blackwood, and Blackwood attempted to persuade Marian to tone it down. Before it could be revised, however, she received a note on June 28 from Barbara Bodichon, who had arrived from Algiers for the summer and had made a point of hearing the London literary gossip: "They assured me all the literary men were certain it was Marian Lewes . . . that they did not much like saying so because it would do so much harm. . . . From their way of talking it was evident they thought you would do the book more harm than the book would do you good in public opinion" (3:103).

Barbara's straight-to-the-mark honesty was the turning point. She had brought into the open the fear that the Leweses had prevented themselves from expressing as they battled against Liggins: that the reputation of the novels would be damaged if Marian were known as their author. Now that it had been spoken as an opinion in other minds, it aroused the high-minded pride that had been wasted in responding to Liggins. The next day Marian withdrew her *Times* letter; two days later Lewes wrote to Barbara: "We have come to the

conclusion of no longer concealing the authorship. It makes me angry
to think that people should say that the secret has been kept because
there was any *fear* of the effect of the author's name" (3:106). The
repeated gossip had served a crucial purpose: by externalizing their
fears, it had allowed them to take up a stance of defiance against
them. Moreover, they now entrusted their secret to gossip's circulatory system, making no public statement but allowing the talk about
the authorship to go on as it might, aided by private announcements
to well-placed sympathizers such as Dickens.

It was, however, to be another six months before all the side effects
of the Liggins affair had run their course. After Liggins was dis-
credited as the author of George Eliot's books, and after even Quirk
had been convinced that the author was Marian Lewes, Charles Holt
Bracebridge remained on his hobbyhorse: he continued to link
George Eliot's characters with their supposed originals and to insist
that she had gotten her information from Liggins or from the originals themselves. Marian's strenuous resistance to the idea that she
wrote "portraits" reached its apex in September and October, when
she and Lewes conducted an angry three-way correspondence with
Bracebridge and Charles Bray. The Gwyther letter had heightened
her sensitivity to this matter; at the end of June she had admitted to
the Coventry group that "there are *two* portraits in the Clerical
Scenes; but that was my first bit of art, and my hand was not well in."
The retrospective admission was made in the service of another denial, that *Adam Bede* contained a "portrait" of her father (3:99). Now
Bracebridge, roaming the countryside to find "evidence" of her
sources, was claiming that the characters in *Bede* were portraits of her
aunt and uncle Elizabeth and Samuel Evans, and that she had copied
Dinah Morris's sermon and speeches from her aunt's papers. No
sooner had she announced her presence on the literary scene as a new
kind of realist, than she was accused of retelling actual life stories; the
Bracebridge affair was like a ludicrous nightmare in which the gossiping characters in her books rose up and began to circulate rumors
about their creator. Bray, caught in a sort of replay of his role in the
George Combe matter, tried to play down the importance of Bracebridge's "finding," and came in for his share of indignation from the
furious letter writers in London.

The anger was of a fiercer kind than the anger against Liggins.
George Eliot's creative art was being questioned, and at the same time
Bracebridge's false claims had an uncomfortable underside of truth:

her work was deeply implicated with specific Warwickshire sources. Naturally her arguments emphasized the first point, dwelling repeatedly on the fact that her stories were drawn from "widely sundered" materials, asserting that only fools would fail to see the work of imaginative invention which brought them together. Through a series of detailed letters, George Eliot and George Henry Lewes finally forced Bracebridge into a written retraction of his charges (3:145–79), but the damage to George Eliot's sense of authorship was significant. "It is happy for me that I never expected any gratification of a personal kind from my authorship. The worst of all this is that it nauseates me—chills me and discourages me in my work," she wrote to Bray on September 19 (3:157). And a week later: "I only wish I could write something that would contribute to heighten men's reverence before the secrets of each other's souls, that there might be less assumption of entire knowingness, as a datum from which inferences are to be drawn." Bracebridge's antics were coming to stand for the author's relationship with the whole marketplace of readers, a relationship becoming "more intolerable as the years bring with them that increased facility of communication which makes the conjectures and inferences of local ignorance matter for current circulation throughout the Kingdom" (3:164). The gap between sympathetic individual readers who "recognized her" in her books and an ignorant gossiping public that recognized only a lowest common denominator was being firmly established as a paradigmatic image of her audiences.

Yet Bracebridge was forcing her to think about the relation of realistic art, life stories, and gossip. On October 7 Marian wrote a long letter to Sara Hennell in which she spelled out for posterity the exact nature of her relationship with her aunt, specifying the differences between Elizabeth Evans and the character Dinah Morris. (Sara dutifully published the letter in the *Pall Mall Budget* after her death). "It is not surprising," the letter concludes, "that simple men and women without pretension to enlightened discrimination should think a generic resemblance constitutes a portrait, when we see the great public so accustomed to be delighted with *mis*-representations of life and character, which they accept as representations, that they are scandalized when art makes a nearer approach to truth" (3:176–77). It is difficult to follow the precise logic of this sentence, though it clearly wishes to defend her good art against silly fiction and to scorn the way good art turns into material for scandal in the public mind. But the notion that the reading public, inured to escapist fiction, is therefore "scandalized" by "a nearer approach to truth" gives away its game by suggesting that the scandal is generated by the very connection with life which she was at pains to deny.

By the end of 1859 Bracebridge had been silenced, and most of the other rifts in Marian's relationships had been repaired. John Chapman was permanently estranged, perhaps because of tensions with George Henry Lewes which went deeper than the immediate occasion. But by the end of September, Herbert Spencer, who seems to have been unaware of the animus building up against him in the Lewes household, had reinstated himself as one of her "sympathetic" friends by reading and praising *Adam Bede* in exactly the terms Marian now most required: "I feel greatly the better for having read it; and can scarcely imagine any one reading it without having their sympathies widened and their better resolves strengthened" (8:246). John Blackwood had expressed their joint success by presenting Marian with a pug dog on July 30; she took the dog as "come to fill up the void left by false and narrow-hearted friends" (such as Chapman and Spencer) who could not keep secrets (3:124). But it was not long before Blackwood himself was in the doghouse; his uneasiness after the breaking of the pseudonym underlay a series of cold negotiations and misunderstandings about money and publication which stretched between September and December. Blackwood's quite sensible refusal to become exercised over an advertisement announcing the publication of an "Adam Bede, Jr." by Newby, a London publisher, was also taken as a sign of his indifference to George Eliot's interests. By the time they finally wrote each other explanatory letters and came to an agreement about the publication of *The Mill on the Floss*, Marian was no longer signing herself "George Eliot"; she wished him to understand that he had to accept her existence as Marian Lewes.[13]

In the long run, the pseudonym "George Eliot" worked brilliantly to achieve precisely that triumphant vindication that Marian Lewes desired. Backed by the power of her books, it acquired a kind of independent existence that has, more than a century later, lost none of its effect. Partly because of that autonomous power and partly because it is the only stable name in her large repertoire, "George Eliot" has become the subject of biography as "Currer Bell" could not. Yet the events of 1859 were to have a lasting effect on Marian Lewes's interior experience of authorship. Her immersion in gossip had taken a variety of forms: she had depended on it for praise in her anonymity and information in her pseudonymity; she had suffered from its intrusion and its desecrating challege to her creative process; and she had relied on it for the circulation of information about herself. The immediate effect was to increase her already acute sensitivity to the damaging power of gossip; her response was to withdraw as far as possible from participation in any dialogue about her work. Soon after she revealed her authorship to the Coventry friends, she wrote to them, "But I feel that the influence of talking about my books even to you and Mrs. Bodichon has been so bad to me that I should like to be able to keep silence concerning them for evermore. . . . Talking about my books, I find, has much the same malign effect on me as talking of my feelings or my religion" (3:99). The same sentiment was expressed in her journal in October, after Herbert Spencer had come to dine and praise *Adam Bede*: "We have made a resolution that we will allow no more talk in our house on the subject. I find it destructive of that repose and simplicity of mind which is the only healthy state in relation to one's books: it has the same effect as talking of one's religion, or one's feelings and duties towards one's father, mother, or husband" (8:251–52n). The "effect" she refers to is related to the betrayals of gossip: it is apparently the perception of disloyalty to a private or sacred relationship. In her horrified reaction to having been seen through the anonymity of her narratives, her books became personal secrets not to be violated even in the sanctuary of home.

As Marian Lewes wrote to Sara Hennell, "the annoyance I suffered from Mr. Bracebridge and Co." was one of the reasons for her "morbid" avoidance of talk about her books, "but apart from my own weaknesses, I think the less an author hears about himself the better" (3:405). Her capacity to erupt on this topic became clear three years later, when Sara innocently wondered whether she had written Margaret Oliphant's *Chronicles of Carlingford*, which some had attributed to the author of *Adam Bede*. Sara received a very cold letter in return, rehearsing a list of grievances left over from the events of 1859. A few days later a repentant Marian wrote to apologize for her peevish and irrelevant letter: "I was not at all well, and three years ago, after the appearance of Adam Bede, my nerves were so jarred on the subject of my authorship, that I have never recovered the injury. The only remedy is the one I habitually observe—to fling the subject as far away from me as possible, and avoid either hearing or speaking of it" (4:25–26, 28). The famous rules of the Lewes household, which kept George Eliot from hearing others' praises or criticisms of her books— except the ones especially selected by Lewes—came into being as a result of these experiences.[14] As Lewes explained them to Sara in September 1862, "You can tell me any details (I'm a glutton in all that concerns her, though I never look after what is said about myself) favorable or unfavorable; but for her let her mind be as much as possible fixed on her art and not on the public" (4:59). Lewes's distinction between his own indifference to what was said about him and his attentiveness to George Eliot's reputation is instructive. He knew that her instinct to hide was created by an equally powerful desire to see herself reflected favorably in the glass of public opinion, and he had learned how volatile that particular paradox could be.

Once fixed on her art, George Eliot continued to have a good deal to say about the subject of gossip and its relation to masks, though what she had to say changed as her career settled in and her authorship became accepted and revered. *The Mill on the Floss*, the last novel in which she drew directly upon her Warwickshire childhood, was written during the year of Liggins. At the end of the novel George Eliot drowns not only her childhood but the whole world of her early fiction; there were to be no more allegations of portrait painting. She did not, however, end the novel without leaving in it a record of the anger generated by that turbulent year of uncontrollable talk.

Gossip bursts into the text of *The Mill on the Floss* like a flood of violence. Until the final three chapters the story of Maggie Tulliver has been told as a series of intimate relationships: her audiences are her family and her lovers. Once she returns to St. Ogg's from the aborted elopement with Stephen Guest, the narrative turns to its attack on "the world's wife" with a vengeance that is matched only by the unstoppable power it attributes to the talk of the town. Maggie virtually disappears in this section; gossip is scapegoated as the murderer of her social existence. By the time of the flood scene, she is socially dead; the final "rescue" fantasy takes place in a social, ahistorical time.

In its focus on the elaborated details of sexual scandal, the representation of gossip (bk. 7, chap. 2) feels like an emanation from a mind well practiced in the projection of nightmarish voices. These voices are rendered neither in imagined dialogue nor in narrative summary but in a collective free indirect discourse that evokes the qualities of fearful fantasy. The speakers are nameless and faceless, but the sound of their—ostentatiously female—voices and the insane logic of their judgment is perfectly audible. Although the narrative irony makes it perfectly clear that "the world's wife" is vicious and self-serving, ready to pander to female success and equally happy to kick a fellow woman when she's down, George Eliot's invention of two hypothetical gossip stories instead of one has the side effect of linking gossip more closely with the inner life of its subject. For the two stories told by the narrator on behalf of "the world's wife" are crass distortions of the two sides of Maggie which are in mortal struggle.

The first story—the one that would have been told had Maggie returned to St. Ogg's as a well-dressed married woman—is a potboiler romance in which the handsome hero, overcome by passion for the young girl, sweeps her away against her will and continues to worship her in marriage. In this version the losers are pitied and dismissed from the main plot: Lucy, a passive victim, is sent to the seaside to recover; Philip is consigned to the Continent, where such deformed persons belong. The romantic and ambitious Maggie wishes for this story; her own passion has sketched it out for her. Yet the gossips' success story is exactly the one her conscience disallows, and much painful irony lies in the fact that she has gallantly squelched the one fantasy that gossip would label morally acceptable

The story that is told turns Maggie into a fallen woman "actuated by mere unwomanly boldness and unbridled passion." In this version Stephen is at the mercy of a "designing bold girl," the connection with Philip is a sign of something disgusting in Maggie, and Lucy does not figure except as part of "the Deanes," whose kindness Maggie has betrayed. The actual evidence of Stephen's letter exonerating Maggie is simply woven into the story as a gentlemanly fabrication. Yet this story too is a translation into melodrama of the guilt, remorse, and resignation to a life of penitence which Maggie feels; she has in effect generated the story out of herself. As George Eliot shows the scandal deepening and widening to include and finally vanquish the best counterefforts of the clergyman Dr. Kenn, it begins to seem that her own floodgates are opened by an imaginary situation in which gossip is so grotesquely allied with self-accusation.

The scandal section has its more controlled narrative uses. In an almost ritualistic way it isolates Maggie and prepares her and the reader for a death more gracious than life in society. And it provides a field against which the novel makes as its definition of heroism the ability to resist and transcend what other people say. Maggie's own resistance is part of the obliviousness to gossip which got her into her fix to begin with, but it brings back a bit of her "old proud fire" when she refuses to leave St. Ogg's because of what people are saying about

her. Her pride is dangerous but good: the alternative would be slav-
ishness to what others think. Final accolades of heroism are given out
successively to Mrs. Tulliver, Aunt Glegg, Philip, and Lucy, each of
whom sticks by Maggie in the face of social pressure. Dr. Kenn com-
plicates the rather simple moral sequence when, fearing that he will
lose his influence over his flock, he finally succumbs to his parishio-
ners' wish that he fire Maggie; he makes a compromised decision
because he sees gossip as an unbeatable power and chooses to retain
his audience. Like Farebrother in *Middlemarch*, Kenn raises the question of survival by accommodation from which George Eliot exempts
her major characters.

The vilification of gossip thus serves its turn in a novel that ends by
washing away the limited world in which Mary Ann Evans grew up.
Yet the attack derives its special force from the uneasy relation between the narrator's defense of Maggie and the sexual innuendo of
the gossipers. Maggie herself hears nothing in gossip that is hers; her
head is full of her own voices of self-reproach. It is the narrator who
hears and reproduces voices that are despicable exactly to the extent
that they intersect with Maggie's inner struggle. Like the revealing
reconciliation fantasy of the flood itself, the gossip fantasy gives us a
glimpse of George Eliot at a moment when gossip's threat to the
idealizations of the highly wrought moral life is most angrily resisted.

In August 1860, with the publication of *Mill* behind her and the
prospect of an entirely new sort of historical project ahead, George
Eliot wrote "Brother Jacob."[15] The simplest plot summary suggests
that this much-neglected story is George Eliot's satirical coming-to-
terms with the extended crisis of pseudonymity she had suffered in
the previous year. David Faux, a confectioner with inflated ambitions,
steals his mother's nest egg and runs away to make his fortune in
Jamaica. He turns up again six years later in a nearby English town,
where he begins to make a successful business and social career under
the pseudonym Edward Freely. As he is on the verge of consolidating
his false position through marriage to a local farmer's daughter, he is
unmasked by the appearance of his idiot brother Jacob, who destroys
all his prospects in the new town. This tale, the narrator concludes, is
"an admirable instance of the unexpected forms in which the great
Nemesis hides herself."[16]

"Brother Jacob" is a companion piece to "The Lifted Veil" in the
sense that it fictionalizes a version of Marian Lewes's experience as she
imagined it to be seen by her provincial critics and persecutors.[17] As

in the earlier story, neither the hero nor his antagonists have any claim to sympathy or virtue. But "Brother Jacob" is to my ear a far better piece of writing. Its concrete, socially detailed narration is writing characteristic of George Eliot, though it speaks in a satirical voice she rarely unleashed without its careful hedge of sympathy and moral appeal. The bitterness and depression that pervade the voice in "The Lifted Veil" and in the later letters about Bracebridge and Co. are not in evidence here. In their stead we have the humor and metaphorical playfulness of a story that considers the accusation that George Eliot had stolen other people's stories and transcribed them as fiction, by inventing a character whose attempts to turn stolen guineas into yellow candy lozenges backfire with a vengeance.

David Faux fastens on his mother's private hoard of guineas to finance his escape because he wishes to preserve his share of the legal paternal inheritance by committing a domestic theft that runs little risk of exposure. The "matri-money" is both a secret, locked in a box, and a cherished family tradition; the children love to hear the money rattle in the box. Thus David's theft, like George Eliot's writing—especially in *The Mill on the Floss*—involves running away to capitalize on intimate family secrets. David plans "to abstract the guineas from their wooden box" (6), put them in a bag, bury the bag in a hole, and return later to carry away the treasure. When he is interrupted by his idiot brother Jacob, who recognizes the guineas, he contrives to placate him by giving him yellow lozenges and then by persuading him that burying the guineas and leaving them in the ground will transform them into the lozenges that Jacob craves. Thus will the stolen treasure be "forgotten" until it is exhumed in the form of consumable art.

The metaphorical connections between confectionery and art are · drawn out in the second chapter, which describes "Edward Freely's" career in Grimworth. When the new confectionery shop window is unveiled, the children are spellbound audiences to the display; the realistic side—meats and pies—is "altogether a sight to bring tears into the eyes of a Dutch painter," while the fantasy side—sweets and candies—"might easily have been blended into a faëry landscape in Turner's latest style" (20–21). Freely makes his way as a confectioner by luring romantically inclined housewives away from their own cookery, but he requires other forms of confection in order to achieve his social ambitions, which he fosters by circulating fabulous stories about his adventures in Jamaica and by inventing a rich uncle who, Jane

Eyre–wise, will make him his heir. It is on the basis of such romantic stories, which mitigate the socially undesirability of his position as a confectioner, that Penny Palfrey yearns to be his bride.

These are the fictions that are shattered when the literal-minded idiot brother finds his way to Freely's shop. At that moment David "felt arrested for having stolen his mother's guineas" (45). Jacob has not forgotten; he has come to retrieve them, and when he sees the jar of yellow lozenges he demands "Mother's zinnies" (47). All the fictional transformations of Faux-Freely's career are "arrested" by the single-minded pursuit of the idiot brother, who sees only identities where David sees transmutations. Not unlike George Eliot contending with Bracebridge, David denies Jacob's claim to fraternity; he even attempts to cover his guilt by mouthing moral rhetoric about our duty to have sympathy for idiots. But he has so fatally bound Jacob to him by feeding him with sweets that he cannot loosen the brute hold of his past. As in Marian Lewes's life, the unwelcome reconnection occurs simultaneously with a family rejection, voiced by David's eldest brother Jonathan when he grudgingly carries out the duty of fairly distributing the paternal inheritance.

The idiot brother is a version of Bracebridge and Co., representing the dumb adhesiveness of a literal-minded past connection who wishes to claim "George Eliot" against her will as a purveyor of provincial lives. His idiocy arrests him in a condition of childhood and suggests a past that does not grow up or admit change; Jacob cannot even notice, much less accept, the transformations of David's life. His ubiquitous pitchfork is the threat that requires David to twist and turn in search of strategies to avoid him. In a parody of literary criticism the narrator introduces a "learned friend" who "observed that it was David's guilt which made these prongs formidable. . . . I thought this idea so valuable, that I obtained his leave to use it on condition of suppressing his name" (6–7). In this aside she manages to point to the pitchfork as a external emblem of the guilt David both feels and denies and also to make fun of the whole question of "sources" and anonymity. It is a moment that perfectly captures the wry balance of the story.

The splitting of qualities among the three named brothers in the story—David, Jacob, and Jonathan—also implicates them more deeply with one another through the biblical allusions. David is as much the titular "Brother Jacob" as is Jacob. He is the clever younger son who receives his birthright through deceit, and who flees to his "uncle" to establish a new family fortune and lineage. Jacob, dumb and rural, is an Esau figure. Both are "sons" of Isaac (Evans)—David in his calculating nature, which links him to the Tom Tulliver figure, and Jacob, further split into adhesive Jacob/rejecting Jonathan, as the one who stays behind to maintain the original family configuration. Insofar as David Faux/Edward Freely is a figure for Mary Ann Evans/ George Eliot, he is a George Eliot imbued with the spirit of Isaac Evans, imagined as an Isaac Evans could and would imagine him. Yet compared with "The Lifted Veil" and even *The Mill on the Floss*, the story reads as a sharp but amused epitaph for a period of life that had passed. Marian and George Henry Lewes might continue to dramatize her shrinking from the world's public voice, but George Eliot had made a comic peace with Bracebridge and Co.

By the time she wrote *Middlemarch*, she had also come to a new understanding of the relationship between gossip and the self-comforting fictions of its subjects. *Middlemarch* is a virtual anatomy of all the different ways people can talk about each other. To read the novel with gossip as a protagonist is to recognize how difficult it is to distinguish gossip from other kinds of dialogue, how fully George Eliot had become interested in an objective depiction of the processes through which information about people is circulated, blocked, or distorted.[18] The narrative creates several precisely distinguished and separate circles of gossip and defines every character through a particularized relationship with the talk of others. By the end of the novel every talking circle discusses the Bulstrode-Lydgate affair, now become a genuine scandal; but had Raffles not picked up a stray bit of paper from Rigg-Featherstone's hearth the normal "whispering gallery" of gossip would not, the narrator suggests, have turned into "the opening of a catastrophe" (chap. 41).

While the broad movement from gossip to scandal repeats the pattern set by George Eliot's earlier stories, the representations of gossip itself open a more complex terrain in which the talk of others is not only inevitable but often essential to the circulation of information needed by members of the community. More important, both gossip and scandal tell the truth in *Middlemarch*—not the truth their subjects acknowledge but a kind of truth they have fearfully or scornfully repressed. Because of this penetrating dialogue between gossip and individual repression, the novel persistently resists one of its most popular readings, as a story of desiring subjects blocked, broken, or excluded by community opinion.[19]

In *Middlemarch* the sheer range of dialogue about absent others challenges the reader to define the activity of gossip. Is Mrs. Cadwallader a gossip when she brings James Chettam the news that Dorothea is engaged to Casaubon? When she insinuates that Celia is interested in him? When Fred asks Rosamond what Mary said, is he gossiping? What is Naumann doing when he rhapsodizes on Dorothea at Rome? Is James Chettam a gossip when he tries to persuade Mr. Cadwallader to interfere in Dorothea's engagement to Casaubon? What about the hospital board when it meets to discuss the candidacy for the post of hospital chaplain? Is the attack on Brooke's estate management in the *Trumpet* gossip or politics? When Farebrother is asked to discuss Fred with Mary, or when he brings news about Fred's doings to the Garth household, is he gossiping?

Such activities have to be set against more outright forms of gossip: the spread of rumor and speculation clustering around Lydgate—his medical practice, his association with Bulstrode, and his engagement to Rosamond—and to a lesser extent around Ladislaw. George Eliot devotes a long chapter (chap. 45) to rumor about Lydgate in which she concentrates fully on the misinterpretations of him which prepare his fall: the uneducated fear he wants the hospital as a source of corpses to cut up, the surgeons resent his refusal to make his fees dependent on dispensing drugs. In such analyses, and in briefer ones about Ladislaw, it is clear that true gossip might be defined as talk laden with titillating fantasy or innuendo that draws conclusions from a lack of evidence and arises from distrust, jealousy, or hostility. Nevertheless, such talk is part of a continuum that includes almost all the talk in the novel and all the shades of meaning and feeling which distinguish gossip from something else.

There is, for example, a fine line between gossip and getting information to people who need to know it. Mrs. Cadwallader performs a service when she tells James Chettam of Dorothea's engagement; she spares him considerable humiliation. Celia twice breaks through the hush-up atmosphere created by gossip to give her sister vital information, about Sir James's intentions and about Casaubon's will. The whole of chapter 59 is devoted to the chain of gossip which finally and belatedly ends with Rosamond telling Will about his role in that will; the news is exactly suited to the banalities of Rosamond's romantic imagination; yet her breaking of confidence comes as a great relief in the conspiracy of silence that constitutes the courtship of Will and Dorothea. When George Eliot returns to the "world's wife" theme in chapter 74, she satirizes the gossiping women less for the quality of their dialogue than for the obstruction they pose to Mrs. Bulstrode's need for information about her husband.

This theme illuminates Sir James Chettam's role in the novel: he is the gossip fearer, always vigilant about the reputation of his family, always haplessly trying to get someone else to prevent actions that threaten to stir up gossip. He wants others to undo the Dorothea-Casaubon marriage, keep Mr. Brooke out of politics, keep Dorothea from knowing the contents of Casaubon's will, get Ladislaw out of town, and then, ironically, prevent Dorothea from "meddling" in the Lydgate scandal—all to maintain, without his overt interference, the dignity of his position. When he wants Dorothea to know the gossip about Will and Rosamond he delegates the dirty work to Mrs. Cadwallader. Failing to halt any of the gossip-worthy courses of action he deplores, Chettam is a comic reminder that the effort to prevent gossip is equivalent to putting a ban on life.

The tactful Mr. Farebrother is his corrective, for Farebrother takes on the complex responsibility of mediating between individuals and the gossip about them. Speaking out against ill-founded rumor is only his easiest task; Farebrother's story is all about the sensitive application of rules for when to say what to whom. He knows gossip about Lydgate before the new doctor comes to town, but he tells no one except Lydgate himself that he has heard of him. He mounts a campaign to sensitize Lydgate to the opinions of his colleagues and another to defend Lydgate in the town's professional circles; unlike the masterpiece of tact and honesty that is his mediation of the Fred-Mary courtship, these honorable efforts fail. In the end it is tact itself that is finally found wanting: after Farebrother has heard gossip about Lydgate's debts, offered help, and been rebuffed, he is unwilling to repeat the intrusion on Lydgate's pride in the bribery scandal. Dorothea's leap of faith in Lydgate shows up Farebrother as a coward; yet his fear that what gossip says may be true is only a special extrapolation from the pattern set by the novel itself.

For gossip in *Middlemarch* is always the externalization of a repressed truth. Bulstrode's case lies at the center of this pattern, not only because what Raffles knows of him is true but because Bulstrode himself can see the story only when he is faced with its appearance in others' eyes: his repression of his stepdaughter's existence and his hush money to Raffles "was the bare fact which Bulstrode was now forced to see in the rigid outline with which acts present themselves to

onlookers" (chap. 61). For other characters, too, gossip provides the
disturbing shock of the true. Casaubon's sexual unfitness for marriage is apparent to everyone but himself and Dorothea. The random
gossip about Ladislaw's "shady" background is corroborated by the
news Raffles brings. Celia's relay of gossip forces Dorothea to see
James Chettam's friendship as the courting she has been highmindedly repressing; Casaubon's will, his final act of gossip, propels
her into love with Will under "the effect of the sudden revelation that
another had thought of him in that light" (chap. 50). Lydgate is told
by town talkers two facts that he strenuously denies: that he has linked
his professional ambitions to Bulstrode's money and that he is courting Rosamond Vincy. Even the bribery scandal contains its uncomfortable seed of truth, as Lydgate recognizes when he wonders if he
would have left Raffles's death uninvestigated had he not accepted
Bulstrode's check. Only the gossip generated by professional competition or provincial ignorance is presented as seriously false; it is undeniable that Lydgate is victimized by medical scare stories and professional jealousy.

Because resistance to the "petty medium" of gossip is resistance to a
truth about the self, the linkage of moral heroism with the power to
defy gossip is a complicated matter in *Middlemarch*. Mary and Caleb
Garth's refusals to have anything to do with their employers' scandalous doings—last-minute will burnings, mysterious blackmailers—
only make them firmer links in the chain of catastrophe. Lydgate
carries around a fantasy of heroic resistance in which all gossip is
defined as "silly conclusions which nobody can foresee"; yet even the
heroic stance carries with it the seeds of defeatism: "It was as useless
to fight against the interpretations of ignorance as to whip the fog"
(chap. 45). And Lydgate's visible actions—his vote for the hospital
chaplaincy, his engagement to Rosamond, his financial dependence
on Bulstrode—are ones in which the posture of defiance blurs only
his own vision of the fact that he has at least partially become what the
talkers say he is.[20]

Against this tragic limitation we should presumably place the transcendent innocence of Dorothea and perhaps the successful resistance to public opinion in her love affair with Will Ladislaw.[21] Yet the
obliviousness to gossip celebrated in this marriage is won only
through a process of exquisite sensitivity to gossip's power. Dorothea's
generous faith in Lydgate—"I believe that people are almost always
better than their neighbours think they are"—is fueled by a derailed

wish to defend Ladislaw from the gossip that separates them: "Some of her intensest experience in the last two years had set her mind strongly in opposition to any unfavourable construction of others" (chap. 72). That "intensest experience" is primarily her inner cherishing of a belief in Ladislaw's goodness against the Chettam-Cadwallader version of Ladislaw as a "low" philanderer. Dorothea's susceptibility to gossip emerges during Will's second farewell scene, when she suddenly suspects him of leaving to escape Rosamond rather than herself; when his final outburst makes it clear that he loves her, her joy includes the relief of vindication: "He had acted so as to defy reproach, and make wonder respectful" (chap. 62). When she goes to clear Lydgate in Rosamond's eyes only to find Ladislaw in the midst of an apparent love scene, the psychological entanglement of the two situations is represented by the plot: suddenly Dorothea becomes Rosamond, a woman who instantly believes that the gossip about her lover is true. In her anger Will becomes "a detected illusion," one "among the crowd" (chap. 80); her noble mission to "save" Rosamond's marriage has as its premise the idea that Ladislaw is what her friends have been calling him. Thus she is as dependent on Rosamond's vindication of Ladislaw as Rosamond is on her belief in Lydgate; and when Will comes for the final interview she goes to meet him with a renewed sense of love as vindication, "a sense that she was doing something daringly defiant for his sake" (chap. 83). This is not a love that turns away from gossip but one that is nourished by resistance to it.

Ladislaw's side of the story is even more entirely shaped by his resistance to what he imagines others will think of him. In his sensitivity he preempts the terms of Casaubon's will before he knows of it; when Brooke tries halfheartedly to keep him away from the Grange, Will thinks, "Her friends, then, regarded him with some suspicion? Their fears were quite superfluous: they were very much mistaken if they imagined that he would put himself forward as a needy adventurer trying to win the favour of a rich woman" (chap. 51). His determination "to give the lie beforehand" (chap. 55) to that suspicion makes it impossible for him to say anything coherent to Dorothea and begins the muffled comedy of courtship conducted as a joint effort of vindication in which the partners lack necessary information about each other. Will is then subjected to a series of unpleasant revelations—Rosamond tells him about the will, Raffles tells him about his parents, and Bulstrode offers him repentance money—

which only increase his desire to defy the stories that he knows Chettam gossip will make of these matters. "However, let them suspect what they pleased, they would find themselves in the wrong. They would find that the blood in his veins was as free from the taint of meanness as theirs" (chap. 60). He refuses Bulstrode's money in large part because he knows he could not bear to tell Dorothea that he had accepted it, and he begins his last talk with Dorothea by telling her that he has done so. All this adds up to a portrait of a man talented in anticipating what he looks like to others, whose defiance of conventional stories proves a salutary—even a disciplinary—influence on his character. If Will escapes being what gossip calls him, it is because he outwits it at its own game.

Or would, were not his author open to every conceivable twist of that game. When George Eliot, in a chapter that must surely have amused her, follows the chain of gossip which ends with Rosamond telling Will about the will, she puts in Rosamond's mouth the story of romantic love which is in fact the story of Dorothea and Will. "It is really the most charming romance: Mr Casaubon jealous, and foreseeing that there was no one else whom Mrs Casaubon would so much like to marry, and no one who would so much like to marry her as a certain gentleman; and then laying a plan to spoil all by making her forfeit her property if she did marry that gentleman—and then—and then—and then—oh, I have no doubt the end will be thoroughly romantic." And she adds, "I dare say she likes you better than the property" (chap. 59). Like every other light-minded gossip Rosamond fails to comprehend the rage of peculiar feeling this news arouses in Will as he storms out, saying, "Never! You will never hear of the marriage!" Yet she is right, as all the Middlemarch gossips are right in their ways; it is really the most charming romance.

If gossip in *Middlemarch* functions as a mirror of what the subject represses, the stories of Bulstrode and Casaubon reveal that George Eliot knew what she was up to: it is not gossip but paranoia that kills in this novel. In these two characters she explores the pain of audience consciousness in extreme forms, saving her utmost horror for those to whom the world is nothing but a "whispering-gallery." Casaubon's existence is determined by his fear of being seen by others; like his cousin Ladislaw, he has keen suspicions about what others suspect, but unlike him, he has no talent, energy, youth, or passion to oppose his fears. "To let any one suppose that he was jealous would be to admit their (suspected) view of his disadvantages: to let them know that he did not find marriage particularly blissful would imply his conversion to their (probably) earlier disapproval. It would be as bad as letting Carp, and Brasenose generally, know how backward he was in organizing the material for his 'Key to all Mythologies'" (chap. 37). Casaubon suspects others—notably Dorothea, who comes to embody his hostile imaginary audiences—"without confessing" his failures to himself (chap. 42); he has thoroughly projected his fears upon others, who loom over him and paralyze his every endeavor. Casaubon—like a part of George Eliot's creativity—seems to die of being seen; his forced intimacy with Dorothea is the beginning of his end.

The question the narrator asks about Bulstrode might equally apply to Casaubon: "Who can know how much of his most inward life is made up of the thoughts he believes other men to have about him, until that fabric of opinion is threatened with ruin?" (chap. 68). In Bulstrode's case the answer seems to be "all of it"; the horror of his story lies less in the evil of his past crime than in the psychological machinations through which Bulstrode constructs a personality that will do anything rather than risk the disgrace of exposure. Bulstrode's imagination is coarser than Casaubon's; he does not seem to intuit that everyone except his wife hates him already, that the "fabric of opinion" is his own fabrication. Yet his fantasy of an approving world is no less a projection than Casaubon's repressed choruses of disapproval; and it is equally fragile. Like his scholarly counterpart, his life shrivels into nothing in the face of exposure.

In both stories the narrator is most effectively sympathetic at the moments when the dread of exposure is most intensely imagined. Nevertheless, the slaves to how things look—including Rosamond— are the villains of the novel; self-consciousness is a greater threat than gossip if only because it creates a dangerous vulnerability to a talking world that no one can escape.[22] In the universe of *Middlemarch* it is necessary for sanity and survival to admit the talk of others into an open—if openly resistant—dialectic with the self.

Middlemarch brought George Eliot to the height of her fame, but it did not alter her wish to remain visible only in the public privacy of her texts. Her resistance to contributing information for biographical sketches and her desire to regulate what others saw and thought of her continued after Lewes's death, through the final "scandal" of her marriage to John Cross, and even beyond her death, in the carefully edited version of *George Eliot's Life* which Cross produced. The recognitions of *Middlemarch* did, however, have a sequel: in the strangely intimate essay "Looking Inward," the male narrator Theophrastus Such entrusts his audience with a directly autobiographical image of the writer's self in hiding. In this last work George Eliot's fearful desire to be seen and discussed by her audiences was turned into confessional comedy and rehearsed for their benefit.

Impressions of Theophrastus Such is concerned with exposure: several of the sketches in this heterogeneous text are portraits of writers in the critical marketplace; others satirize the self-delusions that certain character types impose upon their acquaintances. The opening essay, "Looking Inward," purports to be an autobiographical confession in which "Such"—the English surname suggests a particularly placed and comic version of the generic figure—offers an apology for the satires that follow by asserting his inward complicity with the follies of others. "Dear blunderers, I am one of you," he claims; and the essay ends with a reiteration of this point, now made with the full George Eliot rhetorical regalia: "But there is a loving laughter in which the only recognized superiority is that of the ideal self, the God within, holding the mirror and the scourge for our own pettiness as well as our neighbours'."[23] The hyper-self-consciousness of Such's narrative as a whole may, however, suggest George Eliot's special need to apologize for her indulgence in the outright satire—the "evil-speaking"— she had licensed herself to practice when she adapted the convention of the Theophrastan "character" essay.[24] The intense and circular introspection of Such certainly goes far beyond anything that would have been necessary to make the official point of fellowship in folly. In fact, his self-underminings undermine the official point as well, for they consistently emphasize the psychological gap between him and his audiences.

"Looking Inward" is about the possibility, or the impossibility, of writing autobiography to be read by others. The essay opens with this question: "It is my habit to give an account to myself of the characters I meet with: can I give any true account of my own?" (3) Such is immediately overtaken by his consciousness that others—while not knowing what he knows of himself—are all too likely to know things he does not know about himself; that is, he is instantly threatened by the critical potential of his audience. "Is it then possible to describe oneself at once faithfully and fully?" he asks again; and again his imagination leaps to his audience: it is possible to reveal the truth about oneself unintentionally, as Rousseau does, "from what he unconsciously enables us to discern" (6–7). Such, whose main problem lies in his belief that no one is interested in hearing what he has to say, is simultaneously freighted with the fear that others will see too well what he prefers to conceal.

"Looking Inward" dramatizes the fear of constructing a "false view of her relations with others" which Marian Lewes had observed when she read the autobiography of Harriet Martineau (6:371); it also includes pious strictures against the autobiographical revelation of material that gossips about living others or shows human nature in "its lowest fatalities, its invincible remnants of the brute" (6). But its most autobiographical moments—moments when the narrative sounds suddenly neither like the semicomic Such nor like the pietistic Eliot narrator—are the ones in which the imagination of a responding audience is most fully present. This voice breaks through when Such is confessing that he would simply rather not hear the critical things others say about him: "In brief, after a close intimacy with myself for a longer period than I choose to mention, I find within me a permanent longing for approbation, sympathy, and love" (8). It returns when he describes turning to the act of writing to escape the sense of invisibility that accompanies his talent for sympathetic listening to others. As a friendly listener he is nothing but an audience (a strategy he has developed in order not to feel like a disappointed outcast from the human condition), but writing "brings with it the vague, delightful illusion of an audience nearer to my idiom than the Cherokees, and more numerous than the visionary One for whom many authors have declared themselves willing to go through the pleasing punishment of publication." This fantasy audience is "a far-off, hazy, multitudinous assemblage," a projection of the self which makes "approving chorus to the sentences and paragraphs of which I myself particularly enjoy the writing." It is necessarily hazy, for if any face becomes distinct, it "is sure to be one bent on discountenancing my innocent intentions; it is pale-eyed, incapable of being amused when I am amused or indignant at what makes me indignant" (17). Such is more cowardly—or less ambitious—than his creator, for he will submit his work only posthumously, but he shares with her a knowledge of the necessary illusions that make writing possible in the first place.[25]

Theophrastus Such never answers his own questions about whether it is possible to give a faithful account of the self; the self and its audiences reach a draw in their competition for true knowledge of character. He remains stuck between his wish not to know anything about his audience which is not a projection of himself and his recognition that an audience may see more about him than he wants them to know. George Eliot's rather good-natured portrayal of his dilemma includes, for the first time, a sentence that grants her audiences the right to gossip: "I am not indeed writing an autobiography, or pretending to give an unreserved description of myself, but only offering some slight confessions in an apologetic light, to indicate that if in my absence you dealt as freely with my unconscious weaknesses as I have dealt with the unconscious weaknesses of others, I should not feel myself warranted by common-sense in regarding your freedom of observation as an exceptional case of evil-speaking" (7). The creation of a first-person narrator who says, however reluctantly, "I talk about you, you talk about me," makes a last little rent in the veil of silence with which George Eliot had attempted to obscure her active participation in the arts of gossip and satire. In a move that connects her final work with the male narrators of her earliest stories, she recovers her masculine persona in full view of her audience, as if to suggest a truth about the whole of her career: that the wearing of the mask is the most revelatory mode of all.

SIX

Ambition and Womanhood

I feel that my besetting sin is the one of all others
most destroying, as it is the fruitful parent of them
all, Ambition, a desire insatiable for the esteem of
my fellow creatures.

—Mary Ann Evans to Elizabeth Evans,
March 5, 1839

In the fall of 1859, with Liggins and Bracebridge still uppermost in
her mind, Marian Lewes wrote to Cara Bray about her inability to feel
joy in her successful authorship. "I often think of my dreams when I
was four or five and twenty," she wrote. "I thought then, how happy
fame would make me! I feel no regret that fame, as such, brings no
pleasure, but it *is* a grief to me that I do not constantly feel strong in
thankfulness that my past life has vindicated its uses, and given me
reason for gladness that such an unpromising woman-child was born
into the world" (3:170). It is hardly surprising that her first experience of fame, so deeply tinged with infamy, should leave her with a
sense of disappointment. The sentences are compelling for another
reason, because of the way she rewrites her youthful ambition for
fame as something else.

Beginning her life as a fiction writer, she had imagined that her
painful past would be redeemed by her writing. Now she specifies, to
the correspondent whom she identifies with the life of the feminine, a
more explicit idea of her writing as a redemption of failures in womanhood. While she might have felt elated because her young dreams
had begun to come true—that the ambitions of the past had led her to
the present—she instead represents a process in which she plays a less

active personal role: her past life has "vindicated its uses," while she, the erstwhile unpromising woman-child, should look on in (womanly) thankfulness. The notion that writing redeems her questionable womanhood is complicated by the syntactical split between the personal being and the impersonal life of writing, and then further complicated by the implication that writing has after all failed to redeem her sad past; that it has rather given her continuing occasion for grief. The transformation of youthful ambition into a site of specifically feminine splitting and conflict marks one of the most troubled nodes of feeling and self-representation in George Eliot's repertoire. Although it is intimately linked with the issues explored in the last chapter, the conflict about ambitious womanhood has a trajectory of its own, which may be traced from the earliest writings of Mary Ann Evans to the end of her life. This chapter will follow the thorny path of that Victorian contradiction, as George Eliot represented it in letters and fictions.

Long after the painful experiences of 1859 had faded into memory softened by further success and increased public esteem, Marian Lewes continued to define ambition in ways that transformed it into something other than a drive toward artistic creation or achievement. After the publication of *Felix Holt* in 1866, she responded to a letter from the American journalist Harriet Pierce, demonstrating a propensity to dramatize her melancholy for her most distant audiences."My consciousness is not of the triumphant kind your generous joy on my behalf leads you to imagine. Exultation is a dream before achievement, and rarely comes after. What comes after, is rather the sense that the work has been produced within one, like offspring, developing and growing by some force of which one's own life has only served as a vehicle, and that what is left of oneself is only a poor husk." Once again, the notion of joy in achievement is replaced by a formulation which simultaneously implicates writing with a specifically feminine body and distances it. The "force" that creates writing is separated from the will or the personal ambition of the writer through a metaphor that feminizes the process as maternal generativity and then offers a "postpartum" vision of creation as a devastator of the personal body and being. The process is feminine in the sense that pregnant womanhood is a passive vehicle, but it does not offer womanly joy as a reward; rather, the drive of writing leaves behind a suffering and depleted self.

As this letter develops, Marian Lewes emphasizes the disconnection between personal ambition and writing: "Before that, I was too proud and ambitious to write: I did not believe that I could do anything fine, and I did not choose to do anything of that mediocre sort which I despised when it was done by others. I began, however, by a sort of writing which had no great glory belonging to it, but which I felt certain I could do faithfully and well." Now that she has become a novelist (a condition that by implication does involve a certain glory) ambition is further separated from public fame: the fiction "has been thought a great deal of—but the satisfaction I have got out of it has not been exactly that of ambition. . . . Having done it, one finds oneself the reverse of proud" (8:383–84). Her refusal to name exactly what "the reverse of proud" might be suggests her reluctance to display even the pride of professed humility in her public rhetoric.

Yet overweening ambition still lingered, as a power insatiable by any actual achievement. So Marian suggested in a letter to her friend Maria Congreve, written just as she was beginning to imagine the character of Edward Casaubon: "But my strong egoism has caused me so much melancholy, which is traceable simply to a fastidious yet hungry ambition, that I am relieved by the comparative quietude of personal cravings which age is bringing" (5:125). Defining ambition as a personal hunger that feeds melancholy, she inverted, in conformity with her moral code, the connection she may have known as a deeper truth: that her melancholy was a source of her artistic drive.

The representation of ambition as a form of impotent suffering, laid out in excruciating detail in the portrait of Casaubon, had its strategic uses as well as its truth. By separating her ambition from her achievement and transforming it into suffering, George Eliot could feminize and conceal it, both to her own satisfaction and for the benefit of her audiences and admirers. Her responses to fan letters consistently replace the image of the successful author with one of the desponding soul. A representative example occurs in a letter to Frederic Harrison, who had corresponded with a very hardheaded author about the legal issues in *Felix Holt* and subsequently wrote to praise the novel. Marian responded: "Please to imagine as well as you can the experience of a mind morbidly desponding, of a consciousness tending more and more to consist in memories of error and imperfection rather than in a strengthening sense of achievement—and then consider how such a mind must need the support of sympathy and approval from those who are capable of understanding its aims" (4:300). Even to her fellow author Harriet Beecher Stowe,

George Eliot introduced herself in her first letter as someone with a "mental sickness," wishing that Stowe "could have a momentary vision of the discouragement, nay, paralysing despondency in which many days of my writing life have been past, in order that you might fully understand the good I find in such sympathy as yours" (5:29).

There is little doubt about George Eliot's actual susceptibility to depression. Yet her willingness to broadcast primarily that aspect of her creativity suggests how necessary it was to her to be seen as a sufferer rather than as one of the ambitious, authoritative narrators of her books, and to transform praises of her work into healing balm for a trembling sensibility.[1] In the letters her admirers are never part of the large audience figured in the sales totals of her books; they are souls gifted with a singular ability to understand her and thus to sustain her ever-failing faith. So, even at the height of her fame, she fended off any shadow of acknowledgment that she might be regarded as an applauded public figure. This rhetorical impulse had a long history: since adolescence she had been both stimulated and unsettled by the visible image of achieved artistic ambition.

In Mary Ann Evans's early letters, the most emphatic target of her relentless evangelical self-criticism is her desire for an appreciative audience—an audience she attempts to create through the very activity of self-disparagement. The strength of the desire and the vehemence of the prohibition first appear in the earliest known George Eliot manuscript, the schoolgirl essay titled "Affectation and Conceit," written around the age of fourteen.[2]

The young writer's stated ambition is to make a distinction in eighteenth-century style between two weaknesses of character: "I perceive that Mrs. Spectator has very much in my opinion confounded the two follies affection [*sic*] & conceit." (The slip of the pen is almost perfectly revealing in the context that develops.) Mary Ann Evans has difficulty making the distinction because her two terms keep intertwining with each another, although she does manage to argue that "affectation" is the artificial "assumption of some merit which we do not really possess"—and know we do not—whereas "conceit" is a false notion of superior worth whose possessors "pride themselves upon gaining the admiration and envy of the world at large." The two vices accompany each another, and when the illusion that sustained conceit has vanished, affectation takes over in an effort to continue winning praise from its audience. The long and rather confused opening paragraph that argues these points is followed by two shorter ones in which affectation is decried as it occurs in women vain of their appearance and then bewailed in more extreme language as the writer considers "the nobler sex": "If it is so despicable in women oh how far more contemptible it is in man." It is quite clear that the writer's identification and passion are reserved for "the nobler sex," whose particular claims to superiority are not limited to bodily appearances.

It is also clear that Mary Ann Evans cannot separate the notion of superiority—she does not broach the idea of talent—from the repugnant idea that it is simply an illusory ploy designed to reap praises from others. The ploy is dangerously transparent: if the affected persons could see "how easily their disguise is penetrated, it is to be hoped that they would be as disgusted with their own conduct as those are, upon whom they practise it." The conceited man finds himself "aping some odd or eccentric manner or style, eagerly desiring to be the admired and envied one of the ⟨comp⟩ society ⟨to which he may belong⟩ in which he may move." The revision reveals the young writer's fears: such a performer does not "belong" to the society from which he demands adulation. The sense of superiority is already allied with a retributive fate of isolation.

Both affectation and conceit are imagined more vigorously as relationships with audiences than as self-deceptions. And the true animus of the essay, where the writing becomes powerful and metaphorical, lies in its depiction of the love of praise as a dangerous addiction. Of the conceited man: "Adulation and praise is his food and without a constant daily supply of this unwholesome nourishment, he cannot be said to live; when then he perceives that what he has flattered himself has procured him this necessary dish, begins to tire or cease to please his audience, he of necessity turns to some other art by which to call up the dying embers of their praise & wonder." Such men may "lay traps for a little incense even from those whose opinion they cannot be said to value." The affected woman is even more an addict: her need for admiration is compared to that of a drunkard who "turns to his wine to drown his cares." By the essay's conclusion "the desire of applause" has become its overt subject. To cure oneself of it "is to take care to cast away the love of it upon all occasions, that are not in themselves praiseworthy." The qualifying phrase is the revealing turn; it admits the possibility of occasions that *are* in themselves praiseworthy. What these might be remains undefined by the young essayist, who is quite probably engaged in eliciting a teacher's praise for her precocious and rather affected imitation.

Four or five years later, casting away the love of praise took more tortured forms in Mary Ann Evans's personal letters. In March 1839 she wrote to her aunt Elizabeth Evans in terms that reveal how thoroughly she tried to protect herself against a fear that her own ambition was a form of deception. She accuses herself of being "willing to obtain credit for greater knowledge and deeper feeling than I really possess. Instead of putting my light under a bushel, I am in danger of ostentatiously displaying a false one" (1:19). After chastising herself for not making better use of her provincial circumstances, she produced this audacious sentence: "I feel that my besetting sin is the one of all others most destroying, as it is the fruitful parent of them all, Ambition, a desire insatiable for the esteem of my fellow creatures." Although it masquerades as the confession of a scrupulous young evangelical, everything about that sentence is questionable, from the paradox of destructive fruitfulness and the central godlike position of the personifed "Ambition" to the self-dramatizing definition of this "sin" as a desire for personal esteem disconnected from any object or achievement. Her struggle for spiritual perfection is an exercise in ambition quenching, she continues; yet even religious feeling is subject to "the dominant corruption": "I make the most humiliating and appalling confessions with little or no corresponding feeling." Thus she gives a final twist to the screw she has been applying to herself by admitting that her confessions, including the ones in the previous sentences, are in themselves affectations, "ostentatious displays" produced for audiences. That her own self-criticism should be a performance is the most "humiliating and appalling" confession of all. But if even this confession is merely formulaic, she readmits the possibility of performance, implicitly granting the creative power of ambition, "the fruitful parent" of all her "sins." The self-undoing so characteristic of her adolescent writing conceals, in its devious way, a saving reservation.

The subject of her struggle against ambition seems to have been a special part of the dialogue with Elizabeth Evans, the one woman in the family who had had a public career. It returned in a letter of December 1840, when Mary Ann's fears about her future were sharpened by uncertainty about where and with whom she was to live. She reports that she is attempting to "allow myself no leisure for dreaming about my *worldly* future"; "I earnestly desire a spirit of childlike humility that shall make me willing to be lightly esteemed among men; this is the opposite of my besetting sin, which is an ever struggling ambition" (1:73). In letters to Maria Lewis she could not, however, repress her tendency to compare herself playfully to the great men of literature and learning, even if the comparison was intended to demonstrate her inferiority (1:92).

Musical performance was especially suspect to this young evangelical eye, because it combined achievement with self-exhibition. As John Cross tells us, Mary Ann Evans was a good pianist, "the best performer in the school" at the Miss Franklins'. His informant recounted Mary Ann's readiness to perform for school visitors and her hysterical retreats from her audience after she had done so: "On being released, my mother has often known her to rush to her room and throw herself on the floor in an agony of tears."[3] Wishing to perform, and knowing that she should not wish it, the young girl fled from the moment when, the music ended, attention would be turned on her person. But the anguish of conflict may have been strengthened by an additional sense of shameful pride at being presented by adults to other strangers as a performing wonder. The Liggins affair was not the first occasion in Mary Ann Evans's life to mix the experience of artistic success with humiliation and retreat.

Cross also attests to George Eliot's lifelong love of music, "and especially oratorio."[4] It was oratorio that took the blame for the eighteen-year-old's attempt to cleanse herself of the sins of ambition.[5] On September 4, 1838, Mary Ann wrote to her school friend Martha Jackson that she had attended an oratorio "where, I think, I said farewell to all such expenditures of time and money. I think nothing can justify the using of an intensely interesting and solemn passage of Scripture, as a rope-dancer uses her rope, or as a sculptor the pedestal on which he places the statue, that is alone intended to elicit admiration" (1:9–10). Art is display for praise; the syntax carries a suggestion that it is *only* that. The singers are engaged in mere "exhibitions of skill"; nevertheless, they have tantalized her with images of an artist's life: "Would it be consistent with millenial holiness for a human being to devote the time and energies that are barely sufficient for real exigencies on acquiring expertness in trills, cadences, etc.?" She thinks not, even though the romantic voice breaks in to consider that "without them we should never have an opportunity of appreciating the beautiful powers of the human voice when carried to their highest point of improveability." That argument too is resisted by her attempt to deny art its special character and discipline: the same reasoning, she claims, could lead to an acceptance of opera dancing, horse racing, and even intemperance.

Two months later she has extended the private ban on artistic performance to a depressed denial of her own talent: "I am not fitted to
decide on the question of the propriety or lawfulness of such exhibitions of talent and so forth because I have no soul for music," she
writes to Maria Lewis (1:13). She repeats her qualms about the "ac-
quirement of an expertness in so useless (at least in ninety-nine cases
out of a hundred) an accomplishment" and professes disgust that
beautiful scriptures "be taken on the lips of such a man as Braham (a
Jew, too!)." All of these pious objections signal a half-concealed
struggle against her strong desire to become an artist; she wishes to
convince herself that such a life is exhibitionistic and useless, that it is
blasphemous and deceptive, that it represents the very image of self-
display before an audience which she rejects in herself. There is, once
again, a reservation: the hundredth case. There is an unmarked reservation as well: all her images of artistic activity involve the public
display of the performing or performed body.

During her years as assistant editor of the *Westminster Review* (1851–
1853), when she ran the journal under John Chapman's nominal
editorship, Marian Evans discovered that formal anonymity and the
virtual invisibility of her role created a working situation in which her
intellectual ambitions could freely play. The letters of those years
reveal the perfect ease with which she took on both intellectual and
managerial authority. Once focused on the work at hand—whether it
was assuaging the tempers of ruffled contributors, comparing the
merits and foibles of writers, or discussing the intellectual commitments of the journal—nothing prevented her from exercising the full
force of her powers. Her letters to Chapman display a blunt camaraderie of tone and complete confidence in her editorial judgment;
those to George Combe, with whom she maintained a steady correspondence, coolly mix intellectual exchange with tactful stroking designed to shore up his wavering support of the *Review*. Such freedom
of authority was itself authorized by the formal split between the work
of the journal and the public name attached to it. The position of
official feminine subordination could even prove positively useful:
Marian appealed to it during a particularly delicate interchange with
Combe, as she tried to discourage him from forwarding a set of testi-
monials: "If I were sole editor of the Westminster, I would take the
responsibility on myself, and ask you to send them through me, but
being a woman and something less than half an editor, I do not see
how the step you propose could be taken with the naturalness and

bienséance that could alone favour any good result" (8:90). She may have been confident that Combe would be deaf to the deep irony that accompanied that strategic staging of gender.

When Marian Evans became George Eliot, she continued the official cover that had served her so well as editor, practicing her art in the double invisibility of writing for publication under a male pseudonym. From the beginning of her career as a fiction writer, she was drawn to representations of her struggle with ambition and the revelation of ambition in public performance. Both of the lead characters in her first two stories, the curate Amos Barton and the singer Caterina Sarti, are ambitious performers who suffer from their self-exhibitions. In the second tale, "Mr. Gilfil's Love Story" George Eliot began a long preoccupation with female artists—usually singers—whose art is fueled by "unwomanly" excesses of angry or rebellious feeling. Extending from Caterina Sarti to the multiple singing actresses of *Daniel Deronda*, these figures create a little history of their own, in which we can see George Eliot working out the uneasy relation between the power of the artist's voice and the public display of the performing female body.[6]

"Mr. Gilfil's Love Story" is not an appealing tale; the narrator displays almost as much disguised contempt for the heroine as do the characters who trifle with her feelings. Caterina Sarti does, however, come into existence as a full-grown character during those passages that describe her power of playing and singing music. And that power is presented as a double-edged blessing: it is responsible for Tina's dangerously ambiguous social position at Cheverel Manor, and it is the single, therapeutic channel for the consequent violence of her emotional life.

Rescued as a baby after the death of her Italian father, whose brief moment as a tenor vanishes quickly with a loss of voice and a decline into poverty, Caterina is brought up in Cheverel Manor with the intention of turning her into a sort of genteel household servant, but the discovery of her "rare gift of song . . . associated her at once with the pleasures of the drawing-room," and "the servants began to understand that Miss Sarti was to be a lady after all" (chap. 4). In fact, however, she is something a little less than human, a household pet who sings on command, miniaturized by Sir Christopher Cheverel, who calls her the "little monkey," by philandering Anthony Wybrow, who calls her "my little singing bird," and by the narrator, who calls her "dark and tiny, like a gypsy changeling," a "little southern bird," a

"poor bird," and so on. Since she is not really a lady, Wybrow sees no
harm in trifling with her affections; since she is almost a member of
the family, she sees no barrier to cherishing her passion for him. In
short, her singing puts her in the drawing room, where it allows
Wybrow to meet her—and to see her, the woman on stage, as an
object of sexual dalliance.

George Eliot chastises Tina's passion as a wasting, vindictive, jealous love, but she has constructed a situation that would justify more
social forms of rage and frustration if the narrator were not colluding
so fully with the patriarchal objectification of Tina as a pathetic little
bundle of emotion. When she acts on her feelings the narrator turns
her explicitly into the object of the reader's gaze: "Look at her stoop-
ing down to gather up her treasure" begins a paragraph describing
Tina's tearful cherishing of Wybrow's picture (chap. 12); when she
thinks of the dagger she is turned into a fully formed gothic image:
"See how she rushes noiselessly, like a pale meteor, along the passages
and up the gallery stairs! Those gleaming eyes, those bloodless lips,
that swift silent tread, make her look like the incarnation of a fierce
purpose, rather than a woman" (chap. 13). The small size and fragility
of Tina's body are so often described that her anger seems an agita-
tion in a thimble—except when it is transformed into music.

Music is her single form of action, "the one thing in which she
ceased to be passive, and became prominent"; it is also the only action
that gives her power over her emotions: "Those full deep notes she
sent forth seemed to be lifting the pain from her heart—seemed to be
carrying away the madness from her brain" (chap. 10). Her mistake, it
seems, is to translate her passion into other forms of action: when she
erupts in bitterness against Anthony she feels only shame and self-
reproach; when she goes to their meeting armed with a dagger and
finds him dead she almost dies herself of guilt. Waiting for that meeting, she throws herself into a Handel fugue, and plays it better than
she could have in happier moments, "for now all the passion that
made her misery was hurled by a convulsive effort into her music."
When emotion finds its expression in "the impetuous intricacies of
that magnificent fugue," it is safe not only from the threat of melodramatic action but from the social shame of self-display (chap. 13).
Music contains and conceals anger, leaving no telltale daggers to signal aggressive intent. Only when it is so channeled is George Eliot
willing to represent Tina's passion as legitimate feeling rather than as
pathetic weakness.

Yet even music must be reformed in obedience to its aristocratic
patrons before the tale comes to an end. After Tina has run away from
the manor and fallen ill of guilt and remorse for the murder she
wanted to commit, she is re-placed in a farmhouse and then a village
parsonage for her convalescence from the ambitions and passions that
Cheverel Manor has aroused and denied. Her recovery is marked by
her return to music—or rather, by music's return to her, when the
striking of a single note "rushed through Caterina like an electric
shock: it seemed as if at that instant a new soul were entering into her
and filling her with a deeper, more significant life." When she repeats
Sir Christopher's favorite song, it becomes an act of forgiveness: "Its
notes seemed to carry on their wings all the tenderest memories of her
life, when Cheverel Manor was still an untroubled home." Her music,
which had conferred an illusion of social power, is now robbed of its
aggression and domesticated as an emotional renewal responsive to
Maynard Gilfil's faithful brotherly love in a formulaic sentence: "The
soul that was born anew to music was born anew to love" (chap. 20).

George Eliot's first rendition of the performing woman betrays a
fantasy in which the pride of talent is transformed into a personal and
social humiliation. Its fear is that the performer is a "little monkey" on
display for the amusement of those who live according to long-
established codes of social propriety; its collusion with the aristocratic
point of view is a measure of that fear. George Eliot was to rewrite this
story in a number of ways, notably in *Daniel Deronda*. But her next
fantasy, the treatment of Dinah Morris, preaching on the village
green, expresses a wishful erasure of these fears when it sets out to
imagine the possibility of a performance that is not an act of self-
display.

Chapter 2 of *Adam Bede* ("The Preaching") is a carefully framed set
piece in which George Eliot attempts to persuade her audience that
Dinah Morris is simultaneously a masterly public speaker and entirely
unconscious of how she produces her effects or how she appears in
the eyes of others. Dinah has three audiences: the Methodist faithful
who have come to hear her message, the skeptical villagers drawn by
the phenomenon of a woman preacher, and the upper-class
horseback-riding stranger through whom the entire episode is fo-
calized; all of them are moved and mesmerized by Dinah's preaching.
As both Ellen Moers and Nina Auerbach have pointed out, it is a
highly theatrical scene, with the whole wide landscape elaborately
established as a backdrop, the setting sun providing a kind of natural

stage lighting for Dinah's features.[7] Yet, apart from the sermon itself, the burden of the scene is the discovery that Dinah is not an actress, much less the provincial religious charlatan that the urban reader expects. That is why the focalizing stranger is necessary to George Eliot's purposes: he mediates between Dinah's religious language and the language of performance, allowing the narrator to sidestep her own promotion of Dinah's preaching.

The stranger is identified late in the novel when he fortuitously appears as the kindly magistrate Colonel Townley, who arranges Dinah's access to Hetty in prison (chap. 45). His position as an upper-class male authorizes her special status here as it does in the preaching scene, but his earlier role is also that of the drama critic, who is both "chained to the spot against his will" by Dinah's voice and an assessor of the whole, "interested in the course of her sermon, as if it had been the development of a drama." The artistic commentary on Dinah's power and the recording of her effect on her other audiences, are ascribed to him; these matters are noted as they systematically override the expectations he brings to the scene. Knowing "but types of Methodist—the ecstatic and the bilious," his first surprise is "the total absence of self-consciousness in her demeanour. . . . Dinah walked as simply as if she were going to market, and seemed as unconscious of her outward appearance as a little boy." This body is neither a sexual nor a performing body, as the narrative emphasizes again when Dinah is said to rely on "no change of attitude, no gesture." Only the face and the voice are the sources of Dinah's power, and both, it is asserted, modulate only in response to internal feeling, the voice sounding "like that of a fine instrument touched with the unconscious skill of musical instinct." When the observer-critic wonders whether Dinah has "the power of rousing their more violent emotions," that power appears as if from within, in her sudden paleness, the deepening of the circles under her eyes, and their "expression of appalled pity." Yet this riveting performance is not an imitation; she is, the narrative insists, "speaking directly from her own emotions." The uncalculated "unconscious skill" of this admirably supple speaker defies belief even when it is read as the emotional response of the sensitive stranger; but it is a good indication of the requirements of George Eliot's most romantic imagination: her fantasy moves toward the notion of a direct channel linking emotion and audience through the musical powers of voice, while the consciously performing body virtually fades away.

This fantasy is reinforced in Dinah's interview with Mr. Irwine, which repeats the the scenario in which the judging upper-class male's predispositions about female preachers are undone. In this dialogue, Dinah's womanliness is confirmed by her utter lack of ambition or embarrassment about her status as "a lovely young woman on whom men's eyes are fixed." She does not even lay claim to a calling, but talks of how "speech came to me without any will of my own"; her first preaching occurs when another preacher is unwell, and she finds herself faced with a waiting and needy audience (chap. 8). The notion that her audiences need her gift is her driving force, as George Eliot wished it to be her own. "If there is any truth in me that the world wants, nothing will hinder the world from drinking what it is athirst for," she wrote to John Blackwood after receiving a welcome fan letter about *Adam Bede* (3:241). If preaching, or writing, responds to a necessity, it cannot be regarded as a display of inappropriate ambition.

The moment Dinah is regarded as a sexual woman, however, the spell is broken. When Adam Bede looks at her as an object of interest, "Dinah, for the first time in her life, felt a painful self-consciousness" (chap. 11). Suddenly she apprehends herself as the object of another's gaze, and her public power wanes. In Dinah's case the final sacrifice of preaching is explained not as an inevitable concomitant of her marriage but as an attempt to avoid raising false ambition in less gifted women. "Most o' the women do more harm nor good with their preaching—they've not got Dinah's gift nor her sperrit," Adam explains to a skeptical Seth (Epilogue). The harm they do, apparently, is to display themselves in public without Dinah's power to override every predictable category of response; just so George Eliot worried that her own career might encourage the ambitions of lesser writers and fill the world with more bad literature. Thus she delivers a final muffled blow to the argument of the preaching scene staged many pages earlier, retreating to a warning that even the performer miraculously free of self-display may feed dangerously into the ambitions of the ordinary woman.

Dinah's successor is Mirah Cohen Lapidoth of *Daniel Deronda*, who performs with a similar lack of self-consciousness, though with a far more believable reliance on the professional training that has made her a serious artist with a practical dedication to music. Like Dinah but far more concretely, Mirah is surrounded by images of the stage to which she was bred; her virtue, too, consists in her miraculous ability to dispel theatricality in the very act of performance. All the drive that would place her carefully practiced art onstage is siphoned off into the figure of her disreputable father, in whose hands ambition takes the form of pimping; her quest for a mother defined as "good" guarantees her female immunity from theater life through a sort of genealogical magic. Linked in these ways to the fantasy that controls the figure of Dinah, Mirah nonetheless belongs to a significantly different era in her author's confrontation with ambition and performance. Once George Eliot had become unmistakably famous, her consciousness of these matters took new, though equally complex, forms.

Fame, with all its concomitant praise and applause, seemed to exacerbate rather than to allay Marian Lewes's confict about ambition. Beginning in the late 1860s and continuing through the writing of *Middlemarch* and *Daniel Deronda*, the letters express a new phase of anxiety about her own writing and a renewed intensity of criticism concerning the production and circulation of bad literature. Her suffering now took the form of testing herself against her earlier work and fears of repetition or "excessive writing." The new anxiety served an old purpose: to deny or at least depersonalize the now-apparent connection between her ambition and her high achievement. Because she had achieved financial success, she now had also to defend herself against the idea that she wrote only for fame and fortune: increasingly, she found rhetorical ways to disengage herself from the literary marketplace she had conquered.[8]

Her tendency to separate ambition from the act of writing was now subtly modified: ambition became allied with an economic view of literary activity. Her own writing, on the other hand, was legitimated by the belief that her audience needed her ideas; she represented herself to others as someone who could continue to write only so long as she had something new, true, and necessary to tell her readers. Too much writing could be read as a sign of ambition unmasked; were she to betray such a sign she might become one of those superfluous and immoral writers who, in her opinion, spread their disease through the marketplace. In her late note "Authorship" she deplores the connection between the "spread of instruction and the consequent struggles of an uneasy ambition," and she asks, "How or on what principle are we to find a check for that troublesome disposition to authorship arising from the spread of what is called Education, which turns a growing rush of vanity and ambition into this current?"[9]

Marian Lewes's personal comments on unnecessary writing reveal, however, that her moral standard served as a barrier against a complete recognition of her own position in the world of professional writing. When she told John Blackwood the news of Anthony Trollope's resignation from the Post Office in 1867, she added, "I cannot help being rather sorry. . . . it seems to me a thing greatly to be dreaded for a man that he should be in any way led to excessive writing" (4:392). Apart from its sidelong glance at Trollope's already immense productivity, this remark implies that Trollope will be led (further?) astray if he and his family become financially dependent on his novels; she is loath to promote Trollope from amateur to the professional writer she had always been. Some of her warnings were addressed to Alexander Main, the young man who wrote long letters of effusive praise and compiled the *Wise, Witty, and Tender Sayings* that repeated and recirculated George Eliot's sentences throughout the marketplaces of the realm. This fact seems to have been forgotten in her willingness to be the fountain of wisdom that Main made of her; as he was editing the first round of *Sayings* in 1871 she wrote to him of her difficulty in persuading herself to bring her books into print, "Especially as I have the conviction that excessive literary production is a social offense." As she struggled with *Middlemarch*, "I am haunted by the fear that I am only saying again what I have already said in better fashion. . . . Every one who contributes to the 'too much' of literature is doing grave social injury" (5:185, 212). The literal repetition and republication of what she had already said does not, it seems, qualify as "too much."

When she asked Blackwood in 1874 to do a collection of her already published short poems, the theme of overproduction recurs: the poems are a set of ideas she wants to propagate, "else I should forbid myself from adding to the mountainous heap of poetical collections" (6:26). Beginning *Daniel Deronda*, that most ambitious of tasks, produced similar images; she wrote to Elma Stuart of her doubts: "For our world is already sufficiently afflicted with needless books, and I count it a social offense to add to them" (6:113). She also wrote in her journal for January 13, 1875, of her "fear lest I may not be able to complete it so as to make a contribution to literature and not a mere addition to the heap of books" (6:116). The moral integrity of her whole career was dependent on a perpetual proof of regenerated talent; as she wrote to Blackwood in 1874, "To write indifferently after having written well—that is, from a true, individual store which makes a special contribution—is like an eminent clergyman's spoiling his reputation by lapses and neutralizing all the good he did before" (6:76). Her identification with the clergyman betrays the contradiction in her construction of herself as a writer who is personally disconnected from the life of her books: when she imagines herself as a moral teacher set apart from commercial and literary worlds, she acknowledges that reputation is connected with persons, not with books. If she ceased to practice what she preached even her early work would be retroactively tarnished. Yet for all its contradictions, her willingness to inhabit the role of sage may be read as her defense against the alternative: the part of the ambitious artist whose next performance would provide fuel for the volatile world of sellers and critics.

These attempts to disengage her work from a literary marketplace in which books were being transformed into commodities stemmed not only from a belief that her writing was "literature," but from the fear that her fame would be threatened by a world in which books were simply articles of consumption. After *Felix Holt* was published in 1866, George Eliot worried about "the enforced dearness of good books" (4:316), and Blackwood heard of her vexation that the three-volume edition had not sold out because libraries found them too expensive. "I sicken again," she continued, "with despondency under the sense that the most carefully written books lie, both outside and inside people's minds, deep undermost a heap of trash. I suppose the reason my 6/ editions are never on the railway stalls is partly of the same kind that hinders the free distribution of Felix. They are not so attractive to the majority as 'The Trail of the Serpent'; still a minority might sometimes buy them if they were there" (4:308–10). It is not difficult to see that her quite consistent representation of the book trade as "a heap of trash" with which she does not want to be identified is linked by inversion to her desire to imagine a whole trainload of commuters reading the works of George Eliot. It was in response to feelings of this sort that she and Lewes concocted the overwhelmingly successful marketing plan of publishing her next novel, *Middlemarch*, in eight separate parts over the course of a year.

George Eliot's somewhat ingenuous insistence on her exceptionality with regard to the literary marketplace may be connected with that other sort of exceptionality she claimed in the matter of gender definition. In 1867 she was led, both by John Stuart Mill's proposal of an amendment to enfranchise women and by Emily Davies' solicitation of her support for the founding of Girton College, to make statements about the desirability of serious educational opportunities for women.

The letters in which she recorded those statements are notable for their extreme caution and indirection. It was a subject on which she did not want to be pressed; she did not wish to confront in public the difference between her ideological commitment to the idea that men and women have naturally distinct spheres of influence and her own gender-crossing career.[10] In May 1867 she followed up on a dinner-party conversation in a letter to John Morley about the question of the franchise. "I repeat that I do not trust very confidently to my own impressions on this subject. The peculiarities of my own lot have caused me to have idiosyncrasies rather than an average judgment," she wrote (4:364). "I do sympathise with you most emphatically in the desire to see women socially elevated—educated equally with men, and secured as far as possible along with every other breathing creature from suffering the exercise of any unrighteous power," she wrote to Clementia Taylor, who was working for the suffrage. "But on this special point I am far from thinking myself an oracle" (4:366). Mrs. Taylor may well have been baffled by the immense generality of this "sympathy."[11] "There is no subject on which I am more inclined to hold my peace and learn than on the 'Women Question [*sic*],'" Marian wrote two years later to Mrs. Nassau Senior. "It seems to me to over-hang abysses, of which even prostitution is not the worst" (5:58). What exactly she might have meant by this extraordinary image of mass female fallenness is not so clear as her feeling that the "Women Question" was very dangerous territory indeed.[12] Her reliance on an essentially conservative view of "woman's mission" served, like her self-construction as a writer who transcended the literary marketplace, to buffer her against the connection between her womanhood and the immense literary ambition that any audience so inclined might read in her life and work.

Marian's argument for the distinct function of men and women was based on physical and physiological difference: in her view women suffer bodily more than men, and therefore they acquire a compensatory "moral evolution" that underlies their "special moral influence" through love and affection. The experience of living in the body is, she argued, "the deepest and subtlest sort of education that life gives" (4:364, 467–68). When it came to higher education, she was willing to support it as a means to unite men and women in their moral apprehension of the duties of life (5:58). "Complete unity and sympathy can only come by women having opened to them the same store of acquired truth or beliefs as men have, so that their grounds of judgment may be as far as possible the same," she told Emily Davies, as part of a letter of advice about how to represent the Girton College project to a male audience (4:468). But her support was hedged by the anxiety that women might use their education for revolutionary purposes, instead of recognizing "the great amount of social unproductive labour that needs to be done by women, and which is now either not done at all or done wretchedly" (4:425). She did not allow herself to express her anxiety directly until some years later, when she was firmly established as an icon. Emily Davies reported on a visit in September 1876 during which George Eliot worried about containing young women's ambition: "She hoped that my friend would teach the girls not to think too much of political measures for improving society—as leading away from individual efforts to be good, I understood her to mean. . . . She said, was there not a great deal among girls of wanting to do some great thing and thinking it not worthwhile to do anything because they cannot do that? I said there might be, but I had not come across it" (6:287).

George Eliot's rather pathetic anxiety that young women might feel as she herself had felt—though presumably with less justification—was a reflex of her anxiety about the publication of her own ambition. She was right when she wrote to John Morley that "the peculiarities of my own lot have caused me to have idiosyncrasies rather than an average judgment," although she was unwilling to spell out what those idiosyncracies were. She implied simply that she was an exception and went on to announce her conviction that the goal of human evolution was "more clearly discerned distinction of function" between men and women "(allowing always for exceptional cases of individual organization)" (4:364). Such an individual organization is apparently a kind of biological condition, one that remains outside the normal evolutionary process: if the "unpromising woman-child" had turned into a very promising artist, such adaptations were not necessary for female children who turned more ordinarily into socialized women. That was the way she wished to situate her peculiarities in relation to the subject of women in the abstract. In the imaginative work of her last decade, however, George Eliot began to probe the dangerous subjects her social dialogues had refused to engage.

The new phase of anxiety that accompanied George Eliot's success at midcareer also generated her most searching representations of ambitious concert singers, the poem "Armgart" (1870) and the many-sided investigation of musical careers in *Daniel Deronda* (1876). The question of ambition preoccupied her during the period of poetry writing between 1866 and 1870 and led finally to the new beginning of *Middlemarch*, a novel about ambitions that fail. Several of the poems are about music; "The Legend of Jubal" and the minor poem "Stradivarius" specifically pursue aspects of the relationships among ambition, fame, and artistry. The portraits of Armgart and Alcharisi are particularly remarkable achievements, however, because they contain, in tensely compressed forms, a full range of the conflicts George Eliot was inclined to suppress in her representations of herself.

"Armgart" is the only poem George Eliot wrote in fully dramatic form. Its four major voices—two female, two male—clash in unmediated conflict throughout, as though their parts had been written for a vocal quartet singing passionate and argumentative music. The absence of an explaining, moralizing narrative voice may account for the special strength of the poem, which Henry James found "the best thing, to our sense, of the four" major poems collected in *The Legend of Jubal and Other Poems*.[13] The dramatic form certainly creates the impression that George Eliot was calling into confrontation the most important voices in her consciousness. The poem opens on the moment of success: Armgart has just achieved her first operatic triumph singing the male role of Gluck's Orpheus in some unnamed European capital. Her complete embrace of art, ambition, and fame celebrates fearlessly what her author feared to display, but the form of the poem represents that embrace as dangerous: success is followed a year later by a diminution of voice, experienced by Armgart as a loss of identity and a cause for suicidal despair. The loss of voice plot, repeated in *Daniel Deronda*, was the formal equivalent of George Eliot's anxiety that she could not go on writing as well as she had, that she could not sustain her career in a way that would make a genuine contribution to literature.

But the poem does much more than this chastening form might suggest. Armgart is portrayed as a keenly intelligent woman, capable of seeing and resisting the ideologies of womanhood levied against her by both male and female voices: the voice of Graf Dornberg, the aristocratic suitor who loves her fame because he wishes to appropriate and subdue it to womanly maternity, and the voice of Walpurga, the lamed cousin who plays the role of submissive wife to Armgart's glorious career. In the end Armgart's independent survival is assured when she links her mission to that of her musical mentor, the failed composer Leo. The shedding of ambition enforced by the poem is succeeded not by a recognition of common womanhood but by a selfless withdrawal and dedication to the future of art.[14]

The Armgart of the first scene, just returned from her triumph, speaks arias of self-adulation in which art, audience, fame, and the merging of the self with a larger grandeur of creation are all mixed together in wonderfully romantic rhetoric. Her ambition is forthright and egotistical, although it is clothed in the belief—a version of George Eliot's own argument to herself—that she is rich with deserved praise because she is a blessing to her audiences; she compares herself to "the summer's sun, that ripens corn / Or now or never," and declares fame "the benignant strength of One, transformed / To joy of Many."[15] From the start, however, Armgart's account of herself is doubled by Leo's corrective commentary, as though the ambitious and the chastising voices in George Eliot were singing a duet. Leo, like the stranger in *Adam Bede*, gives his equally proud account of the performance from the vantage point of the audience, but he consistently chides Armgart for actions that betray the prima donna rather than the artist. He objects to an additional trill—the musical ornament that the young Mary Ann Evans had worried over—as a sign of pandering to the audience; he accuses her of loving the jewel bestowed by a royal patron and of harboring a very down-to-earth sense of ambition. She happily admits to it all and imagines a life of spreading fame and glory, while he reminds her that the first heady sensation of triumph comes but once. Although Leo is assigned the case for separating art and ambition, there is a sense of camaraderie and teasing which mingles the voices of the two artists in an exchange from which the others are necessarily excluded.

The exchange between Armgart and the Graf which occupies the long second scene is, by contrast, pure deadlock. The Graf's is the patriarchal voice, the voice that tells "Mr. Gilfil's Love Story" and at least part of *Adam Bede*; his first images of Armgart reveal his kinship with the earlier narrator: "Poor human-hearted singing-bird! She bears / Caesar's ambition in her delicate breast / And nought to still it with but quivering song!" (73). He offers a number of cynical arguments—notably that artistic promise wins more praise than a life of steady achievement—which Armgart immediately sees through and rejects. His vow to marry her and respect her art is clearly undermined by his espousal of the most conventional ideology of woman's place as a mother, as well as by his disappearance when he hears of

Armgart's loss of voice. Armgart's dissection of his promises is the most compact and efficient attack on patriarchal arguments to be found in George Eliot's work—and it is fully supported by the plot of the poem. The Graf is unmasked as one of those who participate in nineteenth-century diva worship as a way of cherishing the fantasy that he might increase the value of his own rank by mastering the artist. Yet his serpentlike arguments are part of George Eliot too, not only because they are allied with her own earlier work and her proclaimed ideology of gender but also because they feed the fear about sustaining her power that plagued her as she was writing the poem. "Have you thought / How you will bear the poise of eminence / With dread of sliding?" the Graf asks Armgart, offering her shelter from "striving in the race" (94). Four years later Marian misquoted the line to Blackwood as she agonized over the composition of *Deronda*: "As to confidence in the work to be done I am somewhat in the condition suggested to Armgart, 'How will you bear the poise of eminence, With dread of falling?'" (6:75).

The Armgart of the first two scenes is a counterimage, a woman immune to the doubts, scruples, and patriarchal sympathies that assailed her creator. Her canny feminist defense suggests a larger pattern in George Eliot's work: the feminist voice may be clearly heard when it opposes a voiced and represented patriarchal argument (as it does, for example, in the "Prelude" to *Middlemarch* or in the critique of the male-dominated educational system in *The Mill on the Floss*), but George Eliot cannot structure a work on positively feminist principles that would threaten the arrangements of gender in the social order itself. Even though Armgart is right to resist the Graf, the poem takes an inevitable turn to destroy the triumph of her success.

A year later, her voice diminished after a serious illness, she plunges into the despair and terror of one who has made a great sacrifice only to find that it was made for nothing. Her fear of becoming ordinary—"the millionth woman in superfluous herds"—is deepened by the terror of being imprisoned in the strength of her passions. Early in the poem we hear of Armgart's belief that singing is a "channel for the soul" that would otherwise burn forests and sympathize with murderesses; she believes what the narrator of "Gilfil" understands about Caterina, that music is a transformative and legitimate channel for female emotional violence (75). Now she feels the doctor's "cures" as "a lava-mud to crust and bury me, / Yet hold me living in a deep, deep tomb, / Crying unheard for ever!" (111–12).

Her audience has already forgotten her, another singer is ready to take over her roles, and she is left to contemplate the horror of the ordinary woman's lot with the passion of an extraordinary sensibility. The horror is deeply felt and scornfully expressed; Armgart is no less single-minded about it than she was in celebrating her earlier glory. She is to George Eliot what song is to her, a channel for the direct expression of stifled but volcanic feeling; like the melodrama of opera, the poem allows George Eliot to dramatize strong versions of single emotions as her prose narratives never do.

Inevitably, the voice of conscience rises up to confront Armgart with the predictable George Eliot doctrines: Walpurga's voice of common womanhood sounds the themes of sympathy for hidden sorrows and the consolation of fellowship, and accuses Armgart of egotism and the betrayal of other women, reminding her that "noble rebellion lifts a common load" (131). But although Armgart learns something from this voice, she does not succumb to its temptations to guilt and sacrifice; they are the female obverse of the patriarchal ideology she rejected in the Graf. Instead, she dismisses Walpurga abruptly when Leo walks in, and she translates Walpurga's ideas into sympathy and identification not with other women but with her fellow artist. Thus the poem makes a significant turn at its end—a turn to the special fellowship of art.

For the first time Armgart questions Leo about his own career, learns of his failed ambitions as a composer, and identifies her loss with his. To his delight she decides not to make a career as an actress but to become a teacher carrying on Leo's tradition of musical training. As he has done, she will bury her losses and invest her talent in a new generation, eschewing the summer's sun of performance for the slow sowing of other futures. And in recognition that Walpurga is a person with her own desires, she will move back to Freiburg, Walpurga's beloved hometown. The sacrifice of ambition is finally made in the name of art and in honor of two personal affections. The voices of Caterina Sarti and Dinah Morris were domesticated and reinscribed in the patriarchal order, but this poem embraces the life of the uprooted, the marginal, the displaced, and celebrates the non-genealogical continuity of musical tradition. Stripped of its performative gloss, the art of music becomes an idealized alternative to empty aristocratic display.

The portrait of Armgart, like the one of Alcharisi, makes a visible link between female ambition and female anger; it blatantly dramatizes George Eliot's lurking suspicion that feminine ambition is based on an angry or overpassionate rejection of the ordinary woman's life. Yet in its characteristic move to disconnect ambition and fame from the practice of the artist's life, the portrait is akin to the stories of the patient male figures in "The Legend of Jubal" (1869) and "Stradivarius" (1873). The latter is a slight poem, based on the idea that Stradivarius's soul as well as Bach's and Joachim's is expressed in a performance of the "Chaconne"; the always invisible violin maker is imagined in dialogue with a cynical painter, defending his long life of painstaking good work against the lures of easy routes to fame. "Jubal," however, is a full-blown allegory of the artist's life.

After he invents music and teaches it to his own tribe, Jubal goes off on an ambitious quest for new experience and inspiration, "sowing music" for earth's civilizations as he goes (*Jubal*, 28). His quest presses on to new landscapes until he arrives at the ocean that symbolizes the end of his long creative life; then he turns home, yearning to be greeted and welcomed by his own people. He arrives in the midst of a festival in which his name is celebrated in communal song, but he is unrecognized, beaten with flutes, and cast aside as an impostor; his "name" and his mere bodily self are entirely dissociated: "The immortal name of Jubal filled the sky, / While Jubal lonely laid him down to die" (38). After this climactic couplet the poem turns to consolation; as he fades into an anonymous grave Jubal has a vision of a heavenly audience, a "gaze" or "face" that sees his life whole, validates its sacrifices, and renews his dedication to the spirit of song. But George Eliot's fear that fame might be alienated from a personal sense of achievement or recognition could hardly be more tellingly expressed. Jubal's death is the tragic vision of the very situation on which she had always insisted in her career: the separation of the performing body from the impersonal dissemination of the work.

Daniel Deronda places the troubling questions of ambition and performance at center stage. The novel breaks open the associations latent in George Eliot's earlier work, making a kaleidoscope of repetition and variation in which the many facets of the problem become brilliantly visible. Mirah Lapidoth's story recapitulates the most conventional Victorian idea that stage life for women is exploitation and prostitution; her rescue extracts the integrity of her talent—her singing voice—from its theatrical trappings. In the story of Gwendolen Harleth, George Eliot for the first time gives her sympathetic attention to the tragedy of performative ambition in an unexceptional woman.[16] In the portrait of Leonora Charisi, the association of female ambition and rage is specified as a direct resistance to the power of the father; the diva is clothed in black and flame-colored purgatorial robes of fear as she continues to the end to defend the "right" of her talent against the ghost of the father she defied.[17] All the stories contribute to a searching investigation of performance as a profession, and of its costs. The new directness represents not so much an ideological change as a kind of self-analysis, an articulation of the strands of feeling and thought which had been implicit in George Eliot's representation of performance from the beginning. The investigation generates at the same time a narrative theatricality and a reactively harsh plot structure that punishes and exorcises the will to perform.

In the simplest sense, *Daniel Deronda* contrasts the virtues of the antitheatrical and unambitious—Daniel and Mirah—to the torments of the damned, the performers Gwendolen and Alcharisi. Both Daniel and Mirah reject the stage despite their singing talents, associating it conventionally with illegitimacy, marginality, exploitation, and the ordinary (or Christian) social construction of Jewishness.[18] Mirah can act no one but herself, cannot see what is "theatrical" about dressing as a poor Jewess singing to rich Christians when it is "all real," and is unambitious for anything but the recovery of love (chap. 39). Daniel's ambition is on hold, blunted (while in training for its Zionist destiny) by his feminine capacity to energize others' lives rather than his own. But the narrative itself makes no such easy division between the stage and social life. The novel opens on the act of Daniel's gaze trained on Gwendolen at the gaming table and becomes, as Alexander Welsh has said, a drama of watchers and performers which extends into the intimacy of marriage.[19] Conversations, widely spaced and tensely set, are theatrical dialogues conducted against a narrative backdrop of prolonged and secret introspection. Both Gwendolen and the former diva Princess Halm-Eberstein live the horror of acting their daily and domestic lives. The meeting of Deronda and his mother is a command performance that undoes his long-cherished fantasy of sympathetic reunion. Even the love story of Daniel and Mirah is, as the Princess scornfully calls it, "poetry—fit to last through an opera night" (chap. 53). The fantastic tale begins as Daniel's voice, singing Rossini, conjures up "an impersonation of the misery he was unconsciously giving voice to" and enters "the inner world" of the suicidal Mirah; when he rescues her she returns the words of the opera to him (chap. 17). The story comes to its long-delayed climax in the confessional coloratura of Alcharisi, which releases Daniel from the spell of arrested motion and allows him to take up his love and his work. The operatic nature of the whole tale self-consciously draws even the political mythology of the novel into the realm of art.

It is perhaps just this narrative conflation of the theatrical and the ordinary that necessitates George Eliot's disciplinary strictures about the professional rigor of the artist's life. Klesmer's education of Gwendolen draws a strict line between middle-class self-display in the drawing room and the work of the professional actress or musician. Through him George Eliot elaborates her fear that theatrical success might inspire unwarranted ambition in the untalented woman; at the same time she produces an ideal of the artist's life which hovers as a redemptive possibility above the image of the theater as a profitable showing of the female body.

Gwendolen's theatricality has, however, a far deeper resonance than appears in the scenes of Klesmer's tutelage. Her story focuses directly on the dangerous slippage between performance and secret, unwomanly passion which had always been an implicit part of George Eliot's resistance to the idea of display before an audience. The theme had emerged in *Middlemarch* in the story of the actress Laure, who intentionally kills her actor husband on stage when her foot slips during a dagger scene. In this story of a mediocre actress George Eliot had conflated the alternatives—music or violence, music instead of violence—that she had established in Caterina Sarti and Armgart; Laure's rage against ordinary marriage is both expressed and concealed within the fiction of performance. The compressed parable of *Middlemarch* flowers into the story of Gwendolen, and not only in the developed story of matrimonial murder. George Eliot's fantasy of performance as an accidental revelation of the self's darkest secrets comes fully to light when Gwendolen's "imitation of acting" the role of Hermione is interrupted (chap. 6).

Gwendolen's character emerges from that part of George Eliot which had feared that her ambitions were nothing but a ravenous desire for praise. Like an embodiment of that desire, Gwendolen unashamedly arranges her life in order to display herself to audiences and elicit admiration. The Offendene theatricals in which Gwendolen plays Hermione's statue coming to life are arranged simply for the purpose of bodily self-display, but they climax instead in a moment of self-revelatory terror. When the panel accidentally flies open to reveal the picture "of the dead face and the fleeing figure," Gwendolen freezes "like a statue into which a soul of Fear had entered." Gwendolen reveals herself as the antithesis of Hermione's redemptive womanhood; at the moment when Hermione melts into love, she freezes into fear. Klesmer, the touchstone, sees something genuine and protects it, pretending that the very convincing moment of terror is part of the performance. Gwendolen is mortified, yet the "fits of spiritual dread" she is ashamed of having others see are, the narrator suggests, her only redemptive possibility, the only "fountain of awe within" a character too terrified to love.

The narrative treatment of this incident makes a direct connection between Gwendolen's need for an audience and her existential condition. She is threatened by solitude or by vast landscapes in which she senses "an immeasurable existence aloof from her"; her sense of assertion and power is dependent on having "human eyes and ears about her." The image of the dead face and the fleeing figure, is on the one hand, an active dread of abandonment and death, on the other, a prefiguration of her guilt at the drowning of Grandcourt, which—in the narrative logic pervading the novel—makes the later event a necessary fulfillment of the internal condition. George Eliot's understanding of Gwendolen's need for performance and praise to ward off the ghosts of deep childhood fears is a self-understanding, a reclamation of her own adolescent harshness. Yet the novel demands that the heroine be cured of that need in the most extreme terms: her appetite for admiration is replaced, through the endurance of near bigamy and near murder, by an unending torment of remorse.

Gwendolen's punishments for the crime of defining her life through the gaze of the other are prolonged and strenuous; yet in her character George Eliot is willing to define and explore an existential condition she had never broached before. Similarly, she is ready to expose in the words of Alcharisi a stunningly direct connection of artistic ambition with antipatriarchal rage, but only by condemning her to purgatorial suffering. Alcharisi endures the power of the patriarchal as it works within the psyche of the rebellious daughter, a power that causes her to cut short a rightfully successful artistic career. Her terror of losing her voice, rather than a genuine loss, is what sends her to the shelter of an aristocratic marriage after some "forgetful" lapses in intonation; the terror is a measure of her absolute need to be preeminent on stage, to maintain the glory of her talent, against her father's will and against the knowledge that she has given her

child away for the sake of her ambitions.[20] The stress of family betrayal which pressures Alcharisi's stage career sheds some light on
Marian Lewes's own demand that her books be incomparable to other
writing in the literary marketplace; by the time *Daniel Deronda* was in
the works she had on her mind not only the family rejection that
resulted from her irregular marriage with Lewes but the deaths of
two stepsons who had been shipped off to South Africa to make their
colonial fortunes as best they could.[21] The self-punishment of Alcharisi's unloving marriage in exile attests to the burden of female
guilt temporarily allayed only by the guarantee of a world-class talent.
It is not her only punishment. Alcharisi spends a good portion of her
time with Daniel defending her choices against her father and her
son, only to have Daniel become an embodiment of his grandfather
before her eyes; caught in the patriarchal myth of motherhood, Daniel cannot, for all his sympathy, understand or condone her failure to
love him.

George Eliot's persistent story of the frailty of a life dependent on
fame is rewritten here: the physical loss of voice which breaks Armgart's career becomes in Alcharisi the threat of psychological subver-
sion from within. Arrested—as George Eliot had feared for herself—
in midcareer, Leonora Charisi becomes the Princess Halm-Eberstein,
condemned to acting the domestic loves she does not feel. Because
she has built her career on the rejection of domestic ties, she must
now live out her domestic life as though she were on stage. Unlike
Armgart, she has constructed the necessity for this alternative
through her very adherence to the patriarchal imperatives she defies;
she punishes herself endlessly for her defiance, but she is unable to
give it up. Even her "submission," the passing of her father's tradition
to Daniel, is theatrically constructed as the necessity "to obey something tyrannic" that seems to come from outside herself (chap. 51).

Read from the inside, Alcharisi's life story is a moving commentary
on the immense psychological difficulty of sustaining an "unwomanly" artistic life that denies and defies its past determinants.
Read from Daniel's perspective, as the writing of the scenes demands,
the theatricality of Alcharisi's self-presentation is, if not horrifying, at
least sufficiently alienating to suggest George Eliot's own difficulty in
containing this exaggerated specter of herself. Alcharisi's understanding of others as characters in plays, her self-proclaimed inability
to love, her apparent pleasure in acting the role of the woman tortured by ghosts returning from her past to force her submission—all

this melodrama collects, sharpens, and finally exorcises the fascination with theatricality which pervades *Daniel Deronda*. When Alcharisi exits, the exorcism is complete.[22] The story of ambition fueled by rage and subverted by guilt hands the victory over to the father, whose will is more than fulfilled in Daniel's acceptance of his inherited task. In the end Alcharisi becomes just what she had feared, a link between male generations.

In the narrative I have been tracing, the special importance of *Daniel Deronda* lies in its indication of George Eliot's deepening ability to imagine the psychological determinants of her own proscriptions, desires, and fears. If her own high ambition was fired by a fear of repetition, it acted by finding its newness in a more scourging exploration of long-familiar issues. To the end, however, she refused to make a direct association between the achievement of her life and the force of her own ambition. John Cross represents her response when he urged her, after their marriage and the end of her career as a novelist, to write an autobiography: "'The only thing I should care much to dwell on would be the absolute despair I suffered from of ever being able to achieve anything. No one could ever have felt greater despair, and a knowledge of this might be a help to some other struggler'—adding, with a smile, 'but, on the other hand, it might only lead to an increase of bad writing.'"[23] The ambition is fully present in its negative form of despair; the self-aggrandizement is there too, in the claim to singular depths. The justification of her writing as an art that fulfilled a need in others comes into play for a moment, raised only to be quenched by the old prohibitive fear, turned against the fledgling ambitions of others. George Eliot was ready to teach others to suffer but not to aspire. On its face, her statement recapitulates the story of Dinah Morris, who withdraws from preaching so that she will not stir lesser talents to unjustified ambition. In its depths, it carries the stamp of Alcharisi, who could not justify her life unless there was no talent like her own.

SEVEN

George Eliot's Stepsons

Sons are heavy hostages to the powers at work in
our lives.
—Marian Evans Lewes to John Blackwood,
August 5, 1869

On July 24, 1859, sixteen-year-old Charles Lee Lewes began an important new correspondence. Full of a sense of the occasion, he supplied himself—aided perhaps by his headmaster's wife—with an elaborately decorated letter paper, edged with birds, flowers, and curlicues printed in red, blue and gold. "Dear Mother," he began in his well-formed schoolboy's hand, "Thank you very much for the watch."[1]

Eleven days earlier Charles and his two younger brothers, Thornton Arnott and Herbert Arthur Lewes, had heard for the first time that their parents' marriage had been broken for five years and that when they returned to England from the Hofwyl School in Switzerland, where they had been placed since 1856, they would be under the care of their father and the friend they had heard of as "Miss Evans"—who, it turned out, was none other than George Eliot, author of *Adam Bede*, the celebrated new novel they had been eagerly waiting to read.[2] Of this critical visit to his children, George Henry Lewes wrote in his journal, "I unburthened myself about Agnes to them. They were less distressed than I had anticipated and were delighted to hear about Marian. This of course furnished the main topic for the whole day." It is not clear whether he told them that the four children at home in Kensington with Agnes Lewes, to whom they had been sending greetings and kisses in their letters, were not their full siblings.[3] It is apparent, however, that he wished to prepare his sons as fully as possible for "the domestic changes, and future arrangements" (3:116) and that one of his missions was to establish the beginnings of a dialogue between them and Marian which would also prepare her to assume the role of their stepmother when Charles left school the following year. Since Agnes was "Mama," Marian was to be "Mother," and the boys were to write to her as if she were a person they knew and loved.

Perhaps this seemed a less bizarre task to them because they had for years been writing to adults whom they almost never saw. George Henry Lewes visited his sons at Hofwyl once a year for three or four days; their mother had never been there, and they did not make visits home. In any case, Charles's first letter to his new "mother" perfectly fulfills his father's wishes. As an aspiring pianist, he could write to Marian about their shared interest in music, and he filled his long and touching first letter with observations that would help her to know him through that topic. Attentive as he was to the adults around him, Charles may even have been thinking of Marian's unconventional gender position when he wound up his letter by observing "how curious it was that I had never heard of a woman's playing the violin, have you heard of one? That they don't play on wind-instruments I can well understand, but I don't see why they should not play the violin, as well as piano, guitarre [*sic*] or harp." And he signed off: "Give three kisses to Father, one for each of us, and tell him to give you the same for us. I remain, dear Mother, Yours affectionately, Charles Lewes." The language of family affection, fostered in his earlier correspondence with his father, is transferred wholesale to Marian Lewes.

Her prompt answer to his letter attempts to cement the musical bonds, though it reads as a painstaking invention of a new parental voice in a vacuum. "I look forward to playing duets with you as one of my future pleasures," she begins, "and if I am able to go on working, I hope we shall afford to have a fine grand piano" (3:125–27). She wishes that she were one of the ladies who do play the violin so that they could play sonatas together. Her strongest impulse in this uncomfortable situation, however, is to establish a carefully moral voice, one that wishes to control the incursion of unformed young manhood into her life by subjecting it to her adult perspective. Charles had been saving up for a watch throughout the previous year, but she has sent him one as a present "because you had earned it by making good use of these precious years at Hofwyl. It is a great comfort to your

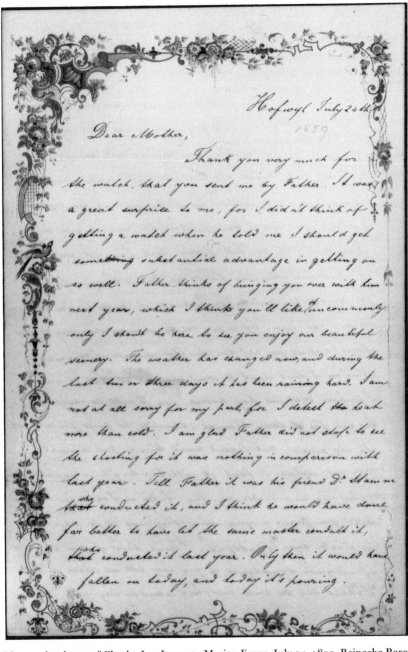

Hofwyl July 24th
1859

Dear Mother,

Thank you very much for
the watch, that you sent me by Father. It was
a great surprise to me, for I did n't think of
getting a watch when he told me I should get
something substantial advantage in getting on
so well. Father thinks of bringing you over with him
next year, which I think you 'll like uncommonly
only I shan't be here to see you enjoy our beautiful
scenery. The weather has changed now, and during the
last two or three days it has been raining hard. I am
not at all sorry for my part, for I detest the heat
more than cold. I am glad Father did not stop to see
the shooting for it was nothing in comparison with
last year. Tell Father it was his friend Dr Stamm
that who conducted it, and I think he would have done
far better to have let the same master conduct it,
that who conducted it last year. Only then it would have
fallen on today, and today it's pouring.

Manuscript, letter of Charles Lee Lewes to Marian Evans, July 24, 1859. Beinecke Rare
Book and Manuscript Library, Yale University.

father and me to think of that, for we, with our grave old heads, cannot help talking very often of the need our boys will have for all sorts of good qualities and habits in making their way through this difficult life. It is a world, you perceive, in which crossbows *will* be *launisch* sometimes and frustrate the skill of excellent marksmen— how much more of lazy bunglers?" She was referring to Charles's complaint that the crossbow had acted up and prevented him from getting any prizes in the annual Hofwyl archery competition; the slightest hint of immaturity in Charles's letter had brought out the moralizing narrator in her. The self-critical and obedient Charles could not have failed to absorb some sense of the anxiety with which Marian Lewes looked forward to the task of helping to establish three teenage boys in productive and respectable lives.

The boys' apparent willingness to call her "Mother" without further ado was not met easily either. Once again, in the year of name changes and name challenges, she faced the dilemma of how to sign herself. "Remember you are always giving a pleasure when you write to your loving mother," she wrote rather stiffly to Charles, and signed, "Marian Lewes." Her second letter to him (October 7, 1859) ends with many quotation marks: "Kisses 'over the water to Charlie!' from His affectionate 'Mother' Marian Lewes" (3:179). By November 26, however, she had relaxed her letter-writing style and found her signature: "Your loving Mutter" (3:215–16). The translation into German—the chief language of the Lewes sons during their school years in Switzerland—seems adequately to have represented the "translation" of actual motherhood into the pseudostepmotherhood of Marian Lewes; it was to remain the name by which Charles—and the others intermittently—addressed her.

Begun as she was reimagining her own childhood through *The Mill on the Floss* on one hand, and waging war with Liggins on the other, the new parental correspondence was a prelude to "a new epoch" (3:232) in Marian Lewes's life. The decade of the 1860s was framed by the crises of her stepmotherhood. Charles came home to live and find a career in July 1860; Thornton also left school and required re-settlement in that year. In 1863 both Thornie and Bertie posed serious questions of vocation and demanded a great deal of parental arrangement and worry. In 1869 Thornie returned from colonial life in Natal and died of spinal tuberculosis in Marian's arms. These three intense periods of crisis were offset by periods of calm, and by the wholly successful domestication of Charles Lewes in the Eliot-

Lewes household. For Marian Lewes, parental responsibility offered both a new sense of legitimacy and a new source of guilt and anxiety. She could vindicate her womanhood through her family and through the care she took to bind Charles to her in affection and honor; yet her inability to do for Thornie and Bertie what she could do for Charles acquainted her intimately with the experience of parental failure.

Marian Lewes's struggle to answer to the demands of her stepmotherhood and the transformations of her parental experience into fiction are the subjects of this chapter.[4] *The Mill on the Floss* has always been understood as the last of the fictions to be generated directly from her provincial childhood, but its publication in 1860 also marked a farewell to little sisterhood and a reorientation in Marian's experience of family life. After it, new perspectives and new characters enter the George Eliot repertoire. Substitute parents begin to populate every novel, and young male characters are cast less frequently as charmingly feckless sexual seducers (along lines inspired by John Chapman) than as troubled or restless seekers who need vocations and help from parental figures or morally guiding women.[5] The quite various characters and experiences that Charles, Thornton, and Herbert Lewes brought into their parents' lives are part of the story and help to account for the many versions in which George Eliot imagined the young man's crisis and turned it about in scrutiny, revision, or compensation.

Agnes Jervis Lewes and George Henry Lewes had five children, three of whom survived: Charles Lee, born November 24, 1842, Thornton Arnott, born April 14, 1844, and Herbert Arthur, born July 10, 1846. By 1856 the Lewes boys had a little brother and two sisters whose father was Thornton Hunt; in 1857, while they were at Hofwyl, Agnes bore her third and last daughter to Hunt.[6] During the spring of 1856, when Charles was thirteen, Lewes was searching for a good school, perhaps one in Germany, which would also remove his boys from contact with both his and Agnes's extramarital relationships. Marian's Warwickshire connections were called upon for help. Her old friend John Sibree turned down a request to be a temporary tutor, but Sara Hennell produced a circular for the Hofwyl School near Bern, Switzerland, an establishment for international students run on modern secular lines by Dr. Eduard Müller. Although Charles once observed rather wistfully in a letter to his father that they were

the only English boys at the school who were actually from England
(July 15, 1857), their letters show that the boys' sense of exile was
largely overcome by the excellence of the school, the wide range of
indoor and outdoor activities, the many school excursions, and the
parental care afforded by Dr. Müller and his wife. After the two older
boys had been at Hofwyl for a year, Lewes took Bertie to join them in
the summer of 1857. Marian reported to Sara Hennell that he had
"found the boys more improved than he had ventured to hope in one
year. . . . their dispositions seem to be under a favourable influence. . . . Altogether, we are very thankful for Hofwyl" (2:383). For
four years, she could rest in the knowledge that substitute parents
were doing their job. Hofwyl accommodated the boys even during
school vacations. They sometimes complained that there was nothing
to do in August, and they looked forward eagerly to Lewes's rare
visits, but they did not openly challenge the rule that they were not to
come home. It is possible that they had their own theories about what
went on there, but they wrote letters as though they assumed an intact
family with a peripatetic father.

During those years Marian Lewes's acquaintance with her stepsons'
characters was formed in the same way as our own must be—through
the letters they wrote to their parents at Agnes Lewes's address.
Charles, the responsible eldest child, comes through his pages as an
increasingly attractive, modest, disciplined, and domestic character.
Though not particularly quick to learn, he made up for it by working
hard and consistently at his studies and especially at his beloved piano.[7] His letters reveal a propensity to systematic listing and a fidelity
to accuracy in fact; an early letter to Agnes reports on the boys' play at
soldiers with the equipment left in the school's attic by a previous
generation of students, and goes ploddingly through the line of boys
in their military formations (8:165); another one, to George Henry
Lewes, lists in order the new row of animal cages in which boys kept
pets or fowl (March 29, 1857). Concert programs and excursion itin-
eraries are reported in full detail. On July 25, 1858, he corrects
Lewes's "mistake in saying 18 years ago you were a bachelor and in
Vienna because next November I shall be 16 and the baby before me
would have been 17 and therefore you could not been 'a gay young
bachelor then.' You must 18 years ago have just been married or at the
time you speak [of] a 'sighing lover.'" Lewes might have learned something from this passage about his children's attentiveness to his personal affairs, but the moment is particularly characteristic of Charles's

consciousness of domestic life, marriage, and children, as well as his occasional mildly ironic humor.

Charles's letters suggest his close attachment to his mother and his interest in women. He tended to address his early letters to Agnes; whereas Thornie wrote for his father, Charles excelled in reporting for motherly eyes details about clothes or bedding and was quite conscious of what his mother might like to hear. Writing to his father on July 15, 1857, Charles tells him, "Many things have been occurring this and last month which I thought then of writing, but those are more sorts of things Mama likes to hear." He yearns for Lewes's arrival, but adds, "It's a great pity Mama can't also come. That *would* be pleasure!!!" Mrs. Müller figures in his letters; he is happier when she is present. And as he comes to his last year at Hofwyl, one learns from his letters, as one could not from his brothers', that there are girls in the world.

His own nurturing impulses were expressed in his attention to Bertie's experience of Hofwyl. Before Bertie arrived, Charles considered how well Bertie would take to Hofwyl, where he "would be able to indulge in his favourite sports, such as gardening, fishing, soldiers etc. etc." (8:165), but he also worried that Bertie would need an interpreter because his French was inadequate (July 15, 1857). Later Charles defended his backward younger brother, reporting on another student who "reads infinitely worse than Bertie" (April 21, 1858) and admiring his natural talent in gymnastics and piano playing. "Fancy though at the age of nearly 13 his spelling his own name Arthur, Artheer! I think otherwise he's learning to spell pretty well although I occasionally hear of tremendous mistakes having been committed by him" (April 17, 1859). Charles's own English syntax, like that of his brothers, occasionally showed signs of German construction; their instruction in various languages required the boys to switch back and forth between English and German script as well as syntax.

Charles's absorption of his parents' anxieties included a meticulous awareness of money and economy. By January 1858 he was lecturing Agnes Lewes not only about her failure to answer his letters and his fear of letters getting lost between Hofwyl and England but about preventing those at home from sending packages to them through the mail, "for it costs much to [*sic*] much. If we want any thing we must buy it in Bern or go without it." Charles, a money saver, lists what francs he has, and mildly chides his brothers for their feckless ways: "Thornie at the end of the month has never got a sou for he spends the pocket money on grub"; Bertie's "soon went in rabbits with which he soon got disgusted" (8:191). In his first letter to Marian Lewes he proposed that they go halves on building a library of piano music, providing her with a detailed account of how much various editions cost. Although she could assure him of the likelihood that her work would finance a new grand piano, she would have found Charles's responsibility in matters of small sums as compatible with her own inclinations as his love of music. His veracity was also capable of good-humored sharing in the new family secret of George Eliot's identity. "Isn't the author of A.B. not yet discovered, Mrs. Empson told me that a gentleman in the train told her it was certain it was a lady, and Mrs. Crookenden had a notion that it was very possibly my mother and asked me if my mother had never written books. I of course told her 'no,' which was 1/2|1/2 true" (November 20, 1859). Charles's willingness to play around with the idea of his two "mothers" suggests how gracefully he was to accommodate himself to his new life.

Thornton Lewes provided his new stepmother with an instructive letter on the "contrast between Charlie's and my character," which "can be seen very well in that, whereas Charlie usually sits at home, with Mrs. Müller, or playing the piano, I am breathing the fresh air in the woods, in the marsh, in the villages, every where, when I can get permission or cheat the masters, which of course is not considered a sin by schoolboys, not even Dr. Müller would say against it" (January 23, 1860). The sentence captures a good deal of Thornie's propensity for self-dramatization and his willful, though oddly honest and innocent defiance of authority. As his contrast announces, he lived in a thoroughly male-oriented world, imitating his father in writing, wordplay, imaginative charm, and the collection and classification of natural species, but also obsessed by war, guns, and male heroics in battle. At eleven, he followed the Crimean War with interest, turning holiday sandcastles into major battle sites.[8]

As the only Lewes son to inherit his father's gift for language, Thornie carried on Lewes's delight in literary parody of all kinds, and it is sometimes difficult to tell whether he is actually representing his life as an adventure story or whether he is conscious of tongue-in-cheek self-parody. An envelope marked (in his own hand) "Thornton's Juvenilia," preserved at Yale, contains fragments of stories and poems written between 1855 and 1860 and testifies both to his large ambition and to his inability to finish most of his projects. The majority of the poems are fragments of epic battle narratives, irregularly rhymed, and showing great delight in imagining moments of hand-to-hand combat in medieval settings. (One of his heros wears a crown filled with hand grenades, bombs, pistols, and glass). A prose fragment written in 1859 attempts to transform a schoolboy episode into a midnight adventure tale. Two shorter completed poems are imitations of Wordsworthian verse. A story titled "The magic wand, or, The good and evil Genii," written at age eleven and elaborately dedicated to G. H. Lewes, tells the tale of a king of "Afrasia" with two sons, the elder corrupted by the evil influence of "Tomcat-Spitfire," the younger—the hero, of course—encountering a battle or two on every page in his redemption of his father's kingdom. In all these efforts Thornie demonstrates a good ear for the sound of various literary styles and genres. His early schoolboy letters display signs of his ambiguously playful self-dramatizing fantasy in the elaborate signatures, followed by "Given under my hand this day—"

Living intensely in his own world of butterfly chasing, bird shooting and stuffing, stamp collecting, and poetry, Thornie wrote letters in which affection and charm shared space with demands. Whereas Charles chose a feminine letter paper to begin his correspondence with Marian Lewes, Thornton's first sentences to her strike the pose of literary courtesy: "For the first time do I seize the pen to begin a correspondence which is to be lasting, and which affords me much pleasure, and answer your letter to Charlie. We received your letter at St. Moriz in the canton of the Grisons, some three hours walk from Italy. You can imagine how glad we were to get it, as being the first from you. It put a touch to our happiness on the journey" (8:242). He seemed anxious, however, to keep his new stepmother in a separate category from his father. In a postscript, he told her "When you receive a letter from me, if at the bottom of the envelope there is a p.M. = pro Matre, it is for you, if not, it is for Father." During the next few years he delighted in teasing George Eliot about her fame; in one letter from Edinburgh (November 3, 1861) he writes, "I am getting on at an intense rate; steam is up; high pressure express; and away we go! Does your feeble imagination twig the metaphors?"

Deference to the adult world was not part of Thornie's vocabulary. His letters are full of requests—for stamps, with detailed lists of the kinds he requires, or books of natural history, or the money he expects for his birthdays. He was ready to appeal to Marian in order to chastise his father for failing to fill his stamp orders correctly. His school reports were extremely mixed, and Thornie was both sensitive to and resentful of his father's admonitions to work harder. He and Lewes had several struggles when Thornie was refused permission to do something he wanted—get a gun with which to shoot birds more effectively, or be confirmed along with some of his classmates—and Thornie made it clear that he bowed to parental authority only because it *was* authority, not because his request was illegitimate. After he had left Hofwyl and had at last been given money for a rifle, he sent his parents a portrait of himself posing nonchalantly in full formal dress, holding the rifle at an artistic angle. "G. H. Lewes Esq!" he begins, "Does not thy conscience tell thee, that thou owest me a letter? Answer and look me straight in the face if thou dost not. But as you cannot do that, I hereby enclose my portrait, that you may look straight in the face, admire the singularly beautiful features and expression, the powerful biceps, the broad chest, the iron legs, and the never failing gun of your 'second' son Thornton" (February 17, 1861).

Thornie's genial imperviousness to the needs of the adults in his life also made him the only one of the boys who even tried to cut through the mysteries of parental behavior. After a year at Hofwyl he wrote to Lewes, "Are you now in London or where are you? Please give me an account of your proceedings, and write as soon as possible as we are very dull without any letters" (8:178). As the Leweses were planning the trip to Italy that was to be their last fling before they took on responsibility for the boys, Thornie wrote to Marian, "When you go to Italy, it is understood that we three imps should go with you, is it not? I suppose it is! For if Father won't have it, you must make him agree" (January 23, 1860). And as the time of their meeting approached, Thornie required an immediate answer from his father about the problem of his two mothers: an English schoolmate who had met Agnes would be there when Marian came. What should they do? He and Charles had decided that Empson should be let in on the secret, and only awaited Lewes's permission to tell him. (March 20, 1860; 8:259–60). Permission was denied. Whereas Charles was ready to participate willingly in keeping the adult secrets, Thornie could confront them with the awkward implications of their secrecy. Although his letters are full of optimism and boisterous trust in his own future, he was not made to tell people what they wanted to hear.

His younger brother, Herbert, on the other hand, struggled to meet the standards of a family he may have found rather overwhelming. When Bertie was nine, his father described him briefly in a note to John Sibree as "*very* backward, because for some years his health was delicate, and I did not like his being at school" (8:153). Bertie's battle with written language seems to have had a deeper origin, however; even after several years at school he was notably unable to command syntax and spelling. His first letter home after arriving at Hofwyl in July 1857 reports that people are kind to him and offers an interesting glimpse of Thornie: "The boys tease Thornton very orfan when he gose to cach buterfluies, they all follo him and tease hime." Two years later he attempted to persuade Lewes to let him stop taking piano lessons: "I do not want to learn music any more I could get on better alone, I should practis more than I do I have not learnt much with the master who gives me lessons I dersay you think I aught to still have lessons but I shall not learn well with him I learn much better alone" (8:252). A few further repetitions were necessary in order to satisfy him that his point had been made. Yet Bertie wished to please his formidable parents and took great pains over his first letter to Marian, which he began, "Dear Mother! I hope you will be satisfied with my letter, which I now write to you about the journey, 1st day and 2nd day we did not have much to walk" (August 26, 1859). "I take pains to write and to spell," he confided to Lewes two days earlier (August 24, 1859). "I am writin a letter to Mother about the journey. I am very pleased with the journey indeed. The only big letter that I can not do well is D, it is very difficult to make. I hope Mother will be satisfyed with my letter."

Bertie's writing and spelling did improve by the time he left Hofwyl, and he seems to have been adept at the fishing, skating, and wrestling that are the main topics of his letters. Marian Evans allowed herself a moment of humor on his account when she quoted Bertie to Sara Hennell: "Bertie, our third boy, writes, 'I am learning about man: we have got a skeleton of a man. It is very *nice* and interesting'" (October 13, 1859; 3:181). But for the most part the parental letters are silent about this least-known and least-promising child, who remained at Hofwyl for three years after his brothers left in 1860.

By 1859 Marian was regularly referring to "our boys." Her consciousness that the end of *The Mill on the Floss* would herald the end of her beloved tête-à-tête with Lewes is expressed in letters written as the year came to a close. Taking a break for letter writing after completing book 3 of *The Mill*, she wrote to Barbara Bodichon on December 5 that their plans for the spring of 1860 were unclear: "At present we expect Charlie, our eldest boy, to come to us at Easter, and we think of staying here, till it is quite settled, what his destination is to be. My novel will not come out till Easter, and until it is out of my hands, I shall think of no migration" (3:228). On the same day she complained—and boasted—to Sara Hennell that she was not exactly on a bed of roses: "I have four children to correspond with—the three boys in Switzerland, and Emily [her niece] at Lichfield" (3:229). To Francois D'Albert-Durade, her mentor from Geneva days, she could afford to reveal a bit more. Her new work will be published at Easter, she reports, and "at Easter our eldest boy will come home from school, and that will make a new epoch in our domestic life, for hitherto we have lived alone. I hope my heart will be large enough for all the love that is required of me" (3:232).

By the end of December it had become clear that Charles would not return at Easter. An English schoolmate had changed his plans, and Charles did not want to travel home alone; instead, the Leweses decided to plan a long-desired trip to Italy and pick up Charles on the way home. "*We* shall have a young face next Christmas," Marian wrote to Sara Hennell, who was entertaining young people herself, "—and we are meditating a flight to Italy when my present work is done, as our last bit of vagrancy for a long, long while" (3:238). This "fructifying holiday before the boys are about us, making it difficult for us to leave home," as she put it to John Blackwood, had taken shape as a final fling of pleasure before parental responsibilities closed in (3:249). The internal pressure of emotion with which she raced to the finish of *The Mill on the Floss*—"getting her eyes redder and *swollener* every morning," said Lewes (3:269)—may have been intensified by the knowledge that she would soon have to turn from indulgence in her own childhood sorrows to the task of providing guidance for a quite conventional young man of seventeen.

Marian Lewes met her stepsons in Bern on June 24 and 25, 1860, after Lewes had spent an initial day with them alone. There is no available account of those days except for the factual recording in Lewes's journal (3:306n.). One of the matters discussed, however, would have been Thornie's future, for although the plan had been that only Charles should return home, it was suddenly decided that Thornton would also leave Hofwyl to be more specifically prepared for a career. He was not to accompany them back to London; whether he wished to remain at Hofwyl until his prospects were fixed or whether he was not invited to join his parents and brother is unclear. As he spent a good deal of the summer doing nothing in particular, it is likely that Marian and Lewes had agreed that Charles was the only one of the boys who could spend any extended time in their household without entirely disrupting their life. This policy, with its decided split between the familial absorption of Charles and the "farming out" of Thornton and Herbert, was to remain constant throughout their lives. Thornie spent three days in London with the family at the end of September, after which Lewes took him to Edinburgh and installed him in the High School there to prepare for the Indian civil service exam. Lewes had consulted Blackwood for help in finding an Edinburgh family with whom Thornie could board: "I want him to have the advantages of family life; and at the same time to have someone over him to replace me" (3:327). Thoroughly conscious of Thornie's needs for parental discipline and family socialization, Lewes seems at the same time to have been sure that a substitute parent would have to supply them.

The second half of 1860 began for Marian Lewes a period of high anxiety and depression. Although she wrote to Sara Hennell in glowing terms of their visit to Italy as "one of those journeys that seem to divide one's life in two by the new ideas they suggest and the new veins of interest they open," there is some evidence that she was also experiencing a split in her life which she did not wish to describe. At the end of the letter she forbears from commenting on the "skeleton" of facts she has told Sara, "for the rest of my mind is too full of cares and duties of a serious prosaic kind for me to be very expansive just now" (3:311–12). To the D'Albert-Durades, whom they had visited with Charles on the way home, she confessed, "I am rather weighed down with anxiety now, dear Maman, and find life, even in the middle of my many blessings, still a difficult and sometimes a toilsome journey" (3:313–14). What were they to do with Charles? Where would he find work; where would they have to live? Although she was strenuously committed to creating a home for this one of Lewes's boys and to representing their family life in the most loving terms, the effort of doing so took a large toll on her mental and physical health. She was forty years old and knew that she would have no children of her own; yet she was called upon to support three adolescent boys through the difficult transition to lives of adult work enjoined on many Victorian boys by the age of seventeen.

The special sadness that is often noticed in descriptions of Marian Lewes at this time, and in the 1860 portrait of her drawn by Samuel Laurence, was probably created at least in part by this combination of circumstances.[9] By January 1861 she could represent her new role with a certain distance on her propensity to internalize tensions about the boys: "I begin, you know, to consider myself an experienced matron, knowing a great deal about parental joys and anxieties. Indeed I have rather too ready a talent for entering into anxieties of all sorts" (3:373–74). It is also during this period that both she and Lewes began to describe her books as children. Lewes wrote to Blackwood in July 1859 that "Mrs. Lewes," after a reviving trip, "will rock the cradle of the new 'little stranger' with fresh maternal vigour" (3:117), and Marian, a month into her stepmotherly duties, joked to him that she was "naturally jealous for 'The Mill,' which is my youngest child" (3:335). Throughout her career, her interest in thinking about the creative process as one of gestation and organic growth attests to a deeply individual use of the conventional metaphor.[10] Its emergence at the moment when Marian became an active stepmother suggests a wish to acknowledge that her primary womanly energies were reserved for the nurturing of her books.

Marian managed to express her depression by focusing on the need to move into London so that Charles could be near his work, rather than on the children themselves. Aided by the kindness of Anthony Trollope, Charles was nominated to compete for a vacancy in the Post Office, and the Leweses spent July of 1860 coaching him daily for the civil service examination. Charles was first in the examination and was appointed to the clerkship, where he began work on August 15 (3:326, 331). In the six weeks since he had arrived in London, his life's career had been efficiently established. "Magnificat anima mea!" Marian wrote to express her relief, "The dear lad is fairly launched in life now" (3:332). Her descriptions of Charles are consistently appreciative. "I think we are quite peculiarly blest in the fact that this eldest lad seems the most entirely lovable human animal of seventeen and a half, that I ever met with or heard of: he has a sweetness of disposition which is saved from weakness by a remarkable sense of duty," she wrote to Charles Bray after two weeks with her new stepson (3:324). This line was developed in a letter to D'Albert-Durade: Charles is "precious to us" and "an exceptional boy—he is wonderfully sweet and gentle in disposition without any want of force and manliness; he is particularly tender and good to me and adds greatly to our happiness" (3:348). Her journal, summing up the year 1860, notes that the time since the summer journey "has not been fruitful in work"; yet it attests to "the comfort we have found in having Charles with us"

(3:308). Charles's lucky combination of attentiveness to mothers and disciplined interests was serving them all well.

Although Marian was determined to imagine herself as the provider of a domestic moral education for the young man, she did not take easily to the sacrifice of their home on the outskirts of London. Town life would be "the most desirable thing for Charles," she wrote D'Albert-Durade," and of course we are anxious to provide a home for him that shall be the best moral education in the critical years between seventeen and twenty one" (3:347). "We are preparing to renounce the delights of roving and settle down quietly, as old folks should do, for the benefit of the young ones," she wrote to Barbara Bodichon (3:342). But she could not bring herself to buy a house in London, although they came near to doing so; finally they rented an unattractive house in Harewood Square as a "preliminary experiment" that lasted from September to December 1860, when they moved again to 16 Blandford Square (3:345). The sense of disruption is apparent everywhere in the letters, and her November journal entry notes, "The loss of the country has seemed very bitter to me" (3:360). "I languish sadly for the fields and the broad sky; but duties must be done, and Charles's moral education requires that he should have at once a home near to his business and the means of recreation easily within his reach," she wrote to D'Albert-Durade. "In three years, I hope, we shall be free to go beyond the smoke for ever" (3:363). When she is talking about houses, she does not hesitate to dramatize her sense of difficult self-sacrifice; her imprisonment in the city is swallowed as a three-year term.[11]

The experience of 1860 confronted Marian Lewes with several kinds of self-division.[12] In "adopting" Charles and sacrificing her health and spirits for the sake of his development, she was proving to herself and her correspondents that she was as responsive as any other woman to the Victorian morality of motherhood. The idea of Lewes's children solidified her status as "Mrs. Lewes," as she was at pains to point out to a correspondent who had called her Miss Evans: "For the last six years I have ceased to be 'Miss Evans' for any one who has personal relations with me—having held myself under all the responsibilities of a married woman. I wish this to be distinctly understood; and when I tell you that we have a great boy of eighteen at home who calls me 'mother,' as well as two other boys, almost as tall, who write to me under the same name, you will understand that the

point is not one of mere egoism or personal dignity, when I request
that any one who has a regard for me will cease to speak of me by my
maiden name" (3:396). The name of "mother" reinforces the fiction
of "Mrs. Lewes," which in turn protects the purity of adolescent children; thus Marian, bolstering her anomalous position, calls upon her
correspondent's own sensitivity to the taboos that protect family life.
At the same time, however, she was exquisitely aware that her relationship with Charles would have to be invented through patient
domestic work, and conscious that she relied heavily on the work of
other substitute parents to allay her guilt about the care and teaching
of Thornton and Herbert. Her hope that Charles might help to nor-
malize her status in the community contended against her suppressed
resentment at the drain on resources of time, energy, mental freedom, and money which the boys represented. It was at this moment
that the idea for *Silas Marner* "thrust itself" upon her.

The idea for the story "came to me after our arrival in this house,
and . . . thrust itself between me and the other book I was meditat-
ing," Marian noted in her journal during the November spent at
Harewood Square (3:360). The internally resisted move to Harewood
Square had been made on September 24; three days later Thornie
had arrived for his three-day sojourn. Immediately after he left,
George Eliot began *Silas Marner*.[13] "The other book" was of course
Romola, which had been conceived during the Italian journey, but
Marner seems also to have displaced an undisclosed plan for "another
English story" mentioned to Blackwood in an August letter (3:339).
Split as it is between the stories of a successfully adopted girl baby and
the maimed fortunes of the Cass brothers, *Silas Marner* incorporates
and transforms many of Marian Lewes's immediate maternal con-
cerns.

The linked double plot of the fable is a subtle vehicle for an oblique
rendering of the simultaneous gain and loss of motherhood which
Marian experienced in her early forties. [The magical story of Silas
and Eppie isolates the wishful elements: social redemption by adop-
tive parenthood, and the desire for a beautiful, unformed girl child
with no remembered history that might separate her from a perfect
connection with her parent. The story of the Cass brothers and Nancy
Lammeter dramatizes experienced anxieties and resignations: the
unmothered Cass boys threaten to waste their lives along with their
father's money, and their murky history is morally connected to Nancy Lammeter's brave but saddened childlessness. The perfection that

many readers experience in reading this fable testifies to the extraordinary coalescence of old images and new emotions which allowed George Eliot to write so directly, and so indirectly, of a current preoccupation.[14] Her successful transformation of family concerns into the stuff of fabular history might be measured by the fact that Thornton Lewes was one of the tale's most ardent admirers.[15]

The ways in which George Eliot projects herself in Silas Marner are manifold and have often been told.[16] Both are weavers and wanderers, known for their cleverness, wearing a faint air of incipient criminality, falsely accused of stealing and unable to answer their accusers, separated and outcast from a severely religious past, living internal lives completely at odds with the prevailing opinions about them. Yet the identification with an alienated hoarder was also one of the oldest self-images in Mary Ann Evans's vocabulary. It appears in a religious poem written at the age of nineteen, in which the speaker casts off all beloved earthly things in a series of stanzas, each ending in "Farewell!"[17] Of the ten stanzas, only one speaks an original image:

> Books that have been to me as chests of gold.
> Which, miser like, I secretly have told,
> And for them love, health, friendship, peace have sold,
> Farewell!

The series of metaphorical displacements, from the secret life with books to the literal hoarding of gold to the golden hair of the miraculously appearing child, indicates that the image of hoarded gold had always signified a guiltily unshared wealth of antisocial life rather than the accumulation of money itself. Silas's own love of his guineas has to do with the companionship of their familiar "faces" rather than with their purchasing power; he thinks of his half-earned guineas "as if they had been unborn children" that allow his imagination to move into the future (chap. 2).[18] When Eppie's human face is substituted for the guineas, he is still reluctant to share her, and the successive stages of his resocialization are marked by the necessity of doing so. Only in this way does the story mildly suggest the old conflict activated when Marian Lewes began to share her husband and household with his son.

For the most part the Silas-Eppie story is a fairy tale of substitute parenthood which derives its appeal from its understanding of impossible wishes. The transfer of Eppie from her mother to her new forty-year-old father is performed when both adults are unconscious; it is naturalized by the erasure of choice. Silas's weaving is interrupted by Eppie's needs, creating no tension but the anxiety of perfect love. Discipline is abandoned, but Eppie grows up perfectly anyway, "the burden of her misdeeds being borne vicariously by her father Silas" (chap. 14). The narrative repeatedly insists that Eppie reconnects Silas with his forgotten past, and especially with his mother and dead little sister, after whom Eppie is named; in fact, Silas is transformed into a maternal figure himself.[19] By the end of their story Lantern Yard, the scene of Silas's betrayal, is literally wiped off the landscape.

It is the Lantern Yard story, however, which shadows forth the possibility that substitute families might be as cruel as natural ones. The relation between William Dane and Silas Marner parallels that of the Cass brothers; in both cases the "evil brother" steals from the father figure (in Lantern Yard the senior deacon, a childless widower) in a way that inculpates the innocent and muzzled brother. The figure of a young man sneaking off with the parental bags of gold—here as in "Brother Jacob," and again revised in Tito Melema's sale of his foster father's rings—seems to have been a powerful one in George Eliot's imagination at this time.

In the story of the Cass brothers the image is grounded in the absence of the loving mother's discipline. Without this "fountain of wholesome love and fear" (chap. 3), without "the sweet flower of courtesy"(chap. 9), the Cass sons, "kept home in idleness," have "turned out rather ill" (chap. 3). Nancy Lammeter's little provincial codes of household order do not prevent her from being a redemptive maternal force in the Cass manor; Godfrey, the son who yearns for domesticity, is made good by his marriage to her. In the second part of the fable, when Godfrey is said to be about forty, the narrative turns, for the first and only time in George Eliot's fiction, to examine the conjunction of a successful womanly redemption with the fact of childlessness. Both the emptiness of Nancy's lot and the parental yearning of Godfrey's are occasions for the production of sentences that demonstrate the clarity with which George Eliot could formulate, master, and exempt herself from the stresses of her own emotional life. Of Nancy the narrator says, "This excessive rumination and self-questioning is perhaps a morbid habit inevitable to a mind of much moral sensibility when shut out from its due share of outward activity and of practical claims on its affections—inevitable to a noblehearted, childless woman, when her lot is narrow" (chap. 17). Of Godfrey's continual fretting after a child: "I suppose it is the way with all men and women who reach middle age without the clear perception that life never *can* be thoroughly joyous: under the vague dullness of the grey hours, dissatisfaction seeks a definite object, and finds it in the privation of an untried good. Dissatisfaction, seated musingly on a childless hearth, thinks with envy of the father whose return is greeted by young voices—seated at the meal where the little heads rise one above another like nursery plants, it sees a black care hovering behind every one of them, and thinks the impulses by which men abandon freedom, and seek for ties, are surely nothing but a brief madness" (chap. 17). From her double position as childless woman and anxious parent, she understood both kinds of fantasy.

In sketching the story of the Cass attempt to reclaim Eppie as Godfrey's natural daughter, George Eliot was aided by a model less intimate than her own. In 1846 Charles and Cara Bray, themselves childless, had adopted Bray's natural daughter Elinor, born to his longtime mistress.[20] Nelly Bray lived with the family from infancy until the age of nineteen, when she died of pulmonary consumption, tended lovingly by Cara and Sara Hennell. In her twenties, then, Marian Evans had become familiar with a situation that offered the burdens and satisfactions of motherhood to two very close friends; when she later "inherited" Lewes's children she began writing to Cara and Sara with a greater sense of equality in the matter of stepmotherhood. ("I used to feel your elevation above me continually in the attitude of mind you showed about Nelly's education and your sense of your relation towards childhood generally," she wrote to Sara in July 1864, when Nelly 's illness had become acute [4:158]). The story of Nancy Lammeter, whose superstitious belief forbids her from meddling with Providence by choosing to adopt a child but who believes that the father by blood has a greater claim than any foster father, may be derived in some way from the experience of Cara Bray. Yet Nancy—unlike Cara and like Marian Lewes—is deprived of the opportunity to bring up an infant; the question of adoption is raised only when Eppie is eighteen and devoted to Silas Marner, and Nancy, having once resigned herself to childlessness, must resign herself over again to the knowledge that she might have had Eppie as a baby if Godfrey had been honest with her. It is in the presence of her forgiving but unrelentingly noncompensatory vision that the wedding which ends *Silas Marner* is most properly celebrated.

During the months when George Eliot was imagining how Eppie

and Nancy rehumanize and redeem male households, Marian Lewes worked at loving and domesticating Charles. In a mood of New Year's assessment, she wrote to Blackwood on January 1, 1861, "I suppose I shall never love London, or believe that I am as well in the streets as in the fields . . . but the duty of staying in it, has a counterbalancing pleasure when one has a great boy, who is learning to love home better than anything outside it" (3:369). The new "family trio" (4:70) may have recalled the old days of life with another father and son, Robert and Isaac Evans; it is possible that Marian's frequently expressed gratitude about Charles's temperament was underscored by memories of stress in the earlier family triangle. The success of her and Lewes's efforts may be judged from the tone of the letters exchanged with Charles during their first trip abroad after his homecoming. Beginning a pattern that was to extend throughout their lives, Charles remained in Blandford Square as housesitter while the Leweses made for Florence (and further preparation for *Romola)* between April and June 1861. "Charles, meanwhile, will keep house here, and work like a nigger at his music, as we are going to give him the privilege of having lessons from Brindley Richards while we are away," Marian wrote to Sara Hennell, imitating her stepson's slang (3:404). Charles had already given every indication of his delighted participation in shared family languages; a letter of his dated February 4, 1861, written to Dorking, where the Leweses had gone for a quick restorative, begins, "Ducks! 'Arrived and past the usual How d'ye does?' your son thinks he will tell you how he came home, how he found home, and what he did at home!" The story of his mundane adventures slides, in Lewes fashion, into literary self-parody: "Presently your young Taugenichts came to a place where two roads met. Hercules am Scheidewege! Neither a figure of Virtue, nor a figure of Vice came to prove the young Hercules." Assured of their interest in hearing every domestic detail, he tells them what he had for dinner and how he didn't know how to carve the meat; beginning his lifelong secretarial duties, he reports on the mail, and forwards the letter—from Trollope— which might be important. His sense of ease and delight is obvious.

Writing about themselves in the third person was one of the family languages; the trio quickly became "the Mutter," "the Pater," and "the Boy," as though they had developed this way of making themselves a family while simultaneously acknowledging the new role each was playing. Throughout his adult life Charles received the salutation "Dearest Boy." Marian's first line to Charles during the 1861 journey,

The Priory,
21. North Bank,
Regents Park.

Tuesday

Dearest Boy

In sending you Ripley's letter I missed putting in a note to tell you that I had written to him decidedly advising him to remain in his present situation. The letter from Mr King was exceeding kind, & I think he is a friend who would help R. to get another place if that in his own Establishment were closed. The newspaper work would make R. happier as well as being in money. — If you have anything to say to me, come round in the morning, because of visitors in the afternoon — 8 of them on Sunday.

Thy loving
Mutter

Manuscript, letter of Marian Evans Lewes to Charles Lee Lewes, November 11, 1879. Beinecke Rare Book and Manuscript Library, Yale University.

appended to a letter from Lewes, reads "Die Mutter thinks of her dear Boy very much and loves him better than ever now she is at a distance from him" (3:407). That she could truthfully tease him in this way suggests that she and Lewes had found it quite easy to talk about her needs and anxieties with the mother-conscious Charles. She did not hesitate to comment in letters to Charles about her acknowledged talent for being physically uncomfortable or about her distaste for living in London; he was apparently drawn into emotional service as readily as he accepted the increasing requests for secretarial work on the home front. For his part, Charles was at least reported to be an adoring disciple; Lewes wrote to Blackwood in May 1861, "It would interest you to see her with the eldest, who *worships* her, and thinks no treat equal to having her all to himself for an evening to make, and be made much of. Among the many blessings that have come to me late in life this of seeing the perfect love between her and the children is one of the greatest; perhaps because it was one of the rocks ahead" (3:421). Unconscious of the many rocks to come, Lewes made the most of this opportunity for dramatizing Marian's success as a step-mother.

She also took frequent opportunities to paint ideal moral pictures in her representations of Charles, which abound in the rhetoric of improvement. "Our dear boy Charles is increasingly satisfactory to us, improving constantly and applying himself with admirable resolution and good sense to the everyday work of life," she wrote to D'Albert-Durade (3:448); to a distant acquaintance she added to her complaints about London, "But he is a dear, precious boy, worth a great deal of sacrifice for the sake of preserving the purity and beauty of his mind. He is very tender to us old people and pets us very much" (3:449). Such language seems a necessary counterpart to her continuing sense of sacrifice. In October 1861, when Charles was about to take his vacation in Switzerland, Marian wrote, "We shall enjoy our dual soli-tude; yet the dear boy is more and more precious to us from the singular rectitude and tenderness of his nature" (3:460); in another letter Charles "shows the rare combination of thorough manliness and gentle purity" (4:8). The frequent references to Charles's purity and tenderness make it clear that she wished to see her domestic project as a protection of innocent youthful development from the moral evils of the masculine public world. As she wrote to Charles himself, "Mutter . . . feels herself quite bathed in blessings—always reckoning one of them to be her boy—who will grow so good, so good—better than any of her books" (4:30).

Such moral formulations had their self-serving aspects; they worked also to muffle her underlying sense that Charles was a quite ordinary person. In May 1862 Anthony Trollope reported to Lewes that Charles was not doing well in the Post Office; his associates "say that he utterly fails in making himself useful" (8:300). Trollope speculated that Charles's Swiss education was to blame, making him better at German and French than in English. Lewes was "completely upset," as he recorded in his journal (May 17, 1863; 4:34). Once apprised, Charles was able to mend his ways and win a promotion the following year; his problem as Marian stated it in her journal was "only slowness of apprehension and of execution" (4:42). When Charles surprised them by becoming engaged at the age of twenty-one to Gertrude Hill, a gifted contralto four years his senior, Marian described her earlier suspicion that Gertrude "would hardly fall in love with our amiable bit of crudity. That was a mistaken parental notion, however" (4:154). In implicit contrast to herself, she described Charles to Sara Hennell at the time of his twenty-second birthday: "He is as happy as the day is long—and very good—one of those creatures to whom goodness comes naturally. Not any exalted goodness, but everyday serviceable goodness such as wears through life" (4:168). Now that her official parental duties were nearly over, she was free to allow a shade of honest feeling into her correspondence. She was also free to express her pleasure in "our dear old tête-à-tête, which we can't help being glad to recover" (4:161, 177).

Charles Lewes married Gertrude Hill on March 20, 1865, and went to Hampstead to live in a household of women, including Gertrude and the two old aunts who had brought her up. In 1866 Gertrude had a stillbirth; later she bore three daughters, Blanche in 1872, Maud in 1874, and Elinor in 1877. Charles's capacity for family affection and service seems to have been inexhaustible. He continued his secretarial service to the Lewes household whenever they were out of London, vetting and abstracting the contents of their voluminous mail and performing innumerable commissions for them. After one particularly long series of notes with requests for errands, his father wrote him on June 9, 1871, from a retreat in Shotter Mill: "Dearest Boy, I hope you are not bored by our commissions—mais que veux-tu? Nous n'avons que toi!" According to his half sister Ethel, Charles visited

Agnes Lewes and her children every Saturday afternoon in Kensington.[21] His letters are unfailingly sociable, amiable, sensitive, responsive, and full of details, particularly of musical performances.

Charles's apparent adoration of Marian Lewes continued well beyond his marriage. He either felt or knew he was supposed to feel a deep and responsive deference to the wisdom of George Eliot. In a letter written when he was twenty-eight, he complains a bit about the shortness of "Armgart," and then corrects himself: "Your writing like great music is always revealing fresh thoughts. One ought constantly to be reading over again instead of impotently longing for more." He goes on to tell her how seriously he has taken some advice of hers, to cultivate deep impressions rather than formulating opinions, and resolves to do exactly what she recommends (July 2, 1871). His most intense emotional service was required, however, after his father's death, when he was for a long period the only person admitted to Marian's presence. "I shall be constantly with her. At present and for some little while to come I am almost living here," he wrote to Bessie Parkes Belloc on December 6, 1879 (7:87). During this period of crisis and after the marriage to John Cross, Charles's language is so closely identified with Marian's that he almost seems to have re-created her anxieties within himself. Letters written to her during her honeymoon with Cross respond precisely to her concerns and buoy her up with reassurances. "I continue to rejoice and rejoice and never to weary of thinking of your new spring of happiness," he wrote on May 23, 1880; "when I am with congenial people we expatiate with delight on your new life." The letter reiterates every conceivable source of positive response to the marriage, along with comic incidents: "I find from a letter addressed to you from the New York Herald office in London that there has appeared in the papers a contradiction of your marriage! The N.Y. Herald calmly asks you to inform him 'what was the cause of the contradiction?' Is not that delicious?" With his finger right on the pulses of the moment, Charles tells her finally, "I think that is really the gravest charge you will have to bear from your friends, that you did not trust them sufficiently to tell them. However as soon as they see you or hear from you, this feeling will I know at once disappear." The generosity to Cross continued after George Eliot's death, when Charles wrote him emotional letters in praise and support of the *Life*. Marian Lewes's four years of maternal sacrifice had, in Charles's case, been more than repaid.

The family trio never became a quartet or a quintet. Marian poured her maternal energies into the relatively gratifying task of nurturing Charles, but the occasional presences of Thornton and Herbert were to be endured. Thornie in particular was not a domesticable animal; when his father described him to John Blackwood, who kept an eye on him during his time in Edinburgh, he clearly felt that there was something missing in Thornie's social makeup. "The young bear wants licking into shape, but there is real power in him," he wrote on January 31, 1861; and six months later, comparing him to Blackwood's son, "It would indeed be a great gain to Thornie if he could catch something of Willie's savoir faire. He wants *rounding*" (3:375, 434). Marian's letters do not find language for Thornie's character at all—a sure indication of stress—until after he left for Natal in 1863, when she wrote to D'Albert-Durade, "Thornton, our second boy, who is at once amiable and troublesome, easy and difficult to manage, has caused us considerable anxiety" (4:117). The contradictions suggest a kind of obliviousness to ordinary codes of behavior and career planning which rendered useless any of her attempts at guidance.

Thornie spent a few weeks in the London household during the summers of 1861 and 1862, passing the first two of his exams for the Indian civil service and then going off to his beloved Hofwyl. When Marian's letters mention him, it is with a sense of strain. The rhetoric of improvement, which is applied so lavishly to Charles and was even to turn up in later representations of Bertie, is notably absent. Thornie is primarily associated with noise. After he went off to Switzerland in August 1861, Lewes wrote to Blackwood, "The house will now resume its quiet, much to Mrs. Lewes's benefit. She allows herself to be preyed upon dreadfully by the boys—she can't say No" (3:445–46). "Young gentlemen of seventeen have often immense resources for boring their elders," Marian wrote to Blackwood after Thornie had returned to Edinburgh (3:463). She calls him "our noisy hopeful, Thornie—'Sturm und Drang'—as one of our friends has christened him"; during the 1862 visit she complains—as usual, to the distant D'Albert-Durade—of "a general impression that life is made up of large boys with robust voices and bright spirits. The weather too is of the most oppressive—rainy and close" (8:290; 4:46).

The crisis came in the summer of 1863. Thornie failed his final Indian civil service exam, having decided he was not interested, and Lewes brought Bertie home from Hofwyl. All three boys were at home, the younger two with no clear prospects. As Lewes consulted his connections for a farming placement for Bertie and Thornie re-

fused to consider any course of action except his "fixed idea of going
to fight for the Poles against the hated Russians" (4:117), Marian
recorded brief indications of her intense anxiety. In May, "We are up
to the ears in Boydom, and imperious parental duties" (4:84). By the
end of July, "Conceive us, please, with three boys at home, all bigger
than their father! It is a congestion of youthfulness on our mature
brains that disturbs the course of our lives a little" (4:94). At the
beginning of September, with a move to a new house (the Priory)
imminent, "We are still in a nightmare of uncertainty about our
boys—awaiting one letter here and another there, and feeling in
many ways the wide gap between theoretic longing and possible practice" (4:106). True to her lifelong ban on writing down descriptions of
family trouble, Marian came as close as she could in this general
formula to expressing her sense of frustration and failure. She expressed it more fully through illness and by escaping to Richmond for
two weeks in September, leaving the rest of the family to wrestle with
Thornie's destiny. Barbara Bodichon finally offered the solution, suggesting emigration to colonial life in Natal and writing to friends
there on Thornie's behalf. On October 16 Thornie was, as Lewes put
it in his journal, "*at last* shipped off to Natal, well equipped with
funds, outfit, and letters, to seek a career for himself there" (4:111–
12). Bertie, after various other plans had fallen through, landed on a
Scottish farm, where, Marian wrote, he "seems to have had his wits a
little sharpened by change of circumstances" (4:119).

Thornton Lewes's letters from Natal are extraordinary pieces of
writing. The parental audience must have been torn between tears
and laughter, admiration and terror; for a contemporary reader they
form a pathos-ridden record of a very young man attempting to
survive by his wits in a frontier colony where no certain principles of
law had as yet prevailed. Thornie's wits were simultaneously innocent
and tough, literary and concrete. He fell in with every money-making
scheme that crossed his path, and each one failed; yet he seemed to
retain his buoyancy and resiliency, not learning suspicion or regret.
The style of his letters is always authoritative, even when they record
the many collapses and failures which are never understood as results of his own errors or misjudgments.

Thornie at nineteen was evidently delighted to be set loose from
parental authority, for which he had an increasing intolerance. In
Edinburgh he had physically attacked the Mr. Robertson with whom
he boarded when he was (he felt unjustly) reprimanded for coming in

too late at night; he told the story to his father with great and righteous pride, including a little drawing of Robertson's bruised face
(8:294–95). Not long after his arrival in Durban, he wrote, along with
enthusiastic descriptions of the scenery, about an acquaintance sure
"of his dignity in being a man, and as such having to obey no man. I
wish the happy hour had tolled for me; still there's nobody out here
who has a word to say to me, and Pater's so far off that his authority is
not worth much, so I ought to feel independent. Thanks, Pater for
the 80£" (January 28, 1864). It was typical of Thornie to express such
sentiments in oblivion of his intended audience, rendered with the
same honest goodwill as his affectionate inquiries about people back
home. He enjoyed telling about his antics aboard the *Danietta,* as
editor of a renegade ship's newspaper called "'the Danietta Blunderbuss,' which gun explodes every Wednesday morning punctually at 8
1/2 a.m, and is extremely popular," and as the espouser of evolutionary theory: "I have consequently been set down as an atheist and a
fool, but that does not matter as it furnishes subjects for chaffing me,
and as I stand it of course, you know how, I am very popular. You
remember explaining to me that the human child in an early stage
had a tail, well—when I informed the Daniettese of this it created a
roar of laughter, and the consequence is that there are constant allusions to my tail" (November 14, 1863). His delight in shocking women
and parsons was indulged when he appeared at a ship's fancy ball
dressed as the Devil, sporting "a yellow tail with a red tip" (December
30, 1863).

Thornie's letters were infrequent, written between upcountry adventures, but they were long, lively, and detailed. Like any young
Englishman of his time, he was easily drawn into the racist politics of
Natal; the Xhosa were "Kafirs," and the Boers, their habits first described in an authoritative-sounding sociological account as lacking in
personal cleanliness but "warm and hospitable . . . if properly
treated," were later to become his primary associates (August 29,
1864). His first plan was to become an upcountry trader. "The wild,
free and easy, independent life suits me wonderfully. If you could
only see me you would say it agreed with me" (August 29, 1864). After
his second trading venture, he was bankrupt and in debt, working as a
"Kafir storekeeper and general Bottlewasher," his precious guns sold
for oxen, which have "departed this life" (June 12, 1865). For the next
year and a half he seems to have vegetated and done odd jobs for
people, except during the period of his participation in the Basuto

War: "It is clear to me that fighting is my destiny." He joined first the Natal Frontier Guard and then a commando group of Free State Boers to fight off the Basuto, who were resisting Boer incursions into their territories. His long desire to be a literary warrior took shape in a document written December 26, 1865, titled "From your own Correspondent—his first battle." The description, in full-blown military-narrative style, recounts the events of December 5, when Thornie participated in what amounted to a ragged Boer cattle raid on the Basuto, which he described as an important military encounter and illustrated with a labeled map of the terrain.

By 1866 Thornie was at loose ends, in need of money from home, and a bit discouraged. He believed, however, in a Boer promise to reward their commando fighters with free farmland along the Boer-Basuto border, a scheme designed to prevent Basuto encroachment on the farms Boers considered their property. On the basis of this promise, he asked that Bertie be outfitted and sent out to join him, promising a three-year commitment to "take Bertie on" and sounding very professional about the increasing value of the land and the supplies they would require (June 2, 1866). In August and September 1866 Lewes spent three weeks preparing Bertie for the venture; Bertie arrived in Durban early in November, to find that the farm promise had fallen through. Undaunted and armed with Lewes's fresh supply of cash, the brothers bought a remote farm in the Transvaal which Thornie described to Lewes in glowing terms on December 9, 1866. They called it "The Falls of the Assagai." "There can be no doubt but that both our vocations were mistaken 'till we were sent farming to South Africa. We shall have the model farm in a very few years," Thornie announced on April 10, 1867. In the next few months the farm took shape despite a series of mishaps, with Bertie earnestly and diligently applying his Scottish farming methods to the South African terrain and Thornie sending vivacious, enthusiastic letters. Marian's sense of relief was evident in a July letter to Maria Congreve: "They are established in their purchased farm, and are very happy together in their work. Impossible for mortals to have less trouble than we" (4:378–79).

The trouble she had private cause to expect was not long in arriving. By September, Thornie reported that he was in so much pain "from sciatica" that he could hardly work (September 16, 1867). In March it was clear that their first year's crop had failed, though Thornie was certain that the next year's would be "splendid"; his pain had now been self-diagnosed as kidney stone, and he had found some relief from homeopathic remedies (March 9, 1868). By October, however, there was no concealing the extent of their desperation, and Thornie set himself to the task of applying once again to his father for assistance. The letter he wrote to Lewes on October 12 is an astonishing document. Like earlier requests for money or help, this one is a detailed account of why such help is necessary, written by a person who cannot stand to imagine himself in the posture of neediness. It begins with an extended account of the failure of a speculation that had been intended to bring them a quick fortune: having heard rumors of a chief who wished to trade ivory for blankets at an excellent rate of exchange, Thornie and Bertie had bought blankets and set off on an expedition, only to find that two young men had arrived before them to relieve the chief of his ivory. Following hard upon a failed hunting expedition, the expenses of this venture had left them "on our last legs." What Thornie has learned from these failures is that he must try again and get to the chief before the other white men do: "One lives and learns." His first request for money, then, is to finance what he imagines will be a successful foray into the ivory trade. Only after pursuing this latest obsession at length does he come to the matter of his health.

"So much for that: the next I am sorry to say is again a demand for money but of such vital importance that I do not hesitate in applying to you," he began. "The fact is this, that with this stone in the kidney and other internal complications, for there is something serious besides the stone, I am gradually wasting away. . . . I can't do a stroke of work of any sort, I can hardly stoop to touch the ground, I can't sit up for half an hour, all I can do is lie down, then get up and walk about for half an hour, then lie down again." Detailing more facts of his intense pain, he concludes, "In fact if I were 50 instead of 24, I should have quietly walked some fine day over our waterfall; but while there is youth there is hope." Still embarrassed by the expense to his father, Thornie indicated a pride of unwilling dependence which may have given a particularly sharp edge to Lewes's misery in receiving the news: "It is my last chance in life, and you are the only person I can apply to, so I don't hesitate to make the application" (8:433–34).

The letter arrived in London three months later, on January 6, 1869. On New Year's day, Marian Lewes had written with unusual confidence in her journal, "I have set myself many tasks for this year—I wonder how many will be accomplished?—A Novel called

Middlemarch, a long poem on Timoleon, and several minor poems"
(5:3). Some short poems and forty experimental pages of *Middlemarch*
were written, but her actual task for 1869 was to preside over the
death of Thornton Lewes.[22] From May 8, when he showed up, "many
weeks before the time at which we thought it possible for him to get to
us" (5:34), until October 19, when he died, life at the Priory revolved
around Thornie's condition. Partly because his (probable) spinal tuberculosis was never definitively diagnosed, the dramatic fluctuations
in his daily or weekly state created a roller coaster of hope and fear in
the household.

Thornie seems to have been both a demanding and a brave patient.
Before large doses of morphia dimmed his mental powers in August,
he was eager for conversation and entertainment in the intervals of
his pain. Although the Leweses hired a nurse, "we spend several
hours of the day by his side"; "our days have been broken into small
fragments" (5:40, 44). Barbara Bodichon came "twice a week to sit
with Thornie, and she is wonderfully clever in talking to young
people" (5:41). Charles and Gertrude spelled his parents when they
needed breaks for their own recoveries. The stress and the loss of
time to concentrate on writing took their inevitable physical and psychological toll. On July 6 Lewes described "Polly" to Barbara as "weak
and wailing" (5:46). In her own dignified diction, Marian wrote to
Harriet Beecher Stowe that she and Lewes had "felt our own health
and nervous energy insufficient for our needful activity of body and
mind. He is at present no better and we look forward to a long trial"
(5:47). By the end she had so emotionally exhausted herself that she
described herself as "shattered in body and mind"; Lewes took her to
the country and forbade any letters or visits "that would heighten the
strength of home associations" (5:65).

At least according to Lewes's account, it was Marian who was the
more emotionally unprepared for Thornie's death. After returning
from their month of seclusion, he wrote to Blackwood, "She had
lavished almost a mother's love on my dear boy, and felt almost a
mother's grief. I was better prepared, having never from the first held
much hope of his recovery, and for the last three months having
almost ceased to wish it, since it *could not* have been more than recovery into a state of constant helplessness and pain" (5:66). The letter
suggests that Lewes had had Marian's hysteria to look after as well as
Thornie's. Although he typically cast them in such roles, it seems clear
that Thornie's death evoked in Marian an especially intense and com-

plicated set of feelings, which erupt into letters only in the most fragmentary ways.

Although Lewes could express his feeling that Thornie's death had
been preferable to life as a dependent invalid, Marian—to whom the
latter prospect would have loomed as a potential destroyer of her
ability to work—spoke rather of her immersion in the powerful and
expiatory act of nursing. To Cara Bray, with whom she now shared
the experience of watching a stepchild die, she emphasized the moment of death: "Nurse and I raised him and his last breathings were
quite peaceful. When death comes, it always seems worse than anything else—but it is not really so. I am too crushed now to feel that the
dear boy is saved from a life of almost certain deprivation and helplessness" (5:60). To Barbara Bodichon she wrote, "It has cut deeper
than I expected—that he is gone and I can never make him feel my
love any more. Just now all else seems trivial compared with the powers of delighting and soothing a heart that is in need" (5:60–61).
Caught up in the emotion of the ministering angel, she did not perhaps realize how much she revealed in her wish to "make" Thornie
feel her love. She did, however, link his death with that of her father
twenty years earlier, which had elicited her fiercely solitary passion of
nursing. "Death had never come near to me through the twenty years
since I lost my Father, and this parting has entered very deeply into
me. I never before felt so keenly the wealth one possesses in every
being to whose mind and body it is possible to minister comfort
through love and care," she wrote to Harriet Beecher Stowe in consol-
idation of their womanly experience (5:71). The linkage with Robert
Evans helps to explain some of the intensity of her feeling; both the
unconventional intellectual daughter and the exiling stepmother
were inwardly required to dramatize their womanly nurturance of the
dying and to assert its precedence over the will to autonomous mental
work.[23]

What feelings the Leweses had about the scattering and wasting of
Thornton's talents in futile South African adventures were too private
for letters. Marian touched upon them only in some indirect sentences to Blackwood, written in August while Thornie had a brief
period of remission. Blackwood was planning to place his son at
school in London, and Marian trusted he had chosen "a satisfactory
Master for your Boy, whose future will probably make a large part of
yours. Sons are heavy hostages to the powers at work in our lives"
(5:51). Her first sentence emphasizes the power that grown children's

lives may exert on the destinies of their parents, but the second revises and reverses the formula, implying that the powers that made her an artist and an outlaw stepmother have victimized or limited her stepsons. Along with the interesting reversal, the stern generality of this rather chilling formula attests to an underlying tangle of contradictory anxieties and guilts.

The more usual strategy for confronting Thornie's sad story was, however, similar to the one that had come into play when Charles was part of the household. Both Marian and Lewes emphasized the sweetness of Thornie's moral nature, as they had never done before. "There is joy in the midst of our trouble," Marian wrote in May to Maria Congreve, "from the tenderness towards the sufferer being altogether unchecked by anything unlovable in him. Thornie's disposition seems to have become sweeter than ever with the added six years; and there is nothing that we discern in his habits or character to cause us grief" (5:40). In the journal entry recording Thornie's death she wrote, "Through the six months of his illness, his frank impulsive mind disclosed no trace of evil feeling" (5:60). Lewes took up the same stance in his letter to Blackwood: "A sweeter purer nature than his can seldom be met with; and we look back with peculiar satisfaction at the fact that never once did we discern the slightest trace in him of anything mean or unworthy" (5:66–67). They comforted themselves by these reassurances that six years of rough associates in frontier conditions had not corrupted Thornie's moral nature; they had not, then, been altogether culpable in sending him to Natal. Yet Thornie's consitutional inability to learn shrewdness or prudence had, as much as anything, ensured his failure to create a life there.

When George Eliot returned late in 1870 to "a Novel called Middlemarch," she was ready for a full-blown study of young men in search of elusive vocations. In the parallel stories of Will Ladislaw and Fred Vincy, she imagines the conditions under which young men "intolerant of fetters" (chap. 10) can be brought to see and commit themselves to a single line of work. Those conditions include the civilizing mission of women, represented as the moral anchor of love for a woman who provides an audience for the young man's fluctuations. Dorothea Brooke shares with Mary Garth the function of "a theatre where the audience demands their best" (chap. 24). But young women do not inspire magical transformations in *Middlemarch*; the young men also require the willing patronage of father figures, as well as an accidental confluence of factors that make it suddenly possible for them to focus their talents and imagine themselves in a particular vocation. Giving them all these conditions, George Eliot rewrites Thornie's story of failure in two different ways, again splitting the more wishful from the more pragmatic story. Will Ladislaw, the artistic dilettante and political radical, is an image of the Thornie who wished to follow his father in talent and radicalism, the schoolboy with grandiose ideas of his future greatness. Will's functions in the narrative are largely to provide an alternative to Casaubon and an adoring perspective on Dorothea, but during the brief and easily resolved sections concerning his career, Will is represented in the historical conditions that could allow his talents to flourish in liberal journalism and politics. Fred Vincy allows George Eliot both to create a young man whose repeated mishaps stem from an imperturbably good nature and to dramatize the immense effort and sacrifice such a person demands from the several adults who are generous enough to force him into shape. Both "hopefuls" are new developments in George Eliot's repertoire, and both are discussed in mixed ironic and forgiving tones that bespeak a newly parental voice.

Ladislaw's is by far the more romantic of the two stories. His dilettante fluctuations create hostility in Casaubon and a certain anxiety in Dorothea, but his proud independence leads to a severing of his reliance on Casaubon's money. According to Mrs. Cadwallader he is the kind of "troublesome sprig" who should have been sent off to India (chap. 38), but he is adored by the narrator as a Lewes-like figure of obscure origins and gypsy propensities who makes himself beloved by children, dogs, old ladies, and liberal minds. The narrator's first meditation on Will's grandiosity (chap. 10) makes some fun of him: "Genius, he held, is necessarily intolerant of fetters: on the one hand it must have the utmost play for its spontanaeity; on the other, it may confidently await those messages from the universe which summon it to its peculiar work, only placing itself in an attitude of receptivity towards all sublime chances." Yet the narrative also supports his position. "We know what a masquerade all development is, and what effective shapes may be disguised in helpless embryos." What Will needs is simply "something in particular" to do; with that proviso he is sent to the Continent "without our pronouncing on his future." Responding to those messages from the universe which put Dorothea in his way, Will's theory would seem to be sustained by its results. Because of her, he accepts Mr. Brooke's invitation to Middlemarch; because the Reform Bill is in the air, he discovers the pleasure of liberal journalism. The narrator stresses the accidental quality of this rescue from the dilettante life of uncommitted self-culture, and also the ease with which aspects of Will's nature are given expression: "His nature warmed easily in the presence of subjects which were visibly mixed with life and action, and the easily-stirred rebellion in him helped the glow of public spirit" (chap. 46). Had Thornie's alternative newpaper, the "Danietta Blunderbuss," been an organ of community politics rather than a shipboard rag, what might his future have been?

Fred Vincy's story provides something of a corrective for such fantasies, although it pastoralizes and redeems Thornie's situation by replacing it in a paternalist community that takes Fred's education into its own hands. Fred is linked through the horse-selling episode to the sinister figure of Dunstan Cass, but by the time of *Middlemarch* the portraits of sons who deviously steal from their fathers have run their course. Fred's drains on his elders' pockets are hapless rather than sinister; in this novel it is adults—Featherstone, Bulstrode—who deviously steal from children, and whose money is a source of manipulation and humiliation for the young. The horse-swapping episode is, in this case, George Eliot's attempt to imagine herself into the mind of a Thornie-like character who is duped at every turn by a very male world in which he imagines himself an adept.

Fred goes to the Houndsley horse fair intending to sell his horse ("without which life would certainly be worth little") in order to pay his debts (chap. 23). Instead he swaps his horse for a more expensive one: "The hope of having at last seen the horse that would enable him to make money was exhilarating." The narrative makes it clear that while Fred is congratulating himself on his perspicacious and suspicious reading of the horse dealers' tactics, he is in fact doing just as they wish him to do—paying good money for a horse known for its bad temper. "To get all the advantage of being with men of this sort, you must know how to draw your inferences, and not be a spoon who takes things literally," he thinks, and by morning "he saw . . . clearly the importance of not losing this rare chance." It is a fine reimagining of the authoritative accounts of failed speculations Marian Evans had read in many of her stepson's letters. Fred is also endowed with Thornie's honesty—he goes to the Garths to explain that he cannot pay the money he owes—and with his imperviousness to the effects of his actions on anyone but himself; it is only when Mrs. Garth informs him that the money is urgently needed that Fred feels "for the first time something like the tooth of remorse." Concerned only with avoiding an appearance of dishonor, his imagination has not dwelt on inconvenience and injury to others—an exercise which "is not common with hopeful young gentlemen" (chap. 24). Fred's imperviousness to the frustration he causes in others is represented as a trait both maddening and endearing: "Fred was so good-tempered that if he looked glum under scolding, it was chiefly for propriety's sake" (chap. 23).

The serious illness that strikes Fred immediately after the horse-swapping episode might seem unmotivated by anything but the desire to create a situation in which Lydgate and Rosamond might come together, unless we discern the shades of Thornie in Fred. The illness is said to arise from Fred's horse-buying visits to "unsanitary Houndsley streets," as though George Eliot is directly connecting Thornie's roustabout life in the frontier colony with the illness that caused his death. Briefly playing out the drama of disbelief that a robust young man could have a life-threatening illness, she leaves the sickroom represented only by Mrs. Vincy's offstage concern. The illness acts as a kind of purgative, a guarantee of the new start that Thornie did not have. "I feel as sure as I sit here," exclaims the motherly voice of Mrs. Vincy, "Fred will turn out well—else why was he brought back from the brink of the grave?" (chap. 36). The rest of Fred's story demonstrates that the combined efforts and sacrifices of Caleb Garth, Mary Garth, and Mr. Farebrother are required to make him turn out well.

Fred, who has refused to follow through on the career for which his father has had him educated, must be reeducated by substitute parents. If Dorothea acts as an ideally stabilizing force upon Will Ladislaw, the relations between Mary Garth and Fred Vincy represent the paradigm of womanly taming from the rather different angle of Fred's childish dependence on Mary. The battle between skepticism and faith in the young man's ability to work steadily is played out in the dialogues between the Garth parents; there is nothing ideal about this story of keeping Fred in line except for the sentiments of his mentors. Caleb Garth's outburst, "I say, that young man's soul is in my hand; and I'll do the best I can for him, so help me God!" (chap. 56), is George Eliot's call to exalt the unseen sacrifice of every parental figure whose work goes virtually unnoticed by those who benefit from it. The episode in which Farebrother warns Fred that he has considered taking advantage of Fred's backsliding takes the educative fantasy one step farther, to show Fred, finally recognizing the sacrifices being made on his behalf, promising Farebrother that "your goodness shall not be thrown away" (chap. 66). Mrs. Garth's didactic desire that Fred should understand and be grateful is corrected by Farebrother's method of dramatizing his own self-discipline for Fred's benefit.

Although Fred will always need someone's "bit and bridle" (chap. 68) to keep him on course, George Eliot rewards his essential good nature with a stable and productive life on the land. Her "Finale" lingers on Fred and Mary with affection and humor, paying tribute to the intractibility of his optimism in a sentence redolent of Thornie: "I cannot say that he was never again misled by his hopefulness: the yield of crops or the profits of a cattle-sale usually fell below his estimate; and he was always prone to believe that he could make money by the purchase of a horse which turned out badly—though this, Mary observed, was of course the fault of the horse, not of Fred's judgment." Mary's irony and forgiveness are George Eliot's own.

Marian Lewes's family experience also found its way into *Daniel Deronda*, in the miniature but intensely rendered Gascoigne episode. If the *Middlemarch* stories create promising fictional futures for a stepson who had none, the story of Rex Gascoigne reverses the decision to send the Lewes boys abroad, contributing in this way to the novel's persistent critique of colonialism. Rex's brother Warham, "dismal under a cram of everything except the answers needed at the forthcoming examination, which might disclose the welfare of our Indian Empire to be somehow connected with a quotable knowledge of Browne's Pastorals" (chap. 5), offers a wry glimpse of Thornie's preparations for the Indian civil service exam. Rex himself, described in terms reminiscent of the language attached to Charles Lewes ("enjoying ordinary, innocent things so much that vice had no temptation for him"), is another young man who gets into trouble with his father about a horse, though his mistake is the domestic one of breaking the horse's knees in headlong pursuit of a woman. Made miserable by Gwendolen's rejection of his love, Rex resolves to go off to the colonies to live on the land. In the innocence of his romanticism, he imagines that colonial life would be a bit like playing house (chap. 8). During the ensuing struggle with his father, Rex exhibits some emotional intractibility, but Mr. Gascoigne wins easily: "In my opinion you have no right whatever to expatriate yourself until you have honestly endeavoured to turn to account the education you have received here" (chap. 8). The successful paternal management of an obdurate son suggests a family that functions through the power of a legitimate male line, as Gwendolen's does not. But the sense of affection lavished upon this minor scene suggests a resonance with remembered family struggles concluded with far less definitive parental control. The even greater intensity with which, in chapter 16, George Eliot imagines the young Daniel Deronda's sensitivity and silence on the unexplained subject of his birth links Deronda's sensibility closely with her own. Yet the pain he undergoes when his love for Sir Hugo Mallinger is mixed with a lurking sense of shame may owe something to Marian Lewes's intuitions about her stepsons' struggles to accommodate their family irregularities with outward grace.

By the time George Eliot was imagining the Gascoigne family, she had additional reason to worry about the fates of young men in colonial lands. Herbert Lewes was dying in Natal. Since 1873 his letters had reported painful "neuralgia" in his back and hips; like Thornie he lost a tremendous amount of weight. However ominous those signs may have appeared to his parents, Herbert was not encouraged to return, and he remained in a life of near poverty with his wife and child until he died in Durban at the end of June 1875—a few weeks after the birth of his second child, whom he never saw. Herbert lived and died offstage. He maintained a correspondence with his parents, and Lewes sent him money at every occasion when Herbert suggested a special necessity, but the silence about him in the Lewes letters to others is rarely broken except at the moments of his marriage and his death. The most extensive pieces of writing connected with Herbert are two letters written by the educated Durban couple who had provided a family refuge for Thornie during his early years in Natal, John and Marie Sanderson. (Sanderson was editor of the *Natal Colonist*; his wife was musical and had provided Thornie with many evenings of cultural companionship). When Herbert arrived alone in Durban seeking health, and remained to die, the Sandersons again acted in loco parentis, and provided the Leweses with full factual and emotional accounts of his death (9:158–63). Marie Sanderson, writing to Marian Lewes, noted how they had earlier been struck by "Herbert's good sense and quiet cheerfulness, which contrasted with but did not spoil Thornton's gay, good natured, winning manner"; when she saw Herbert arrive looking just as Thornie had when she had last seen him, "the ghost of his former self," she was "almost too overpowered to greet him" (9:162). The differences in tone between the educated letters of these kind people, Bertie's barely articulate reports of himself, and the extreme distance with which he is mentioned in the Lewes letters, form part of the pathos of this story.

During the year after Thornie's death, Bertie, who had been left alone on their remote farm, became engaged to Eliza Stevenson Harrison of Newcastle, Natal. He announced on December 23, 1870, that he had sold the farm: "I would sooner live in Natal than here, there is more societie. I shall not be quite buried alive as I am here. Mr. and Mrs. Harrison are very glad I have sold the farm. I think it is done for the best" (8:491). At twenty-four Bertie's misspellings were only occasional, but his childlike syntax and his inability to connect one written idea with another had remained. Because he records good and bad facts in the same blunt bare fashion, his letters are nevertheless powerful records of the repeated hardships he seems to have endured with unfailing acceptance. Mr. Harrison opposed the marriage— "They want her to give me up because I am poor"—and refused to give anything to support the young couple; after her father threatened to hit her, Eliza ran away from home and stayed with friends until she and Bertie were privately married (9:16). Bertie sold the Falls of the Assagai for a span of oxen, six horses, and fifteen pounds, and rented another farm nearer to civilization, only to discover after building a house on it that the land was disputed and he had to leave (9:34–35). During the next three years he made shift as he could, in poverty and illness; much of his income came from working as a wagoner "riding timber," and he raised as many sheep as he could afford, filling his letters with accounts of his current numbers of sheep and lambs, or of his losses. His affection for Eliza and his pride in their daughter is evident despite his inexpressive prose; he gamely attempted in the midst of their poverty to keep up his interest in another kind of life, thanking his parents for "Boxes of Books" and money to buy a piano for Eliza (9:102, 106). His last letters, truncated by his illness, maintain the position that he is getting better even as they record new and alarming symptoms. At the last, Sanderson reported, his doctor forbore to tell him he was going to die.

The immense gap in intelligence and sensibility between Herbert and his parents seems to have rendered this relationship both private and remote. Marian briefly noted the news of Bertie's engagement with pleasure and relief in a letter to Cara Bray: "Since Thornie's death we have especially desired this foundation of a lasting companionship" (5:114); her journal reports "a letter from Bertie telling us, to our joy, that he was engaged to a 'well-educated young lady, Eliza

Stevenson Harrison,' and we agreed to write to the young lady's father on the subject to see if any provision could be made for their early marriage" (5:119). Her language gives no hint that she understood the less-than-genteel social circumstances in which they were about to become implicated or that Eliza might be trading on their fame and wealth in her request for intervention. Yet Eliza's letters—as well as some of the letters that Bertie wrote in her presence—suggest that she may have been quite conscious of the benefits to be derived from maintaining a sentimental connection with the two important writers in London; the decision to name the two children "Marian" and "George Herbert Arthur" after people Eliza had never met may suggest either Herbert's naive gratitude and affection or a kind of calculation. Eliza was "well educated" to the extent that she could read, write, and play the piano "a little" (8:491); she could manage to put on elevated diction for a few sentences, but her natural style, on the grammatical level of Bertie's, was histrionic and sentimental. When Bertie's letters rather uncharacteristically tell how little Marian stands on the sofa to kiss the portrait of Lewes, the guiding hand of Eliza may be imagined; her own letters, written after Bertie's death when the Leweses had agreed to support her and the children, are full of "Dear Pater" and "Dear Mutter" and heart-tugging details that attest to her devoted love for Bertie and the children (9:163–65, 179–81).

The Leweses, for their part, banned any occasion for sentiment after Bertie's death. The news reached them in one of their country retreats; they did not announce it or use mourning stationery. More than a year later, Marian explained to John Blackwood that her continued concern for money arose from having "a widowed daughter-in-law and two little grandchildren in Natal," who were "entirely our charge," and that they had not told anyone of Herbert's death because "Mr. Lewes dreaded letters of condolence." It is particularly interesting that this letter should describe her desire to continue receiving royalties on her books as her inclination to "keep up a sort of active parental relation to those grown-up children" (6:303–4); her books were the children who were filling, rather than emptying, both her emotional and her financial accounts.

The few private reports of Bertie's death written after the news arrived in August 1875 are almost drained of affect. Barbara Bodichon heard of it because Marian wanted to explain why she could not contribute at that time to the funds for Girton College (6:161). D'Albert Durade—always a repository of family news—heard of it; so did

Sara Hennell and Emilia Pattison. In these letters Marian spoke of
Bertie's "thoroughly happy" marriage (6:177), describing the pair as
"peculiarly united" through their retired life (6:174); she wished to
emphasize Bertie's separate domestic happiness, along with their own
new responsibility for the widow and children. To D'Albert-Durade,
she explained that they had been "afraid of urging him to come to
England because his disease was of a nature to be encouraged by our
fitful climate" (6:174). It was only in a letter to John Cross, her "Dearest Nephew," that Marian manifested—and attempted to deny—signs
of the guilt which had been hidden behind their silences. "He was a
sweet-natured creature—not clever, but diligent and well-judging
about the things of daily life, and we felt ten years ago that a colony
with a fine climate, like Natal, offered him the only fair prospect
within his reach. What can we do more than try to arrive at the best
conclusion from the conditions as they are known to us? The issue,
which one could not foresee, must be borne with resignation—is in no
case a ground for self-reproach, and in this case, I imagine, would
hardly have been favourably altered by a choice of life in the old
country" (6:165). Along with suggesting that by 1875 an important
level of intimacy had been reached with Cross, this passage hints at
the nature of the private dialogue between Marian and Lewes: the felt
self-reproach argued down by by reason. There had been no opportunity, "in this case," for redemptive nursing. Bertie's death was attributed to a glandular disease latent since childhood, and the matter, as
told to Sara in November 1875, rested under the umbrella of inherited weakness: "The boys seem all to have inherited an untrustworthy
physique" (6:191).

Eliza Lewes had, however, no intention of understanding the un-
written rule, so deeply absorbed by the Lewes boys in their Hofwyl
years, which had kept Thornie and Bertie away from England. Nor
did she quite grasp the fine points of the policy that paid her expenses
in the hope that she would keep her children in Africa as long as
possible. (The Leweses planned, in accordance with a very conventional colonial pattern, that Eliza would keep her children in South
Africa until they were about twelve, when they would be sent to England for their educations. The argument that the benign Natal climate was essential to their well-being also came into play, as it had in
Bertie's case [7:132].) On November 18, 1878, as Lewes lay dying,
Eliza wrote him a letter which would have reached Marian at the
height of her mourning. She began by tugging at the strings of senti-

ment, quoting her children's amused responses to "Grandpa's" addresses to them as "chicks," and moving quickly to a hysterical account of the fears aroused by the current phase of the English colonial violence in South Africa. Rebellious "Kafirs" threatened to break into her house, and the black police supplied to offer protection offended her: "Just fancy dear Pater those nasty dirty black creatures." She concluded with an apology for not writing sooner, "—and yet it is not for want of love for my Pater we know only too well in this large world we have only our good loving Pater and Mutter that cares for us and love us" (9:241). This abject statement of dependency was a prelude to Eliza's intention to come to England. Uninvited, and undeterred by the news of "Pater's" death, she arrived at the end of April 1879—like one of George Eliot's blackmailing characters who enact the return of the repressed—apparently hoping to be invited to live with Marian at the Priory.[24] The children were beautiful but badly brought up by English standards, and Eliza tormented Marian and Charles with her demands for more money. In December, after absorbing various rebuffs, "the Africans" retired to the relatively safe distance of Brighton; Gertrude Lewes arranged proper schooling for young Marian.

Whatever private ironies the young girl's name may have elicited in her famous namesake may have been compounded by the fact that "Marian" was not her own given name; the passing on of an extralegal name from an extralegal grandmother was further ironized when, in the following year, the grandmother legalized her status as "Mary Ann Cross." Meeting the young Marian and George did, however, result in some unusually direct musing on the subject of children, which was recorded by Edith Simcox, who happened to encounter her beloved Mrs. Lewes just as she returned from a first visit with the South African family. "She smiled compassionately at the good friends who think these children will be a comfort and interest to her—of course she is glad to be able to provide for them, but they cannot enter into her life. And yet she said, if the girl had been alone in the world, it would have been a temptation to her; but it was best as it was; she always became a slave to the child or whatever else she lived with" (9:265). Young Marian had passingly retrieved the *Silas Marner* fantasy: what would it have been like to have a beautiful little girl land on her doorstep? More important, she began a chain of reflection which illustrates the elder Marian's view of herself as a kind of emotional monomaniac who must either be swallowed up—enslaved—by her response to another's dependence or remain apart in her own productive life. As her musing continued, "she spoke half in self-reproach of the people who live in so many relations that their life must be always full, whereas she always sent the strength of her feeling in the channel which absorbed it all. It had been so with her father." Of her marriage, "she said it seemed a sort of dual egoism: but then again that it must surely be best to make the nearest relation perfect" (9:266). In the light of the stories I have been telling in this chapter, such reflections suggest that George Eliot's stepsons had never entered fully into her private emotional life, except during the brief periods when their strong needs overwhelmed her; the period of Thornie's dying was the most intense of these. Her acknowledgment of these truths made her feel that her relation with Lewes was egotistical; at the same time her loving care for his sons was part of what was required in order to maintain a "perfect" relation with him.[25] Paradoxically, to love Lewes perfectly was both to nurture his sons and to ensure at least Thornie's and Bertie's absence from the life of "dual egoism"; and it was precisely that paradox that they had managed to live.

Marian's idea that there was an absolute choice between giving herself to others and doing her own work—that is, that she could be either Marian Lewes or George Eliot but not both at once—sometimes expressed itself in metaphors of self-division that came into special play when her stepsons entered her life.[26] In the particular context of Lewes family relations, the repeated metaphors of books as children (which began just at the time the stepsons entered her life and were also used by Lewes, Thornton, and Barbara Bodichon in letters) may well have developed into a shared family language intended affectionately to defuse several unalterable facts: that she was not to bear actual children; that she was not, after all, the boys' "Mother"; and that they all recognized the writing of her books as her primary passion.

Despite the way she liked to imagine her emotional makeup, however, it would be incorrect to establish a theoretical gap between Marian Lewes's stepmotherhood and her writing. Her experience of Lewes's sons profoundly altered what she wrote about and how she wrote about it. Whether her plots and narratives were generated as compensatory fantasies or informed by direct experience—and they were both—her focus on children brought up by substitute parents, and her privileging of fostering over kinship, was a dominant feature of her imagination from 1860 to the end of her career; the experience of her stepsons gave her the authority for those imagined lives. "I like much better to hear of children already born being taken care of, than to be asked to rejoice greatly because a new one is born," Marian Lewes wrote to Barbara Bodichon, a few months after the birth of Charles's second daughter in 1874 (6:69). As Nancy Paxton has pointed out, George Eliot stretched the definition of "maternal" to identify it it with women's creative insight in general, disconnecting it from the fact of procreation.[27] In her moral thinking the human capacity for goodness was far more readily exemplified by selfless adult reponses to young need than it could be by biological parenthood.

At the same time her personal feeling poured itself more easily into elective affinities with younger people than into the task of loving her stepsons. On August 10, 1869, just as Thornie entered a crisis of his illness, she wrote to Emilia Pattison, apologizing for an untoward "effusiveness" of feeling in their last meeting. "But in proportion as I profoundly rejoice that I never brought a child into the world, I am conscious of having an unused stock of motherly tenderness, which sometimes overflows, but not without discrimination" (5:52). Attending on Thornie's painful suffering would have been more than enough to bring on that profound rejoicing, but it was not enough, it seems, to satisfy motherly tenderness. The effort he demanded may in fact have made her all the more conscious of her desire for easy, spontaneous, and unbidden maternal feelings. The second substitute family of adoring young adults which she and Lewes collected around them in the last decade of their lives was, however, to provide yet another arena in which she had to invent and negotiate her tutelary roles.

EIGHT

Old and Young

> One of the memorable events of this closing year to
> me will always be the acquisition of you as a known
> friend—a friend of the only sort I now desire much
> to acquire: one who takes into his own life the
> spiritual outcome of mine.
>
> —George Eliot to Alexander Main,
> December 28, 1871

While she was in her fifties, George Eliot was gradually transformed into the institution, or myth, that has retained its power for
more than a century. It is that myth which Elaine Showalter invokes
when she describes the late nineteenth-century writers, male and female, who had somehow to reinvent the novel after the reign of
"Queen George"; it is that institution which Deirdre David evokes
when she describes how, in literary criticism, "Eliot looms as a monolithic figure; as sybilline sage, extensively celebrated and finely dissected in all her eminent Victorianism and incipient Modernism."[1] As
David goes on to argue, this mysterious transformation occurred during George Eliot's lifetime, powered both by her own invention of
herself as a "majestically sybilline moral voice" and by the need of a
patriarchal culture to defend itself from the "disruptive anomaly" of
an intellectually powerful woman by creating the myth of a masculine
intellect dwelling in a feminine consciousness.[2] Reading the letters of
Marian Lewes's last decade allows us to come at this matter from
another angle and to consider the personal image that she allowed
herself to believe and cultivate in her relationships with the group of
younger worshipers who began to cluster around her in the early

1870s. For it is not at all clear that George Eliot had any intention of turning herself into the cultural icon she—briefly—became, or even that she fully understood the phenomenon to be occurring. The rhetoric of the later letters does suggest, however, that in her final decade George Eliot found herself responding strongly to personal calls upon her power to influence other human beings and that she increasingly allowed herself to be identified with her own narrative voice.

It is tempting to think of the years 1870–1880 as Marian Lewes's "posthumous decade," because they began with so acute a consciousness of her own death. When Thornie died in October 1869, she wrote in her journal, "This death seems to me the beginning of our own" (5:60); and for the next two or three years her letters regularly repeat the notion that her life is on the verge of ending. "I think too much, too continually of death now, almost to the partial eclipse of life—as if life were so narrow a strip as hardly to be taken much reckoning of," she wrote to Charles when one of Gertrude's aunts died in July 1870 (5:110). Having reached the age of fifty, she calls herself and Lewes "rickety old people" with "short lives" when she writes to younger correspondents, and she imagines the birthdays others will have after she is dead (5:120, 76). Thornie's untimely death was not the only experience that lay behind this mood. Marian's mother had died at forty-seven or forty-eight, her sister at forty-five, and she—who shared their propensity for ill health—was highly conscious of physical heredity. The notion that life after fifty was "extra," something added on, seemed to be a kind of relief, a lightening of some burden or task. There is far less melancholy in these anticipations of death than in the anxiety that had colored earlier views of her future, which were laden with the fear that she could not sustain her ability to write.

The embrace of her own death was in part a defense against the prospect that Lewes might die before her. "Oh how short life—how near death—seems to me!" she wrote to Sara Hennell on the verge of her fifty-first birthday. "But this is not an uncheerful thought. The only great dread is the protraction of life into imbecility, or the visitation of lingering pain" (5:122). "The idea of dying has no melancholy for me, except in the parting and leaving behind which Love makes so hard to contemplate," she wrote to D'Albert-Durade two months later (5:135). For her friend the Talmudic scholar Emanuel Deutsch, who was mortally ill in his early forties, she produced an argument against suicide, citing the example of Mary Wollstonecraft's plan to drown herself: "She tells how it occurred to her as she was walking in this damp shroud, that she might live to be glad that she had not put an end to herself—and so it turned out. She lived to know some real joys, and death came in time to hinder the joys from being spoiled" (5:161). To say that Wollstonecraft's death saved her joys from spoiling is a very peculiar way of describing death after childbirth. It reiterates Marian Lewes's habitual notion that her own career might be retrospectively "spoiled" by some future event and suggests in this case how fully her unstated fears clustered around an image of herself aging alone in a socially untenable position.

By 1873 the overwhelming success of *Middlemarch* with its increasing signs of social acceptance in England brought on a period of renewed confidence, and the obsession with her own death diminished. The deaths of some famous contemporaries, coinciding with the growing fame of George Eliot, enlivened the related question of biography and autobiography. How should the life of a writer be retrospectively represented, if at all? How could she prevent the public from paying more attention to her life than to her art? The Leweses followed a consistent policy of refusing to provide biographical information about Marian even when the circulating facts about her life were incorrect; yet they read every contemporary biography and autobiography the moment it appeared. The energy of her recorded responses makes it clear that her attraction to life stories was checked only by her fear that they would betray too much.

Before she became known as George Eliot, Marian reveled in biographies and memoirs; they provided glimpses into hidden emotional lives, and sources of inspiration. "It is a help to read such a life as Margaret Fuller's," she wrote to Clementia Taylor in 1852. "How inexpressibly touching that passage from her journal—'I shall always reign through the intellect, but the life! the life! O my God! shall that never be sweet?' I am thankful, as if for myself, that it was sweet at last" (2:15). When Elizabeth Gaskell's *Life* of Charlotte Brontë came out in 1857 Marian defended it against "some people" who "think its revelations in bad taste—making money out of the dead—wounding the feelings of the living etc. etc. What book is there that some people or other will not find abominable? We thought it admirable—cried over it—and felt the better for it" (2:330). After she had finished reading John Gibson Lockhart's *Life of Scott* aloud to Lewes, she was moved as if Scott were an intimate who had just died: "Sometimes, when I read of the death of some great, sensitive human being, I have a triumph in the sense that they are at rest, and yet along with that, such deep sadness at the thought that the rare nature is gone for ever into darkness and we can never know that our love and reverence can reach him, that I seem to have gone through a personal sorrow when I shut the book and go to bed." Lewes, she tells Sara Hennell, "loves Scott now as well as I do" (3:15–16). The intense emotional identification that biographies stirred in her was a feeling she worked to produce for the readers of her novels. But when it later came to the question of George Eliot biography, she found herself in the position of the "some people" who had disapproved of Gaskell's life of Brontë.

The Bracebridge affair of 1859 was responsible for initiating the particular vehemence with which Marian opposed the circulation of information about her life. During that period and later she pursued a policy of indifference to the inaccurate biographical information that was invented to fill the gaps left by her silence on the subject of her early life. As Lewes wrote in 1861 to the inquiring editor of *Men of the Time*, "Unable to prevent others from writing about her she steadily declines in any way assisting in attempts of which she cannot approve" (3:429). At least twice, however, she was moved to express her actual fidelity to accuracy. When Bracebridge called her a "self-educated farmer's daughter," she wrote sternly to Charles Bray to correct the matter of her father's social position, describing Robert Evans as one who "raised himself from being an artizan to be a man whose extensive knowledge in very varied practical departments made his services valued through several counties" (3:168–69). Her ire was directed at Bray himself, whom she suspected of originating the idea that her father was a "mere farmer." She was attempting not only to protect her father's sense of social class and the long devotion she had given him but also to prevent Isaac from hearing tales that might suggest his wayward sister had exaggerated the drama of her own social ascent. By the mid-1870s the policy had become slightly more flexible; Marian allowed herself to offer a modicum of biographical information to the American literary lecturer Elizabeth Stuart Phelps because Phelps had managed to assure her that she cared more about her works than about her life. For her Marian briefly clarified the county and religion of her childhood, and the dates of her acquaintance with Herbert Spencer and John Stuart Mill (6:163–64).

The tug-of-war between her interest in biography as a study of

character and development and her hatred of the uses to which biographical information was put extended also to her attitude about
letters. "I have destroyed almost all my friends' letters to me," she
wrote to Sara in 1861, "because they were only intended for my eyes,
and could only fall into the hands of persons who knew little of the
writers, if I allowed them to remain till after my death. In proportion
as I love every form of piety—which is venerating love—I hate hard
curiosity; and unhappily my experience has impressed me with the
sense that hard curiosity is the more common temper of mind"
(3:376). She was still smarting from Bracebridge. But she never demanded that her friends treat her own letters in the same way. By
1874 she could return a loaned letter from Sara with the explanation
"I habitually think of death as so near that I see all documents in the
light of things left behind for others, rather than kept for myself"
(6:34–35). Her willingness to leave her letters behind for others was
secured by her knowledge of how careful they had—almost—always
been.

   By 1870 Marian was clearly thinking about autobiography as well.
For her birthday that year Lewes gave her "a Lock-up book for her
Autobiography" (5:123n.). A year earlier Emily Davies had reported
on a conversation with "Mrs. Lewes" during which the subject of
autobiography developed out of a discussion of *The Mill on the Floss*:
"It was impossible for her to write an autobiography, but she wished
that somebody else could do it, it might be useful—or, that she could
do it herself. She could do it better than any one else, because she
could do it impartially, judging herself, and showing how wrong *she*
was. She spoke of having come into collision with her father and being
on the brink of being turned out of his house" (8:465–66). This
report is revealing for several reasons, not least because of George
Eliot's idea that "impartiality" meant turning her life into a "useful"
cautionary tale against the arrogant exercise of intellectual superiority by the young. Such a view of autobiography would explain why
she found it impossible: writing about her liaison with Lewes and the
break with her family, in no matter how moral a way, was not a story
that could be offered up to the youth who were her imagined audience. Yet her wavering about who might write her life story suggests a
force of blocked desire to which Lewes probably responded when he
bought her a book with a lock.

   Around 1870 Marian may have been toying with the idea of an
autobiography like that of Harriet Martineau, which would not see

the light of day until after Martineau's death. Six years later, anticipating the publication of Martineau's autobiography with great interest, she had not proceeded with her own, but she was still thinking about it. As she put it to Sara, "Autobiography at least saves a man or woman that the world is curious about from the publication of a string of mistakes called 'memoirs'" (6:311). On December 31, 1877, however, she pointedly closed her journal: "Today I say a final farewell to this little book which is the only record I have made of my personal life for sixteen years and more" (6:439).

The final farewell to the idea of autobiography was shaped by Marian's responses to the biographies and autobiographies that were published during the decade of her own celebrity. In September 1869 Harriet Beecher Stowe published "The True Story of Lord Byron's Life" in the *Atlantic Monthly* and sent Marian a copy (5:53). The revival of public attention to the connection between Byron and his half sister Augusta Leigh shocked and enraged Marian, who could not bring herself to refer to it except as "the Byron subject" or "the Byron question." She had just been transforming her own difficult fraternal relationship into a pastoral memory of very early childhood in the Wordsworthian *Brother and Sister* sonnets, and the implicit personal threat of having the real issues of that relationship served up for public consumption was translated into the language of indignant social concern. As she wrote to Sara, "nothing can outweigh to my mind the heavy social injury of familiarizing young minds with the desecration of family ties"; the public airing was "a pestilence likely to leave very ugly marks" (5:56). To Stowe herself Marian gently stated her preference that "the 'Byron question' should not have been brought before the public, because I think the discussion of such subjects is injurious socially" (5:71). She was still indignant four years later. Writing to Blackwood in April 1873 about the special possibilities in the relation of brother and sister and the poem she had written about this "one of my best loved subjects," Marian showed that she had made the personal connection: "I was proportionately enraged about that execrable discussion raised in relation to Byron. The deliberate insistence on the subject was a worse crime against Society than the imputed fact" (5:403). Every personal passion, it seems, was now to be filtered through the idea of the young minds who had to be educated to sustain the social fabric.

The specter of Byron revelations haunted Marian's thoughts as she read John Forster's *Life of Charles Dickens* as well. She had many criti-

cisms of Forster's work, but she liked the sections on Dickens's boy-
hood experience and the transcriptions of his letters, while finding
his later years to "wear a melancholy aspect . . . in the feverish pursuit of loud effects and money" (5:226, 6:23). Her preference for
memories of early years remained consistent; as she wrote to Sara in
1876, "All biography diminishes in interest when the subject has won
celebrity" (6:311). But her genuine interest even in the "freshness and
naturalness" of the humor in the extracts from Dickens's later letters
gave way to a diatribe to John Blackwood about "our national habits in
the matter of literary biography. Is it not odious that as soon as a man
is dead his desk is raked, and every insignificant memorandum which
he never meant for the public, is printed for the gossiping amusement
of people too idle to re-read his books?"[3] The fashion of being "titil-
lated by the worst" is, in her view, "something like the uncovering of
the dead Byron's club foot" (6:23)—a displacement that might warm
the heart of any orthodox Freudian.

The anxiety about sexual relations attended even upon her reading
of John Stuart Mill's *Autobiography* in 1873. "The account of his early
education and the presentation of his Father are admirable, but there
are some pages in the latter half that one would have liked to be
different," she wrote to Barbara Bodichon (5:458). She clarified the
vague reference for Barbara a few weeks later, after being reassured
by the public response that "the effect of the book is good": "I feared
then that the exaggerated expressions in which he conveys his feeling
about his wife would neutralize all the good that might have come
from the beautiful fact of his devotion to her" (5:467). She may have
been conveying something of her anxiety about Lewes's own tendency
to encourage exaggerated reponses to her. Yet the fearful notion that
a single lapse could "neutralize" a whole career of "good" revealed
itself again as a deep pattern of consciousness. Writing autobiography
looked risky: it might create a dangerous propensity to reread her
novels in ways she believed she had not intended.

The publication of Harriet Martineau's autobiography in 1877 was
probably the deciding factor in Marian's stance toward biography and
autobiography. Once again, she found the work "pathetic and interesting throughout the childhood and early youth," but she was horrified by Martineau's presentation of her own writings and others' opinions of them. Although it is difficult to imagine any narrative more
alien to the sensibility of George Eliot than the single-minded "tough
lady" voice of Martineau, Marian spoke of the work very personally

when she wrote to Blackwood about it: "The impression on me was one of shuddering vexation with myself that I had ever said a word to anybody about either compliments or injuries in relation to my own doings. But assuredly I shall not write such things down to be published after my death" (6:351–52). She did not waver in her public espousal of the position that autobiography was valuable as the record of struggle but not as a narrative of achievement.

The Martineau case also demonstrated that a right feeling of reticence about family matters in the autobiographer did not secure her from the gossip mongering of others after her death. "I rejoiced profoundly in the conquest of right feeling which determined her to leave the great, sad breach with her once beloved brother in almost total silence," Marian wrote to Cara Bray, who would have understood exactly what she was talking about. But then she discovered that Maria Weston Chapman, who had added "memorials" to the Martineau volumes, had given a full acount of the public quarrel between Harriet and her brother James. "Really there is nothing but imbecility to be pleaded as a reason why Mrs. Chapman's conduct should not be called wicked," Marian wrote in a rare burst of youthful sarcasm (6:353). When Sara Hennell argued that Martineau herself had been partly responsible for publicizing the affair, Marian attacked any person "who has cared about a future life in the minds of a coming generation" who perpetuated personal animosities through her writing. The more she thought about Martineau's book, she said, the more repugnance she felt to autobiography, "unless it can be so written as to involve neither self-glorification nor impeachment of others. I like that the 'He, being dead, yet speaketh,' should have quite another meaning than that" (6:371).[4]

The meaning she had in mind was formulated more explicitly a year after Lewes's death, when Mrs. Thomas Trollope wrote to ask whether there was to be a biography. "The best history of a writer is contained in his writings—these are his chief actions," she replied. "If he happens to have left an autobiography telling (what nobody else can tell) how his mind grew, how it was determined by the joys, sorrows and other influences of childhood and youth—that is a precious contribution to knowledge. But Biographies generally are a disease of English literature" (7:230). Adhering to the Wordsworthian model for the growth of the writer's mind, these sentences suggest a private decision to define *The Mill on the Floss* as her own way of leaving such a "contribution to knowledge." The whole vexed question of her "chief actions" as an adult could then be simplified, by redefining them as her books.

What little rein she gave to her autobiographical impulse was shifted onto the fictional male narrator of the first two essays in *Impressions of Theophrastus Such*—a narrator significantly innocent of any achievement, publication, or fame. Yet the desire to touch other, younger lives through the story of her own remained an active part of Marian Lewes's consciousness. Through her books, because of the projected voice that seemed to have access to the secrets of the human heart, she gathered in a small crop of young men and women who allowed her to feel the force of her influence, and whom she embraced as absorbers and disseminators of her accumulated wisdom. She had little power to choose her disciples; for the most part they chose her, forming an odd assortment of characters who played their parts in George Eliot's later years. Her willingness to allow them into her life when they applied does, however, say a good deal about her desire to play in person the roles she had created for the narrators of her books.

Acting the sage in public pronouncement was something she forbade herself. To her positivist friend Frederic Harrison, who was always trying to enlist the voice of George Eliot in his causes, she formulated her objections in January 1870. "But the fact is, I shrink from decided 'deliverances' on momentous subjects, from the dread of coming to swear by my own 'deliverances' and sinking into an insistent echo of myself. That is a horrible destiny—and one cannot help seeing that many of the most powerful men fall into it" (5:76). Approached from such an angle, Marian betrayed the sense of her own power which she more generally attempted to conceal. Seven years later she was still fending off Harrison's requests by describing her "antithetic experiences": "I wonder whether you at all imagine the terrible pressure of disbelief in my own duty/right to speak to the public, which is apt with me to make all beginnings of work like a rowing against tide. Not that I am without more than my fair ounce of self-conceit and confidence that I know better than the critics, whom I don't take the trouble to read but who seem to fill the air as with the smoke of bad tobacco" (6:387). The feminist Clementia Taylor was also chided in 1878 for pressuring her to take political positions in public: "My function is that of the *aesthetic*, not the doctrinal teacher—the rousing of the nobler emotions, which make mankind desire the social right, not the prescribing of special measures, concerning which the artistic mind, however strongly moved by social sympathy, is often not the best judge" (7:44). By this time the tone of sagedom—the swallowing up of Marian Lewes in her self-defined function—prevails in the very act of refusing to play the role.

Private prescriptions to particular young minds were another matter. George Eliot's idea was that she would contribute to social progress by influencing young men who would shape the world of tomorrow. In November 1867 she wrote to Blackwood of the many "testimonies" she has received from readers, "especially young men, who are just the class I care most to influence" (4:397). By 1869 her new interest in the young had become a dominant theme in her letters. To Oscar Browning, the Eton schoolmaster who was to become a George Eliot worshiper and biographer, she wrote, "The getting older brings some new satisfactions, and among these I find the growth of a maternal feeling towards both men and women who are much younger than myself" (5:5). Robert Browning received a note signed "M.E.[L.]" in which she reported on a private letter praising Browning's poetry in order to convey "the assurance of having fed a valuable young life" (5:41). Such phrases recur in letters to many others; and when George Eliot had the opportunity to put her new theory into practice, she made the most of it. After a visit to Cambridge in May 1873, she wrote to Maria Congreve, "The real pleasure of the visit consisted in talking with a hopeful group of Trinity young men"—an occasion into which Lewes projected "the silent worship of some of the best young men there" (5:412, 415). For the younger generation she was not Marian Evans, who had run away with George Henry Lewes, but George Eliot, who had looked straight at a godless universe and still found reason for reverence.

After Alexander Main entered into correspondence with her, Marian wrote to him that he was "a friend of the only sort I now desire much to acquire: one who takes into his own life the spiritual outcome of mine" (5:229). Such a definition of friendship—as a kind of extraphysical fertilization of the younger by the elder—makes it clear that what she valued most was the private absorption of her narrative voice. Her interest in the idea that the readerly relation is a "spiritual" one recurs in a letter to an American fan whom she knew she would never meet. "Apart from those relations in life which bring daily opportunities of lovingness, the most satisfactory of all ties is this effective invisible intercourse of an elder mind with a younger," she told Alice Wellington (5:367). She had achieved, she thought, what she most wanted: to become for young readers one of the powerful voices in books which had fertilized and sustained her own lonely youth. In her journal she rendered the immense success of *Middlemarch* as "the growth of my spiritual existence when my bodily existence is decaying," and she contrasted that growth to "the merely egoistic satisfactions of fame," which "are easily nullified by a toothache" (5:357).

The notion that she now had a "spiritual existence" that lay apart from her body and her ego was carried over into actual relationships that involved physical meetings as well as correspondence. She was "spiritual mother" to Elma Stuart's "spiritual daughter," a term that also included Emilia Pattison, affectionately named "Figliuolina" and "Goddaughter," Georgiana Burne-Jones ("Mignon"), and, more problematically, Edith Simcox. All these women, along with the whole Cross family, became part of her "spiritual" family, so that the word came to refer not only to the influence she created through her books but to imaginatively invented familial ties that took the place of her actual sundered ones.

Although two of George Eliot's "spiritual daughters," Georgiana Burne-Jones and Emilia Pattison, were women with eminent husbands whom she met through the normal social channels of English artistic and intellectual life, other young presences of the 1870s— Alexander Main, Elma Stuart, Edith Simcox—were decidedly odder characters who found their way to George Eliot through her books, and were admitted into an "inner circle" partly through the encouragement of George Henry Lewes. Lewes is often seen as the orchestrator of the George Eliot cult in the 1870s, and the letters do give evidence that he fostered idolators. He could not have done so entirely against Marian's will, although he was probably more aware than she was of the need to take advantage of any chance to mitigate the effects of the dual isolation into which he felt responsible for leading her. There are signs that he was becoming weary of her tendency to despair, which did not, even after all those years, respond to the medicine of success. As she was writing *Middlemarch*, Lewes complained to Blackwood of her depression: rereading *Felix Holt* had "made her *thin* with misery, so deeply impressed was she with the fact that she could never write like that again and that what is now in hand is rinsings of the cask! How battle against such an art of ingeniously self tormenting?" (5:246). The preparation for *Daniel Deronda* interfered with Lewes's own concentration on his own book, *Problems of Life and Mind*: "I am hard at work and wish she were; but she simmers and simmers, despairs and despairs, believes she can never do anything again worth doing etc. etc. A word from you may give her momentary confidence. Once let her *begin* and on she will go of her own impulse" (6:11). It was still necessary, Lewes felt, to appeal to Blackwood for help in managing this high-strung thoroughbred on which the two of them had placed their bets.

Blackwood himself came in the aftermath of *Deronda* to feel that Lewes overdid it. "She was looking a little worn and I think Lewes fidgets her in his anxiety both about her and her work and himself," he wrote to his nephew (6:253). Blackwood had a preference for Marian, and may have been himself rather fidgeted by Lewes, but it is impossible to know the extent to which Lewes's protectiveness was more necessary to himself than to Marian. His experience of her had made him conclude that endless amounts of adulation were essential, and when new sources of it turned up, he wanted to make the most of them.

Lewes also took pleasure in playing with names. As *Middlemarch* was coming out in 1872 he began to joke good-naturedly about himself and Marian as Casaubon and Dorothea, fearing that "my 'Key to all Mythologies' will have to be left to Dorothea!" (5:291); he later referred to *Problems of Life and Mind* as his "Key to all Psychologies": "How many 'excursus on Crete' she will have to omit one shudders to think" (5:338). (As it turned out, Marian did have to complete and publish the last volume after his death.) His notion that Marian was spiritually akin to Dorothea, along with old jokes about their living in a house called the Priory, may have led to the practice he began in 1875 of referring to her, in letters to the young admirers, as "Madonna." An ordinary enough term in Italian, this name suggests the spirit of play with which Lewes animated the "family" groups of the decade, with their various nicknames; for the sake of younger members it may well have served as a convenient substitute for the not-quite-appropriate "Marian" and the more formal "Mrs. Lewes."

Marian welcomed and fussed over her new "family"; she also fled from them. After 1869 she preferred spending several months of the year working in an English country retreat to the Continental travels that had been their former habit. Away from London and the demands of others, her health almost invariably improved, and she could work uninterrupted, in the knowledge that almost no one knew her address. The search for an appropriate house to rent from May through September became an annual ritual, until the Leweses

bought The Heights at Witley late in 1876. The alternation between a
London life, which was increasingly full of social appearances, and a
country life, to which only a very rare visitor was admitted, thus became the new rhythm of the 1870s, both for the Leweses and for
those who had attached themselves to them. Clearly the need for
adulation was more than balanced by a need to go beyond the range
of any other voices at all.

Alexander Main entered George Eliot's life in a letter forwarded to
the country village of Shottermill in the summer of 1871. The thirty-
year-old Scottish pupil-teacher, a fanatical admirer of George Eliot's
novels who liked to read them aloud on the seashore, wrote to ask
about the correct pronunciation of "Romola." George Eliot's first responses to Main's fervid letters suggest that she quickly identified with
the situation of this young provincial literary sensibility that reached
toward her from the town of Arbroath on the east coast of Scotland.
She treated him as someone who had reflected "on the small insight
and comparison that go to form the ordinary chit-chat judgments on
literature," to whom she could talk seriously about *Romola* as a historical novel influenced by the work of Scott (5:174–75). After Main
responded with what Haight calls "an eleven-page rhapsody on *Romola*" (5:176n), she told him about her own "worship for Scott" and
how it sustained her during her early years; she was undoubtedly
imagining that the chain continued in Main's worship of her. She
invites him to write again if it will be a "solace" to him, though she
does not promise to reply (5:175). Two more epistles about "The
Spanish Gypsy" rewarded him first with a brief acknowledgment,
then with a letter that sealed a more complex fate between them.
Confessing that his letter had made her cry, Marian wrote, "You have
thoroughly understood me—you have entered with perfect insight
into the significance of the poem. . . . In the passages which you
quote from the Fifth Book, you have put your finger on the true key"
(5:185). In this response her sympathy for his position and the consequences of her isolation from any serious discussion of her books with
other people were deeply mixed. Main became an emblem of her true
audience, the fervent and sensitive soul who dwelt beyond the ken of
the literary marketplace.

All the more ironic, then, that he should use her encouragement to
propose a scheme that would insert him into that marketplace under
the colors of George Eliot. A few weeks after the correspondence
began, Main suggested that he select and edit a book of extracts, or

"sayings," from George Eliot's novels. Nothing could have been farther from Marian's idea that the "wisdom" of her novels depended on the context of the whole. As she professed in a letter to Harrison of August 1866, "Aesthetic teaching is the highest of all teaching because it deals with life in its highest complexity. But if it ceases to be purely aesthetic—if it lapses anywhere from the picture to the diagram—it becomes the most offensive of all teaching" (4:300). Nevertheless, she allowed Lewes to encourage the project, although she disengaged herself from it as much as possible. The pleasure she took from a mind that responded directly to the appeals of her narrative voice was mixed with the probably consolatory notion that she was allowing Main to exercise and develop his literary and moral talent.

Lewes immediately promised Main that he would act as a go-between with Blackwood. When Blackwood quite naturally demurred at the prospect of such a charlatan scheme, Lewes argued that it would "deepen and extend the reputation of the works by bringing distinctly before people's minds what they only see indistinctly, the marvellous wealth of thought and feeling which the works contain" (5:195). Blackwood got the message; he read Main's letters, invited him down to Edinburgh, and found him innocent enough: "very quaint and thoroughly trustworthy I should say" (5:206). The *Wise, Witty, and Tender Sayings of George Eliot*—a title fashioned primarily by Lewes, who took it upon himself to become Main's literary adviser—came into being with great rapidity and was published in time for Christmas 1872.

Main organized his excerpts by novel, dividing the space for each work into quotations from "George Eliot, *in propria persona*," and from the language of certain characters.[5] In order to suggest the variety of tones in George Eliot's discourse, the excerpts were not rendered chronologically within each novel; in some cases passages close together in the text are presented as quite separate gems, so that the sense of a narrator's mind working its way through a subject is lost. But because Marian was so enthralled with Main's "power of putting his finger on the right passages, and giving emphasis to the right idea" (5:208) and because she responded to the volume by telling Main that she had looked through it "with that sort of delight which comes from seeing that another mind underlines the words one has most cared for in writing them" (5:229), the contents of the collection are quite telling. They are also perfectly predictable. Main did what anyone else would have done: he chose those passages in which the narrator widens the focus of her story and talks to her reader over the heads of her characters in those grand George Eliot generalizations. He had an eye for the pungent metaphor as well as for the moral or psychological insight; when it came to characters' speeches his selections inadvertently make the point that George Eliot's characters in their moral and aphoristic moments sound a good deal like versions of the narrator got up in various dialects. There is no doubt that Main did a creditable job of putting his finger on passages that are simultaneously rich and extractable; the book is not an embarrassment. But insofar as Marian was being something more than polite to a passionate provincial youth, the project reveals that she privately agreed with Main's idea that her most preacherly voice was most central to her fictional meaning. As he fulsomely put it in his preface, "She has for ever sanctified the Novel by making it the vehicle of the grandest and most uncompromising moral truth."[6] After the *Sayings* were in print, Marian continued to defend Main's special powers to Blackwood, who privately called him "the Gusher": "It is a great help for me to have such an indication that there exist careful readers, for whom no subtlest intention is lost" (5:231). Her blindness to the irony of cutting the books into pieces in order to make less careful readers attend to Main's underlinings signals the extent of her isolation from ordinary audience response, perhaps her mistrust of its existence.

The publication of the *Sayings* did not satisfy Main's desire for connection with George Eliot. Although he knew enough never to meet her in person, he wished to remain "one of the valued possessions in our spiritual estate," as she generously called him in a letter of 1875 (6:147). The letters that passed between them suggest that a kind of emotional push and pull had been created, to which the Leweses made themselves vulnerable: Main panics when a delayed response makes him imagine the worst; Lewes reprimands him, coddles him, and assails him with accounts of the great author's diffidence, while Marian goes on repeating that his reading of her work means so much to her, compelling him to produce more commentary. In March 1873 Lewes came up with a plan to deflect Main from his concentration on George Eliot worship, suggesting that he excerpt Boswell's *Life of Johnson*, weeding out all the extraneous matter contributed by Boswell himself (5:396). This rather absurd project sounds like a joke on the notion that Main had made himself George Eliot's Boswell without insisting on his own voice; nevertheless, it was done—badly enough so that even Lewes panned it.

Main was in any case more interested in adding a *Middlemarch* section to his new edition of the *Sayings*, for which he also submitted a new preface. Blackwood was horrified and sent it to Marian for her comment. "It seems to me that our friend puts the case rather too strong in favour of his compilation as compared with the Works," he hinted tactfully (5:456). Her response is the only written record of her actual doubts about Main's procedures. If his preface were true, she writes, "I should be quite stultified as an artist. Unless my readers are more moved towards the ends I seek by my works as wholes than by an assemblage of extracts, my writings are a mistake. I have always exercised a severe watch against anything that could be called preaching, and if I have ever allowed myself in dissertation or in dialogue [anything] which is not part of the *structure* of my books, I have there sinned against my own laws." Blackwood made no bones about rejecting Main's revisions after this, and the original preface was retained in all subsequent editions. Yet in spite of her "doubt about the desirability of the 'Sayings,'" Marian did not attack Main himself, who, she claimed, did not misunderstand his own words as his audiences were likely to do. Protecting him against Blackwood's skepticism, she repeated that Main had shown "a very fine instinct in his extracts and mode of arrangement, and I would not for the world undervalue his affectionate labours" (5:458–59). The key to the episode remains ambiguous: Marian's desire to cultivate reverence in the "affectionate labours" of the young is supported by her unacknowleged yearning to be heard as the preacher lurking within the artist. What Main had offered was in any case different from what she heard from Lewes, who made professional assessments of her work, or from Blackwood, whose praises were always about the lifelike qualities of her characters. Main gave the early signal that "George Eliot" would come to signify the widely ranging contemplative voice of her narrative art.

After 1873 the correspondence continued, settling down into polite epistolary dialogue and parental advice on the Leweses' part. But Main came up in November 1877 with another scheme: a George Eliot birthday book, to imitate *The Tennyson Birthday Book* which had come out earlier in that year. Marian did not put her foot down even then. She wrote to Blackwood that she would leave the decision up to him, after declaring her hatred of "puffing, gaudy, claptrappy forms of publication, superfluous for all *good* ends. But anything graceful which you consider an advantage to the circulation of my works we are not averse to" (6:423). Blackwood knew how to read such stances well enough to go ahead with the publication of a gaudily bound volume which he described as a necessary catering to the taste of the colonial class who would be its chief buyers (7:58). Unhappy with the way Main had made his selections, Marian criticized him for including too many versions of the same idea, and for using too little of *Daniel Deronda*—a novel that in any case had completely evaded Main's grasp of George Eliot's narrative range (6:433). The birthday book set off a fear that her writing was repetitious—a fear that had also surfaced when she looked at the *Sayings* some years earlier and wondered whether there was any change from her past to her present "self" (5:229). The flattening out that was the natural result of Main's method of choice was forgotten in her identification with her own narrative pronouncements.

Alexander Main was the perfect audience for those pronouncements because he made himself into the reader that the George Eliot narrator so urgently works to create. A quite different brief exchange of letters makes an amusing comment about what could happen when Marian Lewes attempted to play the moral mentor to a more recalcitrant literary audience. In May 1874 James Thomson, the forty-year-old poet, sent her a copy of his long poem, "The City of Dreadful Night." "Dear Poet," she addresses him, "I cannot rest satisfied without telling you that my mind responds with admiration to the distinct vision and grand utterance in the poem which you have been so good as to send me." The remainder of the note makes it clear that she could not rest until she had made an attempt to turn the younger writer into more morally acceptable paths. She trusts that he "will soon give us more heroic strains with a wider embrace of human fellowship in them," and reminds him that the lot of a poet includes some "affectionate and even joyful" recognition "of the manifold willing labours which have made such a lot possible" (6:53). Thomson replied in June, informing her that her trust "I fear will prove to be misplaced" and showing his fine potential as a parodist. "I certainly have an affectionate and even joyful recognition of the willing labours of those who have striven to alleviate our lot, though I cannot see that all their efforts have availed much against the primeval curse of our existence," he declared and ranted on in that vein for a few sentences. Then he told her why he had sent the poem in the first place: "because I have always read, whether rightly or wrongly, through all the manifold beauty and delightfulness of your works, a character and an intellectual destiny akin to those of that grand and awful Melancholy of Albrecht Dürer which dominates the City of my poem." Two days later he corroborated his dark kinship by sending a George Eliot–like note of remorseful second thoughts: he had forgotten to qualify his general statements with the admission that his poem "was the outcome of much sleepless hypochondria. I am aware that the truth of midnight does not exclude the truth of noonday, though one's nature may lead him to dwell in the former rather than in the latter" (6:60–61). George Eliot, who hoped to conceal her melancholic tendencies within her teacherly role, was, so far as we know, effectively silenced.

In 1872 Marian Lewes received a letter from another fervent Scot who was to require a good deal of epistolary caretaking during the next eight years. Elma Fraser Stuart, a widow of about thirty-five living with a young son in Dinan, Brittany, introduced herself to George Eliot by sending her a carved wooden book-slide along with a letter of worshipful gratitude. "If you please," she began, "long ago people were allowed the boon of offering a present in thanks for good received." After begging George Eliot to accept the book-slide she had made for her, she wrote, "What for years, you have been to me, how you have comforted my sorrows, peopled my loneliness, added to my happiness, and bettered in every way my whole nature, you can never know: till the Great Day of Squaring accounts comes; and then— there will be so many, so many who tell the same story; blessing you: that I feel impelled to speak now, when I could be heard."[7] Marian heard the accents of worship clearly enough and was not displeased. She granted Stuart their "spiritual companionship" and told her that "there is no wealth now so precious to me (always excepting my husband's love) as the possession of a place in other minds through the writings which are the chief result of my life." She also commented on the carved book-slide as an object of religious import. "My eyes see much more in it," she said, "just as they see much more than marble where pious feet and lips have worn a mark of their pressure" (5:244).

Her decision to use a prose that answered fully to the emotional overtones of Elma's letter may have been based on the assurance that her correspondent lived abroad and was unlikely to manifest herself again. Nothing could have been further from the truth. Elma waited a year before she sent her next gift—an oval mirror carved in walnut with flowers, birds, laurel, and Marian Lewes's initials—accompanied by a letter that described her joy in doing the work—"for was it not to lay at your feet?"—and enclosed a photograph of her son, Roland. "I do not exactly know why I enclose the likeness of my dear little son," a postscript ran, "but I think it must be the same feeling that moved mothers of old, when 'They brought young children unto Him.'"[8] Marian's reply emphasized Lewes's joy in the gift more fully than it did her own, although she assured Elma that she had "raised very blessed feelings in two souls" and gave her leave to tell her anything she liked about her life, past or present (5:375). By September 1873 the gifts had begun rolling in—a letter case, a purse, a Shetland shawl—and an agreement that Elma should visit the Leweses in their country retreat had been reached. "I confess I tremble a little at the prospect of your seeing me in the flesh," Marian wrote, and told Elma to "imagine a first cousin of old Dante's—rather smoke-dried—a face with lines in it that seem a map of sorrows" (5:437). She was not loath to feed her young worshiper's mythic impressions. After the meeting on October 3, Marian sent a requested lock of her hair and signed herself "with motherly interest, Your affectionate Friend" (5:442). Lewes, after another box of gifts had arrived, expressed his sense of the risk in the meeting: Elma might have been quite different from what her letters expressed. "However, in this case you were just what we thought you were" (5:462–63). With an amused idea of the connection between the two Scottish fans, he had sent Elma a copy of Main's *Sayings* and planned to follow up with the Johnson extracts.

The relationship was launched. By the following March, Elma was designated a spiritual daughter, and Roland became "my adopted grandson," who received the grandmotherly advice to "be handsome in all ways—chiefly in that best way of *doing* handsomely, as the heroic Roland of these times" (6:71). Elma, an interesting character in her own right, had been trained in wood carving by Parisian carvers who had gone to Dinan for refuge during the Franco-Prussian War, and had later worked further in Paris ateliers; she helped to support herself and educate Roland through the practice of her craft, until she became debilitated by an illness that began in 1874. She continued to send elaborate pieces of her work, along with more intimate gifts of slippers, belts, and shirt patterns to protect her idol from the cold; it is only in letters to Elma Stuart that we can find Marian Lewes discussing the fine points of underwear. Elma was to pursue her connection with the famous author beyond their deaths; she arranged to be buried in the grave next to George Eliot's in the Highgate Cemetery and had her tombstone commemorate her as one "whom for 8 1/2 blessed years George Eliot called by the sweet name of 'Daughter.'"

The group of Marian's letters to Elma Stuart is noteworthy because it is our only record of her at work in the role of motherly mentor. Such counseling was more usually confined to intimate conversation; although both Georgiana Burne-Jones and Emilia Pattison confessed their marital troubles to Marian, her letters to them give little hint of any but the most ordinary social connection except in the affectionate nicknames and endearments, and the special concern for their health. A single letter to Mrs. Burne-Jones suggests the tenor of their dialogue: Marian encourages her to think of the good in her life and less to ask "how shall I enjoy?" than to think "how we shall help the wounded and how find seed for the next harvest—how till the earth and make a little time of gladness for those who are being born without their own asking." Presumably as a consolation for her husband's infidelity, Georgie is urged on in her Latin studies, "to conquer a little kingdom for yourself there" (6:72–73). Edith Simcox disposed of George Eliot's letters to her, most likely in some private ritual; her own letters have disappeared as well, so that our accounts of that relationship rely on Edith's journal, "The Autobiography of a Shirt Maker," which was begun some three and a half years after the commencement of her relationship with George Eliot. Only Elma Stuart saw fit to link her name repeatedly with that of her great idol. Roland Stuart, himself a worthy initiate in the George Eliot cult, published after his mother's death a collection of George Eliot's letters to her, which he then deposited in the British Museum. He excised a postscript to a letter of January 1875, in which Marian had expressed her anxiety that others might misinterpret her in the act of playing the moral counselor: "Please not to let anyone read my letters except yourself" (6:113).[9]

Elma Stuart's emotional forthrightness and her habit of demanding Marian Lewes's opinion and advice about details of her character and conduct elicited from Marian a strongly maternal and sometimes disciplinary voice. She accepted the task Elma imposed on her of helping her to become a better person. Although she demurred a bit about the hyperbole in Elma's letters, she told her, "In one point, dear, you cannot be hyperbolical, and that is in believing that my strongest desire for you is that you should feel helped by me to be—what you are so well capable of being—'a joy, and blessing, and comfort and strength to others.' You see I am using your own words, which are very precious to me. Only don't try what is too difficult—too great a risk of failure" (6:82). When she learned from Edith Simcox that Elma was experimenting with valerian and opium, she became "grievously anxious" about Elma's responsibility in matters of health and lectured her vehemently about squandering her energy and getting too little sleep (6:84–85). When Elma accused herself of intolerance, that arch-sin of George Eliot's fiction, she received a lengthy reply that complicated her self-criticism by suggesting that there was a certain virtue in righteous indignation at "ugly conduct" (6:112). Elma was unrelenting in her pursuit of abegnation for her imagined "sins"; after some of her talk had made a servant smile, Marian had to begin a letter of April 1876 with "You grieve your mother by dwelling on your innocent bit of hyperbole as if it were a sin. We are not so dull as to require every word to be literal or else to have an elaborate commentary" (6:242). When Elma proved her altruism by agreeing to take charge of a dying old lady's dog, she received a full measure of George Eliot rhetoric about the joy of fellowship (6:327). And when Roland reached the age of separation from his mother, a good deal of advice was required in order to help Elma let him go.

For all the superiority that was built into her role, Marian also represented herself as needing Elma's trust. "How can you leave your parent so long in ignorance about you?" she demanded in a note written after some months of silence in 1875. "We long to have some assurance that you love us still" (6:190). When Roland wrote in 1877 about a severe stretch in Elma's illness, Marian replied that the suffering of a loved one should not be left unknown. "I should like to make you promise that you will never hide your pain or sorrow from me" (6:399). Full of endearments, her letters to Elma do suggest the release of a maternal passion blocked not only by her childlessness but by the truncated relationship with her own mother. At the same time, she was careful to keep the relationship with Elma from intruding on the realm of her literary career. When Elma wished to distribute copies of an article about George Eliot, Marian ordered them destroyed: "You could not hinder the suspicion that we had prompted the distribution—that would be the immediate conclusion of ordinary minds, and would by and by become their absolute statement" (6:230). One of the prices she paid for her acceptance of worshipers was the difficulty of containing what they might do in print.

Of the young worshiping women who might write about her, the most talented was Edith Jemima Simcox, who paid her first visit to the Priory in December 1872 when she was twenty-eight years old.[10] She was a person whose accomplishment and energy Marian Lewes might well have admired as examples of all that she could not do herself.

Well versed, like her famous mentor, in several languages, Edith was both a journalist and a dedicated social activist. She was a campaigner for the radical reorganization of labor, a union organizer who addressed both middle- and working-class groups, and a delegate to the Trades Union Congress. A believer in the cooperative movement, she helped found Hamilton and Company, a women's cooperative shirt-making enterprise, and shared its management with her colleague Mary Hamilton for eight years. In 1879 she was elected a member of the London School Board and worked to ensure compulsory non-religious education for all children.

Despite all this independent activity, Edith Simcox's relationship with her idol, as she rendered it in her journal "The Autobiography of a Shirt Maker," bordered on the abject. Throughout her thirties, Edith was passionately, ecstatically, miserably, and hopelessly in love with Marian Lewes. Beginning in May 1876 she began to keep the journal, now a 175-page manuscript with entries dating until January 1900; nearly two-thirds of it relates to the years 1876–1881. In it she recorded every detail of her meetings with Marian and Lewes, her own strongly fluctuating feelings of joy and despair, and the ways in which she attempted to get control over her feelings and regulate her impulses to walk over to the Priory at every plausible occasion. She was in fact producing a kind of clandestine biography, the most intimate account we have of George Eliot's final years. As Edith wrote at the beginning of her entry for December 29, 1880, the day of George Eliot's funeral, "I am not afraid of forgetting, but as heretofore I record her teaching while the sound is still fresh in my soul's ears" (9:323). Combined with her acute observation of the object of her obsession, such detailed recording makes it possible to glimpse Marian Lewes's conversational flexibility and her mentor's dilemma through the screen of Edith's intense projections.[11]

Edith had chosen Marian as the single important audience to her life and found it possible to value what she did only as it passed through the consciousness of her beloved. While the journal allows us to see Marian's attempts to fend off Edith's kisses without either disallowing them or directly acknowledging their sexual nature, it also shows how she attempted to chart a course between acting as Edith's counselor and deflecting the full force of Edith's dependence on her judgment—a course that caused her worshiper no little pain. In 1877 Edith published the first of three books she was to write under the influence of George Eliot, *Natural Law: An Essay in Ethics*, and sent it to

Marian at Witley, dedicating it to her "with idolatrous love" (9:203n). Hearing nothing of it for months, she visited the Priory in November 1877 to a continued silence on the subject. Her first impulse was to have the book withdrawn from the market (9:200). Some days later she managed to maneuver the conversation toward a discussion of the book; she had, she thought, "implied that her approval or blame ended everything for me. . . . Of course she has never known how every word of hers enters into my flesh, but this much she said to me now: That there had been nothing that jarred on her in reading the book. . . . the general impression was of sympathy" (9:203). And Edith goes on for some pages noting the equivocal praise that George Eliot had to bestow. She places her own interpretation on George Eliot's reluctance to recommend the book to a friend: "because the said lady would have known I was a friend of hers and so might either I suppose have identified us too much, or have attached less weight to the supposed echo" (9:204). No one could have had a more personally acute understanding of Marian Lewes's strategies of generalized evasion.

When Edith was asked to stand for the school board, she wrote to Marian "at least [to] wonder how if I had the power of choice she would want me to choose."[12] There is no evidence that Marian was anything but noncommittal, though it seems clear that she supported Edith's social work and wished her to value it more than she did. "I will force myself to remember your crushing prophecy," Edith wrote on the day of George Eliot's funeral, "—that I was to do better work than you had—that cannot be, My Best! and all mine is always yours, but oh! Dearest! Dearest! it shall not be less unworthy of you than it must."[13] A few months earlier, angry with Marian after her marriage to Cross, she had written, "I must not tell her how much she has herself done to kill the ambitions to which she now appeals" (9:315).

Privately, Edith lavished religious language at least as extravagant as Elma Stuart's on her idol, at one point praying to her every night.[14] After her death, pronouns referring to George Eliot are capitalized. When Marian asked her to refrain from calling her 'Mother,' confiding that "her associations otherwise with the name were as of a task and it was a fact that her feeling for me was *not* at all a mother's" (9:283), Edith meditated on the dilemma of her love in a single surviving unsent letter of March 1880: "Do you see darling that I can only love you three lawful ways, idolatrously as Faber the Virgin Mary, in romance wise as Petrarch, Laura, or with a child's fondness for the mother one leans on notwithstanding the irreverence of one's longing to pet and take care of her" (9:303). At this point, after Lewes's death and before the Cross marriage, she was attempting to make herself central to Marian's emotional life by identifying herself with Lewes. Instead, she was virtually shut out of her idol's life for nine months. When she was finally invited to pay a visit, it turned out to be a final one, three days before George Eliot's death.

Both before and after the final year, Edith's possessive jealousy fastened on other admirers, especially John Cross and Elma Stuart. With Elma she maintained an ambivalent independent friendship; she sometimes discussed her critically with Marian Lewes, who drew her toward more sympathetic perspectives. The journal records several conversations in which Marian attempted to turn Edith's attention toward men and marriage, and to chastise her for incivility to Cross in particular. "Was she afraid of my poisoning Johnny's shirts?" Edith teased (9:199).[15] "The fatal Johnny," as Edith called him, had a suspicious tendency to outstay her in visits to the Priory (9:212). Yet Edith was sensitive enough to the signs of Marian Lewes's pleasures. When she called on February 1, 1880, "Young Johnny and Eleanor Cross were there when I arrived and outstayed me." But, as she reflected later in the entry, "I think perhaps what wearies her least is the ardour of a single-minded youth—with which she has some natural sympathy and at all events can feel a dramatic interest" (9:293).

Edith's obsession did not prevent her from being capable of insightful and disinterested biographical observations. Her rivalry with John Cross extended after George Eliot's death to the question of which of them would write her biography. By the time Cross made his decision to take on the work, Edith had already visited the haunts of Mary Ann Evans's childhood and had interviewed some of her friends. In her journal of February 5, 1882, she recorded a conversation with Barbara Bodichon, who had told her "that Cross neither could nor would write the life, and that the mission would and should come to me."[16] It is tempting to wonder whether the reputation of George Eliot would have had a different history had Edith Simcox loosed her far more penetrating and literary sensibility on that project. As it was, she contented herself with publishing "George Eliot, a valedictory article" in the *Nineteenth Century* of May 1881. The intimate vagaries of her love were transformed into a set of Paterian fictional sketches and published as *Episodes in the Lives of Men, Women, and Lovers* (1882). Nor was she displeased by the reticence of the *Life* that Cross produced.

He had, after all, been primed for that task, chosen as the youthful repository of George Eliot's last autobiographical stories. As he wrote to Barbara Bodichon soon after Marian's death, "She talked to me a great deal about you. In fact a great deal of our talk during our short married life was about old days and I think I know all her feelings to her friends very thoroughly" (9:325–26).

John Cross's earlier role in the extended Lewes "family" of the 1870s was that of a practical adviser who connected them with the outside life: he handled their investments, found them their house at Witley, did some of the town errands that Charles Lewes might otherwise have done, and introduced them to lawn tennis and badminton. Yet he shared with Alexander Main, Elma Stuart, and Edith Simcox the propensity for mother worship: all these young adults had close attachments to their actual (widowed) mothers, which were supplemented and exaggerated to the ideal in the image of an all-understanding George Eliot. The Cross family was also at least part Scottish, described by Lewes to Elma Stuart as "our fervid Scotch friends at Weybridge" (6:322). The national temperament was clearly appealing to Marian Lewes, who characterized Mrs. Meyrick, her favorite maternal character in *Daniel Deronda*, as a "happy mixture of Scottish caution with her Scottish fervour and Gallic liveliness" (chap. 46).

It was the whole Cross family rather than John himself who first became important to the Leweses. Herbert Spencer had introduced Lewes to the mother and daughters during a walking trip in 1867, but the families came together after the Leweses met Mrs. Cross and John in Rome in April 1869. Some of Marian's most concrete and humorous letters of the period were addressed to Anna Cross, matriarch of the brood of ten young adults, and a widow six years Marian's elder. Mrs. Cross shared with Barbara Bodichon the distinction of being the only friends to whom Marian familiarly wrote of her husband as "George." By 1871 Marian and Lewes were making frequent visits to Weybridge, where the country air and family cheer promised to restore their health and spirits; they spent several Christmases with the Crosses, who absorbed them into their midst without requiring the intense mentorial roles enforced by the other worshipers.

In fact, the special charm of "Nephew Johnnie" was that he could be teased, confided in, and depended on. By 1872 he was already helping them look for a country house, for which Marian thanked him in a mixture of affection, self-deprecation, and humorous dependence: "It is so much easier to imagine other people doing wise things than to do them oneself! Practically I excel in nothing but paying twice as much as I ought for everything. On the whole, it would be better if my life could be done for me and I could look on" (5:340). After Cross set them up with an elaborate badminton outfit in November 1877, she thanked him in playfully flirtatious prose. "Still—which would you choose? An aunt who lost headaches and gained flesh by spending her time on tennis and Badminton, or an aunt who remained sickly and beckoned death by writing more books? Behold yourself in a dilemma! If you choose the plump and idle aunt, she will declare that you don't mind about her writing. If you choose the pallid and productive aunt she will declare that you have no real affection for her. It is impossible to satisfy an author" (6:415). Her "aunthood" could embrace serious letters explaining to Johnnie her positions on religious conformity, literary questions, or the death of Bertie Lewes, but it was clearly less of a task than spiritual motherhood. At least before his mother's death and their courtship, John Cross appears to stand alone among the young George Eliot worshipers as a refuge from the psychological dependencies with which the others had both graced and burdened her.

When Edith Simcox reread *Daniel Deronda* in 1879, she noted in her journal that she found it a more depressing book than the others. "I am more struck by the pathos of Gwendolen's rejection than by the healing power of Daniel's virtuous conduct and counsel," she wrote (9:275). This remark is not simply an indication of her personal identification with Gwendolen's position as the abandoned moral dependent. She was responding to everything that George Eliot had learned and extrapolated from her relationships with worshipers, everything she forebore to indicate in personal writing or conversation, which made its way into the startlingly original depiction of Daniel's mentorship. The story of Gwendolen Harleth and Daniel Deronda challenges the religious ardor with which George Eliot had written about acts of confession and sympathy in earlier novels, replacing it with a keen and troubled scrutiny of the unexamined motives that lock confessor and dependent together in an unequal relation. If Edith could write, after hearing the abrupt and surprising news of Marian's departure for the continent in May 1880, that she was "only hurt in an unavoidable way by the feeling how far away all the determining conditions of her life are from me, and a rapid thought that it was an irksome task to her to feel bound to give so much account of her doings, because my love was covetous," it was because she had perfectly understood the dilemma of Daniel Deronda (9:305).

The process through which Gwendolen Harleth and Daniel Deronda come into connection is repeatedly described as a kind of mutual coercion. The word appears in the novel's first paragraph describing Daniel's response to the vision of Gwendolen gambling: "Why was the wish to look again felt as coercion and not as a longing in which the whole being consents?" (chap. 1). Gwendolen feels differently coerced by the implicit judgment in Daniel's gaze and experiences his redemption and return of her pawned necklace as an unwelcome assumption of power on his part: "He knew very well that he was entangling her in helpless humiliation: it was another way of smiling at her ironically, and taking the air of a supercilious mentor" (chap. 2). Many chapters on, when Gwendolen is said to be well into the process of transforming Daniel's power into her own dependence, the narrative returns to the notion of coercion in a passage of suggestive unintelligibility:

> Without the aid of sacred ceremony or costume, her feelings had turned this man, only a few years older than herself, into a priest; a sort of trust less rare than the fidelity that guards it. Young reverence for one who is also young is the most coercive of all: there is the same level of temptation, and the higher motive is believed in as a fuller force—not suspected to be a mere residue from weary experience.
>
> But the coercion is often stronger on the one who takes the reverence. Those who trust us educate us. And perhaps in that ideal consecration of Gwendolen's, some education was being prepared for Deronda. (chap. 35)

Several questions are raised here. The first has to do with the implicit comparison of "young reverence for one who is also young" to young reverence for one who is older; George Eliot seems here to be making a sort of private transfer of her own mentorial situations to the (overtly) sexually charged relationship of Gwendolen and Daniel. But why such a relation is "the most coercive of all" remains blurry. What does "there is the same level of temptation" mean? That each of the young participants feels temptation equally? What kind of temptation? to power? to sexuality? to dependence? And why is it more equal than a pair of old and young might feel? Exactly in what direction is the coercion flowing in this sentence? The "But" at the beginning of the next paragraph suggests that the first kind of coercion is exercised by the priest figure, but the context does not bear that interpretation out. It seems more likely that all the coercion is exercised by the dependent, who believes more fully in the younger, unwearied guide. Or perhaps George Eliot's shorthand is meant to suggest a mutual danger: of too much temptation for the mentor and too much belief for the dependent. Yet her inability or unwillingness to get it clear suggests a disturbance about the mutuality of "coercion" which is not resolved by this apparent explanation.

"A sort of trust less rare than the fidelity that guards it" raises other questions. Here the cryptic phrase turns a different area of the balance sheet in Daniel's favor: if he "guards" Gwendolen's confidences well, he will be more worthy of them than most confessors are. The shift of attention from Gwendolen's act—the internal creation of Daniel as her priest—to Daniel's response—the assumption of "fidelity" in a role not of his making—gives him a new moral advantage and leaves aside the actions through which he initiated Gwendolen's response in the first place. The focus on Daniel intensifies in the second paragraph, where "coercion" is transformed into "education," and the narrator invites us to understand what is about to unfold as Daniel's educative process.

What exactly is the education prepared for Deronda? Unlike other educations in George Eliot novels, it is never named, only experienced. A short answer might go something like this: "This is what happens when you put yourself in a position of moral superiority and wisdom and someone takes you up on it." What happens includes the horror of having to hear unwelcome confessions, the helpless frustration of seeing that wise words are useless to help another person, the acknowledgment that it is not the words and the voice but the person himself who is needed, the necessity of acting more sympathetic than one feels, and finally, the recognition that the superiority of the confessor is a form of deception, a self-withholding which allows others to make mistaken projections of their desires. This is the education through which George Eliot brings the ultimate value of sympathy into serious question. As Neil Hertz has put it, "What would happen, she seems to be asking herself, if the *Middlemarch* narrator had to engage with the characters he had been merely observing?"[17] Although George Eliot attempts to persuade us of Gwendolen's internalization of Daniel as a "standard," she is more intent on scrutinizing the contradictions of a position that resembles the one she had acquired when "George Eliot" became a person as well as a voice.

Daniel's power to compel Gwendolen is established primarily through a series of narrative assertions. Gwendolen's initial anger at Daniel's redemption of her necklace is changed after her engagement "into a superstitious dread—due, perhaps, to the coercion he had exercised over her thought—lest that first interference in her life might foreshadow some future influence." This otherwise unexplained transformation is then declared to be a kind of self-fulfilling prophecy: "And superstitions carry consequences which often verify their hope or their foreboding." Once she has met Daniel at Diplow, the dread is transformed again, into "an uneasy longing to be judged by Deronda with unmixed admiration—a longing which had had its seed in her first resentment at his critical glance." It is Daniel's gaze which, the narrator explains, is simultaneously responsible for and innocent of creating Gwendolen's response: his eyes "seemed to express a special interest in every one on whom he fixed them, and might easily help to bring on him those claims which ardently sympathetic people are often creating in the minds of those who need help. In mendicant fashion, we make the goodness of others a reason for exorbitant claims on them" (chap. 29). This passage, whose "we" hardly even pretends to be on Gwendolen's side, casts Daniel as the victim of his own externally projected aura of sympathetic identification.

The next time Gwendolen's attitude is explored is the first of two scenes in which the separateness of Daniel's life is expressed through her approach to a room in which he is sitting with his back to her. Now, "in some mysterious way he was becoming part of her conscience, as one woman whose nature is an object of reverential belief may become a new conscience to a man" (chap. 35). By the end of this chapter the religious imagery appears: Daniel becomes a priest, and Gwendolen begins her secret rites of faith, which are shaken and then recovered in chapter 48 when Grandcourt implies that Mirah is Deronda's mistress, and Gwendolen rushes off to Mirah for assurance that he is "good." Throughout, the narrator denies that Gwendolen's approaches to Daniel—her direct personal questions and quick retreats—have anything to do with "coquetry"; they conceal, rather, the fascinated worship that opens up her capacity to love.

The development of this capacity, set off by Deronda, is represented both as Gwendolen's salvation and as the fault of her mistaken egoism, which fails to separate Daniel's person from his message.

After the drowning of Grandcourt her ability to confide in Deronda allows her to receive his forgiveness and saves her from complete psychological collapse; her demands for his attention thereafter produce from him language that restores her capacity to hope. "But the new existence seemed inseparable from Deronda: the hope seemed to make his presence permanent." Attempting to bring us to some sympathy with this position, the narrator begs us to imagine the feelings of a person being saved from fire: "She had flung herself into his opened arms and clung about his neck that he might carry her into safety. She identified him with the struggling regenerative process in her which had begun with his action" (chap. 65). Daniel, having stumbled into a relationship fraught with transference and countertransference for which he has no names, has given her little evidence that she should not do so.

The climax of Gwendolen's "redemption" has then, in George Eliot's terms, to be the moment when she is shocked out of her self-obsession by the revelation of Daniel's other life. Yet the sense of emotional wreckage in the penultimate chapter overshadows the predictable moral message. Gwendolen has chosen Daniel as her single meaningful audience, and staked her inner life on his recognition. She has become obsessed with being "made better," though her ability to become better remains an open question. Her mentor has other things on his mind; she is left to struggle on alone. Take heed, idolators.

The ways in which Gwendolen compels or coerces Daniel are dramatized with more emotional precision. Gazing thoughtfully at a gambling woman and returning her pawned necklace may not be exactly like writing a George Eliot novel, but they have their similarities: to a susceptible reader, the narrator George Eliot created is experienced as a being who can see into the secrets of the readerly heart, whose words chastise impulsive actions with elaborate second thoughts. Although the consequences of Daniel's intervention are determined by the specific neuroses of the woman in question, we are never quite left to forget—as Gwendolen does not let Daniel forget—that he was the one who started it all. Daniel's education is initiated by the triggering of his impulse to rescue: "Persons attracted him, as Hans Meyrick had done, in proportion to the possibility of his defending them, rescuing them, telling upon their lives with some sort of redeeming influence, and he had to resist an inclination, easily accounted for, to withdraw coldly from the fortunate." In Gwendolen's case that impulse is implicated with sexual attraction, "the fascination of her womanhood" (chap. 28). George Eliot's decision to cast the mentorial relationship as a situation in which hidden sexual desires may be cherished, if not expressed or even acknowledged, suggests how clearly she understood that the currents flowing between her and her idolators of both genders were intensified by the charge of concealed sexual interest.

Once the relationship is launched, the emphasis falls on Gwendolen's power to compel Daniel to play his role. During most of their dialogues, we are situated so as to experience Gwendolen's incursions through Daniel's consciousness, while she remains the more opaque. Gwendolen's rapid alternations between childlike questioning and proud cynicism "might alternately flatter and disappoint control" (chap. 35); they certainly succeed in pulling Daniel into her emotional currents. The very general, George Eliot–like pronouncements that Daniel makes in an attempt to give her a moral education are persistently personalized by Gwendolen: his grave and distant "we's" are always turned into "I's" and connected with a provocative description of her own character about which he is forced to take a personal stand. She invites his disapproval in an effort to win his approval—a technique with which George Eliot had been familiar since childhood and had now managed to stimulate in others. Abandoning polite discourse in the midst of elegant social scenes, she parries his gracious evasions by challenging them in sentences beginning "You think I. . . ." As Gwendolen's desperation increases, so does her insistence on Daniel's responsibility for her. When he tries to distance himself, she makes her moral reform into a matter of his choice: "It is you who will decide; because you might have made me different by keeping as near to me as you could, and believing in me" (chap. 45). By the end of the novel Gwendolen will make herself abject in any way that offers a chance of gaining Danel's approval; resentment of his "halo of superiority" turns into "an impulse to humble herself more" (chap. 56); she considers giving up the money Grandcourt has left her if "it would give her the higher place in Deronda's mind" (chap. 64). Blackmailed, in effect, by his own superiority of understanding, Daniel has no choice but to go on responding to her repeated summonses.

In the process he learns that his rhetoric is ineffectual. Unlike Mirah, who requires only a physical rescue to prevent her suicide, Gwendolen cannot so easily be prevented from drowning in her own hysteria. Before the scene shifts to Genoa, Daniel is horrified by the spectacle of her anguish. "Words seemed to have no more rescue in them than if he had been beholding a vessel in peril of wreck—the poor ship with its many-lived anguish beaten by the inescapable storm. How could he grasp the long-growing process of this young creature's wretchedness?—how arrest and change it with a sentence? He was afraid of his own voice" (chap. 48). Yet his voice—its "depth" and tenor continually foregrounded as if it were a separate entity—continues to take on tones that promise more than he can give. By the time Daniel attends upon Gwendolen in the aftermath of Grandcourt's death, he is playing his role in the full awareness that his words and gestures are partial deceptions, telling only a small part of his internal experience.

The climax of Daniel's education is the moment when he experiences the full force of a truth that had earlier come readily from his moralizing tongue. In his first "lesson" to Gwendolen, he responds to her question about why he disapproves of gambling by talking of moments "which force us to see that our gain is another's loss:—that is one of the ugly aspects of life." When she objects that one can't always help it, he answers, "Clearly. Because of that, we should help it where we can" (chap. 29). Having presented himself to Gwendolen only as a voice and presence of sympathetic understanding, having concealed from her the fluctuations of his own destiny, he is finally forced to face her with the facts of his Jewish mission and his engagement to Mirah. This confrontation elicits from George Eliot some of her most embarrassed melodrama: Gwendolen in a sort of trance, crying out that she has been cruel and is now forsaken, Daniel kneeling at her feet, feeling that "she was the victim of his happiness" and begging forgiveness by repeating that he too is cruel. The acute discomfort of this scene lies, I think, in its lack of serious consequences: it is a paroxysm of guilt which is instantly rewarded by Gwendolen's return to a malleable humility. Daniel is freed to go off on his Zionist adventure, where the making of promises about the renewal of a people will be safely ensconced in a political sphere. The revelation that superior sympathy can act as a form of cruelty—can create in fact that "help-less humiliation" which is Gwendolen's first experience of Daniel—is to a large extent dissipated in the narrative attention to Gwendolen's emotional frailty and dependence.

George Eliot treats these matters in a more equable key in the less highly charged arena of Daniel's relationship with Hans Meyrick, where she subjects Daniel to a mild form of therapy for his self-withholding superiority. Daniel gives Hans his first "advantage" when he transforms his personal desire for Mirah into a solemn warning against Hans's use of her as a model to be "exhibited," forgetting in his concealed anxiety that Hans's pictures are unlikely to be exhibited at all. It is one of those moments that shows just how clearly George Eliot understood the self-interested functions of her own moralizing voice. When Hans reveals his romantic interest in Mirah, the narrator makes a virtual confession on Deronda's behalf: he is "conscious of that peculiar irritation which will sometimes befall the man whom others are inclined to trust as a mentor—the irritation of perceiving that he is supposed to be entirely off the same plane of desire and temptation as those who confess to him." "Hans's evident assumption that for any danger of rivalry or jealousy in relation to Mirah, Deronda was as much out of the question as the angel Gabriel" does not, however, suggest to Daniel that he might equalize his relationship with his former dependent. Instead, the narrator ends her paragraph with a mere whiff of irony at Daniel's expense: "Altogether, poor Hans seemed to be entering into Deronda's experience in a disproportionate manner—going beyond his part of rescued prodigal, and rousing a feeling quite distinct from compassionate affection" (chap. 37). When Daniel is finally forced to discuss his own life with Hans, he is, as Hans puts it, "only beginning to pay a pretty long debt." Revealing a momentarily equalizing vulnerability on the subject of Mirah, Daniel is quickly rewarded by Hans's revelation of the secret of Mirah's affections, which immediately restores his "advantage" (chap. 67). As in the Gwendolen plot, the personal secrecy and superiority of the confessor is both questioned and, ultimately, left intact.

In accord with her usual practice, George Eliot imagines an idealized version of the rescue plot in the Mordecai-Mirah-Daniel relationships. Because of the triangulation here, Daniel is relieved of his role as the self-sacrificial source of wisdom, becoming instead the more passive, less powerful vessel who receives the Jewish inheritance from Mordecai and Daniel Charisi and graces it with the acceptable social figure of the English gentleman. His successful literal rescue of Mirah develops into that more incredible fantasy through which the novel transforms him into precisely the object for which Mordecai and Mirah yearn, as though he were the apotheosis of the wish to become what one's dependents most deeply need. The Jewish mission reestablishes a seamless continuity between Daniel's personal vocation and the specific requirements of others, ostensibly repairing the gaps between sympathetic understanding and human effectiveness which have been opened in the Gwendolen plot. Armed with a transfigured, suprapersonal sympathy, Daniel Deronda sails out of psychological space and into the mythic-historical beyond.

In this fashion George Eliot said her own farewells to the moral and psychological entanglements of the novel. Once she had deconstructed sympathy, the fictional form she had shaped was as obsolete for her as it would be for the young writers of the next generation. After the publication of *Deronda*, her letters concern themselves with the mixed reception of the Jewish material; then, without warning, she has produced the satirical critiques of *Impressions of Theophrastus Such*. On the subject of fiction writing there is silence. If a writer's writings are, as she insisted, her "chief actions," her final action was an explicit abandonment of the all-wise narrative voice that had promised so much to many of her readers.

The entanglements of life were another matter. Unlike Daniel Deronda, George Eliot was not capable of holding interviews with Elma Stuart, Edith Simcox, or anyone else to confess her impending marriage to John Cross. Perhaps she had imagined the guilty melodrama of such scenes all too elaborately in the uncanny prolepsis of her fiction making. Perhaps, too, *Daniel Deronda* was both a prediction and a warning about the public creation of "George Eliot" as a cultural hero. Like the private suffering of his creator, Daniel's inward sensitivity is transformed into and concealed by a powerful moral voice, which makes itself subject to exploitation. In the self-exploration of her final fiction, George Eliot was keen enough to point, however surreptitiously, to the vulnerability and even the deceptiveness of that voice. When she fostered reverential idolatry, as she did in the image of the culture-saving Deronda and in the later relations of her life, she did so in the full knowledge of its power to fail.

The multiple transformations of mentorship in *Daniel Deronda* may provide us with an occasion for a final meditation on the confessional analysis of George Eliot's fiction. As I have suggested, the self-presentations of the letters were forged under the pressures of complex emotional and social conditions. Even their frequent expressions of depression and self-doubt, which told truths about Marian Evans's feelings, were effective ways of taking a certain command of her readers' attitudes and reactions. For a person so conscious of how others might misread her, letters were always negotiations between what she had to say and what she imagined her audiences as capable of hearing. In the novels, however, she could develop her thinking simultaneously along two or three separate tracks of a multiplot tale in such a way that the idealized version of events could produce a sublimation of a personal situation, while another story line might attest to the intractibility of very similar issues. In these stories George Eliot demonstrated her endless capacity for self-reflexive meditation on her own formulated positions and her genius for developing the many sides of those meditations into full-blown imaginary situations. If George Eliot, to repeat Henry James's words, "made us believe that nothing in the world was alien to her," it was because she had had from girlhood an extraordinary capacity to ingest "the world" and make it commensurate with the activities of her own psyche.

Throughout this book my aim has been to dissolve monolithic notions of George Eliot's teaching and ideology by suggesting how they emerge from dynamic reactions and counterreactions within her emotional economy. Her professed belief in social evolution was virtually unrepresentable in fiction, and struggled against her strong sense of human intractability. Her special valuation of memory and her doctrine of sympathy were born of reactions to what she imagined as her own transgressions and can be initially understood as the instincts of remorse and repair, rather than as the adopted beliefs of an agnostic humanist or the self-establishing ideologies of a Victorian liberal intellectual. Strangely enough, the intellectual ambition of Mary Ann Evans found part of its eventual fulfillment in George Eliot's creative activity of remorse, which fueled the fictional elaboration of a whole range of perception otherwise sheltered by the personae she created in letters. To this tendency toward self-revising analysis we owe—to take only some prominent examples from the preceding pages—the complex representations of gossip and parenthood in *Middlemarch* and the interrogation of ambition and mentorship in *Daniel Deronda*.

The gap between the letter-writing voices and all the fictional explorations may finally be understood as a matter of social wariness. Marian Evans was a person who found it necessary to keep a series of secrets about her life in an attempt to protect what she could of her readily threatened sense of place in her culture. The languages of high morality and personal sympathy were forged from her experience, but they also worked as her cover stories, the sheer authority of their rhetoric defying their audiences to disbelieve. Her reluctance to confront any direct form of autobiographical writing was of a piece with the fundamental instinct to perform her self-understanding through outward projections. George Eliot must have known—as she knew so much about herself—that her only real opportunity for evoking the many-sided truths of her inward experience lay in the imaginative activity of fiction making.

Notes

1. On Reading Letters

1. Henry James, "The Life of George Eliot," *Atlantic Monthly* (May 1885), reprinted in *Henry James: Literary Criticism*, ed. Leon Edel (New York: The Library of America, 1984), pp. 994–1010. The quoted phrase is on p. 1010.

2. *The Diary of Alice James*, ed. Leon Edel (London: Rupert Hart-Davis, 1965), pp. 41–42.

3. Mary Jacobus describes Alice James's response as an attempt to exorcise her own "parasitic morbidity"; George Eliot functions for James "as the buried self of her own hysteria." See *Reading Woman: Essays in Feminist Criticism* (New York: Columbia University Press, 1986), pp. 249–52.

4. James, "The Life of George Eliot," p. 995.

5. James, "The Life of George Eliot," pp. 996, 1010.

6. James, "The Life of George Eliot," p. 997.

7. Even the polite Henry James felt compelled to say that there was "something a little violent in the system" of Cross's editing. "The Life of George Eliot," p. 996.

8. Cross, 1:v–vi.

9. V. S. Pritchett, review in *New Statesman* (December 11, 1954): 791–92.

10. See "George Eliot in Her Letters," *Times Literary Supplement* (August 10, 1956): 469–70; Anthony West, "The Higher Humbug," *New Yorker* (October 2, 1954): 132–40; Delancey Ferguson, "A Woman of Will," *Saturday Review* (September 25, 1954): 21, and *Saturday Review* (April 7, 1956): 18.

11. Irving Howe, "A Great Writer's Evolution," *New Republic* (October 18, 1954): 18.

12. Geoffrey Tillotson, "The George Eliot Letters," *Sewanee Review* 63 (1955): 500.

13. James, "The Life of George Eliot," p. 1000.

14. George Eliot, *Impressions of Theophrastus Such*, in *The Works of George Eliot* (standard edition; Edinburgh: William Blackwood and Sons, n.d.), p. 17.

15. The most concentrated body of such criticism occurs in an issue of *Yale French Studies* 71 (1986), which is devoted to questions of letter theory, history, and editing. An extended meditation on the dynamics of reading published correspondences occurs in Patricia Meyer Spacks, *Gossip* (New York: Knopf, 1985), pp. 65–91. I return to these essays later in the chapter.

16. Stanley Fish, "What Makes an Interpretive Community?" in *Is There a Text in This Class?* (Cambridge: Harvard University Press, 1980), p. 347.

17. For a brief history and listing of such manuals in England, see Katherine Horn-

beak, "The Complete Letter-Writer in English, 1568–1800," *Smith College Studies in Modern Languages* 15 nos. 3–4 (1934). The form seems to have had an extended nineteenth-century life in the United States, where books of social conduct took particularly practical forms in order to inculcate something like English manners. On American versions, see Harry B. Weiss, *American Letter-Writers, 1698–1934* (New York: New York Public Library, 1945).

18. Samuel Richardson, *Familiar Letters on Important Occasions* (London: Routledge, 1928). Earlier works often cited are William Fulwood, *The Enimie of Idlenesse: Teaching the maner and stile how to endite, compose and write all sorts of Epistles and Letters* (1568); Angel Day, *The English Secretorie* (1586); and Nicholas Breton, *Poste with a Packet of Madde Letters* (1602).

19. *The Complete Letter-Writer* . . . (London: Henry Mozley, 1801).

20. For a contrast with courtly French letter manuals, see Janet Gurkin Altman, "The Letter Book as a Literary Institution, 1539–1789: Toward a Cultural History of Published Correspondences in France," *Yale French Studies* 71 (1986): 32–34.

21. As Ruth Perry has suggested, letter manuals sometimes invented complex moral situations that trained their readers' sensibilities in distinguishing fine shades of meaning. See *Women, Letters, and the Novel* (New York: AMS Press, 1980), pp. 86–90.

22. William J. Dawson and Coningsby W. Dawson, *The Great English Letter-Writers*, 2 vols. (New York: Harper and Brothers, 1908), 2: 11.

23. Howard Anderson and Irvin Ehrenpreis, "The Familiar Letter in the Eighteenth Century: Some Generalizations," in *The Familiar Letter in the Eighteenth Century*, ed. Howard Anderson, Philip B. Daghlian, and Irvin Ehrenpreis (Lawrence: University of Kansas Press, 1966), p. 275.

24. Bruce Redford, *The Converse of the Pen: Acts of Intimacy in the Eighteenth-Century Familiar Letter* (Chicago: University of Chicago Press, 1986), pp. 1–2.

25. Perry, *Women, Letters, and the Novel*, p. 75.

26. The myth of writing as a copy of speech has, of course, been deconstructed by Jacques Derrida. Martine Reid, writing of the fictionality of Stendhal's letters, follows Derrida in her rendering of the myth: "A formal stylization from the very outset, the letter dreams constantly however of a speech whose exact copy it would be, whose ideal nature would assure it a truthful character. The letter claims to *take the place of* speech and through this link with speech, presumed more true than writing, assures itself—in spite of its history, which formalizes and fictionalizes it straightaway—of the same benefits of speech." See "Correspondences: *Stendhal en Toutes Lettres,*" *Yale French Studies* 71 (1986): 166.

27. For a delightful essay that addresses experiential differences between letter writing and conversation, see Robert Wexelblatt, "Six Meditations on Letters," *Midwest Quarterly* 3 (1991): 264–81. Keith Stewart, writing on eighteenth-century criteria for letter writing, also notes the necessity of making the distinction; see "Toward Defining an Aesthetic for the Familiar Letter in Eighteenth-Century England," *Prose Studies* 5 (1982): 181.

28. See, for example, Florence Hartley, *The Ladies' Book of Etiquette and Manual of Politeness* (Boston: DeWolfe, Fiske, 1873), pp. 122–23; Mrs. John Sherwood, *Manners and Social Usages* (New York: Harper and Brothers, 1884), pp. 207–13.

29. See Perry, *Women, Letters, and the Novel*, pp. 68–70, for a discussion of letters as the cloistered woman's way of "being involved with the world while keeping it at arm's length" (p. 69).

30. John Gregory, *A Father's Legacy to His Daughters* (1774; rpt., New York: Garland, 1974), p. v.

31. John Bennet, *Letters to a Young Lady* (Philadelphia: A. Findley, 1818).

32. Hester Chapone, *Letters on the Improvement of the Mind* (London: John Sharpe, 1822), p. vii.

33. Jane West, *Letters to a Young Lady, in which the Duties and Character of Women are Considered,* 3 vols. (1806; rpt., New York: Garland, 1974), xii.

34. See Chapter 2 for a discussion of what conduct books said about women's letter writing itself.

35. Robert Adams Day, *Told in Letters: Epistolary Fiction before Richardson* (Ann Arbor: University of Michigan Press, 1966), pp. 49–50.

36. For a discussion of all the epistolary precursors of the novel, see Day, *Told in Letters,* chap. 4.

37. Along with Dawson and Dawson, *The Great English Letter-Writers* (1908), see, for example, T. Chamberlain, ed., *Selected Letters* (London: James Burns, 1843); Ada M. Ingpen, *Women as Letter Writers* (New York: Baker and Taylor, 1909); R. Brimley Johnson, *English Letter Writers* (London: Gerald Howe, 1927); E. V. Lucas, *The Gentlest Art: A Choice of Letters by Entertaining Hands* (London: Methuen, 1907) and *The Second Post* (London: Methuen, 1910); Edward T. Mason, *British Letters Illustrative of Character and Social Life* (New York: G. P. Putnam's Sons, 1888); George Saintsbury, *A Letter Book* (London: G. Bell and Sons, 1922).

38. See Day, *Told in Letters,* pp. 259–66, for a list of such epistolary miscellanies in the eighteenth century. "It is clear," he says, "that these owe their existence more to the bookseller than to the *epistolier*" (p. 259).

39. Chamberlain, *Selected Letters,* advertisement (n.p.).

40. Dawson and Dawson, *The Great English Letter-Writers,* 2: 9.

41. Dawson and Dawson, *The Great English Letter-Writers,* 2: 16, 10.

42. Ingpen, *Women as Letter Writers.*

43. Lyn LL. Irvine, *Ten Letter-Writers* (London: Hogarth Press, 1932); Cecil S. Emden, *Poets in Their Letters* (London: Oxford University Press, 1959); Elizabeth Drew, *The Literature of Gossip: Nine English Letterwriters* (New York: Norton, 1964).

44. Drew, *The Literature of Gossip,* pp. 14–15.

45. Irvine, *Ten Letter-Writers,* pp. 18–19.

46. See Irvine, *Ten Letter-Writers,* pp. 13–23; and Drew, *The Literature of Gossip,* p. 5.

47. George Eliot, "Woman in France: Madame de Sablé," *Westminster Review* 62 (October 1854), in Pinney, *Essays,* p. 54.

48. For a study that does historicize the feminization of letters, see Mary A. Favret, *Romantic Correspondence: Women, Politics, and the Fiction of Letters* (Cambridge: Cambridge University Press, 1993). Favret charts the late eighteenth-century shift from the fiction of sentimental femininity popularized by epistolary novels to a more politicized idea of the letter which developed during the period of the French Revolution. Although much of her work is concerned with published letter forms rather than private missive letters, she brings a healthy historical skepticism to bear upon attempts to define private correspondence in feminine and intimate terms.

49. There are exceptions. James Anderson Winn, *A Window in the Bosom: The Letters of Alexander Pope* (Hamden, Conn.: Archon Books, 1977), does sympathetically detailed readings of each of Pope's several kinds of correspondence. Richard Ellmann's study of James Joyce's letters, "A Postal Inquiry," in *Golden Codgers: Biographical Speculations* (London: Oxford University Press, 1973), pp. 132–54, describes the various poses Joyce adopts in his letters to various audiences and suggests the continuity between themes in letters and novels.

50. See William Henry Irving, *The Providence of Wit in the English Letter Writers* (Durham, N.C.: Duke University Press, 1955); Anderson, Daghlian, and Ehrenpreis, eds., *The Familar Letter in the Eighteenth Century*; Redford, *The Converse of the Pen*; and Keith Stewart, "Towards Defining an Aesthetic for the Familiar Letter in Eighteenth-Century England," *Prose Studies* 5 (1982): 179–89.

51. Irving, *The Providence of Wit*, p. 3.

52. Irving, *The Providence of Wit*, p. 14; Anderson and Ehrenpreis, "The Familiar Letter," pp. 276–78.

53. Irving, *The Providence of Wit*, p. 20.

54. Anderson and Ehrenpreis, "The Familiar Letter," p. 279.

55. See, for example, Anderson and Ehrenpreis, "The Familiar Letter," p. 270, on the possible link between writing good letters and the knowledge that the recipient had to pay for them.

56. Redford, *The Converse of the Pen*, p. 8.

57. Redford, *The Converse of the Pen*, pp. 9–11.

58. See, for example, Catherine R. Stimpson, "The Female Sociograph: The Theater of Virginia Woolf's Letters," in *The Female Autograph*, ed. Domna C. Stanton (Chicago: University of Chicago Press, 1984), pp. 168–79; Deborah Kaplan, "Representing Two Cultures: Jane Austen's Letters," in *The Private Self: Theory and Practice of Women's Autobiographical Writings*, ed. Shari Benstock (Chapel Hill: University of North Carolina Press, 1988), pp. 211–29; and in the same volume Patricia Meyer Spacks, "Female Rhetorics," pp. 177–91.

59. G. B. Tennyson, "Absent Friends Speaking: The Carlyle Letters," *Prose Studies* 5 (1982): 251; Spacks, *Gossip*, p. 65.

60. Altman, "The Letter Book as a Literary Institution."

61. This section draws on and is indebted to the following work: in *Yale French Studies* 71 (1982): Charles A. Porter, Foreword, pp. 1–14; Mireille Bossis, "Methodological Journeys through Correspondences," trans. Karen McPherson, pp. 63–75; and English Showalter, Jr., "Authorial Self-Consciousness in the Familiar Letter: The Case of Madame de Graffigny," pp. 113–30. Also Patrizia Violi, "Letters," in *Discourse and Literature*, ed. Teun A. Van Dijk (Amsterdam: John Benjamins, 1985), pp. 149–67; and Lawrence Rosenwald, *Emerson and the Art of the Diary* (New York: Oxford University Press, 1988), chap. 1.

62. Bossis, "Methodological Journeys through Correspondences," p. 64.

63. Porter, Foreword, p. 14.

64. Porter, Foreword, p. 7.

65. Showalter, "Authorial Self-Consciousness in the Familiar Letter," p. 129.

66. Spacks, *Gossip*, pp. 65–91, quoted passages on pp. 73–74, 76, and 90.

67. Bossis, "Methodological Journeys through Correspondences," pp. 66–69.

68. Bossis, "Methodological Journeys," p. 73.

69. Bossis, "Methodological Journeys," p. 70.

2. Constructing the Reader

1. Thomas James Wise, ed., *The Brontës: Their Lives, Friendships and Correspondence*, 4 vols. (reprint of 1933 Shakespeare Head edition by Porcupine Press, 1980), 4:156. Further citations from this edition will be indicated in the text.

2. According to a note later written at the head of this letter, "Mr. N. continued his authorship so the pledge was void." Wise, *The Brontës*, 4:157n.

3. Hannah More, *Strictures on the Modern System of Female Education*, 2 vols. (London: Cadell and Davies, 1799), 1:223.

4. Rebecca Fraser, *The Brontës: Charlotte Brontë and Her Family* (New York: Fawcett Columbine, 1988), pp. 62, 73.

5. Miss Lathom's school in Attleborough, 1825–27; Mrs. Wallington's, Nuneaton, 1828–32; the Miss Franklins' school in Coventry, 1832–35.

6. More, *Strictures*, 1:222–23.

7. Thomas Gisborne, *An Enquiry into the Duties of the Female Sex* (1797; rpt. New York: Garland, 1974), p. 111.

8. For a fine study of the contradictions at work in the concept of modesty, including the tension between the assumption that modesty was a natural attribute of womanhood and the anxious necessity to cultivate it, see Ruth Bernard Yeazell, *Fictions of Modesty: Women and Courtship in the English Novel* (Chicago: University of Chicago Press, 1991), especially chaps. 1–3.

9. Patricia Spacks discusses eighteenth-century women whose letters display the tension between self-assertion and self-suppression in "rituals of politeness." See "Female Rhetorics," in *The Private Self: Theory and Practice of Women's Autobiographical Writings*, ed. Shari Benstock (Chapel Hill: University of North Carolina Press, 1988), pp. 177–91.

10. Sarah Stickney Ellis, *The Daughters of England*, in *The Select Works of Mrs. Ellis* (New York: J. and H. G. Langley, 1844), pp. 90–92.

11. John Gregory, *A Father's Legacy to His Daughters* (1774; rpt. New York: Garland, 1974), pp. 36–37.

12. Hester Chapone, *Letters on the Improvement of the Mind* (London: John Sharpe, 1822), p. 82. For a similar double message, see Catharine Macaulay, *Letters on Education* (1790; rpt. New York: Garland, 1974), pp. 180–81.

13. Eliza Ware Farrar, *The Young Lady's Friend* (Boston: John B. Russell, 1837), pp. 282–83.

14. *The Boarding School; or, Lessons of a Preceptress to Her Pupils* (Boston: J. P. Peaslee, 1829), pp. 30–32.

15. Charlotte Elizabeth Tonna, *Letter Writing* (New York: John S. Taylor, 1843).

16. Tonna, *Letter Writing*, p. 43.

17. For a more secular attack on letter writing after marriage as a frivolous and wasteful activity, see Mrs. William Parkes, *Domestic Duties; or, Instructions to Young Married Ladies* (New York: J. and J. Harper, 1829).

18. Tonna, *Letter Writing*, p. 65.

19. Ellis, *The Daughters of England*, p. 90.

20. Ellis, *The Daughters of England*, p. 92.

21. As Janet Dunbar puts it, "Good manners demanded legible penmanship, which accounts for the beauty and character of much Victorian handwriting." *The Early Victorian Woman* (Westport, Conn.: Hyperion Press, 1953), p. 88. Dunbar points out that good handwriting was especially necessary because of the retained habit of crossing letters in order to keep the postage low.

22. She uses the term again in *GEL* 1:5, 8, and 13.

23. *GEL* 2:294.

24. See Fraser, *The Brontës*, pp. 48–61 and 98–114, for descriptions of this relationship and the writing it produced.

25. Mary Taylor, Charlotte's other friend and correspondent, burned the evidence of what was probably a more blunt and expressive correspondence. Charlotte once wrote to Ellen that she had destroyed a note "as I ought to have written to none but M. Taylor who is nearly as mad as myself" (Wise, *The Brontës*, 1:146).

26. The originals of the letters to Martha Jackson have disappeared; Haight prints fragments that had been published as extracts in the 1890s. See *GEL* 1:xlix–l.

27. Irving Howe, "A Great Writer's Evolution," *New Republic* (18 October 1954): 20.

28. Ruby Redinger gives a brief psychological analysis of George Eliot's style, connecting the early letters to the novels, pp. 78–79. I essentially agree with her central sentence: "Her prime need then as later was to conceal her strong and important but self-forbidden aggressive tendencies." I do not agree with Redinger's rather romantic idea of how the style works, however; in her view, the true voice of "imagination" was hidden by the long and complex analytical syntax, which prevented George Eliot from becoming a poet or humorist. Anthony Trollope was on the mark when he said of George Eliot, "Her imagination is no doubt strong, but it acts in analysing rather than in creating. Everything that comes before her is pulled to pieces so that the inside of it shall be seen, and be seen if possible by her readers as clearly as by herself" (quoted in Redinger, p. 60). The notion that the activity of imagination is in itself analytic offers a more accurate insight about George Eliot's peculiar powers.

29. See Neil Hertz, "Recognizing Casaubon," in *The End of the Line: Essays on Psychoanalysis and the Sublime* (New York: Columbia University Press, 1985), pp. 75–96. In this essay the young Mary Ann Evans's apologies for illegibility in handwriting and the identification of Casaubon as a figure for writing reverberate together in a discussion of George Eliot's fear that writing is endangered by its enclosure in the narcissistic imagination.

30. For an extended treatment of George Eliot's uses of direct address in the context of a feminist narratological argument about that technique, see Robyn R. Warhol, *Gendered Interventions: Narrative Discourse in the Victorian Novel* (New Brunswick: Rutgers University Press, 1989), especially pp. 33–44 and 115–33. Warhol distinguishes between distancing, metafictional uses of direct address (which she genders masculine) and engaging, realist uses (called feminine). Although she shows how George Eliot moves between these modes, the dualisms she creates through this scheme sometimes conflict with the many shades of address to the reader that she uncovers. For some unexplained reason, direct address in *Scenes of Clerical Life* is designated only as masculine.

31. She had already experimented with this method in the presentation of Cheverel Manor of "Mr. Gilfil's Love Story"; it seems to have been especially connected with concrete memories of places from childhood. For comment on the effect of this technique, see Warhol, *Gendered Interventions*, p. 36.

32. Graham Martin also reads this passage against the apparent intentions of the narrator in the context of an essay devoted to showing discontinuities between the authorial language and the story of *The Mill on the Floss*. Noting several instances of unacknowledged contempt in the narrative voice, he sees this passage as a confrontation with "the central anxiety whether such people *really deserve to be written about in the first place*." He notes the irrelevance of the historical argument to the stories of Tom and Maggie and concludes that the passage is a rationalization of the narrator's unacknowledged case against the Dodsons and Tullivers as inadequately human. This reading is congruent with my own, although I would say that the anxiety is generated by the unacknowledged expression of rage. Martin's case is, however, made with a

considerable animus against a narrator who pretends to be in control of issues she does not know what to make of. While such an analysis is particularly relevant to the unsolved autobiographical problems in this novel, I contend that similar processes of narration are common in George Eliot; to resent them is to adopt as a standard the notion that fiction is, or ought to be, unified and controlled. See *"The Mill on the Floss* and the Unreliable Narrator," in *George Eliot: Centenary Essays,* ed. Anne Smith (Totowa, N.J.: Barnes and Noble, 1980), pp. 36–54.

33. John Cross may be taken as a representative of such a reader. When he selected a passage about the dangers of novel reading from Mary Ann Evans's letter of March 16, 1839, he cut a sentence that reads: "I shall carry to my grave the mental diseases with which they have contaminated me." His pencil mark crossing out the sentence may still be seen in the original letter.

34. For a brilliant reading of the same instability in different terms, see Neil Hertz, "Recognizing Casaubon," pp. 88–96. Hertz concludes, "The wavering, then steadying of tone in which the narrator addresses the reader may be read as one way of readjusting to the felt instability of the author's relation to her character, to the unsettled sense that it was through an intense identification with Dorothea's experience in Rome that the magnificent previous paragraph had been written, but that the burden of that paragraph was the fictitiousness and the willfulness of such identifications" (pp. 94–95).

35. Graham Martin, for example, calls George Eliot's narrator "the Intourist guide," who constrains the reader's independent movement in the fictional space. *"The Mill on the Floss* and the Unreliable Narrator," p. 37.

36. Henry James, "The Life of George Eliot," *Atlantic Monthly* (May 1885), reprinted in *Henry James: Literary Criticism,* ed. Leon Edel (New York: Library of America, 1984), p. 1000.

3. Mary Ann Evans's Holy War

1. She had apparently met the Brays in May through her neighbor and new friend Elizabeth Bray Pears, but the beginning of the intimacy did not occur until November (1:12on).

2. Charles Bray, *Phases of Opinion and Experience during a Long Life* (London: Longmans, Green, 1885), p. 76.

3. Redinger suggests that Mary Ann Evans may have absorbed from Cara Bray the idea that it was hypocritical to attend church as an unbeliever (pp. 117–18).

4. Redinger, p. 199. For the whole account, see pp. 107–28.

5. Redinger, p. 113 (subsequent page numbers will appear in the text). Redinger's thesis is confused by her insistence on seeing Isaac as the central figure in George Eliot's imagination; thus she begins the account by attributing the Holy War to Mary Ann's growing rift with Isaac (p. 107).

6. In one of his rare asides, Gordon Haight comments on this passage, "Clarissa Harlowe could not have been more sincere" (p. 43). The latent irony about playing the heroine is to the point.

7. This schoolgirl composition is reprinted in Haight, pp. 553–54.

8. Both John Cross and Ruby Redinger point to this crucial turn in thought. Redinger describes the letter as striking "the keynote to the broad tolerance which mani-

fests itself in the novels" (p. 125), whereas Cross, perhaps more cannily, introduces the letter as "an important and noteworthy declaration of opinion on the very interesting question of conformity" (1:87).

9. The most often quoted examples are in the essay reviewing Wilhelm Heinrich von Riehl's books on German folk life, "The Natural History of German Life," published in the *Westminster Review* in 1856. See Pinney, *Essays*, pp. 266–99. Ten years later, and after Darwin, similar metaphors of root and seed figure the redefinition of "radical" social change which George Eliot attempts in *Felix Holt, the Radical*.

10. Pinney, *Essays*, p. 288.

11. Her brother, sister, and stepsister all lived within a five-mile radius of Foleshill, but the surviving correspondence suggests that she carefully organized and regulated visits from them.

12. She reports getting a new copy, with woodcuts, of *De imitatione Christi* on February 9, 1849; it is not clear whether she was previously reading it in another edition.

13. This passage is ubiquitously quoted and often read as a sign of George Eliot's need to find external bonds of law or discipline in fathers. See Redinger, p. 167; and Dianne Sadoff, *Monsters of Affection: Dickens, Eliot, and Brontë on Fatherhood* (Baltimore: Johns Hopkins University Press, 1982), pp. 86–87. It should not be read out of context or without attention to the reworking of the move out of religious discipline which first occurred in the Holy War itself.

14. For a reading of the legacy of the Holy War specifically in terms of George Eliot's representations of fathers and daughters, see Sadoff, *Monsters of Affection*, pp. 65–118. Sadoff's reading of *Romola* as a traumatic confrontation of the issues of the Holy War is especially valuable; as she rightly concludes, the confrontation does not mean that the issues of rebellion against or guilt about fathers are worked through or resolved.

15. This is also the definition of tolerance preached by the narrator who defends the necessity of realistic art in chapter 17 of *Adam Bede*.

16. George Eliot seems to have been capable of concealing from herself the force of her satire. She responded to news of the reception of *The Mill on the Floss* by defending her sympathy for the Dodsons: "Tom is painted with as much love and pity as Maggie, and I am so far from hating the Dodsons myself, that I am rather aghast to find them ticketed with such very ugly adjectives" (3:299). Because these portraits were intimately linked with her family, she was particularly unable to admit their harshness.

4. The Labor of Choice

1. Nina Auerbach, *Woman and the Demon: The Life of a Victorian Myth* (Cambridge: Harvard University Press, 1982), pp. 183–84. See also Carolyn Heilbrun, *Writing a Woman's Life* (New York: Ballantine, 1988), pp. 48–59; Heilbrun says that George Eliot took herself out of the conventional female marriage plot by living with Lewes and so allowed her talents to come into their own after a period of moratorium. Phyllis Rose focuses more directly on the connection between gratified sexuality and the flowering of creativity. See *Parallel Lives: Five Victorian Marriages* (New York: Vintage, 1983), pp. 211–12.

2. Rose, *Parallel Lives*, p. 235.

3. The question of choice is of course closely connected with the intellectual debate about free will and determinism which occupied George Eliot's mind and those of her

contemporaries. I have chosen to readdress this question by coming at it from its "inward springs" rather than treating it as a primarily theoretical problem. Among earlier and more philosophical treatments, George Levine's essay is central: "Determinism and Responsibility in the Works of George Eliot," *PMLA* 77 (1962): 268–79. See also Felicia Bonaparte, *Will and Destiny: Morality and Tragedy in George Eliot's Novels* (New York: New York University Press, 1975), especially the sections on causality and chance (pp. 13–35) and on determinism and choice (pp. 47–62).

4. For biographical narrative about G. H. Lewes, see Rosemary Ashton, *G. H. Lewes: A Life* (Oxford: Clarendon Press, 1991); and Redinger, pp. 227–56.

5. Cross, 1:234–35.

6. In May 1857 Chapman was relieved of this task after Marian announced her "marriage" to her family (8:171).

7. Ashton, *G. H. Lewes: A Life*, pp. 157–58.

8. "Linger, you are so lovely." She was adapting a phrase from Goethe's *Faust*, pt. 1, line 1700.

9. George Eliot, "Woman in France: Madame de Sablé," *Westminster Review* 62 (October 1854), pp. 448–73, rpt. in Pinney, *Essays*, pp. 52–81.

10. In what follows I complicate Alexander Welsh's argument about the way Lewes and George Eliot managed the two secrets, of their alliance and of George Eliot's authorship. Welsh's representation of the alliance as an "open secret" is true, particularly after the pair had returned to England. As I will show, however, the initial period of the union had its effects on George Eliot's representation of secrets before the revelation of the pseudonym which Welsh takes as the watershed in her relations with her public. See *George Eliot and Blackmail* (Cambridge: Harvard University Press, 1985), pp. 113–31.

11. Gordon Haight evades the matter of when Cara and Sara learned the actual nature of the liaison; implying that Cara knew by the time of her letter to Mrs. Combe, he says she "rallied loyally to Marian's defense." See "George Eliot's Bastards," in *George Eliot's Originals and Contemporaries*, ed. Hugh Witemeyer (Ann Arbor: University of Michigan Press, 1992), p. 84. It is equally possible that Bray concealed his full knowlege from his wife in order to give Marian time to disengage herself from Lewes.

12. See the excerpt from Combe's journal in *GEL* 8:118 for his disillusionment with Chapman. On the Combe-Bray response, see also Ashton, *G. H. Lewes*, pp. 155–57.

13. Phyllis Rose, who emphasizes Marian Evans's justified pride in "a triumph of natural morality in the face of absurd and tyrannical laws," also makes the interesting speculation that this very pride increased the strength of the judgment against her. "Had she pretended to shame and remorse, conforming to the popular plot that she had sinned and needed to be forgiven, I think her union with Lewes would have been found more acceptable" (*Parallel Lives*, p. 220). George Eliot imagined this plot in *The Mill on the Floss*, however, and showed how such a path would lead only to further judgment.

14. These letters also contain enough references to Lewes's frequent and casual participation in her life to alert any audience willing to be alerted. See Ashton, *G. H. Lewes*, pp. 137 and 147, for a similar sense that the Brays would surely have begun to guess at the nature of the relationship with Lewes.

15. See Haight, p. 189.

16. Haight seems to participate in the drama of suspense about whether Marian Evans would be dumped by Lewes when he describes the five weeks during which Marian waited alone in Dover after their return from Germany; "these weeks," he

comments, "must have marked the most trying period of her life." He speculates, based on hearsay in Edith Simcox's autobiography, that Marian had declared her unwillingness to return to London as Lewes's wife until Agnes agreed to a permanent separation (pp. 176, 179). The question of the precise relationship between Lewes's separation from Agnes and the affair with Marian Evans cannot be definitively answered; the best discussion of it is in Ashton, *G. H. Lewes*, pp. 132–43. Arthur Paterson, who constructed *George Eliot's Family Life and Letters* (Boston: Houghton Mifflin, 1928) so as to place George Eliot in the most conventionally acceptable light, offers as fact the possibility that Marian Evans sought out Agnes Lewes before the departure to Germany, and received the assurance that there was no chance she would return to her husband (p. 43). If this were so, it would shed interesting light on such scenes as the confrontation between Dorothea Casaubon and Rosamond Lydgate, but the story may have derived from the fiction rather than the other way around.

17. Cross, 1:235–37; Haight, pp. 189–91.

18. Welsh, *George Eliot and Blackmail*, p. 125. Welsh makes this observation as he discusses the typicality of George Eliot's pseudonymous position as a writer in the new age of information.

19. Reviewing Cross's *Life* in 1888, Richard Holt Hutton landed on this letter in order to show that George Eliot herself believed she had done wrong in living with Lewes and that she saw her writing as "expiatory." His essay, "George Eliot's Life and Letters," expresses a remarkable combination of hostility to George Eliot's failure of faith and shrewdness about the sources of intellectual strain in her letters and novels. See *Essays on Some of the Modern Guides to English Thought in Matters of Faith* (1888; rpt. London: Macmillan, 1891), pp. 288–91.

20. See George Levine, "Determinism and Responsibility," for the theoretical formulation of choice and determinism which I assume here.

21. Barbara Hardy, *Particularities: Readings in George Eliot* (Athens: Ohio University Press, 1982), p. 67.

22. Janice Carlisle, "The Mirror in *The Mill on the Floss*: Toward a Reading of Autobiography as Discourse," *Studies in the Literary Imagination* 23 (1990): 193, 195.

23. Welsh, *George Eliot and Blackmail*, p. 146.

24. There have, of course, been innumerable critical stories told about Maggie Tulliver's career, recent ones often informed by psychoanalytic or feminist theories. The novel virtually asks for such readings, and they proliferate because the text offers not only a story about a divided character but a narrative divided against itself. Barbara Hardy comments in a different way on this same phenomenon when she writes of George Eliot's "imaginative representation of ethics and psychology . . . the ability to make us feel that the artist is enlarging investigation, not restricting it." She shows how the extremely open representation of character avoids the usual patterning of the bildungsroman. See *Particularities*, pp. 68–74. The moral undecidability that characterizes this narrative has become a frequent theme in critical accounts.

25. Just about every critical reader of the novel discusses the narrative self-division in one form or another. For an essay especially compatible with my argument here, see Ian Adam, "The Ambivalence of *The Mill on the Floss*," in *George Eliot: A Centenary Tribute*, ed. Gordon Haight and Rosemary VanArsdel (Towota, N.J.: Barnes and Noble, 1982), pp. 122–36. Welsh, who classes *Mill on the Floss* with George Eliot's early "pastoral fictions," shifts the terms of this question by describing the novel's pattern as "a fall that does not take place"; in his view, George Eliot does not allow discontinuity into the life of her character because she had not yet reached the public stage of her career in which

she had to justify a life in which the past was severed from the present. *George Eliot and Blackmail*, pp. 148–49. Yet the novel puts such intense strain on the notion of continuity that it hardly qualifies as a "pastoral fiction."

26. For a discussion of this problem in terms of George Eliot's literary relation to Wordsworth, see Margaret Homans, *Bearing the Word: Language and Female Experience in Nineteenth-Century Women's Writing* (Chicago: University of Chicago Press, 1986), pp. 120–52.

27. See Mary Jacobus, "Men of Maxims and *The Mill on the Floss*," in *Reading Woman: Essays in Feminist Criticism* (New York: Columbia University Press, 1986), pp. 62–79, for a reading of this chapter which accommodates George Eliot within the debates of contemporary feminist theory.

28. See Homans, *Bearing the Word*, pp. 127–31, on the strange mutations into love for natural objects and the rewriting of Wordsworth they enact.

29. Philip Fisher, who also treats this passage in detail, has an equally sharp sense of the stalemate of alternatives in the novel; he emphasizes the world of choice as one of consumerism and collectorship, the world of Stephen Guest which Maggie later refuses. As he puts it, "The continuity that makes life legible, even to oneself, rests on loyalties that destroy the very self that continuity wants to make legible. . . . It is the intensity of perception on both sides of the impasse that creates the energy of the novel and creates, likewise, the stalemate." See *Making up Society: The Novels of George Eliot* (Pittsburgh: University of Pittsburgh Press, 1981), pp. 80–85 and 97.

30. See Gillian Beer's suggestive comment: George Eliot's "men are inclined to accuse women of a will to martydom when what they are observing is a will to independence. In a social order which constrains women, of course, the desire for independence and for martyrdom may prove to have indistinguishable consequences, but they are not indistinguishable in their natures. The reality of choice is crucial in George Eliot's work." See *George Eliot* (Bloomington: Indiana University Press, 1986), p. 84.

31. The "unconscious plot" of the novel can of course be read as a fantasy in which Isaac Evans is punished and killed. See Redinger, pp. 421–28; or Dorothea Barrett, *Vocation and Desire: George Eliot's Heroines* (London: Routledge, 1989), pp. 57–60. I would guess that George Eliot received some perfectly conscious gratification when she allowed herself to put into words some patterns of behavior she had suffered and silently analyzed for the first thirty years of her life.

32. Barry Qualls defines this problem as an evolution in George Eliot's reliance on the value of memory. "What happens to George Eliot's handling of her narrative voice in *The Mill* is that she herself is questioning the value of memory and the value of the memories. . . . Memory fictionalizes the past for our comfort; it does not propel us toward strong vision." *The Secular Pilgrims of Victorian Fiction* (Cambridge: Cambridge University Press, 1982), pp. 158–59.

33. Cross, 3:258–59.

34. Cross, 3:279.

35. Haight dates Cross's first declaration of love in August 1879 and suggests the fluxes of response in George Eliot, pp. 528–30.

36. Haight, pp. 530, 543. Bray's line appears when he describes George Combe's phrenological assessment of Marian Evans, in *Phases of Opinion and Experience during a Long Life: An Autobiography* (London: Longmans, Green & Co., 1885), p. 75.

37. Rose, *Parallel Lives*, pp. 234–35.

38. Redinger, pp. 479–80.

39. The deed of declaration, dated January 31, 1879, is preserved in the Eliot-Lewes collection at Yale. See Haight, p. 523.

40. Perhaps because it is so typical a move, the language of renewed affection has been foregrounded in other accounts of the decision. Phyllis Rose describes the strong-willed George Eliot casting the marriage "as a spiritual discipline, an attempt to avoid selfishness." (*Parallel Lives*, p. 235). Redinger seems to take the formula at face value when she concludes that the marriage to Cross was motivated by a fear of losing the power to love (p. 479).

41. As Don Mills put it, "It is as if she wants to appear as having no wishes of her own. So, in a paradox, the generosity is hers, too, for giving Cross the chance to satisfy his wish to care for her. Perhaps she even means hers to be the greater generosity, the absolute selflessness, since, for herself, she does not describe marriage as offering happiness" (Unpublished course paper, 1990). I am indebted to Mills's reading of the Cross letters, for stimulating the train of thought that led to the concept of this chapter.

5. The Outing of George Eliot

1. Alexander Welsh gives an account of this period from the perspective of George Eliot's not atypical relationship with the literary marketplace, in *George Eliot and Black-mail* (Cambridge: Harvard University Press, 1985), pp. 113–31. His view of the relation between the "open secret" of the liaison with Lewes and the guarded secret of the pseudonym is one of successful management: "The two affairs were inextricably related, and both were successfully managed. The aggressive public-relations secret was made to support and finally to subsume the quietly determined private relation that was its principal source" (p. 123). Thus, in Welsh's view, the Liggins imposture helped to deflect the guilt of the private relation. Judging by large-scale results, Welsh is right in this analysis, but a detailed look at Marian Lewes's responses during this period suggests a far more troubling series of threats to her new sense of herself as a novelist and a realist.

2. Blackwood, of William Blackwood and Sons, Edinburgh, published *Blackwood's Edinburgh Magazine* ("Maga") as well as full-length works.

3. For a discussion of the male pseudonym as "a transformation of gender which granted the author male authority and placed her in a patriarchal tradition of story-telling," see Dianne Sadoff, *Monsters of Affection: Dickens, Eliot, and Brontë on Fatherhood* (Baltimore: Johns Hopkins University Press, 1982), pp. 104–11.

4. Sara's birthday was November 23; they had a tradition of writing to each other at that time.

5. This letter is quoted in Haight, pp. 229–30. Ms. Yale.

6. Both Welsh (*George Eliot and Blackmail*, pp. 116, 128) and Redinger (pp. 336–37) suggest some sort of connection between the new pseudonym and Marian Evans's ability to tell Isaac Evans about her marriage.

7. U. C. Knoepflmacher develops the connection with Mary Shelley in his extended treatment of "The Lifted Veil," *George Eliot's Early Novels: The Limits of Realism* (Berkeley: University of California Press, 1968), pp. 128–61. See these pages for his wide-ranging discussion of the romantic and philosophical implications of the story in its Victorian context. Sandra Gilbert and Susan Gubar also discuss the story at length, because they are especially interested in its connection with a tradition of female

romantic gothic. See *The Madwoman in the Attic* (New Haven: Yale University Press, 1979), pp. 447–77.

8. In "Myth and the Single Consciousness: *Middlemarch* and *The Lifted Veil*," Gillian Beer studies the story as a drama of George Eliot's anxiety about the perils of authorship (in *This Particular Web: Essays on "Middlemarch,"* ed. Ian Adam [Toronto: University of Toronto Press, 1975], pp. 91–115). Ruby Redinger, in line with her central thesis, reads it primarily as the tale of a blocked writer, "a symbolic expression of George Eliot's last serious battle with the dynamics of the creative process" (p. 403). She does also make a connection between the story and George Eliot's doubt about her right "to invade other psyches" in her writing, and particularly in *The Mill on the Floss*. See pp. 400–405.

9. George Eliot, *The Lifted Veil* (Penguin: Virago Press, 1985), pp. 19–20. Further page numbers from this edition will appear in the text.

10. For an important discussion of the story as a "hysterical text" about the woman writer trapped in male visions and previsions, see Mary Jacobus's feminist-psychoanalytic reading in *Reading Woman: Essays in Feminist Criticism* (New York: Columbia University Press, 1986), pp. 249–74. Jacobus describes the hysteric's dilemma in relation to the father who is both desired and deathly (pp. 260–64).

11. Jacobus, *Reading Woman*, pp. 263–74.

12. Haight, p. 283; Redinger, p. 393.

13. The story of the complex disaffection between Blackwood and Marian Lewes is told at length both by Haight, pp. 305–19, and by Redinger, pp. 405–17.

14. In "The Secrets of George Eliot," Alexander Welsh considers the various reasons that may have underlain the "invention" and frequent discussion of a George Eliot who was too diffident and sensitive to bear criticism. His sense of that image as a public relations move corresponds with my own sense that George Eliot was always drawn to play on the boundary between publicity and concealment. Welsh's meditations do not, however, take the painful experiences of 1859 into account. See *Yale Review* 68 (1979): 589–97.

15. The story was not published until July 1864, when it appeared anonymously in the *Cornhill* magazine. George Eliot had given it to George Smith as a present to compensate for his losses in publishing *Romola*. The notion of "giving" a manuscript to a publisher links this transaction to the rumors that accompanied the Liggins affair and demonstrates George Eliot's sensitivity to the question of who made profits from her fiction.

16. George Eliot, *Brother Jacob* (Penguin: Virago Classics, 1989), p. 55. Further page numbers from this edition will appear in the text.

17. The most interesting political and biographical reading of the story to date is by Susan De Sola Rodstein; see "Sweetness and Dark: George Eliot's 'Brother Jacob,'" *Modern Language Quarterly* 52 (1991): 295–317. See pp. 309–17 for an intricate linkage of the story with the Liggins affair which plays out somewhat different parallels from my own. Otherwise, "Brother Jacob" has so far been discussed mainly in connection with *Silas Marner*. It was written in the month before *Marner* was begun, and its focuses on stolen guineas and provincial community are apparent linkages. Peter Allan Dale reads it as a fable about the evils of entrepreneurial capitalism in"George Eliot's 'Brother Jacob': Fables and the Physiology of Common Life," *Philological Quarterly* 64 (1985): 17–35. Lawrence Jay Dessner treats it as the story of *Silas Marner* "turned upside-down" in "The Autobiographical Matrix of *Silas Marner*," *Studies in the Novel* 11 (1979): 251–82.

18. Gillian Beer has shown how the metaphor of circulatory systems organizes the novel, connecting gossip with financial status, in "Circulatory Systems: Money and Gossip in *Middlemarch*," *Cahiers Victoriens et Edouardiens* 26 (October 1987): 47–62.

19. George Eliot's representations of gossip are most often discussed in relation to her idea of community or as the "medium" within which characters must work out their lives. For discussions of community talk as a relatively benign medium, see Steven Marcus, "Literature and Social Theory: Starting in with George Eliot," in *Representations: Essays on Literature and Social Theory* (New York: Random House, 1954); Welsh, *George Eliot and Blackmail*, pp. 135–37; and Elizabeth Ermarth, *Realism and Consensus in the English Novel* (Princeton: Princeton University Press, 1983), pp. 222–56. Ermarth's idea of consensus owes something to Quentin Anderson's essay "George Eliot in *Middlemarch*" (1958), in *From Dickens to Hardy: The Pelican Guide to English Literature*, ed. Boris Ford (Harmondsworth: Penguin, 1963–67), 6:274–93. For discussions of gossip as a leveling force, see Patricia Meyer Spacks, *Gossip* (New York: Knopf, 1985), pp. 195–202; and especially D. A. Miller, *Narrative and Its Discontents: Problems of Closure in the Traditional Novel* (Princeton: Princeton University Press, 1981), pp. 111–29. Since Miller identifies "the" community as the drive toward the "non-narratable," he has to make of it a monolithic force; yet many of his insights complicate this view by suggesting how the desiring subjects are implicated in community opinion.

20. D. A. Miller sees this problem as an instance of "the uncanny" working to make internal choices correspond with external necessity. See *Narrative and Its Discontents*, pp. 117–19.

21. See John Kucich, *Repression in Victorian Fiction: Charlotte Brontë, George Eliot, and Charles Dickens* (Berkeley: University of California Press, 1987), for the argument that this love affair is fed by the internal dialectic between renunciation and desire: "In love, for both characters, the power of external influence is deliberately minimized" (p. 146). This is part of Kucich's larger point, that George Eliot's "favored characters . . . are all made to seem impervious to the judgments of others about them" (pp. 182–83). D. A. Miller represents the opposite pole: "Dorothea and Will are kept apart for so long precisely by their overwhelming consciousness of what people might say" (p. 164). My argument places George Eliot's dialectic between these two positions.

22. See Kucich for a related argument that George Eliot defines egotism as an excessive reliance on the opinions of others. *Repression in Victorian Fiction*, pp. 183–200.

23. George Eliot, *Impressions of Theophrastus Such*, in *The Works of George Eliot* (standard edition; Edinburgh: William Blackwood and Sons, n.d.), pp. 5–6, 19. Other page numbers will appear in the text.

24. For an informative discussion of George Eliot's adoption of this genre, see G. Robert Stange, "The Voices of the Essayist," *Nineteenth-Century Fiction* 35 (1980): 312–30. Stange sees in the work a desire to recover earlier narrative voices, after the impersonal vision of *Daniel Deronda*.

25. Redinger reads "Looking Inward" as straight autobiography, an analysis of George Eliot's "futile attempts to free herself from the cruelly indifferent auditor within her" (p.372). In her account only the efforts of G. H. Lewes stand between George Eliot and the publication failures of *Such*; she does not see the comic self-knowledge in the essay.

6. Ambition and Womanhood

1. Alexander Welsh points out George Eliot's tendency to advertise her sensitivity in her letters, especially to distant readers. In his reading "The repeated formula is itself a

publicizing act, a way of coping with the intrusion of publicity by reversing its direction, almost by celebrating it." See *George Eliot and Blackmail* (Cambridge: Harvard University Press, 1985), pp. 114–15.

2. It is reprinted in Haight, pp. 553–54. The essay is included in a notebook probably used during Mary Ann Evans's time at the Miss Franklins' school in Coventry, 1832–35.

3. Cross, 1:18–19.

4. Cross, 1:32.

5. For a different reading of the "ambition" and "oratorio" letters, see Redinger, pp. 88–93. Redinger sees Mary Ann Evans's resistance to ambition and performance as a fear of her own imagination, her resistance to the idea of audience as a fear of her inner audiences. In a reading of the *Brother and Sister* sonnets, she also sees Mary Ann Evans's fear of success as stemming from a fear of being praised for something undeserved (pp. 53–55). These matters are well introduced but not fully developed, probably because they are controlled by Redinger's two central theses: that the story of George Eliot is a story of allowing imagination its freedom, and that her brother, Isaac Evans, was the major proscribing figure in her mental life.

6. Gillian Beer comments on the singer as a figure through which George Eliot works out the contrast between social confinement and expressive freedom, all the while worrying about the danger posed to the doctrine of sympathy by the exceptional woman. *George Eliot* (Bloomington: Indiana University Press, 1986), pp. 200–228. Others have seen these characters as expressions of the conflict between love and art or as vehicles for the expression of female rebellion and rage. See Kathleen Blake, "'Armgart'—George Eliot on the Woman Artist," *Victorian Poetry* 18 (1980): 75–80; Sandra M. Gilbert and Susan Gubar, *The Madwoman in the Attic* (New Haven: Yale University Press, 1979), pp. 452–55; and Marcia S. Midler, "George Eliot's Rebels: Portraits of the Artist as a Woman," *Women's Studies* 7 (1980): 97–108.

7. Ellen Moers sees Dinah as George Eliot's domestication of the performing heroine in the *Corinne* tradition; see *Literary Women* (New York: Oxford University Press, 1985), pp. 192–93. Nina Auerbach elaborates on the details of the scene, concluding that Dinah's sermon represents "a deeper drama in which sincerity is at one with compelling display" and that Dinah's superiority to Hetty lies in the fact that she is a successful performer with an ability to move an audience. Her argument occurs in an essay that builds on and against Moers's original critique of the theatricality of George Eliot's heroines: "Secret Performances: George Eliot and the Art of Acting," in *Romantic Imprisonment: Women and Other Glorified Outcasts* (New York: Columbia University Press, 1985), pp. 260–63. Auerbach argues for George Eliot's increasing acceptance of self-performance, in a vision of triumphant development which I wish to complicate.

8. Catherine Gallagher has argued that George Eliot's anxiety about authorship can be attributed to her association of writing with the prostitution of the marketplace; she elaborates on the metaphors linking artistic with commercial exchange in the late essays and in *Daniel Deronda*. See "George Eliot and *Daniel Deronda*: The Prostitute and the Jewish Question," in *Sex, Politics, and Science in the Nineteenth-Century Novel*, ed. Ruth Bernard Yeazell (Baltimore: Johns Hopkins University Press, 1986), pp. 39–62.

9. This piece, probably part of the notes for *Impressions of Theophrastus Such*, is reprinted in Pinney, *Essays*, pp. 437–42.

10. For a more sustained discussion of this topic, see Deirdre David, *Intellectual Women and Victorian Patriarchy* (Ithaca: Cornell University Press, 1987), pp. 177–88. David sees George Eliot's discussions of women as "strategies of containment to evade

or deny an intolerable conflict between woman's mind and male authority"—an authority that had authorized her own career (p. 194).

11. See Nancy Paxton, *George Eliot and Herbert Spencer: Feminism, Evolutionism, and the Reconstruction of Gender* (Princeton: Princeton University Press, 1991), chap. 7, for a discussion of George Eliot's view of the suffrage. As Paxton points out, she refused to sign the suffrage petition, but her reluctance to extend the suffrage was not—as *Felix Holt* demonstrates—confined to women.

12. Nancy Paxton assumes that this letter refers to Josephine Butler's campaign against the Contagious Diseases Acts. *George Eliot and Herbert Spencer*, p. 203. If so, Marian's feminist friends had alerted her to very first stages of this campaign, in the fall of 1869; the letter is dated 4 October 1869.

13. James's review of the volume is reprinted in *Henry James: Essays on Literature; American Writers; English Writers*, ed. Leon Edel (New York: The Library of America, 1984), pp. 966–73.

14. Leo's crucial role in the poem is overlooked by most readers, who celebrate Armgart's refusal of the Graf but acknowledge Walpurga's claims for common womanhood against Armgart's horror of losing her exceptional status.

15. George Eliot, *The Legend of Jubal and Other Poems* (standard edition; Edinburgh: William Blackwood and Sons, n.d.), pp. 86, 88. Subsequent page numbers will appear in the text.

16. Ellen Moers points out that the portrait of Gwendolen Harleth is a realistic critique of the dangers of the myth of the performing heroine (*Literary Women*, pp. 196–97). Gillian Beer elaborates the tragedy of Gwendolen as a figure of "woman's absolute distress" (*George Eliot*, pp. 218–28).

17. For full discussions of the power of the paternal, see Judith Wilt, "'He Would Come Back': The Fathers of Daughters in *Daniel Deronda*," *Nineteenth-Century Literature* 42 (1987): 313–38; and Nancy Pell, "The Fathers' Daughters in *Daniel Deronda*," *Nineteenth-Century Fiction* 36 (1982): 424–51.

18. For a generally compatible discussion of theatricality in this novel, see Joseph Litvak, *Caught in the Act: Theatricality in the Nineteenth-Century Novel* (Berkeley: University of California Press, 1992), chap. 5, especially pp. 159–92. Litvak describes "Poetry" as the antagonist to theatricality in *Daniel Deronda* and as a means of making the distinction between "good and bad Jewishness."

19. Welsh, *George Eliot and Blackmail*, pp. 259–79.

20. See Wilt, "'He Would Come Back,'" p. 323, for the connection of the "lapse of forgetfulness" with the memory of the father's power.

21. Thornton Lewes returned from Natal to the Lewes household in 1869 and died six months later of spinal tuberculosis. Herbert Lewes died impoverished, apart from his wife and two children, in 1875 as George Eliot was writing *Deronda*.

22. For a psychoanalytic reading of the exorcism of Deronda's mother as a threatening form of mimesis, "a scapegoating after an ambivalent celebration," see Neil Hertz, *The End of the Line: Essays on Psychoanalysis and the Sublime* (New York: Columbia University Press, 1985), pp. 224–39.

23. Cross, 1:26.

7. George Eliot's Stepsons

1. Ms. Yale. Further quotations from ms. letters held at Yale will be marked only by date in the rest of this chapter; published letters will be designated by *GEL* volume and page as usual.

2. It is possible that "Miss Evans" and one or more of the children had met each other during the early years of her friendship with Lewes. In letters to his sons at Hofwyl, Lewes made a point of introducing her name. Through him she sent a book of poetry and gifts of money; at least twice Lewes sent messages in which "Miss Evans sends her love and hopes that you won't forget her" (November 29, 1857; November 20, 1858). She appears as a person to remember along with other adults the children know—their nurse, and a Mrs. Owen-Jones. Charles dutifully sends greetings to Miss Evans "when you see her" in a number of letters to his father, especially in the first half of 1859.

3. Rosemary Ashton records the strange possibility that "the younger children seem not to have known that their father was not Lewes but Thornton Hunt." She quotes a statement made in old age by Ethel Lewes, which denies the connection between her mother and Hunt and supposes that Charles Lewes would not have visited his mother so faithfully had she been an adulterer. See *G. H. Lewes: A Life* (Oxford: Clarendon Press, 1991), pp. 180–81.

4. Little has been written about George Eliot's relations with her stepsons. The most extensive and sympathetic accounts of their lives and characters may be found in Ashton, *G. H. Lewes*. Margaret Homans has drawn on certain George Eliot letters about her stepchildren to discuss her conflict between writing and motherhood and the figural representation of writing as a form of motherhood. See *Bearing the Word: Language and Female Experience in Nineteenth-Century Women's Writing* (Chicago: University of Chicago Press, 1986), pp. 177–88. In 1928 Arthur Paterson published *George Eliot's Family Life and Letters* (Boston: Houghton Mifflin), a brief biography and selection of letters between George Eliot and George Henry Lewes and their "boys" which aimed to redeem George Eliot's late nineteenth-century image as a stern moral and intellectual Sibyl and to recast her as a figure of family love and affection. Although the collection is quite successful in suggesting the cultivation of family wit and warmth, its treatment of the letters is even more unreliable than is John Cross's. The transcript of the letters was done by Charles Lewes's youngest daughter, Elinor Southwood Lewes (Mrs. Carrington Ouvry; see *GEL* 1:xiii). She and Paterson cut and paste without any indication that they are doing so, misdate letters, and avoid any signs of conflict or stress in the family relations.

5. Gillian Beer notes that the thematic conflict between natural and foster parents becomes important in the fictions of the 1860s; she is particularly interested in George Eliot's versions of kin and descent. See *George Eliot* (Bloomington: Indiana University Press, 1986), pp. 108–12.

6. Ruby Redinger seriously considers the rumor mentioned by Blanche Colton Williams that Charles was the only actual son of George Henry Lewes, but there is no evidence to substantiate it. Redinger, pp. 252–53; Williams, *George Eliot: A Biography* (New York: Macmillan, 1936), p. 95.

7. A school report he copied out for his parents describes him as the most hardworking of the students, but slow to learn (February 16, 1858).

8. Thornton Lewes, a one-page diary of a trip to Ramsgate, August 9–15, 1855. Ms. Yale.

9. See Haight, pp. 337–39; and Ashton, *G. H. Lewes*, pp. 211–12. Haight speculates that the contradiction between her depression in London and her rise in spirits away from London can be explained by "her equivocal marital state," made especially conspicuous since her fame; Ashton seems to agree that social isolation and gossip are at the root of the matter.

10. After completing *Middlemarch*, George Eliot wrote to Alexander Main, "When a subject has begun to grow in me I suffer terribly until it has wrought itself out—become a complete organism; and then it seems to take wing and go away from me" (5:324). U. C. Knoepflmacher asks, "Was there a link between this obsession to give birth to fictional offspring and the sterility enforced by social convention on the loving 'Mutter' of Lewes' three legitimate sons?" "Mr. Haight's George Eliot: 'Wahrheit und Dichtung,'" *Victorian Studies* 12 (1969): 430. The metaphors suggest that the special intensity of her relation to writing may be so linked.

11. Three years later, in 1863, the Leweses bought the Priory, in Regents Park, and based themselves permanently in London.

12. See Homans for a treatment of the split between the egotism of writing and the sacrifice of family responsibility. *Bearing the Word*, pp. 179–188.

13. Haight dates the beginning of the book September 30, 1860 (1:xxvii).

14. George Eliot's letters to Blackwood emphasize the old images; she calls the tale "a story of old-fashioned village life" (3:371) and says that it was suggested by a Wordsworthian recollection of "having once, in early childhood, seen a linen-weaver with a bag on his back" (3:382).

15. Thornie wrote to George Eliot: "Silas Marner is splendid. I like it extremely, prefering [*sic*] it to Adam Bede or the 'Scenes.' And when I had come to the last page I almost got angry at there being no more of it" (8:280–81).

16. See, for example, Alexander Welsh's list in *George Eliot and Blackmail* (Cambridge: Harvard University Press, 1985), p. 165. For an extensive analysis of *Silas Marner's* autobiographical elements, see Lawrence Jay Dessner, "The Autobiographical Matrix of *Silas Marner*," *Studies in the Novel* 11 (1979): 251–82. Dessner makes an eloquent argument for the value of reading fictions as imaginative transformations of deeply felt private experience, but his long list of possible autobiographical elements does not create a particularly coherent vision of the novel's shape. In his reading Marian Lewes's anxiety about whether the boys would accept her as their stepmother is rendered as Eppie's legitimation of the foster parent when she rejects Godfrey in favor of Silas.

17. The poem was copied out in a letter to Maria Lewis on July 17, 1839 (1:27–28); it was also printed in the *Christian Observer* of January 1840.

18. For this reason I resist readings that associate Silas's hoarding with George Eliot's guilt at making money through her writing or with what is sometimes seen as her unnatural greed for money. See Redinger, pp. 438–39; Welsh, *George Eliot and Blackmail*, pp. 167–68; and Dessner, "The Autobiographical Matrix," pp. 257 and 264. Since George Eliot's earnings virtually supported not only the three Lewes boys but also, to some extent, Agnes's children by Hunt, her anxiety about money and her ability to go on providing it had some basis in reality.

19. Nancy Paxton points out how Silas is reconnected to and associated with maternal forces even before he becomes a parent, emphasizing throughout her study of the story how George Eliot valorizes forces other than biological parenthood. See *George Eliot and Herbert Spencer: Feminism, Evolutionism, and the Reconstruction of Gender* (Princeton: Princeton University Press, 1991), pp. 100–116.

20. The story is told by Gordon Haight in "George Eliot's Bastards," in *George Eliot's Originals and Contemporaries*, ed. Hugh Witemeyer (Ann Arbor: University of Michigan Press, 1992), pp. 76–86.

21. Quoted in Ashton, *G. H. Lewes*, p. 180.

22. "Agatha" and "How Lisa Loved the King" were written before Thornie arrived in

London. The *Brother and Sister* sonnets were completed during the summer of 1869; "The Legend of Jubal" was begun.

23. See Redinger, pp. 253–54, for an analysis of this connection. Redinger postulates a recurrence, after Thornton's death, of Mary Ann Evans's feeling that her moral nature would dissolve after the death of her father.

24. See Haight's account, pp. 526–27 and 534.

25. Once, just after Gertrude Lewes's first baby was born dead, Marian allowed herself to express the work of family relations. "Sometimes it requires an effort to feel affectionately towards those who are bound to us by ties of family, but it is as easy to me to love Gertrude as it is to love the clear air" (4:312).

26. See Homans, *Bearing the Word*, pp. 179–88.

27. As Paxton puts it, she "chose to valorize the 'maternal' sensations and emotions that might be felt by all women rather than to idealize the bonds of biological motherhood." She also emphasizes rightly that George Eliot contends with evolutionary theory by exposing the gap between reproductive capacity and readiness for motherhood. *George Eliot and Herbert Spencer*, pp. 24–25.

8. Old and Young

1. Elaine Showalter, *Sexual Anarchy: Gender and Culture at the Fin de Siècle* (New York: Penguin, 1990), pp. 59–75; Deirdre David, *Intellectual Women and Victorian Patriarchy* (Ithaca: Cornell University Press, 1987), p. 162.

2. David, *Intellectual Women*, pp. 164–67.

3. She was taking a common position on the conservative side of the nineteenth-century debate about biography, which focused on whether unpleasant revelations about the personal life of the subject should be made in print. A similar defense of authorial privacy may be found in an article, "Modern Biography—Beattie's Life of Campbell," by W. E. Aytoun, published in the February 1849 issue of *Blackwood's* and reprinted in *Victorian Biography: A Collection of Essays from the Period*, ed. Ira Bruce Nadel (New York: Garland, 1986).

4. For a discussion of the privacy issue in George Eliot's and Margaret Oliphant's responses to Harriet Martineau's autobiography, see Mary Jean Corbett, *Representing Femininity: Middle-Class Subjectivity in Victorian and Edwardian Women's Autobiographies* (New York: Oxford University Press, 1992), pp. 93–97.

5. My remarks are based on the 7th edition of *Wise, Witty, and Tender Sayings in Prose and Verse, selected from the Works of George Eliot* (Edinburgh: William Blackwood and Sons, 1886).

6. *Sayings*, ix. Main's dedication, "To George Eliot, in recognition of a genius as original as it is profound, and a morality as pure as it is impassioned," made Blackwood hesitate: "in her peculiar position I would take out the allusion to morality as it might raise vulgar discussion" (5:212).

7. *Letters from George Eliot to Elma Stuart (1872–1880)*, ed. Roland Stuart (London: Simkin, Marshall, Hamilton, Kent, 1909), xiii–xiv.

8. *Letters from George Eliot to Elma Stuart*, pp. 4–5.

9. *Letters from George Eliot to Elma Stuart*.

10. It seems not to be clear exactly how the initial connection was made. My information about Simcox is based primarily on K. A. McKenzie, *Edith Simcox and George Eliot*

(London: Oxford University Press, 1961; rpt. Greenwood Press, 1978). McKenzie wrote his account, which includes lengthy quotations from "The Autobiography of a Shirt Maker," after that manuscript had been deposited in the Bodleian Library in 1958.

11. Haight transcribed many pages of Simcox's autobiography in *GEL* 9.

12. "Autobiography," October 19, 1879, quoted in McKenzie, *Simcox and Eliot*, p. 30.

13. Quoted in McKenzie, *Simcox and Eliot*, p. 114.

14. McKenzie, *Simcox and Eliot*, p. 110.

15. The whole circle, it seems, ordered their shirts from Edith's cooperative workshop.

16. Quoted in McKenzie, *Simcox and Eliot*, p. 122.

17. Neil Hertz, "Some Words in George Eliot: Nullify, Neutral, Numb, Number," in *Languages of the Unsayable: The Play of Negativity in Literature and Literary Theory*, ed. Sanford Budick and Wolfgang Iser (New York: Columbia University Press, 1989), p. 288.

Index